PENGUIN BOOKS

FRAGMENTS OF AUTOBIOGRAPHY

Graham Greene was born in 1904. On coming down from Balliol College, Oxford, he worked for four years as sub-editor on *The Times*. He established his reputation with his fourth novel, *Stamboul Train*. In 1935 he made a journey across Liberia, described in *Journey Without Maps*, and on his return was appointed film critic of the *Spectator*. In 1926 he had been received into the Roman Catholic Church and visited Mexico in 1938 to report on the religious persecution there. As a result he wrote *The Lawless Roads* and, later, his famous novel *The Power and the Glory*.

Brighton Rock was published in 1938, and in 1940 he became literary editor of the *Spectator*. The next year he undertook work for the Foreign Office and was stationed in Sierra Leone from 1941 to 1943. This later produced his novel, *The Heart of the Matter*, set in West Africa. Other novels include *The End of the Affair*, *The Quiet American*, *Travels With My Aunt*, *The Honorary Consul* and *The Captain and the Enemy*.

As well as his many novels, Graham Greene wrote several collections of short stories, four travel books, six plays, two books of autobiography (published here in one volume), two of biography and four books for children. He also contributed hundreds of essays, and film and book reviews, some of which appear in a collection entitled *Reflections*. Many of his novels and short stories have been filmed, and *The Third Man* was written as a film treatment. Graham Greene was a member of the Order of Merit and a Companion of Honour.

Graham Greene died in April 1991. Among the many people who paid tribute to him on his death were Kingsley Amis: 'He will be missed all over the world. Until today, he was our greatest living novelist'; Alec Guinness: 'He was a great writer who spoke brilliantly to a whole generation. He was almost prophet-like with a surprising humility'; and William Golding: 'Graham Greene was in a class by himself . . . He will be read and remembered as the ultimate chronicler of twentieth-century man's consciousness and anxiety.'

GRAHAM GREENE

FRAGMENTS OF AUTOBIOGRAPHY

A SORT OF LIFE
AND
WAYS OF ESCAPE

PENGUIN BOOKS

PENGUIN BOOKS

Published by the Penguin Group
Penguin Books Ltd, 27 Wrights Lane, London W8 5TZ, England
Penguin Books USA Inc., 375 Hudson Street, New York, New York 10014, USA
Penguin Books Australia Ltd, Ringwood, Victoria, Australia
Penguin Books Canada Ltd, 10 Alcorn Avenue, Toronto, Ontario, Canada M4V 3B2
Penguin Books (NZ) Ltd, 182–190 Wairau Road, Auckland 10, New Zealand

Penguin Books Ltd, Registered Offices: Harmondsworth, Middlesex, England

A Sort of Life first published by The Bodley Head 1971
Published in Penguin Books 1972
Ways of Escape first published in Canada by Orpen Dennys 1980
First published in Great Britain by The Bodley Head 1980
Published in Penguin Books 1981
This omnibus edition, under the title *Fragments of Autobiography*,
published in Penguin Books 1991
1 3 5 7 9 10 8 6 4 2

Copyright © Graham Greene, 1971, 1980
All rights reserved

Printed in England by Clays Ltd, St Ives plc

CONTENTS

A Sort of Life   9

Ways of Escape   159

PENGUIN BOOKS

A SORT OF LIFE

Graham Greene was born in 1904 and educated at Berkhamsted School, where his father was headmaster. On coming down from Balliol College, Oxford, where he published a book of verse, he worked for four years as a sub-editor on *The Times*. He established his reputation with his fourth novel, *Stamboul Train*, which he classed as an 'entertainment' in order to distinguish it from more serious work. In 1935 he made a journey across Liberia, described in *Journey Without Maps*, and on his return was appointed film critic of the *Spectator*. In 1926 he had been received into the Roman Catholic Church and was commissioned to visit Mexico in 1938 and report on the religious persecution there. As a result he wrote *The Lawless Roads* and, later, *The Power and the Glory*.

Brighton Rock was published in 1938 and in 1940 he became literary editor of the *Spectator*. The next year he undertook work for the Foreign Office and was sent out to Sierra Leone in 1941–3. One of his major post-war novels, *The Heart of the Matter*, is set in West Africa and is considered by many to be his finest book. This was followed by *The End of the Affair*, *The Quiet American*, a story set in Vietnam, *Our Man in Havana*, and *A Burnt-Out Case*. *The Comedians* and twelve other novels have been filmed, plus two of his short stories, and *The Third Man* was written as a film treatment. In 1967 he published a collection of short stories under the title: *May We Borrow Your Husband?* His most recent publications are *The Honorary Consul* (1973), *Lord Rochester's Monkey* (1974), a biography, *An Impossible Woman: The Memories of Dottoressa Moor of Capri* (1975: edited), *The Human Factor*(1978), *Doctor Fischer of Geneva or The Bomb Party* (1980), *J'Accuse: The Dark Side of Nice* (1982) and *Monsignor Quixote* (1982). *A Sort of Life* was published in 1971, and a second autobiographical volume, *Ways of Escape*, in 1980.

In all Graham Greene has written some thirty novels, 'entertainments', plays, children's books, travel books, and collections of essays and short stories. He was made a Companion of Honour in 1966.

For the survivors,
Raymond Greene, Hugh Greene
and Elisabeth Dennys

Only robbers and gypsies say that one
must never return where one has once been.

— KIERKEGAARD

An autobiography is only 'a sort of life' – it may contain less errors of fact than a biography, but it is of necessity even more selective: it begins later and it ends prematurely. If one cannot close a book of memories on the deathbed, any conclusion must be arbitrary, and I have preferred to finish this essay with the years of failure which followed the acceptance of my first novel. Failure too is a kind of death: the furniture sold, the drawers emptied, the removal van waiting like a hearse in the lane to take one to a less expensive destination. In another sense too a book like this can only be 'a sort of life', for in the course of sixty-six years I have spent almost as much time with imaginary characters as with real men and women. Indeed, though I have been fortu- nate in the number of my friends, I can remember no anecdotes of the famous or the notorious – the only stories which I faintly remember are the stories I have written.

And the motive for recording these scraps of the past? It is much the same motive that has made me a novelist: a desire to reduce a chaos of experience to some sort of order, and a hungry curiosity. We cannot love others, so the theologians teach, unless in some degree we can love ourselves, and curiosity too begins at home.

There is a fashion today among many of my contemporaries to treat the events of their past with irony. It is a legitimate method of self-defence. 'Look how absurd I was when I was young' fore- stalls cruel criticism, but it falsifies history. We were not Eminent Georgians. Those emotions were real when we felt them. Why should we be more ashamed of them than of the indifference of old age? I have tried, however unsuccessfully, to live again the follies and sentimentalities and exaggerations of the distant time, and to feel them, as I felt them then, without irony.

Chapter 1

1

IF I had known it, the whole future must have lain all the time along those Berkhamsted streets. The High Street was wide as many a market square, but its broad dignity was abused after the first great war by the New Cinema under a green Moorish dome, tiny enough but it seemed to us then the height of pretentious luxury and dubious taste. My father, who was by that time headmaster of Berkhamsted School, once allowed his senior boys to go there for a special performance of the first *Tarzan* movie, under the false impression that it was an educational film of anthropological interest, and ever after he regarded the cinema with a sense of disillusion and suspicion. The High Street contained at 'our end' a half-timbered Tudor photographer's shop (from the windows the faces of the locals looked out in wedding groups, bouqueted and bemused like prize oxen) and the great flinty Norman church where the helmet of some old Duke of Cornwall hung unremarked on a pillar like a bowler hat in a hall. Below lay the Grand Junction canal with slow-moving painted barges and remote gypsy children, the watercress beds, the hillocks of the old castle surrounded by a dry moat full of cow-parsley (it had been built, so they said, by Chaucer, and in the reign of King Henry III it was besieged successfully by the French). The faint agreeable smell of coal dust blew up from the railway, and everywhere were those curious individual Berkhamsted faces which I feel I could recognize now anywhere in the world: pointed faces like the knaves on playing cards, with a slyness about the eyes, an unsuccessful cunning.

And then there remains to be set reluctantly on my personal map the School – part rosy Tudor, part hideous modern brick the colour of dolls'-house plaster hams – where the misery of life started, and the burial ground, long disused, which lay opposite our windows, separated from our flower-beds by an invisible line, so that every year the gardener would turn up a few scraps of

11

human bone in remaking the herbaceous border. Further off to the north, on the green spaces of a map empty as Africa, lay the wastes of gorse and bracken of the great Common which extended to Ashridge Park, and to the south the small Brickhill Common and the park of Ashlyns, where I once saw a Jack in the Green covered with spring leaves, dancing cumbrously among his attendants like the devils I met later in Liberia.

Everything one was to become must have been there, for better or worse. One's future might have been prophesied from the shape of the houses as from the lines of the hand; one's evasions and deceits took their form from those other sly faces and from the hiding places in the garden, on the Common, in the hedgerows. Here in Berkhamsted was the first mould of which the shape was to be endlessly reproduced. For twenty years it was to be almost the only scene of happiness, misery, first love, the attempt to write, and I feel it would be strange if, through the workings of coincidence, through the unconscious sources of action, through folly or wisdom, I were not brought back to die there in the place where everything was born.

At the far end of the long High Street was the village of Northchurch and an old inn, the Crooked Billet. The name, perhaps because of some event which had happened there and had left an ambiguous impression in my mind from veiled adult conversation, always had for me a sinister ring (in the inn I was sure travellers had been done to death), and this gave the whole Northchurch village an atmosphere of standing outside the pale: a region of danger where nightmare might easily become reality. We were never taken there for walks, though this could well have had a natural explanation, for why should any nurse endure the two-mile trudge along the High Street, past the town hall, past the new King's Road, up and down which the commuters streamed twice a day to the station with their little attaché cases, past Mrs Figg's toy-shop where the children would certainly want to linger, past the sinister stained-glass windows of the dentist, along the market gardens, with everywhere that odd gritty smell blowing up from the coal yards and the coal barges?

There was another walk too which we never took when we were in charge of our old crotchety nurse or the nursemaid, and that was the walk along the towing path by the canal. If a sinister atmosphere lay in my mind around the Crooked Billet, a sense of immediate danger was conveyed by the canal – the menace of insulting words from strange brutal canal workers with blackened faces like miners, with their gypsy wives and ragged children, at the sight of middle-class children carefully dressed and shepherded, and the danger too, as I believed, of death from drowning. *The Berkhamsted Gazette and Hemel Hempstead Observer* periodically printed the reports of inquests on those found drowned in the canal; the casualties among the barge children were reputed to be high, and the story that anyone who fell into a lock was beyond rescue was not contradicted in our imaginations by the lifebelt which hung on the wall of each lock-house. I cannot to this day peer down into a lock, down the sheer wet walls, without a sense of trepidation, and many of my early dreams were of death by drowning, of being drawn magnetically towards the water's edge. (So strong did these dreams become in my adolescent years that they affected my waking life, and the margin of a pond or a river would attract my feet, just as a fast car can hypnotize a pedestrian on an otherwise empty road.)

2

The first thing I remember is sitting in a pram at the top of a hill with a dead dog lying at my feet. It was close by the fields which were later to become, thanks to the beneficence of my rich Uncle Edward – known for mysterious reasons as Eppy – the playing-fields of Berkhamsted School, for even the geography of the little town was influenced by the two big families of Greenes (seventeen Greenes resident in one small place would seem even today an unduly high proportion of the population, and at holiday times the Greenes could nearly reach a quarter of a century). The dog, as I know now, was a pug owned by my elder sister. It had been run over – by a horse-carriage? – and killed and the nurse thought it convenient to bring the cadaver home this way. The memory may well be a true one, as my mother once told me how surprised she had been months later by some reference which I made to the 'poor dog'; they were almost the first words I had spoken.

In all these early years I an uncertain what is genuinely remembered. For example I think I can remember a toy motor-car, which now surely – a 1908 vintage toy – might be worthy of a sale at Sotheby's, but since it appears in a photograph of myself and my brother Raymond, this may not be a true memory. My age then was about four, and I wore a pinafore and had fair curls falling around the neck. My elder brother with a proper masculine haircut, an adult of seven, stares fearlessly towards the box-camera, like a future mountaineer of Kamet and Everest, while I still have the ambiguity of undetermined sex.

As children we used to go down to the drawing-room for about an hour after tea, from 5.30 to 6.30, to play with our mother, and I remember the fear I felt that my mother would read us a story about some children who were sent into a forest by a wicked uncle to be murdered, but the murderer repented and left them to die of exposure and afterwards the birds covered their bodies with leaves. I dreaded the story because I was afraid of weeping. I would infinitely have preferred quick murder to the long drawn-out pathos of their end. My tear-ducts in childhood, and indeed for many years later, worked far too easily, and even today I sometimes slink shame-faced from a cinema at some happy ending that moves me by its incredibility. (Life isn't like that. Of such courage and such fidelity we dream only, but in my distress I wish them true.)

As I approach school-age the memories thicken. One vivid memory (I was probably about five) was of passing with my nurse the old alms-houses which leant against each other near the Grand Junction canal. There was a crowd outside one of the little houses and a man broke away and ran into the house. I was told that he was going to cut his throat, nobody followed him, everybody, including my nurse and I, stood outside waiting, but I never learnt whether he succeeded. *The Berkhamsted Gazette* would have informed me, but I couldn't yet read.*

Of all my first six years I have only such random memories as

*Perhaps there is an understandable failure of memory here, for my brother Raymond writes to me: 'You did in fact see the man cut his throat, standing by a first floor window, or the nurse may have obstructed your view. Anyway he succeeded.'

14

these and I cannot be sure of the time-sequence. They are significant for me because they remain, the stray symbols of a dream after the story has sunk back into the unconscious, and they cry for rescue like the survivors of a shipwreck.

There was a particular kind of wheaten biscuit with a very pale pure unsweetened flavour – I am reminded now of the Host – which only my mother had the right to eat. They were kept in a special biscuit-tin in her bedroom and sometimes as a favour I was given one to eat dipped in milk. I associate my mother with a remoteness, which I did not at all resent, and with a smell of eau-de-cologne. If I could have tasted her I am sure she would have tasted of wheaten biscuits. She paid occasional state visits to the nursery in the School House, a large confused room which looked out on the flint church and the old cemetery, with toy cupboards and bookshelves and a big wooden rocking-horse with wicked eyes and one large comfortable wicker-chair for the nurse beside the steel fireguard, and my mother gained in my eyes great dignity from her superintendence of the linen-cupboard, where a frightening witch lurked, but of that later. The wheaten biscuit remains for me a symbol of her cool puritan beauty – she seemed to eliminate all confusion, to recognize the good from the bad and choose the good, though where her family was concerned in later years she noticed only the good. If one of us had committed murder she would, I am sure, have blamed the victim. When she was in an untroubled coma before death and I was watching by her bed, her long white plantagenet face reminded me of a crusader on a tomb. It seemed the right peaceful end for the tall calm beautiful girl standing in a punt in a long skirt with a tiny belted waist and wearing a straw boater whom I had seen in the family album.

An unpleasant memory of those years is of a tin jerry full of blood: I was feeling horribly sick, for I had just had my adenoids out and my tonsils cut. The operation had been done at home. For thirty years after that the sight of blood worried and sickened me, so that sometimes I fainted at the mere description of an accident. In the blitz, before I encountered the first wounded, I was afraid of what my reaction might be until I found that fear and the necessity of action conquered the nausea.

15

Our home until I reached the age of six was a house called St John's, one of the boarding-houses of Berkhamsted School. My father was housemaster there. When he became the headmaster in 1910 we removed to the School House, but I went back to St John's as a boarder at thirteen and most of my memories of the house (and very unhappy ones they are) date back to that time. Before that first climacteric I remember of St John's only the extra piece of garden we had across the road, where on special days in summer we would go and play with the exciting sense of travelling abroad. There was a summer-house there (no such thing existed on the every-day side), and the garden was built up high above the road so that I couldn't see over the bushes to my home which might have been a hundred miles away. It was my first experience of foreign travel. Later I used to think of the two gardens as resembling England and France with the Channel between, although I had never been to France – England for every day and France for holidays.

At the far end of Berkhamsted at the Hall, the great house of the town, lived the family of Greene cousins. The mother was German and the whole family had an intimidatingly exotic air, for many of them had been born in Brazil near Santos, on a *fazenda* which was also the name of the coffee we drank. There were six children, the same number as in our family, and in ages they were inserted between us, our family starting first, as though my uncle, who was the younger brother, had suffered from a competitive spirit and wanted to catch my father up. My own particular friend was Tooter, though it was with his younger sister Barbara that I was years later to make the rather fool-hardy journey through Liberia which I have described in *Journey Without Maps*.

My uncle's children were the rich Greenes and we were regarded as the intellectual Greenes. We would visit them on Christmas Eve for the Christmas tree, my elder siblings staying for dinner. I used to be embarrassed by the carols in German round the tree because I was afraid I might be expected to sing too. The whole affair in our eyes seemed rather Teutonic, for to us the eve of Christmas had no significance at all. Christmas only began the next morning with the crunchy feel of a heavy stocking lying across the toes and a slight feeling of nausea, due to excitement, which bore the family name of 'Narcissus tummy-ache'. I don't remember any Christmas tree in our house, and mistletoe was an embarrassing joke played by our elders. Kissing had no appeal, and I kept well away from the mistletoe if anyone else were around.

On Christmas Eve, at the Hall, the children all had their presents laid on separate tables which were identified by names on cards. I remember being bitterly disappointed once when an adult present, a leather writing-case, on my table, turned out to be there in error: it was intended for my uncle, who bore the same name and who was the Permanent Secretary of the Admiralty and a Knight of the Bath – a title which I found impressive and not funny at all.

Very remote my uncle Graham seemed, and the more important for his dryness and his taciturnity and the glasses which dangled over his waistcoat on a broad black ribbon. Even today I find it difficult to think of him as a little boy riding to school in Cambridge on a donkey. His speech was all 'ehs' and 'ahs'. Perhaps he felt ill at ease with anyone but a civil servant. He died unmarried in 1950 at his home in Harston at the age of ninety-three, looked after by his two old sisters, Helen and Polly, both in their eighties. At the age of eighty-nine he fell under a tube train owing to failing eyesight on his way to attend a sub-committee of the Committee of Imperial Defence which was to discuss the import of reindeer into the north of Scotland. He lay, quiet and self-possessed, beside the live rail while the train moved back and it was found that he had only bruised a rib. With difficulty he was persuaded to return to Harston. There, when he was ninety-one, he fell out of a tree (he was pruning the branches) and for a while he had to take to his bed, but a more humdrum accident proved the fatal one, a year later, when he tripped over a chair on the lawn. He survived quite a while even then, though bed-ridden, having *The Times* leaders read to him every morning, and the first sign of his approaching end was when my old aunts while undressing him removed a toe with his socks. He was a remarkable man, if we had only known it. Having been drummed out of the Admiralty after Jutland by Lloyd George and the Northcliffe

17

Press, he joined his friend Winston Churchill at the Ministry of Munitions. Only recently in a volume of the *Dictionary of National Biography* did I learn of his connection with the world of James Bond – he was one of the founders of Naval Intelligence. Carson told how 'I met Churchill in the prime minister's room and congratulated him on his knowledge of men. "What do you mean?" said Lloyd George. "Well," I said, "Winston has the wisdom to choose for a much bigger job the man you dismissed from the Admiralty".'

My uncle lived in a big house at Harston in Cambridgeshire, and as children we would go there for the summer holidays, though later my elders went away to the Lake District to climb and I was left with my mother and the baby Hugh. (Finally my sister Molly fell off a mountain and got married to the man who photographed her fall – perhaps she admired his presence of mind.)

Harston House was – at least in part – a lovely William-and-Mary house, and it had a large old-fashioned garden very suited to hide-and-seek, with an orchard, a stream and a big pond containing an island, and there was a fountain on the front lawn. We would fix a cup to the handle of a walking stick, and the water so obtained tasted very cold and very pure. The fountain was about two feet deep and a yard across. Once my elder brother Raymond fell in at the age of three, and when asked how he had got out he replied with bravura, 'I struck out for the shore.' The smell of apples seemed to fall everywhere over the garden and the smell of box hedges, and there was a buzz of bees in the hot summer weather. I remember the funeral of a dead bird which was coffined in a Price's night-light box. My elders, Herbert and Molly and Raymond, buried him in what was called the Shady Walk. I was only a minor mourner, being the youngest, too young and unimportant to be priest or grave-digger or chorister.

My uncle was never there when we were. He stayed safely away from any family turbulence in his bachelor flat off Hanover Square. I had a very possessive feeling for the great rambling garden, and I was furious one year when my mother invited another small boy called Harker, the son of the school doctor, to

18

share my summer there. I treated him as a pariah, I wouldn't play with him, I would hardly speak to him. I never showed him how to get water from the fountain, and I knew hiding places that he would never find, so that he was left ambling aimlessly without a companion, bored sometimes to tears. The experience of that terrible long August was never repeated and thereafter I was allowed to stay alone.

It was at Harston I quite suddenly found that I could read – the book was *Dixon Brett, Detective*. I didn't want anyone to know of my discovery, so I read only in secret, in a remote attic, but my mother must have spotted what I was at all the same, for she gave me Ballantyne's *Coral Island* for the train journey home – always an interminable journey with the long wait between trains at Bletchley. I still wouldn't admit my new talent, and I stared at the only illustration all the way to the junction. No wonder it so impressed itself on my memory that I can see with my mind's eye today the group of children posed on the rocks. I think I feared that reading represented the entrance to the Preparatory School (I went through the grim portal a few weeks before my eighth birthday), or perhaps I disliked the sense of patronage which I always detected when I was praised for something others did quite naturally. Only a few years ago at an Edinburgh ceremonial my memory was confirmed by Doctor Dover Wilson, the Shakespearian scholar, who told me that my parents often spoke to him of the difficulty they found in teaching me to read. I detested that absurd book with the engravings which now seem so charming, *Reading Without Tears*. How could I be interested in a cat who sat on a mat? I couldn't identify with a cat. Dixon Brett was quite another matter, and he had a boy assistant, who might easily I thought, have been myself.

I particularly resented my father's interest. How could a grown man, I argued, feel any concern for what happened on a child's walk? To be praised was agony – I would crawl immediately under the nearest table. Until I had grown up I think my only real moments of affection for my father were when he made frog-noises with his palms, or played Fly Away, Jack, Fly Away, Jill, with a piece of sticking-plaster on his finger, or made me blow open the lid of his watch. Only when I had children of my own did I realize how his interest in my doings had been genuine, and only then I discovered a buried love and sorrow for him, which emerges today from time to time in dreams.

I think that my parents' was a very loving marriage; how far any marriage is happy is another matter and beyond an outsider's knowledge. Happiness can be ruined by children, by financial anxieties, by so many secret things: love too can be ruined, but I think their love withstood the pressure of six children and great anxieties. I was in Sierra Leone, running ineffectually a one-man office of the Secret Service, when my father died in 1942. The news came in two telegrams delivered in the wrong order – the first told me of his death – the second an hour later of his serious illness. Suddenly, between the secret reports to be coded and decoded, I unexpectedly felt misery and remorse, remembering how as a young man I had deliberately set out to shock his ideas which had been unflinchingly liberal in politics and gently conservative in morals. I had a Mass said for him by Father Mackey, the Irish priest in Freetown. I thought that if my father could know he would regard the gesture with his accustomed liberality and kindly amusement – he had never disputed by so much as a word my decision to become a Catholic. At least I felt sure that my method of payment would have pleased him. The priest asked me for a sack of rice for his poor African parishioners, for rice was scarce and severely rationed, and through my friendship with the Commissioner of Police I was able to buy one clandestinely.

Both parents have known someone the children have never known. My father had known the tall girl with the tiny waist wearing a boater, and my mother the young dandyish man who appeared in a tinted Oxford photograph on their bathroom wall, with a well-trimmed moustache, wearing evening dress with a blue waistcoat. More than ten years after his death my mother wrote to me. She had broken her hip and she had dreamt unhappily that my father had not come to see her in hospital or even written to her and she couldn't understand it. Now, even when she was awake, she felt unhappy because of his silence. Oddly enough I too had dreamt of him a few days before. My mother and I were driving in a car and at a turn in the road my father had

20

signalled to us, and when we stopped he came running to catch us up. He was happy, he had a joyful smile as he climbed into the back of the car, for he had been let out of hospital that morning. I wrote to my mother that perhaps there was some truth in the idea of purgatory, and this was the moment of release.

For me this dream was the end of a series which had recurred over the years after his death. In them my father was always shut away in hospital out of touch with his wife and children – though sometimes he returned home on a visit, a silent solitary man, not really cured, who would have to go back again into exile. The dreams remain vivid even today, so that sometimes it is an effort for me to realize that there was no hospital, no separation, and that he lived with my mother till he died. In his last years he had diabetes and always beside her place at table there stood a weighing-machine to measure his diet, and it was she who daily gave him his injections of insulin. There was no truth at all in the idea of his loneliness and unhappiness, but perhaps the dreams show that I loved him more than I knew.

The only separation that really existed was from his children. As a headmaster he was even more distant than our aloof mother. At the Easter holidays we would go to the seaside at Littlehampton, travelling with our mother and nurse in a reserved third-class compartment with a hamper-lunch, but my father wisely would always come down alone a few days later second-class. Sometimes he took a winter holiday alone in Egypt or in France or Italy with a friend, Mr George, a clergyman and headmaster. They remained very formal through all the years, calling each other by their surnames, though naturally George has a less formal sound than Greene. I think their holidays were more intellectual than convivial, for I remember my father naming some place in France visited many years before and saying to his friend, 'You remember, George, that was where we drank a bottle of wine.' Once – it was in Naples – they had a curious encounter. A stranger hearing them speak in English asked whether he might join them over their coffee. There was something familiar and to them vaguely disagreeable about his face, but he kept them charmed by his wit for more than an hour before he said good-bye. They didn't exchange names even at parting and he left them to pay for his drink which was certainly not coffee. It was some while before they realized in whose company they had been. The stranger was Oscar Wilde, who not very long before had been released from prison. 'Think,' my father would always conclude his story, 'how lonely he must have been to have expended so much time and wit on a couple of schoolmasters on holiday'. It never occurred to him that Wilde was paying for his drink in the only currency he had.*

My mother's remoteness, her wonderful lack of the possessive instinct, was made much easier for her to achieve by the presence of Nanny, an old woman who came first to look after my elder sister, some thirteen years before these memories begin, and by a long succession of nursery-maids (who never endured very long, for perhaps they represented a threat to Nanny's future). I remember her bent over my bath with her white hair in a bun, holding a sponge. Her temper deteriorated before she retired on a pension, but I never remember being afraid of her, only impressed by that white bun of age.

Before I was old enough to be taken on these holidays to Littlehampton, when all I knew of the sea was from the gossip of my elders, I used to assume that a pile of sand in a timber yard by the canal bank at Berkhamsted was the seaside; it seemed quite unremarkable to me, and I saw no reason to envy my brothers and sister. Indeed I was very content in those days to remain in one place (a contentment which I envy now). On the occasion of King George V's coronation, when I was six, I was given the choice of going to London with my parents and the three elder children to seats procured for them by my uncle Graham or of watching the local Berkhamsted procession in the company of my maiden aunt Maud who lived in the town. The more economical alternative carried with it the right to choose a toy from the toy-shop, and to the relief of my parents I chose to stay.†

*I think this encounter must have been during the Christmas holidays of 1897–8 when his friend Bosie had departed and Wilde wrote of 'ill-health. loneliness and general *ennui* with a tragi-comedy of an existence'.

†I think my decision was the right one. This is how my brother Raymond, who was ten, described the great day: 'We got up at 4.15 in the morning and had breakfast. At Euston we took a cab and drove to Trafalgar

The toy I chose was a table croquet-set, and I remember with irritation how difficult it was to make the hooked hoops stand straight on a tablecloth. In the local procession somebody rode in armour on a horse, impersonating probably the Duke of Cornwall, and this recalled the picture of a knight in a big bound volume of some girls' magazine in the dining-room. (Later I loved *Ivanhoe* and Maurice Hewlett's *The Forest Lovers* and the first stories I tried to write were of the Middle Ages.) The toy-shop was kept by the old woman called Figg in the High Street. One climbed down a few steps into something like a crowded cabin, where on bunk over bunk lay the long narrow boxes of Britain's toy soldiers, quite inexpensive in those days, in an amazing variety which recalled all the imperial wars of the past century: Sepoys and Zulus and Boers and Russians and French. From memories of those first six years I have a general impression of tranquillity and happiness, and the world held enormous interest, even though I disappointed my mother on my first visit to the Zoo by sitting down and saying, 'I'm tired. I want to go home.'

There were terrors, too, of course, but they would have been terrors at any age. I distinguish here between terror and fear. From terror one escapes screaming, but fear has an odd seduction. Fear and the sense of sex are linked in secret conspiracy, but terror is a sickness like hate.

I inherited from my mother a blinding terror of birds and bats. Even today I loathe the touch of feathers, and I remember how one night at Harston a bat came into my bedroom from one of the great trees on the lawn outside. I saw it poke its furry nose first around the curtains and wait to be observed. Next night I was allowed to keep the window shut, but a bat – I was sure it

---

Square. Then we couldn't go on as it was such a crowd, but at last we got to the Admiralty. We waited about two hours and then the procession came by. Soldiers first, then the state carriages with dukes in ermine with coronets. Then more soldiers and state carriages and then the Royal coach and the King with his crown on. Then came more soldiers etc. After dinner it came by again and just as the crown was put on the King's head, the street lamps lighted, 41 guns fired and then we came home and we were awfully tired'. Oh, the fatigues of childhood never to be equalled till old age.

was the same one – then came down the chimney. I shrieked with my head under the sheet, until my brother Raymond came and caught it in a butterfly net.*

Another recurring terror was of the house catching fire at night and I associate it with sticky coloured plates in the *Boys' Own Paper* recording the exploits of heroic firemen. There always seemed to be fires in those days, and yet I never actually saw a fire until I witnessed too many of them in the winter of 1940–41. I think it was later, when I was seven, menaced by the approach of school and a new sort of life, that I was terrified by a witch who would lurk at night on the nursery landing by the linen-cupboard. After a long series of nightmares when the witch would leap on my back and dig long mandarin finger-nails into my shoulders, I dreamt I turned on her and fought back and after that she never again appeared in sleep.

Dreams have always had an importance for me: 'the finest entertainment known and given rag cheap'. Two novels and several short stories have emerged from my dreams, and sometimes I have had hints of what is called by the difficult name of extra-sensory perception. On the April night of the *Titanic* disaster, when I was five and it was Easter holiday time in Littlehampton, I dreamt of a shipwreck. One image of the dream has remained with me for more than sixty years: a man in oilskins bent double beside a companion-way under the blow of a great wave. Again in 1921 I wrote home from my psycho-analyst's: 'A night or two ago I had a shipwreck dream, the ship I was on going down in the Irish Sea. I didn't think anything about it. We don't have papers here as the usual thing, and it was not till yesterday, looking at an old paper, I saw about the sinking of the *Rowan* in the Irish Sea. I looked at my dream diary and found that my dream had been Saturday night. The accident had happened just after Saturday midnight.' Again in 1944 I dreamed of a V.1 missile some weeks before the first attack. It passed horizontally across the sky flaming at the tail in the very form it was to take.

*The fear of bats remains. I had to steel myself later in Angkor Wat to pass a damaged bat flapping on the floor of a passage, while up in the pineapple towers one could see small men on ropes gathering the bats' dung. In those days there were Vietminh ambushes around Angkor, but I would have preferred an ambush to that dying bat.

24

3

Memory is like a long broken night. As I write, it is as though I am waking from sleep continually to grasp at an image which I hope may drag in its wake a whole intact dream, but the fragments remain fragments, the complete story always escapes.

I must have been still under six years old when we all waited through a sunny afternoon in the St John's garden – on the English side of the road – for the chance of seeing Blériot making his London to Manchester flight, but he never passed overhead – it was a long afternoon wasted, when we might have been across the Channel in France, in the holiday-garden.

I hated the very idea of children's parties. They were a threat that one day I might have to put to practical use my dancing lessons, of which I can only remember the black shiny shoes with the snappy elastic and the walk down King's Road, between the red-brick villas on winter evenings, holding someone's hand for fear of slipping. The only children's party I can actually remember was up near Berkhamsted Common in a big strange house, where I never went again; a Chinese amah asked me if I wanted to make water and I did not understand her, so that always afterwards I thought of it as a Chinese expression. Many years later I wrote a short story about a children's party, and another about dancing lessons, and perhaps there are memories concealed in them too.

I have an impression my father used to smack me as a child though I can remember only one specific beating at a later age, perhaps because it woke a sexual interest in me. Once I called my my maiden aunt Maud a bugger and she reported it to my father, who pulled me out from under a table and demanded an apology which I was unwilling to give, not knowing what my offence was. Indeed I never meant to offend her. I was closer to her than to any other of my numerous aunts, most of them officially maiden – Helen who ran a school of Swedish gymnastics and had passionate women friendships, dear muddle-headed Polly who lived at Harston and painted bad pictures and taught Gwen Raverat to draw and wrote ambitious plays for the village institute (the whole conflict between Christianity and Paganism in

25

Northumbria she managed to contain in a one-act piece with fifty characters), the beautiful mysteriously gay Nora (whom we knew as Nono), Alice, the progressive, who ran a school in South Africa and was a friend of General Smuts and Olive Schreiner, Madge, an aunt-by-marriage, the pretty daughter of the Irish poet Doctor Todhunter – she sang songs about 'Away with the gipsies oh' in pre-Raphaelite gowns from Liberty's.

And somehow left out, I think, of all the children's memories except as a figure in the remote background of the sunny garden – one had to peer to see her closer – there was Florence, who lived in her own cottage at Harston. Harston had been colonized by the Greenes almost as effectively as Berkhamsted or, as I was to discover later, St Kitts. The Greenes seemed to move as a tribe like the Bantus, taking possession. Helen, Polly, Alice and Florence were all paternal Greenes, and Florence was the only girl to marry, but as she had no children she returned to the tribe. I remember her as a thin peaky old lady, her face, which had perhaps been beautiful, hidden behind a spotted veil, tied like Queen Alexandra's under the chin. She had none of the gaiety, fantasy and silliness of Polly; she wasn't brusque and masculine like Helen and Alice. She hadn't a family voice at all that one could recognize. It was as though her loss of virginity kept her apart from all the other Greene aunts – she was only Mrs Phillips, the widow of a county schoolmaster. And yet before she married she had been the most romantic of them all. At eighteen she fell in love with a young sailor who wanted to leave the navy and emigrate with her to the wilder parts of Australia, but the wisdom of older relations prevailed. Otherwise Australia might have been colonized too. Four years later a rich brewer in Lincoln wanted to marry her and gave her the *Life of Charles Kingsley*. He was a poor substitute for the young sailor and nothing came of that. There was a Mr Rust, but no one ever knew which of the sisters he had an eye on, so Florence finally settled for Mr Phillips, the schoolmaster. He kept a little monkey who ate oranges, dividing them meticulously, peeled paper off the walls, and put his arms tenderly round Mr Phillips's neck. Would Mr Phillips without the monkey have been enough? Strangely, as an old lady, one thought of Aunt Florence as being always on

26

a visit, from remoter regions even than Alice, perhaps from Australia.

Maud, my mother's sister, was 'the poor relation' who lived alone in a little house near the school and was made use of by my mother as a fourth at bridge and to take me as a convalescent child to Brighton. She vexed my mother by a nervous trick of yawning and sighing at frequent intervals which was apt to discourage her partner, if he was meeting her for the first time. Nothing that happened in Berkhamsted escaped her eye: she was a walking news-letter, and this too was a cause of irritation to my mother, who, perhaps, thought that as the headmaster's wife she was in danger of figuring in the headlines. In later life I loved my aunt for this very quality, and would make journeys from London to have tea with her and hear the latest gossip of Berkhamsted. The headmaster, when he was no longer a Greene, was fair game, and one in particular caused a good deal of sexual scandal at which my aunt scarcely pretended to be shocked. Her ear was very close to the ground. Once I arrived with my brother Hugh unannounced, walking directly from the railway station five minutes away. She opened the door to us, saying, 'When I heard you were in Berkhamsted I put on the kettle for tea.'

It was after I was six and we had all moved to the School House, but before I went to school, that I began regularly to steal currants and sultanas out of the big biscuit-tins in the School House store-room, stuff my pockets full with them, currants in the left, sultanas in the right, and feast on them secretly in the garden. The meal ended always with a sensation of nausea, but to be secure from detection I had to finish them all, even the strays which had picked up fluff from the seams of the pockets. There is a charm in improvised eating which a regular meal lacks, and there was a glamour never to be recaptured in secret picnics on long sunny mornings on the roof of the Hall, our uncle's big house. No stone of it now remains, a building estate has swallowed all – the lawns, the trees, the stables and the meadows, which were to be the scenery of my calf-love. When I see a performance of *The Cherry Orchard* today, it is on that estate I hear the axes falling. I would sit up there with my cousin Tooter, consuming sweets bought with our weekly pocket money (which was twopence, I think) and discussing possible futures – as a midshipman in the Navy or an Antarctic explorer – none of them to be realized, while we watched the oblivious figures in the yard and the stables below from our godlike secrecy and security. The sweets I remember best were white and tubular, much thinner than any cigarette, filled with a dark chocolate filling. If I found one now I am sure that it would have the taste of hope.

A smell which comes back from those years was the smell of a breakfast food which I didn't like. The same smell I noticed later from sacks of grain outside a corn chandler's, and curiously it was the smell too of my carriers' sweat in Liberia in 1935, and yet there in the damp heat and the strangeness, as they lay close around me at night for fear of cannibals, I enjoyed the smell: it had become the smell of Africa.

Post-six too are my memories of being ill – it happened often, but only the dentist left unhappy memories. Till now I have never suffered greater pain than I did then. I remember rolling on the drawing-room floor in agony from an exposed nerve. I don't think he was a very good dentist, and for years after I had left his care I would avoid walking, on the way to Northchurch and the Crooked Billet, past his house and the stained glass window representing the Laughing Cavalier which hid the chair of torture. Later I resented the fact that my parents used to visit a dentist in London – Mr Crick, I felt sure, was as painless as he was expensive.

But of my other ailments I retain only a sense of peaceful darkness, of endless time, of privacy, a night-light burning, and of books bought by my mother for me to read, sometimes ones that bored me, like *The Man-eaters of Tsavo*. Apart from the tonsil operation I can remember only one unhappy illness – the first attack of hay-fever after playing in a haystack with my cousins. Nobody knew what it was, and I seemed to lie awake coughing and gasping for breath all night long. No later attack was so severe, and even the pains of pleurisy, which I had later, were more easily bearable and less frightening; perhaps it was during that night I evolved my fear of drowning – I was able to imagine the lungs filling with water.

There are two stray scatological memories of the time. For

some reason – it can only have been a convalescence – I found myself at Littlehampton alone with Nora, my mother's favourite sister, so much gayer, more elegant and popular than poor Maud, who once burst into tears when my German aunt spoke of the beautiful hair she possessed when she was young. I was too embarrassed by her elegance to tell my aunt that I wanted to go to the lavatory and I fouled my knickers. At six too I made, perhaps it was on the same occasion, a coloured drawing of a bit of shit for the *School House Gazette*, a periodical in manuscript edited by my eldest brother Herbert (I had the rank of office boy). My memory tells me that the drawing was included because it was taken for a cigar, and I was a little annoyed at the mis-understanding, though I put nobody right, and yet recently I have searched in vain for my painting in the pages of the *Gazette* – perhaps the true meaning of it was understood after all.

Apart from the corpse of my sister's pug at the bottom of my pram, the only domestic animal I can remember was a Pekinese called Bicki which also belonged to Molly, for she was the only one of us ever allowed to own a dog. We in the nursery shared a succession of canaries (one broke a blood vessel singing too loud and long), and I once owned two white mice, but when one ate the other and then died of loneliness, I was falsely accused of having starved them, so they were never replaced. My brother Herbert (but that was a long while after) brought home a baby pig which he had won at a fair and lodged it in his bedroom for the night. On the floor below, unable to sleep, I had the strong impression that he was kicking a football around – he was the athlete of the family. The pig was not allowed to stay.

The Pekinese arrived nailed down in a box. It was in a savage temper after a long railway journey, and it remained consistently unamiable towards my sister who owned it and bit her on many occasions. Bicki and I got on well together. Once it was lost after a walk, the police were warned, and eventually many hours later, when the streets of Berkhamsted had been well scoured and messages sent to Boxmoor and Hemel Hempstead and Chesham, it was found asleep under my bed. My mother was always un-favourably disposed towards dogs, until many years later she became attached to a mongrel of my own called Paddy, and after

29

Bicki had bitten the baby Hugh it was sold quickly into another captivity.

The toy I remember most clearly was a fort. It was given me on my seventh birthday. It arrived dismantled, and I stuck the portcullis and walls and towers on to green cliffs by nails which fitted into holes. It was more like a medieval castle than the forts of Liège and Verdun which were soon to be so important in our lives and it was a little unsuitable for the Zulus who sometimes guarded it.

The games we played were: *French and English*. This was a garden game of conflict, but I can remember none of the rules which must have dated back to the Napoleonic wars. It was played by Charlotte Brontë in her childhood.

Hunt the Thimble. A special treat in the drawing-room when there were aunts and uncles about. At Christmas there was always an enormous number of Greene aunts and uncles, since my mother and father were first cousins of the same name, and a great many of them were unmarried and available.

Tom Tiddler's Ground. Played in the garden on the croquet lawn. A game of trespass. 'Here I come on Tom Tiddler's Ground, picking up gold and silver ...'

The Ocean is Agitated. This was played on Christmas Day when the cousins came to tea. It was a kind of musical chairs. One person promenaded round the circle calling out the name of a fish which had then to rise and follow. 'The ocean is agitated by a shrimp ... by a shark ... by a sardine' and finally 'The ocean is agitated by all the fish'. Then came 'The ocean is calm' and there was a scramble for chairs. I didn't care for this game. Even at an early age I found the chant ridiculous.

Hide-and-Seek in the Dark. This was a game containing the agreeable ingredient of fear, and we played it on the ground floor and first floor of the School House with all the lights out and in the big school hall during the holidays.

Hunt the Slipper. We played this rarely, but always at Christmas.

Musical Chairs. This was a ritual part of the Christmas Day tea-party, when the rich Greenes joined us from the Hall. On such occasions we would play in the old school hall, and I don't think anyone enjoyed it except perhaps the aunts and uncles.

General Post. Played on the same occasion, and with as little pleasure. Party games never seemed like real games (which were games without adults). They were obligations like going to church.

There were Charades, too, and Dumb Crambo, a kind of charade without dialogue, and a game called Clumps, which had been played in my father's childhood.

I have the impression that such games are becoming as obsolete as the street games described by Norman Douglas. Certainly I played none of them with my own children, for games like this demand a large family.

There was a real game too, not a party game, played in the old school hall and invented by my eldest brother Herbert, who was always of an adventurous character until he was changed by the continual and sometimes shameful failures of his adult life. We divided into sides and each side started from opposite ends of the hall. The lights had been turned out and one side must reach the opposite wall in the darkness without being caught. Benches had been piled on benches as obstacles. We listened with agreeably tense nerves for the creak of a board, scanned the blackness ahead, and felt our slow way, hands outstretched. I imagined myself a *franc-tireur* of the 1870 war of which I had read in a book of Henty's. War was still romantic, and every summer Herbert organized all-day manoeuvres with our cousins in the country lanes and fields behind the Hall. We carried sandwiches and ginger beer in bottles with glass marble stoppers, and the object of one side was to penetrate unseen to the stables and capture them. Scouting behind hedges, crawling along ditches, making heroic forays across an open space, one experienced the first hint of sexual interest for the enemy – the girl on sentry duty in the stable yard.

There was one entertainment I was not allowed to attend until I was much older. It was given, whenever he visited my parents at Berkhamsted, by an old clergyman called Canon Baldwin, who held the living at Harston. He recited the more grisly scenes from Shakespeare, in the dark of the drawing-room, taking all the parts himself: male and female. Sometimes, listening from a discreet distance in the hall outside, I heard muffled gurgles, chokes and screams, as Duncan lay laced with his golden blood or Desdemona strangled. They were tense occasions for my parents, as a single cough from one of the privileged guests would stop the Canon in mid-speech and he would call angrily, like Hamlet's uncle, for lights. Perhaps it was not surprising that his daughter married Doctor Dover Wilson.

The Canon and my father were great chess-players. My father played for his county by correspondence, but he admitted that the Canon was the better man. The Canon would sometimes take my father for a walk up to the Common and play chess with him on the way. 'I open with Queen's Pawn Two,' he would say, and my father would make the appropriate response, but after about ten moves he lost his sense of the board, and the Canon would announce triumphantly and irrefutably, 'Checkmate.'

clob and decenter a hvam tm keres with his voice blood a Deodmori hamade to hav enotar ocaa ona na roe penmia ia a self-a aoeep acoan ora con a and euter a eutr a lop la Camm to mac apce la ma ie woad hall anp ga ina lica Hamka a unakka agei atdro cora ik wa a por ap orma ina thav as a daughm marnia Dora a howta Waim a a aroe tra boa which my fat cat

Chapter 2

1

SOME time in 1910, when my father became headmaster, we removed from St John's (down the road into the High Street, turn left into Castle Street by the Norman church) to the School House, and that remained our home until my father's retirement in the twenties. The new things which most impressed me were the long path from the street to the front door, on the right the red-brick Tudor school hall and on the left, divided from me only by a flower-bed, the old disused churchyard. There was a white cat which used to sit on the tombstones and it was said by my father to be the ghost of a notorious absentee headmaster in the eighteenth century. When I was sixteen I sat on a gravestone with Peter Quennell and we both read aloud to each other from *The Yellow Book* with a sense of daring and decadence.

At the end of the long path, beyond the house, one reached the tennis-court, and beside the tennis-court was a small flower-garden with a pond full of tadpoles, and a buddleia which in summer swarmed with peacock butterflies. One of my early memories is of catching near the buddleia a female orange-tip which they told me was a very rare specimen, much rarer than the male. After I caught a butterfly I would put it in a poison-bottle, but a scruple always inhibited me from pinning it out in a case as my elders did, so the corpses soon became brittle and from frequent examination fell to powder, and then I threw them away. I wasn't scared of butterflies, but I was deeply afraid of moths – something about their hairy bodies terrified me. I fear them still and I am unhappy with one in the room until I have killed it. Beyond the buddleias lay two greenhouses at right-angles: in the small one were only pot-plants, geraniums and the like, but in the larger were plants of importance, orchids, which my father brought back from sales in London, and green grapes, and there was a deckchair in which my father at leisure moments would sit smoking a pipe and blowing smoke over the grapes to kill greenflies. There were very strict rules about never leaving a door open. I had the impression that the least drop in temperature brought instant death, and indeed I was not far from the truth. Once the gardener, who had the misleadingly responsible name of Charge, got tight and forgot to stoke the stove in the orchid house. All the orchids died including one for which my father had refused three hundred pounds – the equivalent of several thousand pounds today. It must have been a severe blow as it would be for me to have the manuscript of a story carelessly destroyed, but my elder brother cannot remember him even mentioning the matter, nor was the gardener sacked.

Through a gateway by the smaller greenhouse one passed to the croquet lawn, where at the far end were apple trees and a revolving shelter which figured in my first truancy. I don't clearly remember whether it was at this period I tried very hard to kill my brother Raymond by hitting him over the head with a croquet mallet, but I think this violent outbreak came later when I shared a room with him and we woke every morning to a quarrel. Now I shared a room uncomfortably with the baby Hugh, who cried at night and kept me awake.

Walking across the croquet lawn (what a vast estate the whole place seems to me now, when I live, like most of my contemporaries, an apartment-life between bedroom and sitting-room), one came to a wooden fence which separated it from the kitchen-garden and a forest of raspberry and loganberry canes. Sometimes, but not often, we were allowed to pick from them and eat, and I preferred the winy flavour of the large loganberries. Beyond the kitchen-garden, on the right, was the entrance to the school quad, and on the left were the stables, which in those days contained no car, not even a horse, only one donkey called Miranda (she was employed in taking the washing to the laundry), and the cottage of the gardener, Charge. Beyond this cottage and behind yet another wall my father had built the School House sanatorium and near there, in a second kitchen-garden, we children were given small allotments of our own to tend – perhaps six feet square. (I can only remember growing radishes.) My only other gardening activity was to collect snails in a bucket and pour salt on them, so that they exploded into foam. (I was paid so much a

34

hundred for their corpses.) I think I was rather older when I was paid a penny a dozen for killing cabbage-white butterflies with a tennis-racket. This seemed to me a very fine sport, and I can sympathize with the interest the Chinese feel when encouraged to kill flies at sight.*

The School House stood in the street called Castle Street which ran down to the canal. On the opposite side were rather inferior shops, not up to the High Street standard: a sweet-shop (one had to climb steps to enter it) where we bought the mineral waters for our manoeuvres; a jeweller's called Bailey's (an old man with a white beard sat perpetually behind the window with a magnifying glass in his eye mending watches and when they read to me about Moses and the Tablets of the Law, I always thought of him); a stationer's and a pawnbroker's where I once tried to pawn a broken cricket-bat but the broker wouldn't accept it.

I had splintered the bat in a clandestine game, beating in bushes near the canal for a lost ball, and I didn't want anyone at home to see the condition it was in. At some stage between eight and ten I had made friends with two or three town boys of what was called then the working-class, and one summer I used to meet them in secret near some rubbish dumps beside the canal. I would bring a bat and a cricket-ball, neither of which they possessed. (Cricket, even in the preparatory school, was still a game: it only became a sport and therefore feared in the senior school.)

This is one of a few memories which remain to me suggesting some social conditioning. Why otherwise should the meetings have remained secret? There were others. During the 1914 war an old woman lived in Castle Street who prepared tripe, and I was given the idea that this was a far lower occupation than a butcher's – it was 'untouchable', though we frequently ate her tripe with white onion sauce. My mother was deeply offended because the tripe-seller's daughter married an officer in the Inns of Court

*I noticed with pleasure one year when I was travelling in the restaurant-car between Hankow and Pekin that there was a fly-swatter beside every place, but alas! there were no flies left to swat. I remember a glorious day in Freetown in 1942 when I closed the windows of my little office and slaughtered more than three hundred flies in a timed four minutes.

35

O.T.C., which was stationed for a while in the town (the Corps was regarded by the citizens with some pride because it was not an ordinary regiment – every man was a potential officer as well as a potential barrister).

In the Junior School, which I entered about ten, I became aware too of the stigma attached to those who were 'train boys'. A day-boy was as respectable as a boarder, but a train-boy was not. (Claud Cockburn, who lived at Tring only a few miles away, avoided the stigma because he was sent as a boarder to my father's School House.) The idea was fostered by many of the masters. Train-boys were regarded as dirty (no wonder, after half an hour on the L.N.W.R. burning war-time fuel), and the fact that many were aided by L.C.C. grants was held against them too. At a later date my father, who unlike my mother was quite without social prejudice, tried to remove the stigma by giving them a house and a housemaster and calling them Adders, but it was not a very helpful choice of name. It needed moral courage to be friends with a 'train bug', as they were called, but I can't remember any feeling stronger than a certain illicit toleration which I felt towards the dirtiest of the lot. He was once caned in public in my form room by my father for some offence which was never made clear to any of us, but we were accustomed at that age to the moral confusion of adults and we didn't trouble to ask him the reason.

Though my father was completely free from social snobbery I noticed a certain exaggerated interest in royalty which was exhibited by my mother and by the aunts who were temporarily in-waiting around her, and I was obscurely irritated; it seemed to lower our family pride, though I was ready enough to accept the glamour of royalty in fiction, in the imaginary world of Ruritania and Kravonia.

I slept at first in the same room as Hugh, who for a long period, it seems to me now, made me pass hours of sleeplessness with his crying. When I went to bed, I had to creep by a kind of branch line on the main staircase that ran steeply up to my mother's private lavatory, which lay in a tower over the terrace at one end of the school quad. My father never used this lavatory, I think, but the children sometimes did, and at night this narrow climbing stair on the way to bed was the point of terror: anything might lurk there in ambush.

I shared my bed with a multitude of soft animals of which I can remember a teddy bear (the most loved), a glove bear (it came second in my affection because it could not stand alone), and a blue plush bird (it was the age of Maeterlinck). I kept the bird, I think, only for the sake of filling the bed, because I disliked the feel of plush and I have mentioned my terror of birds. When quiet had fallen on the house, the fear of fire would emerge like smoke and I would imagine I had been deserted by all my family. I would drop the teddy bear out of bed and shout for the nurse or nursery-maid to pick it up. When one of them came, I felt assured again that all was normal, and I could sleep, though once I remember getting out of bed and sitting on the top of the stairs in order that I might hear the voices from the dining-room below, the low comforting drone of dull adult conversation which told me that the house was not yet ablaze.

My favourite toys in those days were a clockwork train and lead soldiers. When the soldiers had lost too many limbs to stand up we melted them down in a frying-pan over the nursery fire and dropped them into cold water as people do now in Sweden on New Year's night, seeking omens of the future. (I remember well the unmistakable question mark I fished out of the water one Stockholm night which fixed in lead my doubt of the future.) When I was a bit older (about twelve) I would play with Hugh, who was six, an elaborate war game based on H. G. Wells's book *Little Wars*. In the holidays we were able to use the big tables in the School House dining-hall. We would push two tables together and lay out a whole countryside. There were roads marked in chalk and cottages and forests of twigs and rivers which had to be crossed. One game might last a week, with perhaps two hundred men on either side, quick raids by cavalry and slow advances by infantry, measured on lengths of string, mêlées which led to the capture of prisoners, and bombardments with the two 4·2 naval guns. It was 1916, but war was still glamorous to a child.

I passed too through a Meccano period, adding box to box each Christmas, but I had little skill as an engineer. For hobbies

37

(a hobby is an almost compulsive necessity of childhood) I collected stamps. I sold my collection later to Hugh for cash which he always seemed to have easily available – he must have hoarded his weekly twopences, though I never discovered where, and bought with the proceeds books on Antarctic exploration. (The Arctic never interested me because it was all sea.) I day-dreamed of being taken on an expedition as a sea-scout, and when I was about ten I wrote to Doctor Bruce, the explorer, and criticized several statements in his book on Polar Exploration in the Home University Library. I received a courteous and defensive reply.

I collected cigarette cards too, and for a very brief period, because somebody gave me a special album for them, postmarks, but I found these rather abstract and there was no Stanley Gibbons catalogue to indicate whether Penang was more valuable than Angmering. Crests and postcards too had their appropriate albums, and I remember another toy, a monorail car. I have never seen one since. The thin steel single rails were tricky to fasten and the car never kept to them long, swaying wildly, losing balance and plunging to earth. I should be nervous today of travelling by monorail.

The books on the nursery shelves which interested me most were *The Little Duke* by Charlotte M. Yonge (the memory of this book returned to me when I was writing *The Ministry of Fear* and when I revised the novel after the war I inserted chapter headings from *The Little Duke*), *The Children of the New Forest* by Captain Marryat, the Andrew Lang Fairy Books, the E. Nesbits, of which I liked best *The Enchanted Castle*, *The Phoenix and the Carpet*, *Five Children and It* (the less fantastic *The Would-Be-Goods* and *The Treasure Seekers* never meant much to me). Two incidents from these books have always remained vivid to me, one of terror and one of joyful excitement: the Ugly Wugglies made of masks and umbrellas in *The Enchanted Castle* who suddenly came alive and applauded the children's play from their roofless mouths, clapping empty gloves, and the end of *The Phoenix*, when the magical bird has gone and a great box arrives full of everything the children have ever desired: 'toys and games and books, and chocolate and candied cherries, and paint-boxes and photographic cameras' – Brownies they would have been in those days. I think I read alone, but perhaps it was read aloud to us, Kipling's *Baa Baa Black Sheep*, which was like a warning not to take happiness in childhood for granted. At an earlier period of course there was Beatrix Potter. I have never lost my admiration for her books and I have often reread her, so that I am not surprised when I find in one of my own stories, *Under the Garden*, a pale echo of Tom Kitten being trounced up by the rats behind the skirting-board and the sinister Anna-Maria covering him with dough, and in *Brighton Rock* the dishonest lawyer, Prewitt, hungrily echoes Miss Potter's dialogue as he watches the secretaries go by carrying their little typewriters.

Towards the end of this period in my life I came on Henty. We had on the nursery shelves a long run of Henty, and I particularly liked the dull historical parts. 'The XIVth Hussars proceeded in close order to the top of the ridge. On the right flank were the Second Ghurkas . . .' Rider Haggard I discovered after Henty. My favourite, of course, was *King Solomon's Mines*, but the later adventures of Quatermain bored me. I fell fast in love with Nada the Lily, and because of his savagery I admired Chaka, the great King of Zululand. Later I read *The Brethren* (about the crusades), from which a great phrase remains in my mind to this day, 'So they went, talking earnestly of all things, but, save in God, finding no hope at all', *The Wanderer's Necklace* (a romance of Byzantium in which the hero is blinded by the woman he loves), and *Ayesha*, the sequel to *She*. I didn't at all care for romantic *She*, and found the metaphysical love story sloppy as I find it today (I have always preferred Freud to Jung). But the scene in *Ayesha* when the mad Khan goes hunting with bloodhounds the lord who had courted his wife held me with the strange attraction of suffering and cruelty. 'What followed I will not describe, but never shall I forget the scene of those two heaps of worrying wolves, and of the maniac Khan, who yelled in his fiendish joy, and cheered on his death-hounds to finish their red work.' *Montezuma's Daughter* led me to read and reread a history of Mexico in the school library; the dark night of Cortez' retreat from Mexico City along the narrow causeways haunts me still. What a happy chance it seemed in those days to be the son of the headmaster, for in the holidays all the shelves of the library were open to me, with thousands of books only waiting to be explored.

To Stanley Weyman I must have been introduced fairly early, because I seem to remember my favourite, *The Story of Francis Cludde* (a story of the persecution of Protestants in Queen Mary's reign) being read aloud to me, but it may have been during one of my periodic illnesses. (These agreeably broke up the endless years of childhood: two attacks of measles, a threatened mastoid, jaundice, pleurisy.) There were other Stanley Weymans which were nearly as important to me: *Count Hannibal* (with the masochism of the scorned lover who finally conquers the proud beauty) and *The Abbess of Vlaye*, which perhaps I valued because I had stolen it with some risk from the local W. H. Smith's store. Other books which I have since bought and reread for old time's sake are *The Lost Column*, a story of the Boxer Rebellion, and *The Pirate Aeroplane* both by Captain Gilson. *The Pirate Aeroplane* made a specially deep impression with its amiable American villain. One episode, when the young hero who is to be shot at dawn for trying to sabotage the pirate plane, plays rummy with his merciless and benevolent captor was much in my mind when I wrote about a poker game in *England Made Me*. I bought *Chums* every week and I remember in particular a fine pirate serial which rivalled *Treasure Island* – by what forgotten author? – and a fascinating account of a world war which began with a coolie strike in the Port of London. (I would force my brother Hugh to lie quiet on the sofa for hours while I read it to him.)

The influence of early books is profound. So much of the future lies on the shelves: early reading has more influence on conduct than any religious teaching. I feel certain that I would not have made a false start, when I was twenty-one, in the British American Tobacco Company, which had promised me a post in China, if I had never read Captain Gilson's *Lost Column*, and without a knowledge of Rider Haggard would I have been drawn later to Liberia? (This led to a war-time post in Sierra Leone. At Oxford I had made tentative inquiries about the Nigerian Navy as a future career.) And surely it must have been *Montezuma's Daughter* and the story of the disastrous night of Cortez' retreat which lured me twenty years afterwards to Mexico. *The Man-eaters of Tsavo* on the other hand fixed in me a boring image of East Africa which even Hemingway was powerless to change. Only an assignment to report the Mau-Mau rebellion in 1951 and the sense of continuous danger on the Kikuyu roads was able to remove it.

Poetry at this period meant very little to me. There were many fatuous verses in the anthology we were given in the prep school, like Allingham's 'Up the Airy Mountain' and Tennyson's 'The Brook'. On one occasion we were told to learn any poem we chose by heart, and I got a certain undeserved credit for learning a long ballad about the brave Lord Willoughby, but it was the only poem in the anthology that I found of any interest. 'Horatius' had too many classical allusions, and I was too young to appreciate 'After Blenheim'. 'Barbara Frietchie' was better, but 'Lord Ullin's Daughter' was awful, so awful that it has crept into several of my stories, an inescapable symbol of fatuity.

My severe attitude towards 'Horatius' all the same must have been adopted later at school, for I have come across a questionnaire which I answered when I was seven years old in the *School House Gazette*. (Apparently I received the second prize for my 'confessions' – twelve tubes of watercolours.)

What is your greatest aim in life? To go up in an aeroplane.
What is your idea of happiness? Going up to London.
Who is the greatest living statesman? Don't know any.
Who is your favourite character in fiction? Dixon Brett.
What are the qualities you most admire in men? Good looks.
In women? Cleanliness.
What is your favourite pastime? Playing Red Indians.
What is your pet hobby? Collecting coins.
What is your favourite quotation? 'I with two more to help me will hold the foe in play.'
Who is the author you like best and which book? Scott. *The Talisman.*
Who is the cricketer you most admire? Herbert Greene.
Which is your favourite holiday resort? Overstrand.

41

Aeroplanes. I have mentioned our failure to see Blériot on the London to Manchester flight, so that perhaps the first aeroplane I actually saw was one I watched through the nursery window above the school playing-fields. Suddenly it nose-dived. I heard later that the pilot was an old boy of the school (his name I think was Wimbush). His younger brother was on the playing-fields, he knew his brother was in the plane, and he saw it crash. He walked quickly away down the hill to the school, saying nothing. Often since then watching planes cross the sky, I half-expect to see them fall to earth, as though it were my gaze which had caused that first crash.

Once an airship, captained by an old boy, came down in the grounds of Berkhamsted Castle and remained there for some days on show. The stationer even made picture postcards of it. It was long before I saw another airship, though I can remember being woken and wrapped in blankets and brought to a bathroom window to see a blaze in the night sky from a Zeppelin which had been shot down over Potters Bar.

Being in London. Once a year we were all taken to *Peter Pan.* I loved it wholeheartedly. My favourite scene was the one where Peter Pan fought alone against the pirates with his sword, and narrowly second to it was the moment of enjoyable horror when the green-lit face of Captain Hook appeared at a service hatch and put poison in Peter's glass. The dying Tinker Bell touched me, but never would I consent to call out with the audience that I believed in fairies. It would have been dishonest, for I had never believed in them, except for the period of the play. There was one scene with attractive mermaids which to my great disappointment was cut, for reasons, I think, of war-time economy, from later productions. I could have dispensed more easily with the house in the tree-tops, for I never cared for Wendy, but 'To die will be an awfully big adventure' was a line which echoed through all my adolescence; it only really faded from my mind when death became for all of us a common everyday risk. At a later age, when I was twelve, I was taken to a revival of *The Admirable Crichton.* The heroine, Lady Somebody or other, who dressed in animal skins on the desert island, disturbed me for many nights, and she is one of my earliest sexual memories. Was it Cathleen

42

Nesbitt who played the part? If so, those disturbed nights had been experienced not long before by Rupert Brooke, but it was not 'mother comfort' I sought even at that age. It was some years before I was again so sexually moved by a play, and then it was at *Christopher Sly*. The beautiful actress who played with Matheson Lang and was his wife wore a long white silk nightdress which proved just as exciting as the animal skins.

When we went to London we usually had lunch with a retired colonel of the Indian Army called Henry Wright and his wife, our great-aunt Maud, at 11, Belgrave Road – always known to me as Number 11. Maud had introduced Robert Louis Stevenson to his first great love, Mrs Sitwell, who was tied to an unwanted alcoholic husband, but that, of course, meant nothing to me then. It was the vast chamberpot produced after lunch from the side-board cupboard by Colonel Wright, a relic of Victorian manners, which impressed me. He was my godfather, a bluff man, bearded like Edward VII, who walked with the help of sticks because of gout, I suspect, though he claimed to my brother Raymond that he had a cork leg. Before we left for the theatre he held out a hand to each of us concealing a half-crown piece. He died during the First World War and left me a gold watch. My mother sold it for five pounds and put the money for me into war-savings; for more than a quarter of a century afterwards this was my only inheritance.

In later years, after Colonel Wright's death, we were always taken to the Florence Restaurant in Soho, where to my constant surprise a black man in Oriental costume brought the coffee. I wasn't allowed coffee and I was always afraid we would not get to the theatre before the curtain rose. Grown-ups seemed slow at eating and drinking and too blasé about the theatre to be safe companions, particularly my uncle Graham if he happened to make one of the party. I had the unhappy impression that he had come to see his family and not the play.

Qualities most admired in men. My favourite and youngest uncle, Frank, the only uncle on my mother's side of the Greenes, was tall and good-looking and intellectual. I used to see very little of him at this time except at Christmas which he spent with us. I felt shy of him. He understood me too well, and though I liked him, he was a danger to my privacy. He was a civil servant

43

in the Board of Education and he married the daughter of Doctor Todhunter, the Irish poet, when I was about seven. He was the most literary-minded of all my uncles and aunts and he liked walking. When I was older, he, Raymond and I would go on foot to Boxing-day meets of a local pack, and to this day, as I write, I can feel the hard rungs of the furrows under the feet, see the fumes of the riders' breath, and hear the horns and the shouts sharp as ice. Until the hounds moved off we were never certain that the hunt would not be cancelled and we would lose the cry when the fox was sighted and the dabs of scarlet racing over the winter fields. Frank died in the late 1920s from appendicitis, and except for my cousin St George Lake, killed in France, he was the first relative I had to mourn.

Favourite quality in women. I think my reply to this question was probably motivated by disdain, for I find in the *School House Gazette*, from a Table Talk written by my aunt, that I had a good deal of undeserved contempt for my elder sister Molly and through her for girls in general – a contempt which I was soon to lose. My interjections were pointed and repetitious: 'You are silly, Molly. Girls are so silly.' 'Girls wouldn't know. They know nuffin.' 'Girls are always slow and always last.'

Favourite pastime. I am mystified by my choice, for I can't remember that I ever played at Red Indians, *The Last of the Mohicans* I find to this day unreadable, and it was before the days of Western films. I have a vague memory of a small bow and arrows with a green velvet handhold with which for a time I shot erratically at a target hung on the apple trees. But I was too bad a shot to continue long.

Pet hobby. The coins were any foreign coins which came my way and they were piled together in a box which later contained other treasures: a replica of the *Lusitania* medal said to have been given by the German authorities to the crew of the submarine which sank her and a postcard from the Western front, written to me by my red-haired cousin St George – a form with such printed information as 'I am well', 'I am in hospital', with the inapplicable phrases struck out. He provided me too with a spiked Uhlan helmet containing a convincing bloodstain. I wept a long time at the news that he had been killed, and perhaps I have never again

44

felt a death so keenly. In childhood eternity has no meaning – a child has not learnt to hope.

Favourite quotation. This reply surprises me, for I remember liking better Aytoun's 'The Execution of Montrose', which combined heroism and injustice. A child learns about injustice early.

Favourite author. Scott and Dickens were available to me in an admirable series of square books published by Blackie, the Told to the Children series, with coloured illustrations. *Oliver Twist* was in this series and *Peveril of the Peak*. The original text was preserved as far as possible, but dull descriptive passages were blue-pencilled.

Cricket. My eldest brother was the only cricketer I knew, so my praise was not exaggerated. I remember how at Overstrand I went with him to a county match, and he asked me to collect the autographs of the team, who he thought would be more amenable to the request of a little boy. The captain used my head as a desk to write on, and I experienced much more spiritual elevation than I felt at fourteen from the hand of a bishop at confirmation. Only once, on a later occasion, did I collect a signature, when I ran, in my school cap, after G. K. Chesterton, as he laboured like a Lepanto galleon down Shaftesbury Avenue.

Favourite holiday resort. Littlehampton, where we went at Easter, was thought by my mother to be a vulgar resort in the summer, visited by the wrong people, so that we used to go to Overstrand in Norfolk instead. On the cliffs above lay Poppyland, scarlet fields of poppies known as the Garden of Sleep, and I have always imagined Swinburne's 'Forsaken Garden' to have lain somewhere there. Littlehampton meant more to me, and I remember it better: the goat carriages on the green (I was photographed in one at my ambiguous curly age); the beach of silver sand where sea anemones could be found, which had to be reached by ferry, a foreign place, like the garden across the road, not to be visited every day; picnics in Arundel Park to which we set off by carriage to the sound of clopping hoofs (so that later I loved Alfred Noyes's poem, 'The highwayman came riding, up to the old inn-door').*

*I plead guilty to ingratitude. Thirty years later Noyes threatened me with an action for libel when I wrote a review of his autobiography.

45

The elder children took riding lessons from a Miss Reeves and her groom Keenie, a meagre sour creature, whom nobody liked; even his name was ignoble. I started lessons when I was about eight, and I enjoyed them well enough, but fear mingled with the pleasure. The first time I was off the leading rein, as I approached the big iron bridge that spanned the Arun, my pony took fright and jumped a ditch and a hedge. I gained great credit because I kept in my saddle after the jump and fell off only after a discreet interval, the first of many credits I have received for failing.

2

The school began just beyond my father's study, through a green baize door. The passage led to the old hall where we were able to play in the holidays, another to the matron's room and the terrace. One matron, Miss Wills, embarrassed me on my seventh birthday by kissing me when I brought her a piece of my birthday cake, so that I returned to the family circle, angry and shattered by the experience. My aunt Nono wrote some verses on the subject in the *School House Gazette* – 'Miss Wills kissed me when we met, As I took my birthday cake in . . .' and I had the uncomfortable sense that now the incident would never be forgotten: it had been immortalized by art.

You could get to the school also by going past the dark room and linen-cupboard on the nursery landing, through a glass door, to the dormitories. As I had the freedom of these regions only out of term, they are always empty in my memory – stony, ugly, deserted.

I went to school just before I was eight, as my birthday came in October, after term had started. My form master in the bottom form was called Frost. Later the school was reorganized and he was put in charge of the preparatory school which occupied a house in which my aunt Maud had once lived – it was there that I first read *Dracula* with great fear one long summer afternoon. The memory is salt with the taste of blood, for I had picked my lip while reading and it wouldn't stop bleeding – I thought I was going to bleed to death, one of Count Dracula's victims.

Frost had the reputation of getting on well with very small

boys, but I was a little afraid of him. He used to sweep his black gown around him in a melodramatic gesture, before he indulged his jovial ogrish habit of screwing a fist in one's cheek till it hurt.

Of my first day at school I can remember nothing except that I had to read a passage from *Captain Cook's Voyages*, the set English book that term. I found the formal eighteenth-century prose very dull, and I still do. History was my favourite subject, and when I was about twelve a rather foolish master whom we all despised stated in my annual report, otherwise given up to laconic statements – 'Satisfactory', 'Tries hard', 'weak' and suchlike – that I 'had the makings of an historian'. I was pleased, but considered rightly that it was an attempt to pander favour with my father.

At this period I was not unhappy at school except that, when I was twelve and I was moved into the top junior form, I remained at the bottom of the class for a whole term and lost my confidence. Of the masters I remember a monstrously fat one called Moir with black hair which was thinly streaked across the top of a bald head. Poor man, he must have suffered from some glandular disease which rendered him unfit for military service. He married during the war to everyone's astonishment a pretty young woman who was a temporary mistress; it seemed the mating of Beauty and the Beast. A popular master in charge of one of the junior houses was called Simpson. He was never properly shaved, the five o'clock shadow was there at morning prayers, and he h: d four chins, although he was not otherwise a fat man. He rubbed his hands together in a gloating manner when in form he caught one who belonged to his house in a punishable offence. He would refer jocularly to beatings and he very obviously enjoyed them. In a strange way this made him popular. It seemed to me even then that his boys were collaborators in a pleasure.

I can remember nothing about games, except that once I teased my cousin Tooter, who ran home from the playing-fields, crying. I felt a great shame at this, I knew already in my heart that I belonged on the side of the victims, not of the torturers, and this was a betrayal of all those sunlit afternoons on the roof of the Hall. These were the old playing-fields near the railway station, beyond Berkhamsted Castle, and when war came they were taken

47

over by what was called Kitchener's Army and to this day they are known as Kitchener's Fields. (My rich uncle came to the rescue of the school and lent the governors enough money to buy far better fields at the top of the hill where my sister's pug was killed.)

The only class I actively hated was held in the gym. I was very bad at gymnastics and all life long my instinct has been to abandon anything for which I have no talent; tennis, golf, dancing, sailing, all have been abandoned, and perhaps it is only desperation which keeps me writing, like someone who clings to an unhappy marriage for fear of solitude. I particularly disliked trying to vault or to climb a rope. I suffered in those days, like a character of mine, Jones, in *The Comedians*, from flat feet, and I had to wear supports inside my shoes and have massage from a gym mistress. The massage tickled a little and my soles sometimes ached, but on the whole I found the treatment agreeable, perhaps because it was given by a woman. This must have been between the age of ten and twelve, for it was the war of 1914 which brought a number of mistresses to the school in place of the masters who had joined the army.

The memory of August 1914 is associated with my uncle's house at Harston. The lawn in front of the house had a high wall. One could see over it only by climbing the chunky roots of old trees covered in ivy and swarming with spiders. Troops were continually passing through in these first days and they rested on the village green; once I was sent out with a basket of apples to refresh them. Herbert bicycled in from Cambridge one day with the evening paper announcing the fall of Namur. My brothers and I were delighted at the speed with which it had fallen because the prolonged defence of Liège had threatened a speedy termination of the war. As long as the war continued, we might one day be involved, and the world of Henty seemed to come a little nearer. Perhaps there would be an invasion, as in William Le Queux's famous documentary novel, and Berkhamsted Common, I believed, would be ideal for the exploits of one young *franc-tireur*. Indeed there were dramatic incidents even in Berkhamsted. A German master was denounced to my father as a spy because he had been seen under the railway bridge without a hat, a

48

dachshund was stoned in the High Street, and once my uncle Eppy was summoned at night to the police station and asked to lend his motor-car to help block the Great North Road down which a German armoured car was said to be advancing towards London. A colonel of the Inns of Court O.T.C. was also at the station. 'Five hundred rifles,' he lamented, 'and not a round of live ammunition.' My uncle was sceptical, but he lent his car.

But the war ended too soon for us, and only Herbert became lightly involved, when he was promoted lance-corporal in the H.A.C. He never reached France and one day he returned home without his single stripe. It was only a long time afterwards that I learned the reason – a sympathetic one. He was in charge of a spy who was awaiting execution in the Tower (he added the spy's autograph to his collection), and on the occasion of an air-raid he let the prisoner out of his cell to share the fun. Otherwise we were touched closely only twice – by the death of St George and by the disappearance of our new nurse's fiancé – 'missing, believed killed'. She was a kind dumpy young woman called Olive Dodge with an agreeable face like a penny bun with two currants for eyes (the most you could expect in war-time), and we were sad for her, knowing as our parents told us that there was little or no hope. Yet she never lost her hope and one day the miracle happened – he was discovered in a London hospital with shell-shock. He didn't recognize her, he was plunged in deep melancholia, but she never despaired, and one day she was able proudly to introduce him to the denizens of the nursery, a very tall dark man with a small moustache who spoke hardly at all. They married and lived happily ever after, or so I hope, in Acton.

At some point that year I abandoned the effort of trying to vault or climb a rope or scramble on the parallel bars, and I pretended, whenever that class came round, that I was ill. I would walk up on to the Common and stay there, hidden among the gorse bushes with their yellow flowers until school was over. Once lying flat in the bracken by the side of the road I saw the gardener Charge go by with the family donkey-cart. My parents, when I told them years later, denied that this was possible, because they said he could have had no business up there far away from the laundry and the town, but how could I have imagined

Miranda? Perhaps he was out for his own personal pleasure on a sunny June day. I enjoyed the feeling of being safely hidden among the bushes while he went by, even if I were not yet hunted. The long secret trek through the heather by Alan Breck and David Balfour always for me took place on Berkhamsted Common; it almost seemed a personal adventure, perhaps because my mother was kin to the Balfours of Pilrig, and indeed first cousin to Stevenson himself.

I don't know how long these sporadic escapes went on. They turned at some point (I would guess when I was eleven) into a better organized and a more prolonged truancy. By this time I was having breakfast in the dining-room with my elders, and not in the nursery with five-year-old Hugh and the baby Elisabeth. At the end of breakfast I would gather up my school-books as though going across to prayers.

I should explain that the school day began with prayers of a rather lay variety – masters on a platform, boys below – in what was called Deans' Hall which was named after Dean Incent, the sixteenth-century founder of Berkhamsted School, but also – the position of the apostrophe was important – after Doctor Fry, my father's sinister sadistic predecessor and kinsman by marriage, who had become the Dean of Lincoln.

This Manichaean figure in black gaiters with a long white St Peter's beard sometimes came to stay. After breakfast on these occasions it was my mother's duty to clear the hall outside the dining-room of maids and children, so that the Dean could go to the lavatory unobserved and emerge again unseen by anyone. As a headmaster he had been known as a flogger, and he thus made a life-long enemy of one old Berkhamstedian, later my Oxford tutor, Kenneth Bell, who one day had his cap snatched off by a school bully and was then beaten by Fry who saw him in the street without it. Fry as Dean of Lincoln became a popular lecturer in the United States where he went at regular intervals to procure money for restoring Lincoln Cathedral. On his last voyage, as he returned first-class in a Cunarder, fate overtook him and showed him up as the absurd figure he had always been. He had suffered a stroke before embarking which damaged his powers of speech and his neighbours at table overheard him asking his son Charley,

50

the Vicar of Maidenhead, for certain shocking objects when all he had in mind was a soft-boiled egg. Charley, who for years vainly paid court to my beautiful aunt Nono, was a far more likeable figure. He was so fat that he looked like a black tennis-ball, and to amuse us he would put two chairs together and bounce over them – not jump. 'Bounce for us, Cousin Charley, bounce for us,' we would cry, while my aunt watched with cynical disdain. She couldn't respect a man who bounced.

Instead of going to Deans' Hall I would wait in the garden until I knew the school was safely assembled, for fear that I might meet other boys or masters, and then I would walk up the High Street. My purpose was to steal something to read from the local W. H. Smith's store. I can only remember two occasions, but I think there must have been others: once I stole a copy of *The Railway Magazine* and once, as I have mentioned, *The Abbess of Vlaye* by Stanley Weyman, a sixpenny paperback with double columns. My reading matter thus obtained, I would return home. This must have been an even trickier matter than the theft as I had to go by the windows of the dining-room where the maid would be clearing breakfast, but I suppose at the height I had reached then it was quite easy to stoop below their level. That danger safely past I would go cautiously out to the croquet lawn, past the buddleia and the butterflies, and swing the summerhouse round so that it faced a flower-bed and the sanatorium wall; there I sat comfortably in a deck-chair and read my stolen book until the school broke up for lunch. I followed the same routine, without the foray to the High Street, in the afternoon, and recklessly I carried my truancy on until the last day of term. I was in the form of a Mr Davis and my father, who was making a rapid tour of the classrooms on the last day, was asked by Davis how my illness was progressing. It must have been quite a shock for my father who knew of no illness in his family. He came back home and out to the shelter where I was discovered . . . or rather I think he sent my mother. (Perhaps the search was proceeding in many directions at once.) I was told to go to bed, and when I was in my nightshirt my father came up and caned me.

This is the only beating I can remember, but at school I would invent apocryphal stories of having been cruelly flogged – it gave me the status which a headmaster's son lacked. I was in the middle of some story of brutal cruelty during a break between classes in the quad when a 'scrumming' took place. This was a strange kind of lemming drive which at intervals afflicted the lower school. A rumour would start that an extra half-holiday was going to be given (which happened fairly frequently during the war, whenever an old boy had been decorated with a D.S.O. or an M.C. A V.C. ranked as a whole holiday, but this only happened twice.) The rumours, however often they proved to be wrong, caused the whole junior school to press up against the terrace during a break and stay crammed there until my father would appear and send us packing. Occasionally the rumour proved true and so confirmed the idea that we had actually caused the half-holiday by our scrumming.

Magic and incantation play a great part in childhood. There was a tuckshop by the fives-court which was only open, because of war-shortages, to boys of the senior school. As a junior I would stand outside reciting an accepted formula, 'Treat I', to any older boy as he came out, and occasionally one would detach a morsel of bun and hand it over. The favourite purchase was a penny currant bun with a bar of chocolate inside, though it was seldom that any chocolate was included in the exiguous treat. I suppose we were always a little hungry in the war years. There were no potatoes and little sugar and we grew deadly tired of substitutes – rice and honey-sugar. My sister Elisabeth, who was around two at the time, would have hardly eaten anything at all during our nursery meals if I had not named each spoonful after a war-leader, though what their names could possibly have conveyed to her I cannot imagine. 'This is General Joffre,' I would say, popping in a dreary spoonful of suet, 'and this is General French . . . Hindenburg . . . Allenby.'

The clouds of unknowing were still luminous with happiness. There was no loneliness to be experienced, however occupied the parents might be, in a family of six children, a nanny, a nursemaid, a gardener, a fat and cheerful cook, a beloved headhousemaid, a platoon of assistant maids, a whole battalion of aunts and uncles, all of them called Greene, which seemed to bring them closer, and invariably at Christmas that old bachelor

52

friend who in those days formed part of any large family gathering, a little mocked in secret by the parents, a little resented in
secret by the children. The six birthdays, the Christmas play, the
Easter and the summer seaside, all arrived like planets in their
due season, unaffected by war. Only in the clouds ahead I could
see that there was no luminosity at all. Yet anything, I felt, anything, even a romantic death, might happen to save me before my
thirteenth year struck.

Chapter 3

1

I HAD passed thirteen and things were worse even than I had foreseen. I lay in bed in the dormitory of St John's, listening to the footsteps clatter down the stone stairs to early prep and breakfast, and when the silence had safely returned I began trying to cut my right leg open with a penknife. But the knife was blunt and my nerve was too weak for the work.

I was back in the house of my early childhood, but the circumstances had changed. The garden across the road, France across the Channel, was now closed to me: I could no longer set foot in the chintzy drawing-room where my mother had read aloud to us and where I had wept over the story of the children buried by the birds. In those early days I had not even been aware that there existed in the same house such grim rooms as those I lived in now. Even the door by which I entered the house was a different one, a side door like a service entrance, though no servant would have endured the squalor we lived in.* There was a schoolroom with ink-stained nibbled desks insufficiently warmed by one cast-iron stove, a changing-room smelling of sweat and stale clothes, stone stairs, worn by generations of feet, leading to a dormitory divided by pitch-pine partitions that gave inadequate privacy – no moment of the night was free from noise, a cough, a snore, a fart. Years later when I read the sermon on hell in Joyce's *Portrait of the Artist* I recognized the land I had inhabited. I had left civilization behind and entered a savage country of strange customs and inexplicable cruelties: a country in which I was a foreigner and a suspect, quite literally a hunted creature, known to have dubious associates. Was my father not the headmaster? I was like the son

---

*Memory often exaggerates, but some twelve years ago, because I had started a novel about a school, I revisited the scene and found no change. I abandoned the novel – I couldn't bear mentally living again for several years in these surroundings. A leper colony in the Congo was preferable so I went to Yonda in search of a burnt-out case.

of a quisling in a country under occupation. My elder brother Raymond was a school prefect and head of the house – in other words one of Quisling's collaborators. I was surrounded by the forces of the resistance, and yet I couldn't join them without betraying my father and my brother. My cousin Ben, a junior prefect, one of the rich Greenes, had no such scruples and worked covertly against my brother, gaining much popularity in consequence, so that I felt the less sympathy for him when he was later imprisoned, without warrant or reason, in the second German war under Regulation 18b. Injustice had bred injustice.

Though children can be abominably cruel, no physical tortures were inflicted on me. If I had possessed any skill at games I might even have won a tacit acceptance into the resistance movement, but I hated rugger only one degree less than I now hated cricket – a sport which at six years old I had loved as a game. 'Runs' I enjoyed, for then I could be alone in the solitude of the countryside, and at this period of my life I loved the country. It was my natural escape-route. On the wide stretches of Berkhamsted Common, seamed with the abandoned trenches of the Inns of Court o.t.c. among the gorse and heather, and in the Ashridge beechwoods beyond, I could dramatize my loneliness and feel I was one of John Buchan's heroes making his hidden way across the Scottish moors with every man's hand against him.

I grew clever at evasion. Truancy was impressed as the pattern of my life. To avoid fielding-practice I invented extra coaching in mathematics after school; I even named the master who I said was teaching me and curiously enough my story was never investigated. I would slip out of St John's with a book in my pocket while others were changing and make my way a little up the hill where a small lane branches off into the countryside. It was one of the most solitary lanes I have ever known; not even courting couples were to be seen there, perhaps because it was hardly wide enough for two to walk abreast. On one side was a ploughed field: on the other a ditch with a thick hawthorn hedge which was hollow in the centre and in which I could sit concealed and read my book. What book? I cannot be sure now. The days of Henty were over – my body was leading my brain in unfamiliar directions. I found extraordinary beauty and passion, I remember, in Sir Lewis Morris's *Epic of Hades*, and perhaps I was reading lines like these spoken by Helen of Troy:

> Was it love
> That drew me then to Paris? He was fair,
> I grant you, fairer than a summer morn,
> Fair with a woman's fairness, yet in arms
> A hero, but he never had my heart.
> It was not he seduced me, but the thirst
> For freedom, if in more than thought I erred,
> And was not rapt but willing. For my child,
> Born to an unloved father, loved me not,
> The fresh sea called, the galleys plunged, and I
> Fled willing from my prison and the pain
> Of undesired caresses, and the wind
> Was fair, and on the third day as we sailed,
> My heart was glad within me when I saw
> The towers of Ilium rise beyond the wave.

Today the lines seem pinchbeck, and yet they retain the secret smell of my hiding-place.

One comes to literature by devious routes, and it was often Stephen Phillips's *Paolo and Francesca* which I carried with me into hiding, just as another boy may be playing truant now with the verse-plays of Christopher Fry. There *were* lines in that banal drama which faltered on the edge of poetry: 'The last sunset cry of wounded kings', 'the childless cavern cry of the barren sea', and I was not critical in the hawthorn hedge.

The danger of discovery lent those hours a quality of excitement which was very close to momentary happiness. Scent to me is far more evocative than sound or perhaps even sight, so that I become attracted without realizing it to the smell of a floor-polish or a detergent which one day I miss when I open my door and home seems no longer home. So in my sixties I seem able to smell the leaves and grasses of my hiding-place more certainly than I hear the dangerous footsteps on the path or see the country-man's boots pass by on the level of my eyes. I remember how in 1944 I spent a rather guilty night of security in Berkhamsted away from the fly-bombs and the fire-watching with my brother

Hugh. Asleep in the Swan Inn I dreamt of the W. H. Smith bookshop down the High Street from which I had stolen *The Railway Magazine* all those years ago, and I smelt the individual smell of the shop which was like the smell of no other Smith's that I have ever known. In my dream I found a book for which I had long been searching on a particular shelf, and so in the morning, before I had breakfast, I walked down the street to see whether my dream might prove true. I was disappointed, the book was not there, but what I noticed at once on entering the shop was that the familiar smell had gone, and without the smell the shop was not the same. I inquired after the manager whom I remembered well: he had died the year before, and I suppose the new manager had changed whatever was the source of the smell which had so long haunted my imagination.

On Sundays we would go for walks, by order, in threes, and the names had to be filled up like a dance programme on a list which was hung up on the changing-room door. This surely must have had some moral object, though one which eludes me today when I remember how deftly the 'Emperor's Crown' used to be performed by three girls at once in a brothel in Batista's Havana. Three can surely be as dangerous company as two, or were the authorities cynical enough to believe that in every three there would be one informer?

The housemaster in my first year was Mr Herbert, an old silver-haired bachelor, whose formidable sister cared for him better than she did the boys. To add to my inextricable confusion of loyalties he happened to be my godfather, mysteriously linked at my birth to look after my spiritual well-being with that formidable gouty Colonel Wright of Number 11, who owned the chamber-pot in the dining-room cupboard. Mr Herbert was certainly not a cynic. He was an innocent little white rabbit of a bachelor, dominated by the dark Constance, his sister; he must have possessed a passion for birds because he later became the private secretary to Lord Grey of Falloden in that statesman's blind retirement. My only memory of him is seated at a desk in the St John's schoolroom on the first evening of my first term there, while each boy in turn submitted to him, for censorship or approval, any books he had brought from home to read. The danger was in the source – home, where dwelt unreliable and uncelibate parents. Anything in the school library was acceptable – even the inflammatory blank verse of Sir Lewis Morris from whom I later learned of the carnal loves of Helen and Cleopatra.

The methods of censorship are always curiously haphazard. In the 1950s I was to be summoned by Cardinal Griffin to Westminster Cathedral and told that my novel *The Power and the Glory*, which had been published ten years before, had been condemned by the Holy Office, and Cardinal Pizzardo required changes which I naturally – though I hope politely – refused to make. Cardinal Griffin remarked that he would have preferred it if they had condemned *The End of the Affair*. 'Of course,' he said, 'you and I receive no harm from erotic passages, but the young ...' I told him, and it was true enough, though I had forgotten the evil influence of Sir Lewis Morris, that one of my earliest erotic experiences had been awoken by *David Copperfield*. Our interview at that point came abruptly to an end, and he gave me, as a parting shot, a copy of a pastoral letter which had been read in the churches of his diocese, condemning my work by implication. (Unfortunately I thought too late of asking him to autograph it.) Later, when Pope Paul told me that among the novels of mine he had read was *The Power and the Glory*, I answered that the book he had read had been condemned by the Holy Office. His attitude was more liberal than that of Cardinal Pizzardo. 'Some parts of all your books will always,' he said, 'offend some Catholics. You should not worry about that': a counsel which I find it easy to take.

School rules, like those of the Roman Curia, are slow to change, however temporary the ruler who inspires them may be. I think the censorship of books from home (which was strictly enforced only, like a customs examination, when one passed the border – parcels from home were exempt) was dropped with Mr Herbert's retirement, but other relics of his government remained – the lavatories without locks, where each newcomer, anxious to perform his morning duty, had to call out 'Number off' in order to learn which of the compartments was empty; and that rule for Sunday walks which made certain that no one, under any circumstances, would ever walk dangerously alone.

But I was not a member of the resistance – I was Quisling's son. I had often to go begging that my name might be included in groups who had no desire for my company, until at last, after a term or two of purgatory, I received permission from my parents to spend Sunday afternoons at home. It was a relief for which I paid dearly in my nerves – a kind of *coitus interruptus* with the civilized life of home, for as evening fell I had to rejoin my companions tramping into the school chapel and afterwards climb the hill to St John's, and then at night the stone stairs to the dormitory – where at this moment in my memory I have lamentably failed to saw open my knee.

Unhappiness in a child accumulates because he sees no end to the dark tunnel. The thirteen weeks of a term might just as well be thirteen years. The unexpected never happens. Unhappiness is a daily routine. I imagine that a man condemned to a long prison sentence feels much the same. I cannot remember what particular item in the routine of a boarding-school roused this first act of rebellion – loneliness, the struggle of conflicting loyalties, the sense of continuous grime, of unlocked lavatory doors, the odour of farts (it was sexually a very pure house, there was no hint of homosexuality, but scatology was another matter, and I have disliked the lavatory joke from that age on). Or was it just then that I had suffered from what seemed to me a great betrayal? This story at least was to have a satisfactory though remote ending.

2

While I was at St John's I must have read Q's novel *Foe-Farrell* three or four times. It was the dramatic story of a man's revenge, and I very much wanted an opportunity for dramatic revenge. As I remember the tale a political demagogue ruined the experiment of a great surgeon by inciting a mob to wreck his laboratory where it was believed that he was practising vivisection. From that moment the surgeon Foe (or was it Farrell?) pursued Farrell (or was it Foe?) across the world and through the years with the sole object of revenge – I think he even found himself alone in an open boat on the Pacific with his enemy, improbable though this may sound. Then, under the long-drawn torture of the pursuit,

59

the characters changed places: the pursued took on nobility, the pursuer the former vulgarity of his enemy. It was a very moral story, but I don't think it was the moral which interested me – simple revenge was all I wanted.

For there was a boy at my school called Carter who perfected during my fourteenth and fifteenth years a system of mental torture based on my difficult situation. Carter had an adult imagination – he could conceive the conflict of loyalties, loyalties to my age-group, loyalty to my father and brother. The sneering nicknames were inserted like splinters under the nails.

I think in time I might have coped with Carter – there was an element of reluctant admiration, I believe, on both sides. I admired his ruthlessness, and in an odd way he admired what he wounded in me. Between the torturer and the tortured arises a kind of relationship. So long as the torture continues the torturer has failed, and he recognizes an equality in his victim. I never seriously in later years desired revenge on Carter. But Watson was another matter.

Watson was one of my few friends, and he deserted me for Carter. He had none of Carter's *finesse* – Carter continually tempted me with offers of friendship snatched away like a sweet, but leaving the impression that somewhere some time the torture would end, while Watson imitated him only at a blundering unimaginative level. Alone he would have had no power to hurt. Nonetheless it was on Watson that I swore revenge, for with his defection my isolation had become almost complete.

For many years after leaving school, when I thought back to that period, I found the desire for revenge alive like a creature under a stone. The only change was that I looked under the stone less and less often. I began to write, and the past lost some of its power – I wrote it out of me. But still every few years a scent, a stretch of wall, a book on a shelf, a name in a newspaper, would remind me to lift the stone and watch the creature move its head towards the light.

In December 1951 I was in the shop of the Cold Storage Company in Kuala Lumpur buying whisky for Christmas which I was going to spend in Malacca. I had just got back from a three-day jungle patrol with the 2/7th Gurkha Rifles in Pahang, seeking communist guerillas, and I was feeling very tired of Malaya. A voice said, 'You are Greene, aren't you?'

A foxy-faced man with a small moustache stood at my elbow.

I said, 'Yes, I'm afraid . . .'

'My name's Watson.'

'Watson?' It must have been a very long time since I had lifted the stone, for the name meant nothing to me at first, nor the flushed colonial face.

'We were at school together, don't you remember? We used to go around with a chap called Carter. The three of us. Why, you used to help me and Carter with our Latin prep.'

At one time, in the days when I still day-dreamed, I would imagine meeting Watson at a cocktail party and in some way humiliating him in public. Nothing could have been more public than the Cold Storage Company of Kuala Lumpur during the Christmas rush, but all I could find to say was, 'I didn't think I was any good at Latin.'

'Better than we were anyway.'

I said, 'What are you doing now?'

'Customs and excise. Do you play polo?'

'No.'

'Come along and see me play one evening.'

'I'm just off to Malacca.'

'When you get back. Talk over old times. What inseparables we were – you and me and old Carter.' It was obvious that his memory held a quite different impression from mine.

'What's happened to Carter?'

'He went into Cables and died.'

I said, 'When I get back from Malacca . . .' and went thoughtfully out.

What an anti-climax the meeting had been. I wondered all the way back to my hotel if I would ever have written a book had it not been for Watson and the dead Carter, if those years of humiliation had not given me an excessive desire to prove that I was good at something, however long the effort might prove. Was that a reason to be grateful to Watson or the reverse? I remembered another ambition – to be a consul in the Levant: I had got so far as sitting successfully for the *viva*. If it had not been for Watson . . . So speculating, I felt Watson sliding out of mind, and when I came back from Malacca I had forgotten him.

Indeed it was only many months later, after I had left Malaya, as I thought, for good, that I remembered I had never rung him up, had never watched him play polo, nor exchanged memories of the three inseparables. Perhaps, unconsciously, that was my revenge – to have forgotten him so easily. Now that I had raised the stone again, I knew that nothing lived beneath it.

3

The last footsteps had receded a long time ago, and I had put away the penknife. If the knife had been less blunt or my nerve had not failed, I wonder how I would have explained the cut knee. But perhaps unconsciously the whole point for me was that the act was inexplicable, like a would-be suicide's uncertain overdose of sleeping pills, something which demands prompt action from outside. Successful suicide is often only a cry for help which hasn't been heard in time.

After a long interval the matron came up to inspect the dormitories and found me in bed. I invented reasons – a feeling of sickness, a headache – which she accepted readily. She was a young woman – though to me then she seemed like all my elders fixed in a kind of static middle-age – who radiated a sense of calm friendliness. The thermometer might accuse me of malingering, but not she. She knew that even a child reaches at a certain moment a psychological limit. I was to stay in bed until after lunch and then take tea in her room. Thus she postponed for another year or more the final act of rebellion. Kindness alas! is often false kindness, enabling one to endure a little longer an almost unbearable situation.

It was on that day that the rain came down in torrents, postponing what I had perhaps stayed in bed to avoid, the weekly parade of the O.T.C. I hated that uniform with the puttees I could never learn to tie with any security or neatness and I dreaded the parades where I always fumbled fixing bayonets or strayed forming fours, under the ironic eyes of Watson and Carter. There was a deadly gravity about these parades because the years of

Passchendaele and Gallipoli were only just over; outside the school chapel there was the list of old boys killed, plaque after plaque in double column, to remind us of the recent years. Most of us were shocked when the Eton o.t.c. arrived for a joint field-day with grey uniforms in place of the sacred khaki and with an undisciplined frivolity, which seemed in our over-serious eyes to deny the virtues of the dead.*

The water flowed in torrents down the hill; the gutters over-flowed, and now it was a flood which I feared, dams breaking, reservoirs overflowing (I had read about it all in Rider Haggard's *Lysbeth*), but even drowning was preferable to the ignoble routine of school. The matron's kindness stood out by its rarity in that world, and perhaps because of its rarity two kind gentle people were drawn together and the assistant housemaster, Mr Dale, whom we had nicknamed Dicker, married the matron.

Dicker was a youngish man in those days (though, of course, to me middle-aged) with a bald head and gold-rimmed glasses and a drawl which sometimes became a slight stutter; a difficulty of communication, one would have said, and yet to those willing to listen he communicated more than any other master, except perhaps my father. Oddly enough he had no difficulty with discip-line, and though he had little obvious popularity, like some of the hearty mud-stained members of the staff, and looked out of place in flapping shorts as he circled the scrum with a whistle in his mouth, no one imitated his drawl, his nickname was innocuous, and the worst joke ever made at his expense was 'Where do the fleas run? Up Hill and down Dale'. Hill, a fine tennis-player and an older man, was Dale's chief friend at the school. Later, when retired, they collaborated in difficult academic crosswords which were published in a Sunday paper under the name of Torque-mada. Some of Dale's kindness must have rubbed off on Hill, for I remember how I was once invited to tea by him and how two

*The o.t.c. bred in me a permanent dislike of uniforms. There was a time in 1942 when the authorities at home wished to put me into a naval uniform. I pointed out that to have proper privacy for my secret work I would have to bear the rank of commander. They suggested the Air Force. In that case I must be a group captain, I replied, and then they surrendered. I could call myself c.i.d. Special Branch, they said, and the danger of a uniform was over.

hours of anchovy-toast and tea-cakes and adult conversation
atoned for a week of misery and postponed again the final breakdown. Perhaps it would have been postponed indefinitely if at that
period I could have comforted myself with Dale's favourite
apophthegm, drawled out in the most distressing circumstances:
'It's all experience.' I remember repeating the phrase to keep my
spirits up in April, 1941, as I shambled fearfully down blazing
Gower Street in the footsteps of our old Jewish post warden,
powerful and imperturbable in his shiny black mackintosh, like a
moving statue in malachite, the stone catching the reflection of
the flames and flares, one of the bravest men I have known and
the most unaware of his own courage.

4

I think it may have been the interminable repetitions in my life
which finally broke me down. A term always lasted thirteen weeks,
and contained two 'half-holidays' as they were called, except in
summer when there were three. Sundays came every seven days
with terrible regularity, like Lazarus with his drop of water; there
were no Saints' Days to vary the week, and once a week came the
dreaded o.t.c. parade.

I tried out other forms of escape after I failed to cut my leg.
Once at home on the eve of term I went into the dark room by the
linen-cupboard, and in that red Mephistophelean glare drank a
quantity of hypo under the false impression that it was poisonous.
On another occasion I drained my blue glass bottle of hay-fever
drops, which, as they contained a small quantity of cocaine, were
probably good for my despair. A bunch of deadly nightshade,
picked and eaten on the Common, had only a slightly narcotic
effect, and once, towards the end of one holiday, I swallowed
twenty aspirins before swimming in the empty school baths. (I
can still remember the curious sensation of swimming through
cotton wool.)

I endured that life for some eight terms – a hundred and four
weeks of monotony, humiliation and mental pain. It is astonishing how tough a boy can be, but I was helped by my truancies,
those peaceful hours hidden in the hedge. At last came the mo-

ment of final decision. It was after breakfast one morning in the School House dining-room, on the last day of the summer holidays, that I made my break for liberty. I wrote a note, which I placed on the black oak sideboard under the whisky tantalus, saying that instead of returning to St John's, I had taken to the Common and would remain there in hiding until my parents agreed that never again should I go back to my prison. There were enough blackberries that fine autumn to keep me from hunger, and I prided myself on knowing every hidden trench. This time it was a quisling who took to the *maquis*. What I cannot remember arranging was any way by which my parents could communicate the news of their surrender.

There was a wonderful sense of release from all the tension and the indecision as I made my way up the long road lined with Spanish chestnuts from the ruined castle to the slope where the Common began. I had to hurry, for here on this open road I might have been intercepted, but the race against time was part of the excitement on that golden autumn day, with a faint mist lying along the canal, across the watercress beds by the railway viaduct and in the grassy pool of the castle. Then I was safely there, on the Common, among the gorse and bracken of my chosen battle-field.

I had brought a book in my pocket, but I was much too excited to read, for I had a whole campaign to plan. There were two routes a search-party might take, the one by the road I had come and another through Kitchener's Fields which entered the Common by a flank. There was one point of vantage, an abandoned firing-butt, from which I could see anyone who approached for a hundred yards around, but there I would be exposed myself and I didn't like the idea of my rebellion ending in an undignified chase. I wanted to be an invisible watcher, a spy on all that went on, and so I moved restlessly among the bushes on the edge of the Common, watching for the enemy, ready to retreat unseen into the depths, like the *franc-tireurs* of Henty or David Balfour pursued by red-coats or Buchan's Hannay.

It was still too early for the invasion to begin. Immediately after breakfast my mother would be busy with the kitchen, the nursery, the linen-cupboard; my father would be shut in his study working on the Scheme – an elaborate game of his own invention consisting of a large board with slots of vari-coloured cards. With its help he was able to ensure that on the school timetable a master was not allotted contradictory duties, to teach Latin Composition to ivb simultaneously with English literature to va. Visiting headmasters were introduced to this Scheme with pride, and I think my father took as much pleasure in shifting a pink card to an empty space or solving a difficult problem with a 'free period' in white as in moving a queen to mate at chess or suddenly disrupting an opponent's attack by castling. He would sit over the board for half an hour at a time, motionless, in the attitude of Rodin's Thinker. No one would surely be bold enough to disturb him, while he was bent over his essential game, with my peace-destroying note.

I think at least two hours must have passed, and I would like to know now what conferences were held, what tactics were suggested, what decisions were made. But it is too late for me to find out. All the protagonists are dead except myself – my father, my mother, my elder sister, even the head housemaid who would have known all. I can imagine the bruit extending, in spite of all precautions, upstairs to the nursery and along the passage to the kitchen quarters: what a murmur of under-housemaids and scullery-maids, and the gardener perhaps leaning in at the kitchen-window to catch the latest report. And all this time I had nothing to do but roam my battlefield from bush to bush. My resolution was quite unchanged. I had asserted my freedom. Let others clean up the mess, I was happy, and never in the future – not even when I played Russian roulette on this same Common – did I experience again the hopeless misery of the years which I was escaping now.

It was time I looked at my exposed flank – a steep clay path between oaks and beeches above Kitchener's Fields. I moved rashly out beyond the cover of the bushes and began to descend, until, turning a corner, I came face to face with my elder sister, Molly. I could have run, of course, but that hardly suited the dignity of my protest, and so I went quietly home with her. It was a tactical defeat, but it proved all the same a strategical victory. I *had* changed my life; the whole future was decisively altered.

Perhaps I was nearer a nervous breakdown than I now care to believe, for a thick haze conceals all that happened next. Did I talk to my sister on my tramp home? I think I must have walked in silent pride. How was I greeted? I remember no reproaches, only a well-warmed bed in the spare-room next my parents', which was used only for more serious ailments than the regular family traffic of colds and coughs. I seem to remember my father sitting on the bed and interrogating me seriously and tenderly, and from that interrogation grew a whole comedy of errors. I suppose I complained of the general filth of my life at St John's, meaning the unlocked lavatories, the continual farting of my companions, but he misunderstood me and believed I had been the victim of some ring of masturbation, so that other investigations were now set on foot among the innocent inhabitants of St John's. The truth was I had not yet discovered the pleasure of masturbation and didn't even know the meaning of the word, though my father in any case probably used some vague abstract expression which was equally applicable to breaking wind.

At this date my brother Raymond had started to study medicine at Oxford and he was hastily summoned home for consultation; my father found the situation beyond him – perhaps he even believed the popular fable of his generation that masturbation led to madness, a threat already existing on both sides of the family. His own father, buried in St Kitts, had been a manic-depressive, and my mother's father, an Anglican clergyman, suffered from an exaggerated sense of guilt and, when his bishop refused his request to be defrocked, proceeded to put the matter into effect himself in a field. We were never told anything about that grandparent and I had always assumed he was dead before I was born. Only a few years ago, in reading Swinburne's letters, I learnt from a footnote that he had not died until 1924, so he must have seemed a living menace at this moment in our lives.*

*As an undergraduate at Trinity College, Cambridge, he had been part-author of a favourable review of the first shocking volume of *Poems and Ballads*. 'Please send me *at once*,' Swinburne wrote to the sinister Hotten in 1867, 'the January number of a Cambridge Magazine called "the Light Blue" containing an article on my Poems.'

My brother, who felt great pride at the trust reposed in him (he was only three years older than myself and in his first year at Oxford), suggested psycho-analysis as a possible solution, and my father – an astonishing thing in 1920 – agreed.

Chapter 4

1

IN age I find myself with an interest in my forebears which I never felt when I was young. In psycho-analysis I was led to think no further back than to my childhood, and my relation with my father and mother. I sought the cause of my rebellion in myself, in my loves and my fears. I didn't see it as only one of a long series of rebellions stretching back into the years before I was born. An ageing clergyman had undressed himself in a field, another had left his family abruptly to seek some golden memory of a time when he was sixteen years old and alone without parents on a Caribbean island. My father and mother too must surely have rebelled, though I do not know the nature of their rebellion, unless perhaps it was in the loving folly of their marriage.

Of my grandparents, it is to my father's father that I feel the closest now. He went out to St Kitts as a boy of fourteen to join his brother in the management of his father's sugar estates, and his brother Charles died of yellow fever two years after his arrival, in 1840. William was alone on the island, in charge of the estates. It was a situation Ballantyne might have taken for one of his boys' books, though I doubt whether he would have included the legend that Charles had left thirteen children behind him when he died at the age of nineteen. William went home after a dose of yellow fever himself. We always leave too soon the Coral Islands where we have been happily wrecked, but the memories of Mount Misery with its head buried in the clouds, of the green wastes of sugar-cane, the black sands of Dieppe Bay, of the little church of Christchurch outside which his brother lay under a grey slab of stone were powerful enough to draw back the middle-aged man from the family life at Bedford with eight children and enough money to live on in reasonable comfort (though the sugar estates on the distant island were producing less and less). For twenty years he had done very little, unlike his energetic brothers who had never lived a Ballantyne life – one was Governor of the Bank of England, another a Tory MP, the third a successful solicitor. William tried a little scientific farming and gave it up; he passed his examinations as a solicitor but he never practised. The only occupation he followed for any length of time was based on a place he called on his letter-heads 'Bleak House, the Plains of Desolation'.

He had become the only active (though none of his activities was very active) director of a peat company – his young partner committed suicide. He would disappear suddenly from Bedford, the large house and the large garden and the large family, leaving no money behind, and the next they would hear of him was from the overseer's hut, the only human habitation among the black bogs (which perhaps recalled the black volcanic sands of the island). He took no genuine part in the enterprise, but he would take long walks with a book in his pocket, and then return at night to the unfinished tramway-line, the half-built hydraulic plant, the rough food, the uneducated conversation in the lamplight and the narrow camp bed. He wasn't made for the family life in Bedford, the games of clumps and snap, the exciting visit of a Mr Rust who set the girls in turmoil. There was a barrier between him and his children. He would sit alone in his study, reading and marking his books. Only his daughter Alice had something of his frustrated romantic nature which would lead her, after his death, to a career in South Africa from which she rarely returned to England with her tales of new exotic friends, Olive Schreiner and General Smuts. I can just remember her with her square kindly sensible face, turning a little masculine with age, an impression of gaberdine. At twenty-two she was writing to her brother Graham: 'When I think of the countries I want to visit, the mountains I want to climb' (her father had written a little book which was printed in St Kitts about his ascent of Mount Misery), 'the rivers, forests and valleys I want to explore, I feel half frantic at the thought that I am getting older and older and am no more likely to travel than I was ten years ago.'

Suddenly in May 1881 – the worst time of year to set out to the Caribbean – my grandfather decided to pack up and leave. Graham saw him off in London and wrote to his mother: 'Did father send you a line from Southampton? I left him at 1 a.m. on Tuesday morning at the Charing Cross Hotel, endeavouring to finish a large cigar. He told me he intended to take very little rest that night, as he wished to be very sleepy on the following, the first night on board. I hope this plan succeeded but I have strong misgivings thereon. If the sea was rough in addition to the seasickness he would have all the additional discomfort of weariness. Our theatre was, after all, badly chosen. We went to *The Lady of Lyons*. A most mournful piece, not at all calculated to raise the spirits of an intending voyageur.'

He wasn't much missed, judging from Alice's letters to her brother Graham in London. Life in Bedford was as exciting as ever, with birthday treats and excursions and tea in the garden and walks by moonlight and the seductive behaviour on a tricycle at Barford of my other grandfather's curate, Mr Humble, and a further visit from the alarming Mr Rust ('He is so utterly inscrutable in his looks, words and deeds, that I know no more what his feelings are than if he were the Sphynx').

In spite of her longing for adventure, when the chance came Alice turned it firmly down. 'Thank you so very much, dear Papa, for your wish to have Florence and me with you for a time, but indeed, it cannot be. It was so very good of you to propose it that it seems ungrateful to refuse it point blank, but I really could not go unless we all went too. Like Mama, I do not like the thought of you being all alone; it seems so dreary for you. But as Mama, I suppose, has written to you all the Pros and Cons for your projects, I think I need not say any more, except to hope that we shall all meet again somewhere or other.' 'Somewhere or other', it must have seemed a chilling phrase to the middle-aged man who had failed to relive his youth under Mount Misery. Less than two months later he was dead of fever.

His grave is the same shape and size as his brother's, but he has failed to leave any impression on the island among all the coloured Greenes. It is Charles, dead at nineteen, forty-one years earlier, who is remembered. Perhaps the legend of his thirteen children is not wholly untrue, for when I visited the island two years ago, in the features of one would-be cousin I thought I saw a close resemblance to my Uncle Graham.

I don't know by what process of elimination my father and brother chose Kenneth Richmond to be my analyst, but it was a choice for which I have never ceased to be grateful, for at his house in Lancaster Gate began what were perhaps the happiest six months of my life. Active happiness depends to some extent on contrast – a lovers' meeting would not be the same without the days of deprivation, and those breakfasts in bed on a tray neatly laid, brought by a maid in a white starched cap, followed by hours of private study under the trees of Kensington Gardens, seemed all the more miraculous after the stone steps, the ink-stained schoolroom, the numbering-off at the bogs, the smell of farts around the showers. And London was there just down the road. I was independent. I could take a bus or tube to any destination. Films and theatres depended only on the management of my pocket-money. There were no Sunday walks in unwanted company. I was growing rapidly into an adult without the torments of puberty.

Only once something happened to disturb the quiet and restful routine. A guest was describing an accident at dinner, and my mind went back to Harston ten years before, a story of two ladies on the Royston road in a carriage: the horse had run away, and one had fallen out and her long hat-pin had pierced her brain. I found myself on the dining-room floor. I had fainted as sometimes I had fainted at early service in the school chapel. I wasn't worried; my imagination had a way of showing me the details of an accident though they were never described, and then I would faint like a medical student at an operation. I was surprised when Richmond took me to a specialist in Harley Street, but I thought no more of it. The incident was forgotten for four years.

Often of an evening I found myself in the company of authors. Richmond himself was one, if only of a book which I found rather dull reading, on educational theory. Walter de la Mare came to the house – the poet I admired most at that time – and wrote his spidery signature in my new-bought copy of *The Veil*. Often with him was his close friend; Naomi Royde-Smith, the editor of the *Weekly Westminster*, who had published Rupert

Brooke's early poems; she was too kind to me, so that a year later I began to bombard her with sentimental fantasies in poetic prose (she even published some of them). J. D. Beresford came too – a novelist crippled by infantile paralysis. *The Hampdenshire Wonder* remains one of the finest and most neglected novels of this period between the great wars, although it was an inferior novel, *Revolution*, which appealed more to me then. One evening we played a game in which each guest in turn had to imitate a vegetable, and I remember how we all simultaneously recognized de la Mare's stick of asparagus. Such evenings were far away from the hours of prep in St John's musty schoolroom. My only duties were to read history of a morning in Kensington Gardens and at eleven o'clock to go in for an hour's session with the analyst.

Kenneth Richmond had more the appearance of an eccentric musician than anyone you might suppose concerned with curing the human spirit. A tall stooping figure in his early forties, he had a distinguished musician's brow with longish hair falling behind without a parting and a face disfigured by large spots which must have been of nervous origin. There were two little girls who were brought up on the principle that children should never be thwarted, with the result that they were almost unbearably spoilt. On Sundays I was left in charge of them for an hour, while Richmond and his beautiful wife Zoe went to a church in Bayswater of some esoteric denomination, where the minister asked the congregation to decide by vote whether they would prefer that evening a sermon or a lecture on a psychological subject. Meanwhile at home I was seeing to it that for one hour a week the children learnt what it was to be thwarted.

I kept perforce a dream diary (I have begun to do so again in old age), and fragments of the dreams I can remember still, though the diary has been destroyed for nearly half a century. There was one dream of which I remember colours of great beauty; there were towers and pinnacles which might have come out of Miss Nesbit's *The Enchanted Castle*, and I heard a bodiless voice intoning, 'Princess and Lord of Time, there are no bounds to thee'; and I remember a nightmare in which I was pursued by sinister Chinese agents and took shelter in a hut with an armed detective, but, just as I felt the relief of security in his company, I

73

looked at the hand holding the revolver and saw that he had the long nails of a Chinaman.

Sitting in Kensington Gardens, reading of the Carolingians in a dull blue volume of Tout, I kept one eye alert for possible adventures among the nursemaids, but the only adventure I had was not of the kind I desired. An elderly man, with an old Etonian tie and a gaze unhappy and shifty, drew a chair up to mine and started to talk of schools. Was there corporal punishment at my school, and did I suppose there were any schools left where girls were whipped? He had an estate, he told me, in Scotland, where everyone went around in kilts, so convenient in some ways, and perhaps I would like to come for a holiday there ... Suddenly he sloped away, like a wind-blown umbrella, and I never saw him again.

When eleven struck in a Bayswater church tower I would cross the road, turn a corner and go into the little house in Lancaster Gate. If I couldn't remember the last night's dream I would be asked to invent one (for some reason if I invented a dream it always began with a pig). Richmond belonged to no dogmatic school of psycho-analysis, so far as I can make out now: he was nearer to Freud than Jung, but Adler probably contributed. There had been a tragedy twenty years before when a patient had killed himself and the coroner had been brutally unsympathetic, and I have the impression that he proceeded very carefully, very tentatively. My life with him did me a world of good, but how much was due to the analysis and how much to the breakfasts in bed, the quiet of Kensington Gardens, the sudden independence of my life I would not like to say, nor whether the analysis went deep enough. In any case, as Freud wrote, 'much is won if we succeed in transforming hysterical misery into common unhappiness'.

There he would always be, sitting behind the desk with his marred musician's face, stop-watch ready, waiting for my coming. Was there a couch, the stock-subject of so many jokes? I can't remember. I would begin to read out my dream, and he would check my associations with his watch. Afterwards he would talk in general terms about the theory of analysis, about the mortmain of the past which holds us in thrall. Sometimes, as the analysis pro-

74

gressed, he would show little hints of excitement – as though he scented something for which he had been waiting for a long while. But so far as my own dreams and associations went, he *told* me nothing; he patiently waited for me to discover the long road back for myself. I too began to feel the excitement of the search. Perhaps, in spite of all the good it did me, the excitement was too heady for a boy and fostered the desire to turn up every stone to discover what lay beneath, to question motives, to doubt – no love would be simple afterwards or free from dusty answers.

The classic moment approached, as in all such analyses, when the emotion of the patient is due to be transferred: a difficult period for the analyst. Perhaps Richmond was trying to provide a subject away from home, for one of the evening callers proved to be a girl who was a ballet-student and one night we went to see her dance. With the added glamour of the stage around her, I nearly fell in love. Exploring London I had found a little bookshop on the Embankment near Albert Bridge and I bought a first edition for a few shillings of Ezra Pound's early romantic poems, *Personae* – he displaced Walter de la Mare in my admiration. So, under the influence of *Personae*, I wrote three sentimental imagist lines to the girl, whose romantic name was Isola ('a future Pavlova' I wrote to my mother), but I never showed them to her, the relation never went further, and I did not see her again. The transference took a more inconvenient route, settling on my analyst's wife, and the moment I feared at last arrived when, sitting in Kensington Gardens, I found the only dream I had to communicate was an erotic one of Zoe Richmond. For the first time I dreaded the hour of eleven. I could, of course, say that I remembered nothing, and Richmond would tell me to invent, and I could trot out the habitual pig, but I was caught sufficiently by the passion for analysis to be repelled at the thought of cheating. To cheat was to behave like a detective who deliberately destroys a clue to murder. I steeled myself and left the Gardens and went in.

'And now,' Richmond said, after a little talk on general theory, 'we'll get down to last night's dream.'

I cleared my dry throat. 'I can only remember one.'

'Let's have it.'

'I was in bed,' I said.

75

'Where?'

'Here.'

He made a note on his pad. I took a breath and plunged.

'There was a knock on the door and Zoe came in. She was naked. She leant over me. One of her breasts nearly touched my mouth. I woke up.'

'What's your association to breasts?' Richmond asked, setting his stop-watch.

'Tube train,' I said after a long pause.

'Five seconds,' Richmond said.

Towards the end of my stay with the Richmonds my rich Greene uncle, Eppy, who perhaps did not wish to be outdone by his intellectual brother, sent his elder daughter Ave to be analysed, and she too stayed in the house. Perhaps if she had come a little sooner my transference would have been directed towards her, for she was a very pretty girl, who, a few years later, was courted by all the Greene brothers, except Hugh who was still too young. Herbert and I particularly entered into rivalry. Tennis on summer evenings, exciting car-rides to the King's Arms in the neighbouring town of Tring . . . there were even moments when my German aunt became worried: another first-cousin marriage in the Greene family would have been a disaster. Now in London with all the opportunities open nothing occurred. In those days at sixteen a boy was still very young. With daring I took her to the first London production of Eugene O'Neill's *Anna Christie* (her family, I learnt afterwards, considered it an unsuitable choice). I was still so heartfree that I could wonder, with cynical amusement, how long it would be before her emotions began to be transferred towards our bizarre and spotty analyst. But I was not there to see. Before that happened (if it ever did) I was returned – repaired – to the world of school.

Chapter 5

1

IT was a life transformed. I was no longer a boarder at that hated brick barracks called St John's, which had become so mysteriously changed from the home of a happy childhood, and I had no fear of the old routine of classes. Classes, when once I had outwitted and outgrown the gym, I had never hated, and I returned to them with the proud sense of having been a voyager in very distant seas. Among the natives whom I had encountered there, I had been the witness of strange rites and gained a knowledge of human nature that it would take many years for my companions to equal, or that was what I believed. Had my grandfather returned to England from the long morning rides among the sugar-canes and the black labourers of St Kitts with the same exhilarating and unbalanced sense of superiority? I had left for London a timid boy, anti-social, *farouche*: when I came back I must have seemed vain and knowing. Who among my fellows in 1921 knew anything of Freud or Jung? That summer I invited Walter de la Mare to a strawberry-tea in the garden with my parents. He had come to lecture in Berkhamsted and I posed proudly as the poet's friend, though I wished my father had been more impressed by his poetry. 'It lacks passion,' he argued with me, and to refute him I showed him a poem in *The Veil*.

> 'Poor hands, poor feeble wings,
> Folded, a-droop, O sad!
> See, 'tis my heart that sings
> To make thee glad.

> 'My mouth breathes love, thou dear.
> All that I am and know
> Is thine. My breast – draw near:
> Be grieved not so!'

He shook his head sadly, remembering Browning. 'Tenderness,' he said, 'not passion.'

77

I found it easy now to make friends. The domination of Carter was over for good. He belonged to another geological age, a buried stratum of school society. A school has many backwaters, but I was at last in the main stream. Instead of those petty gangsters of St John's there were Eric Guest (later a distinguished Metropolitan magistrate), Claud Cockburn, Peter Quennell. I escaped in company with Quennell the loathsome O.T.C. on condition that we both took riding lessons from the gym master, an agreeable red-faced ex-cavalryman called Sergeant Lubbock. I was always a frightened rider and later, when I had left school, I would take a horse out only in order to scare myself with jumps on the Common and escape the deep boredom which I had begun to suffer, a belated effect of the psycho-analysis, or so I believed then, not knowing it would pursue me all my life. Quennell always rode a far more spirited horse than mine, galloped faster, jumped higher. Sometimes returning at a walk down the long road from the Common – the road of my escape – we would pass on a hot summer's day the sweating trudging ranks of the O.T.C. singing a gloomy military song, 'We're here because we're here because we're here,' like a line of Gertrude Stein, and I felt the same compassionate contempt a cavalryman must have felt in the old days for the poor bloody infantry. I no longer ride, but the smell of a horse's coat brings back at once the sense of pride and tension.

Now that I had reached the vith form, work too was transformed. The School Certificate had been safely gained, and I was able to drop mathematics, Latin and Greek and choose the so-called modern side, with French, History and English as the main subjects. There were not many of us and we enjoyed frequent blank periods when we worked alone in the library – beneficiaries from the white cards of my father's Scheme. French, which I never learnt properly to speak, became a fascinating literary language taught by a handsome tawny-faced man called Rawes who had his roots, so it was said, in Portugal and the wine trade and wore in his buttonhole the small green ribbon of a Portuguese decoration, for he had served with the unfortunate Portuguese troops who had been whipped, like porkers to an abattoir, to the mass slaughter of the Western Front. Most boys were frightened by his worldly good looks, his air of military authority, and he was unpopular, but I always enjoyed his teaching, and during his French lessons, when we would spend a whole hour juggling with words in an attempt to translate two or three lines of Molière or a sestet of Heredia, he opened my eyes to the importance of precision in my own language as well.

It was he who introduced me to Lytton Strachey's *Landmarks in French Literature*, and through Strachey I at least imagined for a while that I had become a lover of Racine. How cunningly Strachey went about his persuasion: 'The ordinary English reader today probably thinks of him – if he thinks of him at all – as a dull, frigid, conventional writer.' No boy worth his salt could fail to respond to that challenge, and on long solitary walks – which were for pleasure now and not an escape from cricket, for Kenneth Richmond had made sure that I would be excused all games – I carried *Bérénice* in my pocket in place of *The Epic of Hades*.

It was now I began to develop a love for the landscape around Berkhamsted which never left me, so that Chesterton's rather inferior political ballade '*Of the First Rain*' moves me still like poetry with its key-line: 'A storm is coming on the Chiltern Hills.' Chenies, Ivinghoe, Aldbury have always meant more to me than Dartmoor or the fells of Yorkshire, and the hidden spots of the Chilterns were all the dearer because they were on the very borders of Metroland. They had the excitement of a frontier. There was one dried stream-bed, half hidden in bushes, called the Woe Water because the stream only ran before a war. It ran before the Boer War and in July 1914. I visited it during the crisis of Munich and it was dry, but I failed to return in September 1939. The depth of this country was vertical rather than horizontal, so that a Green Man might be seen dressed in leaves only a few feet away from the school playing-fields, and once talking to a railway porter in a public house near the station I learned that he had not been as far as the High Street five hundred yards away since his wife died fifteen years before. Berkhamsted always reminds me of Rilke's poem, where beyond 'the narrow-chested' suburban houses 'a shepherd leans against the last lamp-post in the gloom'.

It was strange that, while I carried Racine with me on my walks and Ruskin's *Sesame and Lilies*, I was beginning to write the most sentimental fantasies in bad poetic prose. One abominable one, called *The Tick of the Clock*, about an old woman's solitary death, was published in the school magazine. I cut out the pages and posted them to the *Star*, an evening paper of the period, and for God knows what reason they published the story and sent me a cheque for three guineas. I took the editor's kindly letter and the complimentary copy up to the Common, and for hours I sat on the abandoned rifle-butts reading the piece aloud to myself and to the dark green ocean of gorse and bracken. Now, I told myself, I was really a professional writer, and never again did the idea hold such excitement, pride and confidence; always later, even with the publication of my first novel, the excitement was overshadowed by the knowledge of failure, by awareness of the flawed intention. But that sunny afternoon I could detect no flaw in *The Tick of the Clock*. The sense of glory touched me for the first and last time.

Then I attempted the theatre: first, modestly enough, with one-act plays, very tragic and very brutal, set in the Middle Ages, which seemed to give scope to my poor brand of poetic prose. I was much under the influence of Maurice Hewlett and *The Forest Lovers*, and many an Isoult La Desirous found her way into the plays. 'A slim girl, somewhat under the common size of the country, and overburdened with a curtain of black hair; and a sullen, brooding girl who says little, and that nakedly and askance; and in a pale face two grey eyes a-burning.' So the Abbot of Holy Thorn described her, and it was much the same character which attracted me when I read over and over again Maeterlinck's *Pelléas and Mélisande*.

Then another influence succeeded Hewlett. I went to see Lord Dunsany's *If* in which Henry Ainley played the leading part (I had myself played the Poet in Dunsany's *Lost Silk Hat* at a school fête and felt myself his colleague). Immediately afterwards I began to write a fantastic play of which I cannot even remember the title. It celebrated what I liked to believe was the sense of poetry inherent in the ceremony of afternoon tea. In 1920 tea was still one of the important meals of the day, and the most aesthetic.

The silver pot, the tall tiered cake-stand, like a Chinese temple, two kinds of bread and butter, white and brown, cucumber and tomato sandwiches cut razor-thin, scones, rock-buns, and then all the cakes – plum, madeira, caraway seed – the meal had about it the lavishness of a Victorian dinner. My play, I don't know why, except that Dunsany's had taken much the same road, moved from London to Samarkand.

I sent the play to one of the many dramatic societies which existed in 1920, though I didn't fly so high as the Stage Society, and I was excited to receive a letter signed with a woman's name accepting it for production. So up I went to London one morning to meet my first management. The address was somewhere in St John's Wood, a district which in those days still retained the glamour of illicit love-nests. There was a long delay, after I sounded the bell, and when at last the door was opened, it was by an over-blown rosy woman holding a dressing-gown together, who was watched from the end of the passage by a naked man in a double bed. She looked with astonishment at my blue cap with a school crest while I explained that I had come about my play. Then she gave me a cup of rather weak Mazawattee tea (very different from the tea which I had been celebrating) and she became carefully vague, as she scrutinized me, about casting and the date of production. I don't remember that I ever heard from her again, and the society, I am sure, soon ceased to exist. Perhaps my play was the last piece of wreckage at which she clutched, and down with it sank all her dreams of some rich sucker who would put up the expenses, incidental and accidental, of his play (including the quarter's rent and the milk bill and all that went with the double bed at the end of the passage).

Still my play had been accepted. Disillusion came gently, slowly, with no letters in the day's post bearing a London postmark, and I suppose it was then I began to have the dream which continued intermittently for twenty years. In the dream, though still at school, I was an established writer who was making enough money to support himself. Why should I fear examinations when I could simply, by an act of will, abandon all study? What did a university matter to me? Why should I bother about the future and that ugly Anglo-Saxon word of double meaning a 'job'?

81

But in waking life the classes continued without interruption, and the menace of scholarship examinations loomed ahead.

2

For English my father took charge of some of the classes, 'Dicker' Dale of others. Dicker's were the more unexpected. He would read aloud to us, a class of half a dozen only, works which were not on the syllabus, introducing us in his lazy drawl – 'it's all experience' – to Beddoes and *Death's Jest-Book*. But perhaps my father's lessons drove deeper roots. He was an unconventional teacher. His three subjects were English, History and the Latin classics, and they often overlapped, so that a lesson on Robert Browning might well turn into a discussion of Trevelyan's history of Garibaldi's campaigns. The amusement and respect which he inspired in the vith form (far, far distant now were the jeers of Carter and his immature gang who didn't know a thing about the Freudian interpretation of dreams) have been described by Claud Cockburn. 'Nobody but a fool could fail to enjoy a history lesson with Charles Greene. "Speaking", he would say, "of Rome, let me draw your attention to yesterday's events in Paris. Let me draw your attention for a moment, if I may, to the probable – nay, assured – consequences of the machinations of Mr Lloyd George and M. Clemenceau. Let us gaze for a moment into the abyss which now opens before the feet of liberal Europe. Let us not for a moment hesitate to recognize the consequences of the evil acts of these misguided men. And with this in mind, let us return to a thoughtful consideration of the situation which faced Cicero (a shady character) and his associates at the moment of the Catiline conspiracy."'

A letter written to me by Peter Quennell after I had reached Oxford describes my father's manner as he lay, almost on his back, in his deep chair at the end of the table in the library, his mortar-board at a perilous angle (he was never during school hours without gown and mortar-board and it was a shock sometimes to encounter him in his uniform on the home side of the green baize door: it was like a breach of neutrality). I had gone to Oxford a term or two in advance of Quennell carrying with me

82

his introduction to a girl much older than either of us who lived at Boar's Hill. Greatly daring, Claud Cockburn and I invited her to lunch and I sent Quennell what must have been a rather boastful telegram (not that there was anything at all to boast about, for in a letter to my mother I wrote, 'She was very charming, but on the wrong side of twenty'). This was his reply, arranged somewhat in the *vers libre* manner of his *Masque of The Three Beasts* which was about to be published by the Golden Cockerel Press. (The poem had already appeared in *Public School Verse*, and it was said that in the school baths he had been sometimes pursued by his own particular Carters who mockingly recited what seemed to them his loony lines.)

My dear Graham,

Even ironic laughter wants a fine sprinkling of discretion. Next time you take my dear Violet out to lunch you must arrange not to wire to me during your father's period . . .

Your father was in the middle of what I think was an English period. It had become rather historical. The dear old gentleman was lying comfortably on his back – like an inverted turtle.

> – Have you noticed how like a very dear old
> turtle he is becoming? –
> – and we had become gloomy but sonorous –
> over the future of Democracy

And then of course entered Mrs Edmunds* (Mr Edmunds has a new bluff sea captain macintosh which makes him look like a statue waiting to be unveiled

> – and once wore a souwester with it)
> – in a tottering hurry

And your father stopped in the middle of a more than Ciceronian period

> – and heavy gloom and foreboding fell
> upon everybody –

* My father's widowed secretary who had married, for the second time; her new husband was a big humourless master in the Junior School. By her first husband, with a more glamorous Irish name, she had a beautiful daughter with long golden hair falling below her waist. How often I walked up the long High Street almost as far as Northchurch and the Crooked Billet in the hope of catching sight of her. I think not one of us liked the idea of poor Edmunds as her stepfather. He seemed like an intruder on the realms of romance.

83

              – and especially Peter when he heard
          it was for him –
              – and I pictured my father run over in
          Theobald's Road
              or my Cockerel at his last gasp
    And your father made ineffectual efforts to sit up and said in a severe
and entirely cold and disapproving way that I might read it at 12
          – and – suddenly relenting – if I was good – that I might read it
now – and immediately and at once

                                        lest there was an answer
And I read it in icy stillness and while I was still glaring at it
          – in astonishment of mind
          – almost alarm –
your father
          asked in a yet more disapproving way if there was an answer
          but there wasn't
And he slid back to the turtle position
          and the Ciceronian period went on – and the Democracy of
Europe and its fate rolled up again like storm clouds.

Literature can have a far more lasting influence than religious
teaching, and my father's enthusiasm for Robert Browning was
the bacillus of a recurring fever. The edition I still possess of the
poems was given me by him as a Confirmation present, but it was
certainly not a belief in God that Browning confirmed. I had
emerged from my psycho-analysis without any religious belief at
all, certainly no belief in the Jesus of the school chapel, and what
I took from Browning my father might well have thought un-
healthily selective. To recall today any phrase from the Sermon on the Mount I must open the New Testament to find the
words, but some lines of Browning have stayed in my memory
for fifty years and have influenced my life more than any of the
Beatitudes:

          'Better sin the whole sin, sure that God observes;
          Then go live his life out! Life will try his nerves,
          When the sky, which noticed all, makes no disclosure,
          And the earth keeps up her terrible composure.'

          'I never saw a brute I hated so;
              He must be wicked to deserve such pain.'

> 'And the sin I impute to each frustrate ghost
> Is – the unlit lamp and the ungirt loin,
> Though the end in sight was a vice, I say.'

And if I were to choose an epigraph for all the novels I have written, it would be from *Bishop Blougram's Apology*:

> 'Our interest's on the dangerous edge of things.
> The honest thief, the tender murderer,
> The superstitious atheist, demi-rep
> That loves and saves her soul in new French books –
> We watch while these in equilibrium keep
> The giddy line midway.'

With Robert Browning I lived in a region of adulteries, of assignations at dark street corners, of lascivious priests and hasty dagger thrusts, and of sexual passion far more heady than romantic love. Did my father, under that potent spell, not even notice the meaning of the lines he read us? Even in Swinburne I never felt so strongly the drive of desire – the sudden exact detail which could stir a boy physically.

> 'What is the use of the lips' red charm,
> The heaven of hair, the pride of the brow,
> And the blood that blues the inside arm?'

> 'Oh, that white smallish female with the breasts . . .'

> 'Your soft hand is a woman of itself,
> And mine the man's bared breast she curls inside.'

> 'Was a lady such a lady, cheeks so round and lips so red,
> On her neck the small face buoyant, like a bell-flower
>   on its bed,
> O'er the breast's superb abundance where a man might
>   base his head?'

> '. . . . there you stand,
> Warm too, and white too: would this wine
> Had washed all over that body of yours,
> Ere I drank it, and you down with it, thus!'

After an afternoon of Browning it was not to Tennyson's poems that one turned for a comparison: one walked up the

High Street in the fading light, hoping to see a tress of gold hair dangling waist-deep.

'— Ah, but the fresher faces! "Is it true"
Thou'lt ask, "some eyes are beautiful and new?
Some hair, – how can one choose but grasp such
wealth . . . ?"'

In Browning there was the sense of danger, adventure, change: we could leave dull fidelity to the *Lord of Burleigh* and *Sir Galahad*.

As we grow old we are apt to forget the state of extreme sexual excitement in which we spent the years between sixteen and twenty. There was a musical comedy in the early twenties called *The Cabaret Girl*, in which Miss Dorothy Dickson starred. Today it would seem, I suppose, as comic as *The Boy Friend*, but, during my first year after leaving school, I saw it six times, and every time but one in a state of continuous physical excitement. (That one time an understudy had taken Miss Dickson's part.) There is a short story of Sean O'Casey's called 'I Wanna Woman' which is more in the mood of adolescence than romances of calf-love.

We lived in those years continuously with the sexual experience we had never known; we talked, we dreamt, we read, but it was always there, and yet, when I came to write, it was sentimental verse or sentimental prose fantasies which leaked from the pen. And in between the periods of sexual excitement came agonizing crises of boredom. Boredom seemed to swell like a balloon inside the head; it became a pressure inside the skull: sometimes I feared the balloon would burst and I would lose my reason. Then, if it were not term-time, I would beg my brother Raymond to take the train with me to London, an hour away (a workman's return ticket, if one caught an early enough train, cost only about three shillings). We would have lunch in a restaurant in Soho (a five-course half-crown lunch at Pinoli's) and walk down Charing Cross Road looking at the second-hand books. I was soothed by the movements of the crowd and the hard resistance of the pavement under my feet. A country walk in those moods was no solution. Turf yields like a body and the feel of it brought the fever back. Every haystack was the possible scene of bucolic love.

Alcohol began to appeal to me in the innocent form of bitter beer. I was offered beer first by Lubbock, my riding master, whom I visited one evening in summer. I hated the taste and drank it down with an effort to prove my manliness, and yet some days later, on a long country walk with Raymond, the memory of the taste came back to taunt my thirst. We stopped at an inn for bread and cheese, and I drank bitter for the second time and enjoyed the taste with a pleasure that has never failed me since. I had found another alleviation of the boredom-sickness and later at Oxford it served me dangerously well, when for a whole term I was drunk from breakfast till bed.

What a mess those inexperienced years can be! Lust and boredom and sentimentality, a frightened longing for the prostitute in Jermyn Street, where there were real brothels in those days, an unreal romantic love for a girl with a tress of gold and a cousin who played tennis when it was almost too dark to see the ball – in that twilight world of calf-love any number of girls can rehearse simultaneously a sentimental part which never reaches performance. My younger brother and sister had a nurse who ill-treated them and fancied me. I felt a traitor to them every evening when I came and kissed her good night. Like a promise of something further she gave me my first razor, but the promise was not fulfilled. One night when I came up to the nursery before bed I found my mother there, and, to show that I was not ashamed of what I did on other occasions, I went and kissed the nurse quite openly on the lips. I was neither in love nor in lust, and I was glad enough when soon after that she went away, and the children were relieved of her tyranny.

3

I went up to Oxford for the autumn term of 1922 to Balliol* with nothing resolved – a muddled adolescent who wanted to write but hadn't found his subject, who wanted to express his lust

*I had failed to win a scholarship, so why to Balliol? I think my father wisely plumped for a college which at that period was anti-athletic. Also the number of students there, as in a great city, offered the shelter of anonymity.

but was too scared to try, and who wanted to love but hadn't found a real object. I tried to make my aunt Maud into an intermediary between me and the girl with the gold hair, for I was afraid to write to her at home where the letter might be seen by her formidable stepfather, but my aunt after passing her one letter refused to pass another and I don't think I ever received a reply. At the same time I preserved carefully a postcard from my cousin who was somewhere in Germany, and after a little while I tried to persuade myself that I was in love with a young waitress at the George in the Cornmarket who corresponded with me during my first vac and sent me a snapshot. This correspondence too I preserved, making thus a harem out of scraps of paper.

'For love of Love or from heart's loneliness . . .' No one has better expressed than Rupert Brooke in his adolescent verse this state of confused, half-expressed sexuality.

'Pleasure's not theirs, nor pain. They doubt, and sigh . . .' But the genuine pain was not far off: it is possible to grow up between one blink of the eyelids and another.

Chapter 6

1

IT must have been the summer of 1923 that I reluctantly joined my family at Sheringham on the Norfolk coast. I was allowed two hundred and fifty pounds a year by my over-burdened father – a generous enough allowance in those days – and I was able, soon after I went up to Oxford, to reduce the cost to him by winning a history exhibition of fifty pounds. I had twice failed for a scholarship while at school, and I doubt whether my history had much improved in the intervening months, but we still lived in a world of influential friends. My tutor, Kenneth Bell, was an old pupil and disciple of my father's and a governor of my school. I learned from him later that the history exhibition had been awarded mainly on my English essay. 'That poem you quoted,' he said, 'I told them you had written it yourself.' He must have known that I was trying to write poetry, but the poem in fact was one by Ezra Pound which I knew by heart. 'It's the white stag, Fame, we're hunting . . .' Few dons in 1923 had read Pound, and, when I told Kenneth Bell of his mistake, he was not unduly disturbed. The exhibition had to go to someone: better me than another.

Perhaps if I could have saved enough money I would have gone to France that summer and not to Sheringham. Paris at the time lured me more than Athens or Rome. In Paris *Ulysses* had just been published: at the Sphynx, they said, the customers were served by naked waitresses: the Folies Bergère and the Concert Mayol were not regarded as the family entertainments they have since become. But the end of my first year saw me heavily in debt: so many barrels of beer, so many books, shelf upon shelf of them, which had nothing to do with work. At Blackwell's bookshop credit seemed to a newcomer endless (though they liked a little bit sometimes on account), but drinks were ordered through the college buttery and appeared on battels, as college bills were called (there was no credit given there), and as I spent my first two terms in lodgings in Beechcroft Road, far up in north Oxford, there had often been taxis at midnight – which left a deficit for the term ahead. So gloomily, I thought, 'It must be Sheringham this summer', for there I could live at my family's expense.

The younger children, Elisabeth and Hugh, had grown too old for a nurse, and so my kissing-instructress had not been replaced, but instead a governess had been appointed, a young woman of about twenty-nine or thirty – ten years or more older than myself. During the first days at Sheringham she made little impression – my day-dreams were still of my cousin and of the waitress at the George. My brother and sister were happy, I noticed, with her, and she joined cheerfully in our games of cricket on the sands. The first time I looked at her with any interest was at the same instant the *coup de foudre*. She was lying on the beach and her skirt had worked up high and showed a long length of naked thigh. Suddenly at that moment I fell in love, body and mind. There was no romantic haze around this love, no make-believe: I couldn't share it like calf-love with a waitress at the George.

It is strange how vivid the memory has remained, so that I can see the stretch of beach, my mother reading, the angle from which I examined her body, and yet I cannot even remember the first time I kissed her or the hesitations and timidities which surely must have preceded the kiss. For her it was a flirtation which at first, before she scented danger, must have helped the passage of the boring hours, alone in the big nursery at Berkhamsted with two children as companions. For me it was an obsessive passion: I lived only for the moments with her. She began soon to be a little scared of what was happening; every evening of the winter vacation I would go upstairs to the nursery where she sat alone and the slow fire consumed the coals behind an iron guard. My parents must have heard my footsteps night by night as they crossed the floor, just as when I sat below I could hear her movements on the ceiling while I pretended to read. Sometimes during the day she would enlist my sister's aid to hide from me. I took dancing lessons in order to please her, and on Saturday nights we would go together to what were called 'hops' at the King's Arms. To keep up appearances I would have to dance occasionally with some boring wife of a master at the school and surrender her to other arms. Sometimes in the dark schoolroom out of term, on the excuse of teaching my brother and sister to waltz and foxtrot, we had dances of our own when half-kisses could be exchanged without the children seeing.

But the fear set in. She told me how she was engaged to be married to a man working for Cables & Wireless in the Azores. She had not seen him for over a year, and he had become like a stranger to her. Soon he would be returning, and she would have to leave Berkhamsted to marry him. Once when she talked to me of her marriage, she wept a little. I was too inexperienced to press her for more than kisses; marriage for me seemed then to be years out of reach and there was the great difference in our ages. All I could do was urge her to break her promise and I had nothing to offer in exchange. We wrote to each other every week when I returned to Oxford, and her handwriting became so fixed in my memory that when, more than thirty years after we had ceased to write, I received a letter asking me to get her seats for my first play *The Living Room*, I recognized her hand on the envelope and my heart beat faster until I remembered that I was a man of over fifty and she, by now, well into her cruel sixties.

I can see now that my courtship from the distance of Oxford went to comic and selfish lengths. For example I organized a reading of poems by 'Oxford Poets' with what was then the British Broadcasting Company at Savoy Hill. Among others Harold Acton took part, Joseph Gordon Macleod, T. O. Beachcroft and A. L. Rowse, who was the only one to receive a 'fan' letter – it came from an old invalid lady who had found his verses, she wrote, 'consoling'. I read an extract from an attempt on the Newdigate Prize. The subject that year was 'Lord Byron', but my sentimental blank verse lines had nothing to do with Byron – they were directed at Berkhamsted where the governess sat listening, as she had been warned to do. Poor young woman, it never occurred to me what embarrassment she must have suffered, seated before the radio set with my father and mother. Other verses too I poured out to her like letters and sold them to the *Weekly Westminster*, still edited by Kenneth Richmond's friend, Miss Naomi Royde-Smith, or gave them gratis to the *Oxford Outlook* (of which I was conveniently the editor), or sent them to the *Oxford Chronicle*, which paid me five shillings a poem, or the *Decachord*, which paid nothing. There would have been no doubt at home of the subject of my verses. Even the sound of her footsteps on the nursery floor were recorded in plain lines, and my jealousy of the man she was to marry. In one sonnet written in that winter of 1924 I looked forward without relish to my solitary future – 'Eating a Lyons chop in 1930' the sonnet pessimistically began. How could I have imagined that by 1930 I would have been already happily married for two years? But the reality of a passion should not be questioned because of its brevity. A storm in the shallow Mediterranean may be over in a few hours, but while it lasts it is savage enough to drown men, and this storm was savage. Passion had temporarily eased the burden of bore- dom: hope was a panacea, even when it was only expectation of the 'hop' at the King's Arms on the next Saturday night, but there were times – even a governess has holidays and days of freedom – when I realized that my old enemy was merely biding his moment. A manic-depressive, like my grandfather – that would be the verdict on me today, and analysis had not cured my condition.

2

I can remember very clearly the afternoon I found the revolver in the brown deal corner-cupboard in a bedroom which I shared with my elder brother. It was the early autumn of 1923. The revolver was a small ladylike object with six chambers like a tiny egg-stand, and there was a cardboard box full of bullets. I never mentioned the discovery to my brother because I had realized the moment I saw the revolver the use I intended to make of it. (I don't to this day know why he possessed it; certainly he had no licence, and he was only three years older than myself. A large family is as departmental as a Ministry.)

My brother was away – probably climbing in the Lake District – and until he returned the revolver was to all intents my own. I knew what to do with it because I had been reading a book (I think Ossendowski was the author) which described how the White Russian officers, condemned to inaction in southern Russia at the tail-end of the counter-revolutionary war, used to invent hazards with which to escape boredom. One man would slip a charge into a revolver and turn the chambers at random, and his companion would put the revolver to his head and pull the trigger. The chance, of course, was five to one in favour of life.

One forgets emotions easily. If I were dealing with an imaginary character, I might feel it necessary for verisimilitude to make him hesitate, put the revolver back into the cupboard, return to it again after an interval, reluctantly and fearfully, when the burden of boredom and despair became too great. But in fact there was no hesitation at all: I slipped the revolver into my pocket, and the next I can remember is crossing Berkhamsted Common towards the Ashridge beeches. Perhaps before I had opened the corner-cupboard, boredom had reached an intolerable depth. The boredom was as deep as the love and more enduring – indeed it descends on me too often today. For years, after my analysis, I could take no aesthetic interest in any visual thing: staring at a sight that others assured me was beautiful I felt nothing. I was fixed, like a negative in a chemical bath. Rilke wrote, 'Psycho-analysis is too fundamental a help for me, it helps you once and for all, it clears you up, and to find myself finally cleared up one day might be even more helpless than this chaos.'

Now with the revolver in my pocket I thought I had stumbled on the perfect cure. I was going to escape in one way or another, and perhaps because escape was inseparably connected with the Common in my mind, it was there that I went.

Beyond the Common lay a wide grass ride known for some reason as Cold Harbour to which I would occasionally take a horse, and beyond again stretched Ashridge Park, the smooth olive skin of beech trees and last year's quagmire of leaves, dark like old pennies. Deliberately I chose my ground, I believe without real fear – perhaps because so many semi-suicidal acts which my elders would have regarded as neurotic, but which I still consider to have been under the circumstances highly reasonable, lay in the background of this more dangerous venture. They removed the sense of strangeness as I slipped a bullet into a chamber and, holding the revolver behind my back, spun the chambers round.

93

Had I romantic thoughts about my love? I must have had, but I think, at the most, they simply eased the medicine down. Unhappy love, I suppose, has sometimes driven boys to suicide, but this was not suicide, whatever a coroner's jury might have said: it was a gamble with five chances to one against an inquest. The discovery that it was possible to enjoy again the visible world by risking its total loss was one I was bound to make sooner or later.

✳ I put the muzzle of the revolver into my right ear and pulled the trigger. There was a minute click, and looking down at the chamber I could see that the charge had moved into the firing position. I was out by one. I remember an extraordinary sense of jubilation, as if carnival lights had been switched on in a dark drab street. My heart knocked in its cage, and life contained an infinite number of possibilities. It was like a young man's first successful experience of sex – as if among the Ashridge beeches I had passed the test of manhood. I went home and put the revolver back in the corner-cupboard.

This experience I repeated a number of times. At fairly long intervals I found myself craving for the adrenalin drug, and I took the revolver with me when I returned to Oxford. There I would walk out from Headington towards Elsfield down what is now a wide arterial road, smooth and shiny like the walls of a public lavatory. Then it was a sodden unfrequented country lane. The revolver would be whipped behind my back, the chamber twisted, the muzzle quickly and surreptitiously inserted in my ear beneath the black winter trees, the trigger pulled.

Slowly the effect of the drug wore off – I lost the sense of jubilation, I began to receive from the experience only the crude kick of excitement. It was the difference between love and lust. And as the quality of the experience deteriorated, so my sense of responsibility grew and worried me. I wrote a bad piece of free verse (free because it was easier in that way to express my meaning clearly without literary equivocation) describing how, in order to give myself a fictitious sense of danger, I would 'press the trigger of a revolver I already know to be empty'. This verse I would leave permanently on my desk, so that if I lost the gamble, it would provide incontrovertible evidence of an accident, and my parents, I thought, would be less troubled by a fatal play-acting than by a suicide – or the rather bizarre truth. (Only after I had given up the game did I write other verses which told the true facts.)

It was back in Berkhamsted during the Christmas of 1923 that I paid a permanent farewell to the drug. As I inserted my fifth dose, which corresponded in my mind to the odds against death, it occurred to me that I wasn't even excited: I was beginning to pull the trigger as casually as I might take an aspirin tablet. I decided to give the revolver – since it was six-chambered – a sixth and last chance. I twirled the chambers round and put the muzzle to my ear for a second time, then heard the familiar empty click as the chambers shifted. I was through with the drug, and walking back over the Common, down the new road by the ruined castle, past the private entrance to the gritty old railway station reserved for the use of Lord Brownlow, my mind was already busy on other plans. One campaign was over, but the war against boredom had got to go on. I put the revolver back in the corner-cupboard, and going downstairs I lied gently and convincingly to my parents that a friend had invited me to join him in Paris.

For I had to get away somehow from evenings where the ceiling of the room where I sat sounded under the well-known footsteps and all I had for physical expectations were the Saturday night 'hops' or a few minutes pressed together in the dark schoolroom. My rival was soon to return from the Azores and the governess would be married and gone before the long summer vac came round again. The whole episode of my love had lasted less than six months, but even today it seems to have endured as long as youth itself. As for the revolver I was never tempted to take it up again, but it left an influence on my night-life; in dreams even to this day I often raise a revolver to defend myself against some enemy and find it useless because, when I fire, the bullets are discharged without the force to penetrate. A kind of Russian roulette remained too a factor in my later life, so that without previous experience of Africa I went on an absurd and reckless trek through Liberia; it was the fear of boredom which took me to Tabasco during the religious persecution, to a *léproserie* in the Congo, to the Kikuyu reserve during the Mau-Mau insurrection, to the emergency in Malaya and to the French war in Vietnam. There, in those last three regions of clandestine war, the fear of ambush served me just as effectively as the revolver from the corner-cupboard in the life-long war against boredom.

Chapter 7

1

I ONLY stayed in Paris ten days, although it was my first visit abroad. Claud Cockburn and I had become probationary members of the Communist Party at Oxford, and I held a Party card containing three or four sixpenny stamps which represented my monthly contributions. It was a very small branch, though it served both city and university; I doubt if there were more than half a dozen members, and Cockburn and I, with no scrap of Marxist belief between us, joined only with the far-fetched idea of gaining control and perhaps winning a free trip to Moscow and Leningrad, cities which six years after the Revolution still had a romantic appeal. Our mercenary motive was seen through almost at once by a very serious Australian Rhodes scholar who was much older than ourselves and we soon ceased to attend meetings.* But I still kept my card as a souvenir, and with it in my hand I visited the Communist headquarters in Paris, where they were equally puzzled by my youth and my bad French. However I was invited to a meeting that night somewhere around Menilmontant. The working-class quarter was full of policemen in blue steel helmets and Gardes Mobiles who carried rifles, but the meeting nonetheless bored me to exhaustion. Endless messages from branches abroad were read out amid cheers, and soon I slipped away and took the Métro home to my hotel in the Rue Tronchet and the huge blue copy of *Ulysses*, the size of a telephone directory, which I had bought on my first day in Paris at Sylvia Beach's bookshop. Years later, writing *It's a Battlefield*, I used this meeting and the sense of futility it conveyed to describe

*Life's ironies: neither Cockburn nor I were then at all inclined to Communism, but some years later he became a Party member and afterwards left the Party, while I found myself thirty years on, after my experience of the French Vietnamese war and American policy there, in greater sympathy with Communism than ever before, though less and less now with the Russian version of it.

rather unfairly a branch meeting of the Communist Party in London.

This was the only experience which differentiated my visit from that of any other young man in the 1920s. I went to the Casino de Paris to see Mistinguette, to the Concert Mayol to excite myself with naked breasts and thighs, and then back to the small room smelling of urine in the second-class hotel in the Rue Tronchet, passing the Madeleine on my way. The Madeleine in those days was suitably surrounded by aunt-like figures of a certain age who called to me as I went by. But I was too timid to make my first experiment in copulation with any of them, or else they were not young or pretty enough when I compared them with the girls of the Concert Mayol. It was certainly no sense of morality which restrained me. Morality comes with the sad wisdom of age, when the sense of curiosity has withered.

I had one respectable chance of adventure, and there is a touch of vanity in the letter I wrote to my mother about it: someone at least had considered me old enough to marry. 'At the moment I am in a state of utter panic. I have just had two solid hours of French conversation (good for me, I suppose) with a French matron in this hotel. She has a daughter, whom I have not met. I did not meet the mother till this morning. She has been match-making in a most brazen and terrifying manner. She has described her daughter most intimately with regard to character and looks. She has even insisted on my meeting her this afternoon, and corresponding with her from England when I return. She has had the barefaced impertinence, though I assure you I gave her no encouragement, to inquire into my prospects. As though I had asked her blasted daughter in marriage! At any rate she confessed that her daughter was *plus tranquille et plus timide* than herself. And at the end, as she left the room, leaving me limp and help-less, a poor fly hopelessly entangled in the web, powerless even to struggle, she let out her only words of English, "Pardon me, but you see – I am a mozzer." It's lucky I'll be leaving on Wednesday. She can't possibly make me propose in three days. And yet – the Lord knows what she can't do.'

As a distraction from lost love and baffled desire Paris was not a
success, and now that Russian roulette had failed me, I tried
drink instead when I returned to Oxford. For nearly one term I
went to bed drunk every night and began drinking again immediately I woke. I had given up going to lectures after my first
term, judging them less useful than reading; and now, though I
was within a few terms of my final exams, I only had to be sober
once a week when I read an essay to my tutor.

At the end of term there was a ceremony called 'The Handshake', when each in turn had to sit at a table opposite the Master
and the Dean, while his tutor commented on the work he had
done during the term. I was helped as far as the door by two of
my friends, Robert Scott and George Whitmore, who held me
on a steady course through the quad. Then I slumped into a chair
beside Kenneth Bell and faced the Master and the Dean. I don't
think it occurred to either of these two that an undergraduate
would appear before them drunk at that early hour and on such a
serious occasion and they probably put down any strangeness in
my manner to nerves. My tutor recognized my state, but he was
sympathetic. Kenneth Bell and the Dean (who was known as
'Sligger') were the two opposite poles of the college, and they had
little liking for each other. Sligger gathered around him young
men who attracted him by their looks and who played, if only
superficially, the comedy of homosexual inclinations: Bell's
pupils were aggressively heterosexual and were inclined, like
himself, to drink large quantities of beer. So he stage-managed
skilfully what might have been a disastrous Handshake, and I
was released safely into the care of my friends who had a taxi
waiting and they lodged me as though I were something break-
able in the train for Bletchley. The long wait there for the connection to Berkhamsted was enough to sober me. I have never again
in my life drunk quite so heavily over so long a period, but I
have cause to be grateful to that spell of alcoholism: it left me
with a strong head and a tough liver. 'Mithridates he died old.'*

*I think it must have been during this period of perpetual drunkenness
that I unconsciously made an enemy who cropped up nearly twenty years

Now I look back, there seems something a little bizarre about my Oxford days. They certainly do not recall those of Newman or the early pages of *Brideshead Revisited*; perhaps they were closer to Maclean's and Kim Philby's at Cambridge . . .

A small affair of what might have become espionage began innocently enough in early 1924. I had read a book of short stories by Geoffrey Moss called *Defeat* about the occupied zones of Germany. Moss described the attempt of the French authorities in their zone to establish a separatist Palatine Republic between the Moselle and the Rhine. German criminals had been brought in from Marseilles and other ports – pimps, brothel-keepers, thieves from French prisons – to support the collaborators. Even one of the ministers had served a prison sentence. French troops held the crowds back while unarmed German police were beaten unconscious. Only the opposition of the British and American governments put an end to what was known as the Revolver Republic, but it was believed in Germany that at any moment the 'spontaneous' outbreak would be renewed.

I was easily aroused to indignation by cruelties not my own, and the idea of experiencing a little danger made me write to the German Embassy in Carlton Gardens and offer my services as a propagandist. The *Oxford Outlook* was at my disposal, for I was the editor, and to the *Oxford Chronicle*, a city paper, I was a regular contributor, if only of the five-shilling love poems.

I had not expected the promptitude of the German response. Coming back one early evening to my rooms in Balliol I found my armchair occupied, my only bottle of brandy almost finished, and a fat blond stranger who rose and introduced himself, 'Count

---

later in strange circumstances. In 1942 I went up to Kailahun in Sierra Leone near the Liberian and French Guinea border to try to contact some American missionaries in Liberia who possessed a radio transmitter that might prove useful in our watch on the Vichy border. Installed in Kailahun was a district commissioner who didn't disguise his profound dislike of me. So violent did his antagonism prove that I had to have a censorship clamped on his mail, and his letters home proved to be breaking all the rules of security. I still remain in complete ignorance of what happened between us at Balliol.

von Bernstorff.' He was the first secretary of the German Embassy, a man who loved luxury and boys and who frequented a shady club called the Abyssinia in Archer Street, Soho. No one could have foretold that hidden in those folds of flesh was a hero who was to run a Jewish escape-route from Germany to Switzerland during the last war and be executed in Moabit prison.

My days after that seemed to be filled by Germans – there was a very pretty Countess von Bernstorff, the diplomat's cousin, who left a scented glove behind in my room to be added to my adolescent harem of inanimate objects, a young man with a long complicated title, who claimed a nobler and longer descent than the Hohenzollerns, and a mysterious wizened narrow figure with a scarred face, Captain P., whose full name I have now forgotten. Captain P. would turn up at irregular intervals, like someone who looks in at a kitchen door to see if the kettle is boiling. Now that I have worked in the Secret Service myself, I feel I should have smelt him out immediately as an intelligence officer. The day arrived when I called at Carlton Gardens and Count Bernstorff handed me a packet and told me to burn the envelope – which, of course, I kept for some years as a souvenir. Inside were twenty-five pound notes – more than sufficient in those days for a fortnight's holiday down the Rhine and the Moselle.

My father took the affair very seriously. He told me how Lord Haldane's career had been wrecked by his too great friendship for the Germans, and he offered to pay for my holiday himself. I knew that he could ill afford his generosity and I refused the offer. After all, I argued, I was not going to follow the same career as Lord Haldane and was unlikely to attain his eminence.

I asked Claud Cockburn to come with me; we were to be joined in Germany by my cousin Tooter, for neither Claud nor I could speak German. We went inexpensively by the Hook, and as we were laughing with pleasure in the railway compartment to Harwich at the thought of our free holiday and the confiding nature of German diplomats, there slid in beside us thin narrow Captain P. with his duel-scarred face. Our laughter broke abruptly off and we tried to appear the serious observers we were meant to be. I was very sea-sick on the crossing in spite of Mothersil and saw no more of Captain P. – perhaps he was sea-sick too.

Our holiday was uneventful, in spite of the stack of introductions which waited for us in the Cologne hotel. There we met a man called Waldenheim who was the political organizer in the German Volkspartei, and an industrial magnate, Doctor Hennings, who owned a great dye factory outside Cologne and gave us a gargantuan feast in Leverkusen, while he talked glibly of Germany's starvation.

After Cologne we went to Essen and lodged in simple luxury at Krupp's private hotel. In the Ruhr, newly occupied by French troops, 'there was a delightful sensation of being hated by everybody,' I wrote my mother. 'No tourist could be expected in the Ruhr, and I suppose all foreigners are taken for French officials. In the evening we went to a cabaret where we were even more unwelcome, and a rather fat naked woman did a symbolic dance of Germany in chains, ending up of course by breaking her fetters.' I can remember still the menace of Essen where most of the factory workers were on strike: the badly lit streets, the brooding groups. We flirted with fear and began to plan a thriller together rather in Buchan's manner.

At Bonn, then a small provincial university town, we stayed for half a crown a day in a little *gasthaus* built in 1649. On the riverside at night, encouraged by the atrocity stories we had heard in Cologne, we followed innocent Senegalese soldiers in the hope of seeing a rape, which never occurred. At Trier on the Moselle, which had been the centre of the Separatist movement, Spahis in turbans and long cloaks lounged under the Roman gateway, but there were no incidents to excite us. A local editor told us that every letter which left Trier was censored by the French authorities, so I wrote a letter to myself, addressed to 'The Editor of the *Oxford Outlook*', recounting imaginary atrocities by the French and mentioning the day and hour of the train we were to take out of the zone. But there were no soldiers to arrest us on the platform and the letter arrived safely in England unopened – a useful lesson in checking one's information.

Only in Heidelberg, outside the occupied zone, did our introductions provide us with an interesting encounter. There in the bureau of what was called respectably the Society for the Relief of Exiles from the Palatinate we met a kindly middle-aged man in plus-fours called Doctor Eberlein, who frankly explained to us the real purpose of his society. He was a kidnapper. He recruited young men to drive fast cars across the frontier into the French zone where they seized mayors and officials who were collaborating with the French authorities and bundled them back into Germany to be 'tried' for high treason.

In those days, when Hitler was still unknown to us, Doctor Eberlein's adventurous story appealed to me and gave me an idea for the future. When I returned home I wrote to Count Bernstorff suggesting that there might be difficulties in transmitting funds to the secret nationalist organizations in the occupied zone. An Oxford undergraduate would hardly be suspected as a courier ... After some delay Bernstorff replied. He wrote that at present they had no difficulty in transmitting funds, but he had been asked by his 'friends' in Berlin whether I would be prepared to return to the French zone, get in touch with the Separatist leaders and try to obtain some information about their plans for the future. I finished reading the letter with excitement and a measure of pride, for I was being promoted from propaganda to espionage. It was a heady thought for a boy of nineteen, and I am amazed now, in these more security-conscious days, at what both of us had so rashly put upon paper.

Today, I would have scruples about the purpose I served, but at that age I was ready to be a mercenary in any cause so long as I was repaid with excitement and a little risk. I suppose too that every novelist has something in common with a spy: he watches, he overhears, he seeks motives and analyses character, and in his attempt to serve literature he is unscrupulous.

It was an odd schizophrenic life I lived during the autumn term of 1924. I attended tutorials, drank coffee at the Cadena, wrote an essay on Thomas More, studied the revolution of 1688 'from original sources', read papers on poets to the Ordinary and the Mermaid, attended debates at the Union, got drunk with friends; then 'Cross a step or two of dubious twilight, come out on the other side, the novel'. There another life began, where I exchanged last letters with the woman I loved, who was engaged to another man, wrote a first novel never to be published, the unhappy history of a black child born to white parents, and prepared

103

plans with Bernstorff for espionage. All the time Germans were dropping into my life unannounced, arriving from Paddington for the day to see the colleges and drink in my room. Of course my parents had no suspicion of what I was about, but surely my social life during that last year at Oxford must have surprised them a little. 'My gentleman from the Foreign Office, Berlin,' I wrote to my mother, 'was great fun. A real pre-war Prussian, but with a charming wife. In town he had been to *Primrose*, *Saint Joan* and *White Cargo* and explained the contrast in the real blood-and-iron fashion: "You must see all kinds of plays, in order to sympathize with all types of people, for only by sympathizing with them can you dominate them. It also helps in the study of their weak points." I felt all through lunch, which he gave me at the Mitre, that he was trying to discover mine. However *his* weak point was adiposity, and I quite broke his spirit and dominated him thoroughly by dragging him round Oxford at the speed of an express.' Didn't it occur to my parents that their son was keeping somewhat curious company?

Meanwhile I wrote to a right-wing journal owned by the Duke of Northumberland called *The Patriot*, which had supported the Separatist Republic, and offered to be their correspondent in Trier. As I demanded no expenses and wrote from the respectable address of Balliol they were ready to welcome articles so long as I understood, they frankly explained, that I could represent only one point of view, their own. Then I wrote to the French Embassy in London, telling them how I was visiting Trier for *The Patriot* and would be glad of any introductions they could give me. All was set, and with sufficient cunning, when the blow fell. The Dawes Plan was formulated, the Great Powers met together at some Swiss resort, agreements were reached, guarantees were given, and one insignificant recruit to the ranks of espionage was told to fall out – his services no longer required. All the lessons in German I had been taking from a maiden lady in North Oxford had been wasted time.

I often wonder what would have happened if my plans had not been aborted. Espionage is an odd profession: for some it is a vocation, with an unscrupulous purity, untouched by mercenary or even patriotic considerations – spying for spying's sake. Already I had begun to be dissatisfied with the plain gathering of fact and rumour and with its transmission to a single source; the idea of being a double agent had occurred to me. I would be certain, I thought, to learn something of my employers' interests: even the questions I had to answer would have value for the French authorities, and the honest pity which I had formerly felt for defeated Germany had died a quick death after the gormandizing in Leverkusen and the lies of the editor in Trier. Perhaps it was lucky for me that Germany was able to dispense with my services, for the life of the double agent is a precarious one.

Chapter 8

1

PERHAPS, until one starts, at the age of seventy, to live on borrowed time, no year will seem again quite so ominous as the one when formal education ends and the moment arrives to find employment and bear personal responsibility for the whole future. My parents had given me everything they could possibly owe a child and more.* Now it was my turn to decide and no one – not even the Oxford Appointments Board – could help me very far. I was hemmed in by a choice of jails in which to serve my life imprisonment, for how else at twenty can one regard a career which may last as long as life itself, or at the best until that sad moment is reached when the prisoner is released, in consideration of good behaviour, with a pension?

'I've just applied for a sub-editorship on a trans-Atlantic liner,' I wrote to my mother in January 1926, but that was only the last wild throw after many failures and more than six months of virtual unemployment since I left Oxford. I don't even remember whether I had an answer to that particular application.

The last term before I took Finals had been filled with frustrated efforts to decide the future. I don't think my old dream of the Nigerian Navy ever led me very far, but I passed my viva for the Consular Service, having an idea of following in the footsteps of Flecker in the Levant, although in the end I never sat for the examination, for it would have entailed many months of being coached in French. I had at the time a great admiration for some of Flecker's poems and I pictured myself in a caravanserai on the Golden Road to Samarkand or sitting beside a clicking jalousie, full of self-pity and nostalgia, in a Middle Eastern seaport:

*I came down from Oxford with heavy enough debts for those days. I admitted a hundred pounds of them to my father who paid them with hardly a complaint – the rest I worked off slowly during the next year and a half.

>'Half to forget the wandering and pain,
>Half to remember days that have gone by,
>And dream and dream that I am home again!'

More and more the wind-vane of my inclination swung in the direction of the East. I applied here, I applied there ...

For example there was an interview with the Asiatic Petroleum Company. Here I had been helped by my uncle, who was head of the Brazilian Warrant Agency; he had spoken on my behalf to a director. Unfortunately I found my interviewer knew all about a book of verse I had published at Oxford and he regarded this tendency of mine with deep suspicion. No one, he said, who worked with the Asiatic Petroleum Company could have outside interests. I tried hard to persuade him that my small book had been an aberration of adolescence: now that I was mature I had outgrown literature and my only ambition was to make a success in business. When I saw that nothing was of any avail I suggested to my mother that there might be an opening in the company for my eldest brother Herbert to whom unemployment was like a recurring flu – at least he hadn't put himself out of court by publishing a book.*

I had been play-acting to the director, but there was some truth in my desire to cut away from the past. I knew I could never be a good poet, I associated even the act of composition with unhappy love, and my first novel which I had written while at Oxford had never found a publisher. I was ready to wear any mask to escape from myself, and so now I flirted with a less important business opening than Asiatic Petroleum, and one far removed from Samarkand. The Lancashire General Insurance Agency had opened a branch at Oxford under a genial manager with a silky moustache called Captain Harris who was always good for a free drink and a doubtful joke; he was the more popular because he had a plump blonde secretary who hinted, when she was left for a moment without him, at all kinds of possibilities, even a weekend in Paris. Captain Harris offered me, as soon as I should go down, a job at three hundred and fifty pounds a year plus commissions, which might easily, so said the optimistic captain,

*Years later he did publish one of dubious authenticity called *Secret Agent in Spain* – almost a family title.

amount to another eight hundred, but I had my doubts . . . I think I must have made contact with the captain and his girl when I offered to readers of the *Oxford Outlook* a free insurance against failure in examinations. They had only to fill in the coupon on page 37 and in case of failure they would receive a free champagne dinner for two at one of the Oxford restaurants. I suppose Captain Harris insured me against my risks. 'Of course the chief attraction of the dinner,' I wrote home, 'will be its mixed character, and as stupid females have the reputation of being the prettiest, this ought not to be negligible.'

Finals came and went with the future undecided. I managed to get a moderate second in Modern History, my only alpha being in Political Science of which I knew least, but I remembered how I had won my Balliol exhibition with the aid of a poem by Ezra Pound, and I carefully learnt by heart certain passages from authors who had not been required reading – Santayana was one of them – passages sufficiently general in idea for them to fit with a little ingenuity into almost any essay I might be required to write. I was much helped by a game we often played at Christmas called 'Noun and Question'. In this game papers were handed round on which one person would write a noun, concealing it with a fold, another a question. The papers were all reshuffled and drawn from a hat, and a player would have to reply in verse to the question he picked, introducing the noun. One might be faced by such a word as 'skyscraper' and the question 'Who is your favourite character in Shakespeare?' Compared with this game, it was child's play to insert a purple passage of Santayana on *Hamlet* into an essay on Machiavelli's *Prince*.

I never joined the Lancashire General Insurance Agency (although, of course, I suggested it might be a suitable opening for Herbert). Instead I found myself for two weeks an employee of the British-American Tobacco Company, destined for China in two months' time.

From the first I was daunted by the great concrete slab beside the Thames, with the uniformed porter like an officer of some foreign country demanding credentials; in the lift several middle-aged men were carrying files carefully like babies. The director who interviewed me (his name, I think, was Archibald Rose) had the appearance of a senior army officer, perhaps a brigadier, in plain clothes. He was correctly dressed in dark capitalist uniform with a well-tied bow tie, a well-groomed moustache; he had the politeness of a man speaking to his equal in age and position. He would have made a good Intelligence officer, and I have little doubt now that he belonged, however distantly, to the Secret Service. A man in his position, recruiting and controlling men for the Chinese hinterland, could hardly have escaped contact with the 'old firm', and perhaps for that reason he was not scrupulously accurate about the details of the employment. The end justified the means.

'I want university men,' he said in remarkable contrast to the director of Asiatic Petroleum, 'because they have other interests. They can stand loneliness.' It was the best chosen fly he could have attached to his hook. After one year, he said, spent in the treaty port of Shanghai, I would be appointed to some station in the interior with one other companion. The starting salary would be four hundred and fifty pounds a year. I discovered soon after joining the firm that both these facts were inaccurate. I would have to spend at least three years in the Shanghai office and maybe longer, and the salary was three hundred and sixty pounds. What was more important to me, because of my interest in a girl at Oxford, I should not be allowed to marry for the first four years after my appointment and only then with the permission of the directors. If I threw up the job before the end of my first year, I would not only have to pay my return fare, I would have to reimburse the company for my passage out.

I went to work – if you can call it that – almost at once. I was shown into a large office like a classroom where there were rows of desks. I felt as though I were back in the Junior School – how civilized the big library table of the Sixth seemed in comparison. To make the resemblance to school even closer the new boys, some half a dozen of them, were all placed at the front of the class. Now I can remember only two of them. Mr Rose's hook had caught one other university man: he was from Cambridge, where he had played cricket for his college but had not succeeded in taking a degree. The other sat at the desk next to mine. He had been a bank clerk in Cardiff, and he insisted on playing game after game of double noughts-and-crosses, which he invariably won. He was equally knowledgeable on the subject of motor-cycles. My tutor Kenneth Bell had written of me in his recommendation, 'He is a good mixer,' and I tried to live up to this unsound judgement, but noughts-and-crosses palled rapidly. I bought two paperbound copies of *Chinese Self-Taught* and tried to keep my companion occupied, but we made small progress.

There was absolutely no work for any of us to do. Far from being new boys who had to be bullied into learning, it seemed that we were favoured pupils who must be kept happy. We belonged to a privileged class because we were destined for China, though sometimes I felt we more closely resembled pampered prisoners who must not know the fate to which we were being led. Our passages had already been booked, and my heart sank when my companion, busily drawing his squares for yet another game, said, 'We'll be able to do this on the boat going out, won't we?' The excitements of the Forbidden City, the Boxer Rebellion, Captain Gilson's *Lost Column* faded from my imagination, and only an awful inevitability of double noughts-and-crosses took their place. Perhaps we were to be chained together, not only on the boat and on the Shanghai Bund, but in that small up-country station, which had at first seemed so romantic a prospect.

As there was no work to distract us from the enigmatic future, they gave us to read, to help pass the slow office hours, big folio ledgers, and in the pages of insignificant accounts an entry would sometimes stand sharply out: 'For burial of coolie found dead on office steps . . . Radio for son of General Chiang Kai-shek on his twenty-first birthday . . .'

The next week we were to go to the Liverpool factory for a month and watch from eight in the morning till seven at night the way cigarettes were made. Some of the older men were knowledgeable about the foreign substances which were added to the tobacco. There was no practical point so far as I could see in our stint at the factory, for we were to be concerned in all our working future in marketing cigarettes not making them.

I went to see Archibald Rose and told him of my uncertainties. He was a little impatient. After all I was being paid five pounds a week for doing nothing at all. It was time I made up my mind,

110

one way or another. (I nearly offered my brother Herbert in my place.) Then I went back to my lodging in Chelsea and tried to go on with my second novel – I had abandoned all hope for the first.

Conrad was the influence now, and in particular the most dangerous of all his books, *The Arrow of Gold*, written when he had himself fallen under the tutelage of Henry James. I have long forgotten the details of my plot. The setting was nineteenth-century London when Carlist refugees lived around Leicester Square. A young Englishman became involved in their conspiracy. There was a girl, of course, as romantic and ill-defined as Donna Rita. The book was a greater struggle to write than the first had been, for I had now much less hope. How could I abandon the chance of being a businessman, when it seemed my only escape from the hated obsession of trying to make imaginary characters live? I went to Oxford for a weekend to confide my fears, became engaged to be married and sent a telegram to Archibald Rose telling him that I was not returning to the office. I was ashamed of my cowardice, but I couldn't bring myself to face him: I had taken ten pounds of B.A.T. money and ten pounds seemed a lot in those days.

Again I was without a future, for I had no confidence in those five hundred words a day on single-lined foolscap. What did I know of Carlist Spain or Spain at all except from the pages of Conrad? And yet I returned to the place and period three years later with less happy results, because the book was published and can still be found in second-hand catalogues under the title *Rumour at Nightfall*. As for the London refugees my only material lay in Carlyle's *Life of John Sterling* – the one book by Carlyle which I have been able to read with pleasure.

There was the problem of money. I had dropped my allowance when I took my job and I couldn't live at home, for the house was closed and my family at the seaside. It was Sackville Street or nothing. To the young men of my generation, down from the university without work, recourse to Sackville Street was like recourse to the pawnshop in earlier days. Among the 'gentlemen's tailors' stood an office with the Dickensian name of Gabbitas & Thring. I have always, most unfairly, thought of the interview between Nicholas Nickleby and Mr Squeers as taking place there.

There was a Dickensian mustiness about Sackville Street in those days, in the old-established tailors' shops on either side, where prostitutes kept flats on the second floor. The office of Gabbitas & Thring (chief rival of the equally Dickensian Truman & Knightley) might have been that of an old family solicitor, with strange secrets concealed in the metal file-boxes. It was not the cream of educational aspirants which trickled through Sackville Street. I doubt if many young men ever reached Eton or Harrow with the aid of the 'partners', for a man with a first-class degree did not require their help. They were the last hope of those needing a little temporary aid. You pawned yourself instead of your watch.

I had a horror of becoming involved in teaching. It was a profession into which you could so easily slip, as my father had done, by accident. He had intended to be a barrister, had 'eaten his dinners' and taken on the job of temporary master only to tide him over a lean period. Had he been afraid of feeling the trap close, as I was now? I wanted nothing permanent, I explained in near panic, to the partner. Was there not, perhaps, some private tutoring job which was available just for the summer? He opened his file with an air of disappointment: there were certainly good opportunities, he suggested, in the coming school term, for an exhibitioner of Balliol with an honours degree. As for private tutoring I was too late in applying, such men were needed immediately the schools broke up (he whisked over page after page), there was really nothing he could offer for someone of my qualifications . . . I would hardly be interested in this (he had detached a page with the tips of his fingers), a widowed lady living at Ashover, a village in Derbyshire, who required someone to look after her son of eight during the holidays. I would not be asked to live in the house: I would have a room in a private hotel with all my meals, but there was no salary attached. When I accepted, he looked at me with disappointment and suspicion – there must be something disgracefully wrong in my background.

The position suited me, for I had the evenings free when I could work at my novel. The country was beautiful with the grey Pennines standing all around, a few wandering sheep on desolate deserted hills, loose stone walls and occasional cottages with an

112

Irish air of dilapidation. The widow was undemanding. She didn't want her son to be overworked. A little mathematics perhaps in the morning (I had forgotten all I ever knew), a quarter of an hour of Latin (equally forgotten), some games after lunch ... I had what I thought the bright idea of teaching him a little carpentry, though I had never practised it myself. There was a large shady garden which reminded me of my uncle's at Harston with lots of out-houses in which I discovered wooden crates, nails, hammers. I suggested we should build a toy theatre. My pupil agreed readily enough: he was a boy without initiative: he was quite ready to stand around holding the nails. Unfortunately the toy theatre failed to take even a rudimentary shape, so that after two days' work I decided that what we had been making without knowing it was a rabbit hutch. He was quite satisfied, even though there was no rabbit; he was as undemanding as his mother.

Back in the private hotel, which was called Ambervale, I plodded on till dinner time, among the Carlist refugees in Leicester Square, but the oppression of boredom soon began to descend. Once on my free day I walked over the hills to Chesterfield and found a dentist. I described to him the symptoms, which I knew well, of an abscess. He tapped a perfectly good tooth with his little mirror and I reacted in the correct way. 'Better have it out,' he advised.

'Yes,' I said, 'but with ether.'

A few minutes' unconsciousness was like a holiday from the world. I had lost a good tooth, but the boredom was for the time being dispersed.*

The only other distraction lay in the old ladies – a gay crowd who insisted on playing paper games they didn't properly understand after dinner under the direction of an elderly gentleman: 'Famous general beginning with the letter B', the sort of thing to which family life had accustomed me. They were regarded with cynical impatience by the only other young people, a pale slang-

*André Breton once wrote to Cocteau: 'All my efforts are for the moment directed along one line: conquer boredom. I think of nothing else day or night. Is it an impossible task for someone who gives himself to it wholeheartedly? Do understand that I insist on seeing what lies on the other side of boredom.'

ridden schoolboy and a girl with bobbed hair who wanted a hotel flirtation. She went with me to the pub where the landlord showed us into a private room, where we sat gingerly on the edge of a table and kissed dryly, then took refuge in a half of bitter and a gin and lime. She offered me a mongrel wirehaired terrier as a souvenir, which was to be sent by rail from Leicester to Berkhamsted and was to prove the bane of my life. Later the dog played an off-stage part in a play of mine, *The Potting Shed*, and Mr Kenneth Tynan, for reasons which remain mysterious to me, believed that he represented God. At lunch I would share a table with the flapper and her fat mother because the manageress thought it would be nice for the young people to get together. The mother was too shy to talk and whinnied like a frightened horse whenever I spoke to her.

The afternoons were the worst, for then there was not even the pretence of lessons. When I was tired of hide-and-seek for two I invented a game of pirates which involved a lot of physical activity on the walls of the vegetable garden. Luckily my pupil fell off the wall and cut his leg. This, in the eyes of his mother, made mathematics impossible, so now I could read to him all day while he lay stretched in a deck-chair. And so my second job came slowly and undemandingly to an end. My family returned from the seaside, the mongrel dog, called Paddy, arrived by train in a highly nervous condition from Leicester, and I was back at square one in Berkhamsted.

2

Three months of blank days went by, and then I arrived one wet night in Nottingham and woke next morning in the unknown city to an equally dark day. This was not like a London smog; the streets were free of vapour, the electric lights shone clearly: the fog lay somewhere out of sight far above the lamps. When I read Dickens on Victorian London I think of Nottingham in the twenties. There was an elderly 'boots' still employed at the Black Dog Inn, there were girls suffering from unemployment in the lace trade, who would, so it was said, sleep with you in return for a high tea with muffins, and a haggard blue-haired prostitute, ruined by amateur competition, haunted the corner by W. H. Smith's bookshop. Trams rattled downhill through the goose-market and on to the blackened castle. Against the rockface leant the oldest pub in England with all the grades of a social guide: the private bar, the saloon, the ladies', the snug, the public. Little dark cinemas offered matinée seats for fourpence in the stalls. I had found a town as haunting as Berkhamsted, where years later I would lay the scene of a novel and of a play. Like the bar of the City Hotel in Freetown which I was to know years later it was the focal point of failure, a place undisturbed by ambition, a place to be resigned to, a home from home.

1

I HAD come to work on the *Nottingham Journal* unpaid because no London paper would then accept an apprentice. One entered the office through a narrow stone Gothic door, stained with soot, which resembled the portal of a Pugin chapel, and the heads of Liberal statesmen stuck out above like gargoyles: on rainy days the nose of Gladstone dripped on my head as I came in. Inside was a very ancient lift with barely room for two which creaked up a rope to the editorial offices.

The subeditors were kind to me, though I cannot remember that they ever gave me any instruction. Half-way through the evening we had a sweepstake on the football results, to which each contributed threepence, and the winner would stand chips for all and pocket the change. I was unreasonably lucky, so that around eight, more often than not, I would get a breath of fresh air while I fetched the chips from a fish-stall. They were wrapped up in an old copy of the *Journal*, but never in the *Nottingham Guardian*: the *Guardian* was the respectable paper.

In the offices of the *Journal*, unlike the Asiatic Petroleum Company, I found it a positive advantage to have published a volume of verse. The editor of the weekly book-page, a Methodist minister, was kind to me and sometimes gave me a novel to review. The *Journal* prided itself on its literary tradition: the paper might be considered vulgar but at least it was bohemian. Sir James Barrie had once been a member of the staff, and this fact in those days perhaps impressed me more than it would do today. There were the memories of *Peter Pan*, those early stirrings of sexuality aroused in me at *The Admirable Crichton*, and I had even in my omnivorous childhood read *The Little Minister* which stood on the bookshelf in the dining-room at home in an elegant black buckram binding. (Childhood is not afraid of sentimentality.) *Mary Rose*, too, which I had seen with my parents, had left behind a sense of fading poetry like a scent in a drawer and of deeply buried emotions inexplicable without the professional aid of Kenneth Richmond. Mine is an unfashionable taste, but even now it seems to me that the first act of *Dear Brutus*, before the author plunges disastrously into the haunted wood, is almost equal to Wilde at his best.

My haunted and disastrous wood at this moment was Leicester Square and the neighbouring streets of Soho where my hero was wandering lost among the exiled Spaniards whom Carlyle had observed when he first came to London in the 1820's – not in Leicester Square but Euston. I had transposed them, perhaps because the Leicester Lounge and the old Empire Music Hall in their last days were better known to me, and I now transposed them again in my mind's eye to the goose-market of Nottingham. 'Daily in the cold spring air, under skies so unlike their own, you could see a group of fifty or a hundred stately tragic figures, in proud threadbare cloaks: perambulating mostly with closed lips, the broad pavements of Euston Square and the regions about St Pancras new Church. They spoke little or no English; knew nobody, could employ themselves on nothing, in this new scene.' Nor could I speak any Spanish, and the skies of Nottingham, though seldom visible, were even more unlike their own. How could they possibly have come alive on my single-lined foolscap – a word which already had an ominous ring about it?

After the first week in Nottingham I found cheap lodgings for myself and my dog Paddy in a grim grey row with a grim grey name, Ivy House, All Saints Terrace. My landlady was a thin complaining widow with a teenaged daughter, and, when my future wife, Vivien, visited me for a holiday weekend, the girl let down a cotton-reel from upstairs and banged it on my ground-floor window to disturb our loving quiet. My high tea before work consisted almost invariably of tinned salmon which I shared with Paddy, so that most days he was sick on the floor. On overcast mornings, before going on with my hopeless novel, I would take him for a walk in the nearby park where, when you touched the leaves, they left soot on the fingers. Once I took a lace worker to high tea, but she didn't sleep with me for all that. Oxford seemed more than six months away and London very far. I had fallen into a pocket out of life and out of time, but I was not unhappy.

117

Vivien was a Roman Catholic, but to me religion went no deeper than the sentimental hymns in the school chapel. 'Lord Dismiss us with Thy Blessing' represented the occasional mercy of God, and I enjoyed the luxurious melancholy of 'Abide with Me'. The only prize I had ever won at school was a special prize for an 'imaginative composition', given by an elderly master in memory of his son killed in the first world war. It was the first time the prize had been awarded, and being a deeply religious man he was grieved that it should go to a story about an old senile Jehovah who had been left alone in a deserted heaven.

I met the girl I was to marry after finding a note from her at the porter's lodge in Balliol protesting against my inaccuracy in writing, during the course of a film review, of the 'worship' Roman Catholics gave to the Virgin Mary, when I should have used the term 'hyperdulia'. I was interested that anyone took these subtle distinctions of an unbelievable theology seriously, and we became acquainted. Now it occurred to me, during the long empty mornings, that if I were to marry a Catholic I ought at least to learn the nature and limits of the beliefs she held. It was only fair, since she knew what I believed – in nothing supernatural. Besides, I thought, it would kill the time.

One day I took Paddy for a walk to the sooty neo-Gothic Cathedral – it possessed for me a certain gloomy power because it represented the inconceivable and the incredible. There was a wooden box for inquiries and I dropped into it a note asking for instruction. Then I went back to my high tea of tinned salmon and Paddy was sick again. I had no intention of being received into the Church. For such a thing to happen I would need to be convinced of its truth and that was not even a remote possibility.

The impossibility seemed even more pronounced a week later when I returned to the Cathedral and met Father Trollope. I was to grow fond of Trollope in the weeks which followed, but at the first sight he was all I detested most in my private image of the Church. A very tall and very fat man with big smooth jowls which looked as though they had never needed a razor, he resembled closely a character in one of those nineteenth-century paintings to be seen in art shops on the wrong side of Piccadilly – monks and cardinals enjoying their Friday abstinence by dismembering enormous lobsters and pouring great goblets of wine. Poor Trollope, his appearance maligned him. He led a very ascetic life, and one of his worst privations was the rule which, at that period, forbade him to visit the theatre, for he had been an actor in the West End – not a star, but one of those useful reliable actors who are nearly always in demand for secondary roles. First he had become converted to Catholicism (Dr Fry, that former ogre of Berkhamsted, had persuaded his family, who lived in Lincoln under the shadow of the deanery, to oppose his conversion), and then he was driven further by some inner compulsion to the priesthood. There were many plays on his shelves among the theological books – reading them was the nearest he could get to the footlights.

It was some weeks before he told me his story, and it came like a warning hand placed on my shoulder. 'See the danger of going too far', that was the menace his story contained. 'Be very careful. Keep well within your depth. There are dangerous currents out at sea which could sweep you anywhere . . .' Father Trollope had been swept a very long way out, but the turbulent sea had not finished with him yet. He held a high position in the Catholic Nottingham world: he was Administrator of the Cathedral, wellplaced to rise into a hierarchy where men of business ability are valued, but he was deeply dissatisfied with any future which could be represented as success – he hadn't yet sacrificed enough, and a few years after I left Nottingham he wrote to tell me that he was entering an Order, an Order which was to my mind the least attractive of any, the Redemptorist. What had these monks, with an obligation to dwell in all their sermons and retreats on the reality of hell, in common with this stout cheerful man who loved the smell of greasepaint and the applause at a curtain-fall? Perhaps nothing except the desire to drown. A few years later he was dead of cancer.

It was quite a while before I realized that my first impression was totally false and that I was facing the challenge of an inexplicable goodness. I would see Trollope once or twice a week for an hour's instruction, and to my own surprise I came to look forward to these occasions, so that I was disappointed when by reason of his work they were cancelled. Sometimes the place of instruction was an odd one – we began our lesson, perhaps, with a discussion on the date of the Gospels on the upper deck of a tram swaying out to some Nottingham suburb where he had business to do and concluded it with the significance of Josephus in the pious pitch-pine parlour of a convent.

I had cheated him from the first, not telling him of my motive in receiving instruction or that I was engaged to marry a Roman Catholic. At the beginning I thought that if I disclosed the truth he would consider me too easy game, and later I began to fear that he would distrust the genuineness of my conversion if it so happened that I chose to be received, for after a few weeks of serious argument the 'if' was becoming less and less improbable. Bishop Gore in his great book on religious belief wrote that his own primary difficulty was to believe in the love of God; my primary difficulty was to believe in a God at all. The date of the Gospels, the historical evidence for the existence of the man Jesus Christ: these were interesting subjects which came nowhere near the core of my disbelief. I didn't disbelieve in Christ – I disbelieved in God. If I were ever to be convinced in even the remote possibility of a supreme, omnipotent and omniscient power I realized that nothing afterwards could seem impossible. It was on the ground of a dogmatic atheism that I fought and fought hard. It was like a fight for personal survival.

My friend Antonia White many years later told me how, when she was attending the funeral of her father, an old priest, who had known her as a child, tried to persuade her to return to the Church. At last – to please him more than for any other reason – she said, 'Well then, Father, remind me of the arguments for the existence of God.' After a long hesitation he admitted to her, 'I knew them once, but I have forgotten them.' I have suffered the same loss of memory. I can only remember that in January 1926 I became convinced of the probable existence of something we call God, though now I dislike the word with all its anthropomorphic associations and prefer Chardin's Omega Point, and my belief never came by way of those unconvincing philosophical arguments which I derided in a short story called *A Visit to Morin*.

'Oh,' it may be said, 'a young man is no match for a trained priest,' but in fact, at twenty-two, fresh from Oxford and its intellectual exercises, I was more capable of arguing an abstract issue or debating an historical point than I am today. The experience of a long life may possibly increase one's intuition of human character, but the mass of memories and associations which we drag around with us like an over-full suitcase on our interminable journey would weary me now at the start with all such arguments as we indulged in then. I cannot be bothered to remember – I accept. With the approach of death I care less and less about religious truth. One hasn't long to wait for revelation or darkness.

Although I was not received till early February 1926, I must have made my decision some weeks before, for I wrote flippantly to my mother in January, in the course of a letter full of other concerns, 'I expect you have guessed that I am embracing the Scarlet Woman.' The flippancy was fictitious: the fun of the intellectual exercise was over. I had reached the limit of the land and there the sea waited, if I didn't turn back. I was laughing to keep my courage up.

The first General Confession, which precedes conditional baptism and which covers the whole of a man's previous life, is a humiliating ordeal. Later we may become hardened to the formulas of confession and sceptical about ourselves: we may only half intend to keep the promises we make, until continual failure or the circumstances of our private life, finally make it impossible to make any promises at all and many of us abandon Confession and Communion to join the Foreign Legion of the Church and fight for a city of which we are no longer full citizens. But in the first Confession a convert really believes in his own promises. I carried mine down with me like heavy stones into an empty corner of the Cathedral, dark already in the early afternoon, and the only witness of my baptism was a woman who had been dusting the chairs. I took the name of Thomas after St Thomas the doubter and not Thomas Aquinas – and then I went on to the *Nottingham Journal* office and the football results and the evening of potato chips.

I remember very clearly the nature of my emotion as I walked away from the Cathedral: there was no joy in it at all, only a sombre apprehension. I had made the first move with a view to my future marriage, but now the land had given way under my feet and I was afraid of where the tide would take me. Even my marriage seemed uncertain to me now. Suppose I discovered in myself what Father Trollope had once discovered, the desire to be a priest . . . At that moment it seemed by no means impossible. Only now after more than forty years I am able to smile at the unreality of my fear and feel at the same time a sad nostalgia for it, since I lost more than I gained when the fear belonged irrevocably to the past.

Chapter 10

1

I WAS earning nothing and learning very little on the *Journal*, and I had begun again to draw an allowance from my father who could ill afford it. I decided, between one high tea of tinned salmon and another, to leave Nottingham and try once more to find a job in London. I thought I was leaving Nottingham without regret, and I would have disbelieved anyone who had told me then that the city was embedded unforgettably in my imagination, and that the memory of it would stay with me over the next forty years like a photograph of a woman which one preserves in a drawer one doesn't know why, even when the relationship has seemed a long time dead.

Ten years passed before I wrote in a book called *A Gun for Sale* a description of my first morning in the city.

There was no dawn that day in Nottwich. Fog lay over the city like a night sky with no stars. The air in the streets was clear. You had only to imagine that it was night. The first tram crawled out of its shed and took the steel track down towards the market. An old piece of newspaper blew up against the door of the Royal Theatre and flattened out. In the streets on the outskirts of Nottwich an old man plodded by with a pole tapping at the windows. The stationer's window in the High Street was full of prayer books and bibles: a printed card remained among them, a relic of armistice day, like the old drab wreath of Haig poppies by the war memorial: 'Look down, and swear by the slain of the war that you'll never forget'.

The card, with its quotation from Siegfried Sassoon, had been in the window when I arrived in Nottingham in November and it was still there when I left in February.

In 1945, when the second war was over, I began to plan a novel set in Nottingham, and I revisited the city on the excuse of refreshing my memory, though it wasn't a 'necessary' journey, the only kind which in those days we were expected to make. I found the essentials were still the same, though the 'boots' had

123

disappeared from the Black Dog Inn. I wrote no more than the first chapter of the novel before I turned instead to *The Heart of the Matter*, but in 1957 I adapted the idea into an unsatisfactory play, *The Potting Shed*, in which I gave an off-stage part to my unsatisfactory dog. Our walks together along the River Trent and down to the goose-market forced their way into the play, and 'My landlady has a penchant for tinned salmon,' I remarked through a character's mouth. 'My dog likes it, but it often makes him sick. He's not a very good dog – parents unknown.' No, whatever Tynan might think, Paddy was never intended to be God. He was just himself.

I was to continue my effort to write romantic novels for some years to come, but when I finally realized their futility, it was to my memory of the solitary months in Nottingham that I returned for help; there I found a different subject. The furnished room in All Saints Terrace drew me back, like the Common at Berkhamsted, the abandoned trenches, and I made it the home of a libidinous clergyman who, unlike my grandfather, had been unfrocked against his will.

Time since I left Oxford had moved as slowly as the unemployed bands of those days, shifting, with hands spread out, along a pavement edge: the British-American Tobacco Company, the tutoring in the Pennines, the long evening hours on the *Journal* with little to do, the five hundred words a day on a novel which I was half aware belonged to the past and would never be published. Suddenly the hands of the clock swung round as though a hand were correcting the hour. I left Nottingham at the end of January, and in the first week of March I had been accepted on trial as a subeditor by *The Times*.

2

I was happy on *The Times*, and I could have remained happy there for a lifetime, if I had not in the end succeeded in publishing a novel, but not the one I was about to finish when I left Nottingham. My regular hours were from four in the afternoon to eleven at night, though occasionally I was forced to stay later. But more often, while my services remained as little valuable as they had been at Nottingham, I would be sent away before my

124

time, and this worried me. It seemed to me only too likely that I would not survive the period of trial, but finally the leisurely life of the home subeditors (there must have been about ten of us) calmed my nerves and I began to realize I was as safe as though I had entered the Civil Service. No one on *The Times* was ever known to be sacked or to resign. I remember with pleasure – it was a symbol of the peaceful life – the slow burning fire in the subeditors' room, the gentle thud of coals as they dropped one by one in the old black grate.

Ivy House, All Saints Terrace, and my sour widow had been exchanged for a bed-sitting-room in Battersea and a far from melancholy landlady. She was untidy, exuberant and absentminded. Articles of furniture regularly disappeared from my room towards the end of a month to reappear a week later; she had put them in hock to overcome a temporary difficulty. When I went out in the evening to Battersea Station to catch a train to Blackfriars I would pass an imposing building with a notice hanging on the railings: 'It is forbidden to throw stones at the Polytechnic'. Wandering along those streets I was passing unconsciously through the scenery of a future book, *It's a Battlefield*.

My five pounds a week was quite adequate to keep a single man. I was charged, I think, thirty shillings a week for my room and breakfast, and my dinner in *The Times* canteen seldom cost me more than elevenpence – for elevenpence I got two kippers, a pot of tea, and a slice of syrup roll.

Paddy I could no longer retain. I left him at Berkhamsted without regret. Luckily he had wormed his way into my mother's affection. He was the first dog she had ever cared for – perhaps because like a difficult child he was both nervous and independent. He never quite recovered his mental equilibrium after a picture in the drawing-room fell down beside him, and in those days there was no psycho-analyst for dogs.

I had been on *The Times* only two months when the General Strike was declared. *The Times* was the only paper which continued to be issued without interruption from the first day of the strike, although at the beginning it appeared in the form of a single multigraphed sheet. Our success aroused the jealousy of

Winston Churchill, who seized a quarter of our paper stocks for his extravagant *British Gazette*. As the *Gazette* was badly edited, over-printed and maldistributed, great bundles of his journal, manufactured with our paper, were dumped loose around the streets for anyone to pick up. Being one of the editorial staff I was automatically a strike-breaker, and there were moments of drama, even in the quiet of Printing House Square.

Among the notices on the wall of every room there had always hung instructions on what to do in case of fire – if a bell rang three times we were to file out in an orderly way and proceed I forget where. It was an instruction which seemed as far removed from reality as the little book on style with which each of us was supplied, and in which we read that we must not spell 'bunkum' 'buncombe' or 'Marquess' 'Marquis'. Now, when an unmis-takable fire-alarm sounded in the afternoon on the second day of the strike, no one paid any attention. We were all of us a little sleepy, for we had been up the whole previous night while the multigraph machines turned out the famous single sheet of May 5, 1926, Number 44263 of *The Times*, price twopence. We had worked as loaders and packers, for there was little subediting to do, even though the single sheet finally managed to include, apart from news of the strike, a weather report, broadcasting, sport, Stock Exchange, and a Court Page of five lines which might have been written by Sir John Betjeman ('The Prince of Wales return-ed to London from Biarritz last night, travelling from Paris by air'). The machines did not stop till eight in the morning, and then we had all walked home, for there were no trams, no tubes, no buses. Little wonder that not one of us paid any attention at first to the fire-alarm.

The bell rang once, twice, three times. Someone asked with mild curiosity, 'A fire?' After a while the assistant chief subeditor, Colonel Maude, rose and moved with his usual elegant and lei-surely gait into the corridor. He was a man of great courtesy, very tall and slim with a soft blond moustache; you would have taken him for a military attaché but never for a journalist. I remember that he always apologized to me in a low drawling voice when he handed me any work at all – even a small paragraph for the News in Brief on a prize vegetable marrow – and now, when he returned to the room and sat down, it took quite a time to realize that *The Times* – so he was telling us – had been set on fire. He was seated again at the long table, which was usually presided over by the chief subeditor, George Anderson, but it was opening-time and at opening-time Anderson always took a short leave of absence. The strikers apparently had squirted petrol through a grating into the basement and had managed to set alight one of the great rolls of paper which stood there. Maude obviously was not disturbed, there was no copy to deal with, and my fellow subeditors chatted a little while on the subject of fires in general and the feasibility of burning down *The Times*. One of the subeditors was an elderly man who ran a small farm in the country and therefore always dealt with the agricultural page. He told us a few anecdotes about rick-fires, which passed the time until the all-clear sounded. Later that night there was a small fight between the loaders, of whom I was one, and the pickets in Printing House Square; the Sporting Department acted as storm-troops and there were few casualties. Nor was there any bad feeling. The revolutionary atmosphere south of the river died away on the bridges.

More from curiosity than from any wish to support the Establishment I became a special constable and I used to parade of a morning with a genuine policeman the length of Vauxhall Bridge. There was a wonderful absence of traffic, it was a beautiful hushed London that we were not to know again until the blitz, and there was the exciting sense of living on a frontier, close to violence. Armoured cars paraded the streets, and just as during the blitz certain areas, Bloomsbury and Euston among them, were more unhealthy than others like Hampstead and St John's Wood, so Camberwell and Hammersmith were now considered more dangerous than the City. Our two-man patrol always ceased at the south end of Vauxhall Bridge, for beyond lay the enemy streets where groups of strikers stood outside the public houses. A few years later my sympathies would have lain with them, but the great depression was still some years away: the middle-class had not yet been educated by the hunger-marchers. On the side of the Establishment it was a game, a break in the monotony of earning a secure living, at its most violent the atmosphere was that of a

127

rugger match played against a team from a rather rough council school which didn't stick to the conventional rules. 'I'm almost sorry now that it's over,' I wrote home, 'as we had as much free beer as we wanted at the office while it was on.'

There was yet another advantage. I felt accepted now. I even received a silver match-box from the management. My three months' trial was not yet finished, but in the cameraderie of free beer and unusual duties I had become an established member of the staff. Oxford had at least taught me to drink pint by pint with any man.

Of my companions in the subeditors' room (most of them seemed much older than I was) I remember faces and characteristics more than names. The youngest subeditor, apart from myself, was so fastidious that he could eat nothing, he said, which had been touched by the human hand: for dinner in the canteen he took only a cup of tea. Yet he was plump enough, so that he must have had somewhere at home a hygienic source of supply. I would try to tempt him with a tin of sardines, but there was obviously some doubt in his mind as to what happened between the netting of the fish and the tinning. I connected his fastidiousness with his employment, for he was in charge of the Court Page and he had a desk all to himself, loaded with such superior reference books as the *Almanach de Gotha*, Debrett's *Peerage* and Burke's *Landed Gentry*.

There were other faces which returned to me often later in dreams. At least once a year, until quite recently, I dreamt I was entering the subeditors' room after a long absence. I would find an empty chair but not in my old place, and I would feel a sense of shame because I had been away so long and had returned only temporarily (the faces I saw around me were many of them by this time the faces of the dead) I would take Crockford down from the shelf over the coalgrate and check the name of an obscure vicar who had grown a prize vegetable marrow.

3

I can think of no better career for a young novelist than to be for some years a subeditor on a rather conservative newspaper. The hours, from four till around midnight, give him plenty of time to do his own work in the morning when he is still fresh from sleep – let the office employ him during his hours of fatigue. He has the company of intelligent and agreeable men of greater experience than his own: he is not enclosed by himself in a small room tormented by the problems of expression; and, except for rare periods of rush, even his working hours leave him time for books and conversation (most of us brought a book to read between one piece of copy and another). Nor is the work monotonous. Rather as in the game of Scrabble the same letters are continually producing different words; no one knows at four o'clock what the evening may produce, and death does not keep a conventional hour.

The young subeditor gains too some small insights into the vanities of the famous. J. M. Barrie before making a speech would send to *The Times* a typescript which included some passages that his audience must have taken for whimsical impromptus. (His speeches were always printed verbatim in the first person – a distinction he shared only with the Prime Minister.) 'I see the Archbishop of Canterbury smiling sceptically in my direction and wickedly shaking his head ...' I would read this at four-thirty in an after-dinner speech which was to be delivered at ten. Did the Archbishop have a prompt copy?

Another amusement was to discover unconscious obscenities in the copy handed in – not always perhaps unconscious. Charles Marriott, the art critic, was continually trying, or so it seemed, to slip something by, and the correspondence editor himself was responsible, at the time when Hyde Park was much in the news because of the Chiozza Money case, for the headline, 'Blocking in Hyde Park'.

And while the young writer is spending these amusing and unexacting hours, he is learning lessons valuable to his own craft. He is removing the clichés of reporters; he is compressing a story to the minimum length possible without ruining its effect. A writer with a sprawling style is unlikely to emerge from such an apprenticeship. It is the opposite training to the penny-a-liner.

The man who was of chief importance to me in those days was the chief subeditor, George Anderson. I hated him in my first week, but I grew almost to love him before three years had passed. A small elderly Scotsman with a flushed face and a laconic humour,* he drove a new subeditor hard with his sarcasm. Sometimes I almost fancied myself back at school again, and I was always glad when five-thirty came, for immediately the clock marked the hour when the pubs opened he would take his bowler hat from the coat-rack and disappear for thirty minutes to his favourite bar. His place would be taken by the gentle and courteous Colonel Maude. Maude was careful to see that the new recruit was given no story which could possibly stretch his powers, and if he had been chief subeditor I doubt if I would ever have got further than a News in Brief paragraph. At the stroke of six, when Anderson returned and hung up his bowler, his face would have turned a deeper shade of red, to match the rose he carried always in his buttonhole, and his shafts of criticism, as he scanned my copy with perhaps a too flagrant headline, would have acquired a tang of friendliness. More than two years went by, and my novel *The Man Within* had been accepted by a publisher, before I discovered one slack evening, when there was hardly enough news to fill the Home pages for the ten o'clock edition, that a poet *manqué* had dug those defences of disappointed sarcasm. When a young man, Anderson had published a volume of translations from Verlaine; he had sent it to Swinburne at The Pines and he had been entertained there for tea and kind words by Watts-Dunton, though I don't think he was allowed to see the poet. He never referred to the episode again, but I began to detect in him a harsh but paternal apprehension for another young man, flushed with pride in a first book, who might suffer the same disappointment. When I came to resign he spent a long time arguing with me, and I think his real reason for trying to prevent my departure was that he foresaw a time might come when novel-writing would fail me and I would need, like

*I am grateful to Mr Arthur Crook, the editor of *The Times Literary Supplement*, for this characteristic example. 'E. Colston Shepherd, the former aeronautical correspondent of *The Times*, once told me that he was infuriated by a very truncated version of a story he had written with great care. He complained bitterly to Anderson, saying that his story had been very badly cut. "Heavily, my dear Shep, heavily. Not badly. I cut it myself."'

himself, a quiet and secure life with the pubs opening at half-past five and the coal settling in the grate.

No other group of men – not even the air-raid wardens at my post in Gower Street during the blitz nor my fellows later in the Secret Service – have so planted themselves, nameless though they may have become, in my memory. Perhaps this is always the case with a young man's first real job: the impression in the wax will never go quite so deep again. Even those with whom I had only a transient contact are impressed there, Geoffrey Dawson, the editor (whatever his later politics of appeasement I can only remember his kindness to a young employee), Vladimir Poliakoff, the diplomatic correspondent, in a grey homburg hat with a very large brim, who would come into our room to consult the files, carrying with him an air of worldliness and mystery (why was he not reading them next door in the foreign room where he naturally belonged? Perhaps he wished to remain for obscure reasons of state incognito), the medical correspondent, Doctor McNair Wilson, who was, I think, more an authority on Napoleon than on medicine, and in my last year the future editor, Barrington-Ward, a cold complacent man, prematurely bald, who suddenly appeared, like an unspoken threat, unexplained and inexplicable, in the room of kindly old Murray Brumwell, the assistant editor. He had, I can see now, the smooth assured air of a Dauphin, but I thought of him even in those early days as Pecksniff, though Pecksniff had a good head of hair. Later, when I had fallen on evil days and tried to return to *The Times*, he wrote me a letter which Pecksniff could not have bettered. 'Since your day,' he wrote with a vague reminiscence of Longfellow, 'the tents have been folded and moved on.'

4

That summer I finished my second novel and wrote to my mother, 'The gamble of the thing is getting it typewritten, as one has to have two copies against wear and tear. Could you advance me five pounds and let me pay you back at the rate of about ten shillings a week?' They were five wasted pounds, and I can only hope I paid her back. I sent the typescript to Heinemann. It was July, 1926. There was an acknowledgement and afterwards a long silence – it seemed as irrevocably lost as though I had dropped it into the coal-fire of the subeditors' room. Months went by . . . the new year came . . . February . . . March . . . I even began a third book which I soon abandoned, a detective novel, the first of so many unfinished novels – *Fanatic Arabia*, which in spite of its title taken from Doughty began in a London bus station and was never intended to move further than the Midlands; *Across the Border*, an African story, which opened in Berkhamsted; a school novel of a timid boy's blackmail of the housemaster who had protected him; a spy story called *A Sense of Security* . . . Even today, until I have passed a quarter of the course, I am uncertain whether I will be able to reach the end.

The detective story I still believe to have been ingenious. A young governess was found murdered in a country house, and a multiplicity of strange clues baffled the police. Only the local priest recognized behind them a child's psychology and realized where they led – to a small girl of twelve who had committed the crime because her beloved governess was in love with a man. The priest, of course, did not betray the child . . . Now I can detect the various threads of my short experience which intermingled: my sister's governess, jealousy of the man she was to marry, perhaps the long summers at Harston House, even Father Trollope and my new conversion; yet, if I had been asked about the story then, I would have said it bore no relation whatever to my life.

It is better to remain in ignorance of oneself and to forget easily. Let the unemployed continue to lurk around the pubs in Vauxhall Bridge Road and the kidnappers drive out of Heidelberg towards the frontier, safely and completely forgotten; we ought to leave the forgotten to the night. If one day they find their way into a book, it should be without our connivance and so disguised that we don't recognize them when we see them again. All that we can easily recognize as our experience in a novel is mere reporting: it has a place, but an unimportant one. It provides an anecdote, it fills in gaps in the narrative. It may legitimately provide a background, and sometimes we have to fall back on it when the imagination falters. Perhaps a novelist has a greater ability to forget than other men – he has to forget or become sterile. What he forgets is the compost of the imagination.

Eight months went by with no reply from Heinemann, and at last I wrote to remind them of my typescript. I felt sure that this would bring me no luck, and I was not surprised when a bulky package came quickly back. The managing director, Charles Evans, wrote himself, apologizing for the delay. There had been two contradictory reports, so he had wished to read the novel himself and now, in spite of his interest, he regretted ... At the same time he hoped I would show him my next book. That this was a polite formula for a mislaid manuscript seems obvious to me now, but I was a novice and I was so encouraged by his words that I never sent the manuscript elsewhere, content to abide by Heinemann's decision. I would write one novel more, I decided, and, if the third book proved as unsuccessful as the others, I would abandon this ambition for ever. I was established on *The Times*, and marriage would be possible in another year.

I knew nothing of a letter lying in my parents' files, like a little time-bomb, which was to make that future seem doubtful. Perhaps they had forgotten it themselves, as one forgets an unpleasant fact one has lived with for a long time and cannot alter, and it was only my sudden illness which brought it back to mind.

The doctor to whom I complained of recurrent pains was a dangerous man to consult. I had picked him at random as I wandered down a Battersea Street troubled by a sharper stab of pain than usual. His brass plate caught my eye on a house not far from the railway viaduct. Smoke coated his panes, an aspidistra drooped on his window-sill, starved of tea-leaves, and his door vibrated gently as the trains emerged from Clapham Junction. The doctor opened the door himself, a young Hindu, and showed me into a dingy consulting room where he must have been waiting with eastern patience for the sick to seek him out. He judged my pulse and took my temperature and prodded where the pain lay; then he gave me a bottle of medicine ready prepared which he said would do the trick. I think he charged six shillings for the consultation and the bottle. Luckily over the telephone I told my brother, who was now an intern at Westminster Hospital, what had happened, and that night I found myself in a public ward at his hospital to be operated on for appendicitis with the least possible delay. The Hindu doctor stayed in my mind – a symbol of the shabby, the inefficient and possibly the illegal, and he left his trace, with another doctor, on some pages of *A Gun for Sale*.

As I lay in the ward after the operation (in those days they kept the patient at least a week) I began to plan my third novel, the forlorn hope. I called it *The Man Within*, and it began with a hunted man, who was to appear again and again in later less romantic books. But curiously enough there came to me also in the ward, with the death of a patient, the end of a book which I would not begin to write for another six years.

It was our second death. The first we had barely noticed: an old man dying from cancer of the mouth. He had been too old and ill to join in the high jinks of the ward, the courtship of nurses, the teasings, the ticklings and the pinches. When the screens went up around his bed the silence in his corner was no deeper than it had always been. But the second death disturbed the whole ward. The first was inevitable fate, the second was contingency.

The victim was a boy of ten. He had been brought into the ward one afternoon, having broken his leg at football. He was a cheerful child with a rosy face and his parents stayed and chatted with him for a while until he settled down to sleep. One of the nurses ten minutes later paused by his bed and leant over him. Suddenly there was a burst of activity, a doctor came hurrying in, screens went up around the bed, an oxygen machine was run squeaking across the floor, but the child had outdistanced them all to death. By the time the parents reached home, a message was waiting to summon them urgently back. They came and sat beside the bed, and to shut out the sound of the mother's tears and cries all my companions in the ward lay with their ear-phones on, listening – there was nothing else for them to hear – to Children's Hour. All my companions but not myself. There is a splinter of ice in the heart of a writer. I watched and listened. This was something which one day I might need: the woman speaking, uttering the banalities she must have remembered from some

134

woman's magazine, a genuine grief that could communicate only in clichés. 'My boy, my boy, why did you not wait till I came?' The father sat silent with his hat on his knees, and you could tell that even in his unhappiness he was embarrassed by the banality of his wife's words, by the scene she was so badly playing to the public ward, and he wanted desperately to get away home and be alone. 'Human language,' Flaubert wrote, 'is like a cracked kettle on which we beat out tunes for bears to dance to, when all the time we are longing to move the stars to pity.'

After two weeks I returned to *The Times*, but perhaps because I had returned too soon, I fainted my first evening at work. I was given another week's holiday and went to Brighton, as I had so often gone in the past with my aunt after a childish sickness. I thought no more of the affair, unaware of the time-bomb ticking in my mother's desk. (I have the little machine before me now, a letter written five years before, in 1921, to my father by Kenneth Richmond.)

My mother wrote to me in Brighton asking me when I returned to London to go and see my old analyst. I was a little puzzled, but I was pleased at the thought of seeing him again; I was aware that he had deliberately severed our relationship, for fear that I might come to depend on him, but to me he represented the happiest period of my life. One night at Brighton I was sitting quite alone, or so I thought, in one of the shelters on the front, when a voice spoke to me unexpectedly in the darkness. 'Good evening,' it said in the accent of old age.

'Good evening,' I replied, trying to see through the night.

'I am Old Moore,' the voice said. So perhaps I should have been warned.

Kenneth Richmond no longer lived in the trim little house in Devonshire Terrace off Lancaster Gate, but a larger and darker house without any memories for me. We talked a little of my second novel and he offered to help me in my search for a publisher, but I felt sure this was not the purpose of my invitation. And then, speaking as unexpectedly as Old Moore on the Brighton front, he reminded me of what I had quite forgotten, the occasion when I had once fainted at his dinner table. Afterwards he had taken me to see a specialist in Harley Street: a small dark intense

135

man whose features are now confused in my memory with those of the actor Ernest Milton and of Colonel de Castries of Dien Bien Phu.

'Your mother tells me you are engaged to be married,' Richmond said. 'Now about this fainting attack at *The Times* . . .'

I remembered how the specialist had questioned me about earlier attacks of fainting in the summer stuffiness of the school chapel. Many children, I told myself, went through such a phase.

'Doctor Riddick diagnosed epilepsy,' Richmond said.

Epilepsy, cancer and leprosy – these are the three medical terms which rouse the greatest fear in the untutored, and at twenty-two one is unprepared for so final a judgement. Epilepsy, Richmond went on, could be inherited: I must consider the risk carefully before marriage, and he sought to comfort me by pointing out that Dostoievsky too had suffered from epilepsy. I couldn't think of a reply. Dostoievsky was a dead Victorian writer, not a youth without a book to his name who had pledged himself to marry . . . 'Let me see your novel,' Richmond said, meaning to be kind. 'What is the title?'

'*The Episode*,' I said.

I left the house and began walking fast towards South Kensington, the King's Road, Oakley Street, the Albert Bridge, away from *this* episode. When I got home I wrote a letter; they had left things rather late, I said, before informing me. Poor souls, I can sympathize with them now as I read the letters which were written to them on the same day by Richmond and Doctor Riddick. Doctor Riddick's was frightening, even in its moderation. 'The attacks to which he is occasionally subject are, I think, epileptic; but since he has lost consciousness in three only, there is a reasonably good chance that, with suitable treatment, the condition may be arrested.' The treatment seemed to consist of good walks and Keppler's Malt Extract. Richmond's letter was more encouraging, and my mother in pencil has pathetically underlined all the optimistic phrases she could find, perhaps to comfort my father – 'quite likely to clear up completely' . . . 'no cause for alarm' – even the phrase about Dostoievsky is trotted out and surprisingly underlined, but then follows what I think was unfair and dangerous advice: 'We agreed that Graham ought not to be told what is the matter in any terms that included the word epilepsy.'

Was the diagnosis right? With the hindsight of forty years, free from any recurrence, I don't believe it, but I believed it then. I remember next day standing on an Underground platform and trying to summon the will and the courage to jump. It was not my new Catholicism which restrained me. There was no theological despair in what I felt. I was simply tired out by the thought of starting a completely different future than the one I had planned. But suicide requires greater courage than Russian roulette, the trains came and went, and soon I took the moving staircase to the upper world.

My next thought was of an elderly priest. Father Talbot, of the Oratory. I had been passed on to him – a fashion priests have – by Trollope, and I had spent many agreeable hours with him in discussion and argument at his quiet chambers in the Oratory, as unclerical as rooms in college. He was a man of very liberal views, and surely, I thought despairingly, he would have some answer to my greatest problem: that if I were epileptic, I must avoid having children. Surely there must be some cranny of canon law or moral theology that would contain a ruling for just such a case as mine.

He asked me to go out with him, and for the next hour we drove in a taxi, crossing and recrossing the same rectangle between the Brompton Road and Bayswater, just as we crossed and recrossed the same lines of argument. Under no circumstances at all was contraception permissible. 'The Church forbids me to marry then?'

'Of course we don't forbid marriage.'

'Do you expect married people to live together without making love?'

'The Church expects you to trust God, that's all.'

Up and down, over and over, a useless embroidery which made no pattern.

How differently he would have answered my question today, telling me, I have no doubt, to follow my conscience, which even then was elastic enough for almost anything. Catholics have sometimes accused me of making my clerical characters, Father

Rank in *The Heart of the Matter* and Father James in *The Living Room*, fail unnecessarily before the human problems they were made to face. 'A real priest,' I have been told, 'would have had something further to say, he would have shown a deeper comprehension, he wouldn't have left the situation so unchanged.' But that is exactly what in those days, before John Roncalli was elected Pope, the priesthood was compelled to do. There was no failure in comprehension. Father Talbot was a man of the greatest human sympathy, but he had no solution for me at all. There was only one hard answer he could honestly give ('the Church knows all the rules,' as Father Rank said), while the meter of the taxi ticked away the repetitions of our fruitless argument. It was the Rock of Peter I was aware of in our long drive, and though it repulsed me, I couldn't help admiring its unyielding façade.

My misery did not last long. My brother, by this time a doctor, was the first to question the diagnosis, and then the medical correspondent, Doctor McNair Wilson, who had been in the subeditors' room when I fainted, confirmed that he had seen no symptom whatever of epilepsy.

6

I married, and I was happy. In the evenings I worked at *The Times*, in the mornings I worked on my third novel. Now when I write I put down on the page a mere skeleton of a novel – nearly all my revisions are in the nature of additions, of second thoughts to make the bare bones live – but in those days to revise was to prune and prune and prune. I was much tempted, perhaps because of my admiration for the Metaphysical poets, by exaggerated similes and my wife became an adept at shooting them down. There was one, I remember, comparing something or someone in the quiet landscape of Sussex to a leopard crouching in a tree, which gave a name to the whole species. Leopards would be marked daily on the manuscript, but it took a great many years for me to get the beasts under control, and they growl at me sometimes yet.

One day in the winter of 1928 I lay in bed with a bad attack of flu, listening to my wife in the kitchen washing up the breakfast things. I had posted copies of the typescript to Heinemann and

The Bodley Head about ten days before, and I was now resigned to a long delay. Hadn't I waited last time nine months for a refusal? Anyway, uncertainty was more agreeable to live with than the confirmation of failure. The telephone rang in the sitting-room and my wife came in and told me, 'There's a Mr Evans wants to speak to you.'

'I don't know anyone called Evans,' I said. 'Tell him I'm in bed. Tell him I'm ill.' Suddenly a memory came back to me: Evans was the chairman of Heinemann's, and I ran to snatch the telephone.

'I've read your novel,' he said. 'We'd like to publish it. Would it be possible for you to look in here at eleven?' My flu was gone in that moment and never returned.

Nothing in a novelist's life later can equal that moment – the acceptance of his first book. Triumph is unalloyed by any doubt of the future. Mounting the wide staircase in the elegant eighteenth-century house in Great Russell Street I could have no foreboding of the failures and frustrations of the next ten years.

Charles Evans was a remarkable publisher. With his bald head and skinny form he looked like a family solicitor lean with anxieties, but a solicitor who had taken an overdose of some invigorating vitamin. His hands and legs were never still. He did everything, from shaking hands to ringing a bell, in quick jerks. Perhaps because the flu had not entirely departed, I expected at any moment the legendary figures of Heinemann authors to enter the room behind me, Mr Galsworthy, Mr John Masefield, Mr Maugham, Mr George Moore, Mr Joseph Hergesheimer. I sat on the edge of the chair ready to leap up. The bearded ghost of Conrad rumbled on the rooftops with the rain.

I was quite prepared to hear what I had always understood to be the invariable formula – 'of course a first novel is a great risk, we shall have to begin with a small royalty' – but that was not Evans's way with a young author. Just as he had substituted the direct telephone call for the guarded letter, so now he brushed aside any ancient rite of initiation.

'No publisher,' he said, 'can ever guarantee success, but all the same we have hopes . . .' The royalty would begin at $12\frac{1}{2}$ per cent, with a fifty-pound advance, he recommended me to take an agent, for in the future there might be subsidiary rights to deal with ... I went out dazed into Great Russell Street. My day-dream had never continued further than a promise of publication and now my publisher (proud phrase, 'my publisher') was suggesting even the possibility of success.

He was as good as his word, selling more than 8,000 copies of the novel, so that I was all the more unprepared for the failures which succeeded it. In the flush of that success I would have refused to believe that success is slow and not sudden and that ten years later, with my tenth novel, *The Power and the Glory*, the publisher could risk printing only 3,500 copies, one thousand copies more than he had printed of my first novel.

The Man Within is very young and very sentimental. It has no meaning for me today and I can see no reason for its success. It is like the book of a complete stranger, of a kind for which I have never much cared – and this makes another judgement on the book yet more mysterious to me. My uncle Eppy – the rich worldly business uncle of the Brazilian Warrant Agency – wrote to me: 'It could only have been written by a Greene.' I thought of my parents, I thought of all those aunts and uncles and cousins who had gathered together at Christmas, and of the two unknown Greene grandfathers, the guilt-ridden clergyman and the melan-cholic sugar-planter dead of yellow fever in St Kitts, and then I thought of the novel, the story of a hunted man, of smuggling and treachery, of murder and suicide, and I wondered what on earth he was driving at. I wonder still.

7

Leaving *The Times* was even more difficult than joining it and took almost as long. A few months after the publication of *The Man Within*, while I struggled with another novel, *The Name of Action* (the only good thing about the book was its title and that was suggested to me by Clemence Dane), I wrote to Charles Evans a blackmailing letter: I told him I must choose between *The Times* and novel-writing – I couldn't continue to do both. He replied offering me, if I chose to resign, six hundred pounds a year for three years (half to be supplied by my American publisher) in return for three novels. I did so choose, but how was I to set about it? I had been happy on *The Times*, I couldn't just write a letter to the manager and walk out. I consulted George Anderson, and we held long dialogues together, while he reasoned with me. I had a great future, he assured me – one day, if I were only patient for a few more years, I might hope to be the correspondence editor. Already, when the correspondence editor was on holiday, I tasted the glory of deputizing for him and this brought me into direct contact with the editor, Geoffrey Dawson himself. Closeted with the editor every afternoon at four o'clock I argued the merits of the letters and we decided which was to lead the page. I was exalted by the contact, especially when, as sometimes happened, I won the argument and even perhaps secured the promotion of one of Walter Sickert's frequent letters which offended Dawson's tidy mind by being almost illegibly written over large sheets of lined paper in thick black ink, apparently with a matchstick and usually with an impenetrable smudge over an operative word, a calligraphy which suited his savage *non sequiturs* on subjects far removed from painting.

At last Anderson realized how strong was my determination to leave, but he agreed that first I must have a word with the editor, and the editor was hopelessly elusive. There were even moments when I wondered whether Anderson had warned him of my intention. If I tried to make an appointment he was heavily engaged, if I went to his room it was empty or he was busy with a distinguished visitor. It was weeks before I caught him – I had the uncomfortable sense of doing something beyond the bounds of polite manners like wearing a bright coloured tie with a dinner jacket. Indeed I began to believe that no subeditor had ever before resigned from *The Times*, just as no one had ever been sacked from the paper since the ungentlemanly days of Lord Northcliffe. Dawson, when I cornered him at last, took the conversation urbanely into his own hands. He said he understood that I had written a novel, and he congratulated me on its success – his wife had demanded a copy from her circulating library. *The Times*, he assured me, would have no objection if I continued to write novels in my spare time. The art critic, Mr Charles Marriott, had done so for many years, and even the dramatic critic, Mr

141

Charles Morgan, had published one or two. Indeed the time might have almost come to try me out with an occasional third leader. However, if my mind were really made up, he could only say it was a rash and unfortunate decision.

I had a further interview before leaving on 31 December 1929, with the assistant editor, Murray Brumwell, who resembled an elderly schoolmaster and perhaps for that reason always transformed me into a tongue-tied pupil. It was too late to argue with me now, he said, but he would implore me to take care of my health and not to overwork. I smiled a little, thinking how I had been doing two jobs and working eleven hours a day. It was only later I realized that overwork is not a matter of hours and that he had good reason.

So I left the coal-grate and the faces under the green eye-shields, faces which remain as vivid to me now when the names of their owners are forgotten as those of close friends and women I have loved. In the years to come I was bitterly to regret my decision. I left *The Times* the author of a successful first novel. I thought I was a writer already and that the world was at my feet, but life wasn't like that. It was only a false start.

Chapter 11

1

THE conditions of writing change absolutely between the first novel and the second: the first is an adventure, the second is a duty. The first is like a sprint which leaves you exhausted and triumphant beside the track. With the second the writer has been transformed into a long-distance runner – the finishing tape is out of sight, at the end of life. He must guard his energies and plan ahead. A long endurance is more exhausting than a sprint, and less heroic. One may sometimes envy Radiguet and Alain-Fournier whom death forestalled before they embarked on the long cross-country run.

The Man Within was, it is true, the third novel I had completed, but the first two had been clumsy exercises. I had been in training only, and there still remained other possibilities – British-American Tobacco or the Lancashire General Insurance Company. With all its faults of sentimentality and over-writing *The Man Within* was professional. I found myself committed to the long-distance race.

I sometimes find myself wishing that, before starting the second novel, *The Name of Action*, I had found an experienced mentor. If Robert Louis Stevenson had been alive* he would have been only ten years older than I am now, and perhaps I would have found the courage to consult him in distant Samoa and have sent him my first book. He had always seemed to me 'one of the family'. I had lived as a boy on the fringes of his world: his relative and biographer, Graham Balfour, had come to our house, my beautiful aunt would often arrive from a stay with his friend Sidney Colvin and his wife, the former Mrs Sitwell, whom as a young man Stevenson had loved and whom he had met in the house of my great-aunt Maud of Number 11. Names which

---

*It is seldom realized how short was Stevenson's career: he began his first attempt at a novel (and abandoned it) when he was twenty-five, and he died at forty-four.

appeared in his Collected Letters were photographs in our family album. In the nursery we played on the bagatelle board which had belonged to him. Surely from my relative in Samoa I might have received better and more astringent counsel than from my publisher, Charles Evans, who was determined to shut his eyes to the disastrous failings of his young discovery. I even received an enthusiastic telegram from Evans welcoming the typescript of the second novel – how could I tell how bad it really was? Evans must have known, but he was determined to keep it dark for the time. He had a reputation for discovering young writers, and he couldn't admit a mistake too quickly.

I don't think I ever really believed in the book in spite of the telegram. I know I despaired of it often, as I plodded with my unlikely hero through the streets of Trier, on my last holiday before I left *The Times*. In most of my novels I can remember passages, even chapters, which gave me at the time I wrote them a sense of satisfaction – 'this at least has come off'. So I felt, however mistakenly, with the trial scene in *The Man Within*, and later with Querry's voyage in *A Burnt-Out Case*, with the three-cornered love scene in *The Quiet American*, the chess game in *Our Man in Havana*, the prison dialogue in *The Power and the Glory*, the intrusion of Miss Paterson into the Boulogne chapters of *Travels with my Aunt* – I don't think a single book of mine has failed to give me at least once a momentary illusion of success except *The Name of Action*. When I think of the novel now I remember only my facile use of the geography of Trier, which I had first visited on my German expedition with Claud Cockburn, the echoes of my unpublished Carlist novel *The Episode* (a young man caught up idealistically in a disappointing revolution), and my discovery that a simple scene of action, a police pursuit through the night streets of Trier, was quite beyond my power to render exciting. I was failing dismally at what seemed to have come so naturally to Buchan, Haggard, Stanley Weyman. My long studies in Percy Lubbock's *The Craft of Fiction* had taught me the importance of 'the point of view' but not how to convey physical excitement.

Now I can see quite clearly where I went wrong. Excitement is simple: excitement is a situation, a single event. It mustn't be wrapped up in thoughts, similes, metaphors. A simile is a form of reflection, but excitement is of the moment when there is no time to reflect. Action can only be expressed by a subject, a verb and an object, perhaps a rhythm – little else. Even an adjective slows the pace or tranquillizes the nerve. I should have turned to Stevenson to learn my lesson: 'It came all of a sudden when it did, with a rush of feet and a roar, and then a shout from Alan, and the sound of blows and someone crying as if hurt. I looked back over my shoulder, and saw Mr Shuan in the doorway crossing blades with Alan.' No similes or metaphors there, not even an adjective. But I was too concerned with 'the point of view' to be aware of simpler problems, to know that the sort of novel I was trying to write, unlike a poem, was not made with words but with movement, action, character. Discrimination in one's words is certainly required, but not love of one's words – that is a form of self-love, a fatal love which leads a young writer to the excesses of Charles Morgan and Lawrence Durrell, and, looking back to this period of my life, I can see that I was in danger of taking *their* road. I was only saved by failure.

The Man Within had sold 8,000 copies; *The Name of Action* barely passed a quarter of that figure. The reviewing of novels at the beginning of the thirties was at a far lower critical level than it has ever been since. Gerald Gould, a bad poet, and Ralph Strauss, a bad novelist, divided the Sunday forum between them. One was not elated by their praise nor cast down by their criticism, and the third novel which I had now begun was as false and even more derivative than *The Name of Action*.

2

I had left *The Times* with enough money to live on for three years, and so, to make that money go further and to give me a room in which to work, we moved into the country. We had found a thatched cottage (that pastoral Georgian dream of the industrial twenties), with a small garden and orchard, up a muddy lane on the edge of Chipping Campden. It was to rent for a pound a week (the limit of what we could afford), and we moved our few belongings there, including a newly bought Pekinese with a great passion for dustbins. There was no electric light and the Aladdin lamps smoked if we left them for a few minutes alone. We were a scared couple that first night, with no sound of accustomed traffic, only a hooting owl. After darkness fell, on the evening of our arrival, I was summoned by a knock to the back door and saw an unknown countrywoman standing outside, holding a dead rat by the tail.

'What do you want?'

'I thought yu'd be interested,' she said, swinging it to and fro.

There certainly were rats, they pattered and rustled and squeaked in the roof and they remained noisy in our thatch until a man consented to come with a ferret and drive them out. In his tight breeches with his pointed face he looked like a ferret himself – it was said in the village that he had starved his wife to death.

After a few weeks we began to lose our fear of the strange country and life became happy enough, until the future started to cast a shadow. It was a life rich with new pleasures – the local wines, made out of almost anything vegetable, which could be bought from the brawny landlord Rathbone at the Volunteer (they had no effect on the head but a great effect on the legs), home-brewed bitter at the Noel Arms which was kept by the stepfather of a boy called Nigel Dennis, and an almost endless variety of walks, north, south, east and west, to Moreton-in-Marsh and Chipping Norton, Evesham and Broadway and Blockley and Bourton-on-the-Water. (The Pekinese, over-exercised by fifteen-mile walks, developed hysteria and had to be destroyed.) There were apples from our own garden and Cos lettuces which I had grown myself with the help of a gypsy gardener called Buckland who came once a week and put all the snails aside for his own supper.

The life of a village is intimate and dramatic. There is a sense of community. People talk. In a city there may be a suicide in the next street and you will never hear of it. It is difficult for me to understand how I could have spent hours with the bloodless creatures of my new novel, *Rumour at Nightfall*, which was yet another story of the Carlist rebellion, but set this time in a Spain I had never visited. It was as though I were unable to cut the

146

cord which bound me to that still-born book, *The Episode*. Didn't I sometimes in a lucid moment measure the sentimental cardboard figures of my fancy against the people I met every day between the muddy lane where I lived and the Live and Let Live Inn? I don't remember. Perhaps – even more important – I should have measured them against my own experience, against the memories of flight, rebellion and misery during those first sixteen years when the novelist is formed.

There had been, if I was to trust my uncle, something at least of the Greene character in *The Man Within*, if only that irrational desire to escape from himself which had led one Greene grandfather out of the Church and the other to die in St Kitts. A writer's knowledge of himself, realistic and unromantic, is like a store of energy on which he must draw for a lifetime: one volt of it properly directed will bring a character alive. There is no spark of life in *The Name of Action* or *Rumour at Nightfall* because there was nothing of myself in them. I had been determined not to write the typical autobiographical novels of a beginner, but I had gone too far in the opposite direction. I had removed myself altogether. All that was left in the heavy pages of the second was the distorted ghost of Conrad. Only once, and that at the very beginning, had the book moved with a semblance of life, when a colonel played the part of a priest and heard the confession of one of his men, dying from a wound. It was a clumsy rehearsal for a scene better rendered ten years later in *The Power and the Glory*.

3

I find in my diary of that period some of the comedy and drama of the Cotswold life which was going on all around me.

'Mass was taken by the priest from Foxcote; with a housekeeper he lives alone in a great old house above Ilmington, and sometimes wakes to see an owl sitting on his bedpost. The books in the library are allowed to go to rack and ruin for want of attention. He studies astronomy and preaches temperance and goes about the country on a knock-kneed horse. The landlord of the Seagrave Arms at Weston-sub-Edge, from whom I get the parsnip wine, serves him often with tea. According to him it is a distinction to have a knock-kneed horse. Only a good horse goes knock-kneed.'

'A troop of strolling players, which gave performances here the other day, apparently quarrelled at Eynsham and divided. One family has come back here and is holding weekly dances at the town hall for a living. Cresswell, the rich deaf architect, who lives in the square, objected to the noise of motor-bicycles and has forced them to stop the dances at midnight. He tried to have moved the Wednesday sheep market which has been held in the square for hundreds of years, but in this he failed. He hunts, indeed with fishing it is his sole amusement, and in retaliation the farmers have warned him off their land. This is driving him from Campden for Campden's good.'

'Father Billsborough at Mass, preaching on Missions: "What a glorious sight! Seven thousand Zulus coming to Communion. We don't see that in England."' (It was always a joy to listen to Father Billsborough, the most loved man in Campden. I remember him when he asked for money to clean his little church, speaking of ' Millions of dead flies breeding away on the ceiling'.)

'A lot of didicoes and travellers about, which are the local names for gypsies and tramps. A woman came to the door with a baby and a basket of clothes-pegs yesterday, and this morning at breakfast someone was singing in the lane. The tramps all seem to carry kittens with them on trolleys.'

'There was a band of pea-pickers at the station, a rough-looking man with a wooden leg, his wife (a worn, curiously refined woman) and his three children, two girls of about six and four, and a boy who could not have been more than two. We got into conversation. I found it hard to understand what the man said, but suddenly realized that he was telling me that the boy had "the smartest upper-cut since Jimmy Wilde. You go down on your knees to him and he'll give you a couple before you know where you are. Nothing can hurt that child. He fell off a hay-wagon yesterday and a car ran over his neck in Evesham once and he got up laughing." The pea-picker had once been a boxer himself and claimed to have been England's hope as a heavy-weight, but apart from his leg his hands had been ruined by labour. He held them out, calloused and trembling. "Your son

148

will be champion instead," I suggested. "Oh," he said, "I've a better son than this, twenty-three years old, but he's lost his nerve. If the bookmakers put up one thousand pounds he wouldn't fight. He went to Birmingham against a man heavier than himself and he knocked him out so he never got up again." "They couldn't do anything to him?" I asked. "They kept him hanging about for four months, and now nothing will tempt him to fight."'

Of Charles Wade and his manor at Snowshill (Wade was a great collector of antiques with an estate in St Kitts, and he had built a remarkable model railway and village in the grounds of his manor): 'Wade, until late in the evening when nearly everybody had gone. hardly spoke at all. Bow-legged in knickerbockers and bedroom slippers with dark greying hair bobbed over his shoulders, a blue striped shirt of the "gents haberdashery" kind and a black evening tie; when he speaks he mouths his words and leaves them inchoate as though he were not used to speaking at all, and when he laughs at some rather obvious joke of a farcical physical kind he bellows like a child with open mouth. His collection is as much a toy to him as his model railway and village, and he reads nothing but Jeffery Farnol and that aloud, making appropriate noises with pieces of old iron. He can be suddenly insulting, and sitting on the floor in front of a log fire, the only light, I had a terror that he was going to insult me with a suddenness which would leave me at a loss. I lay in bed that night discussing him, and the thought of his thin walnut face and his open mouth laughing made my flesh creep.'

'In the High Street a butcher shook young living rats out of a steel cage for the fat foxhounds to eat, which sprawl with bloodshot eyes and stupid bodies on the grass gnawing bones. The villagers gathered at their doors and watched with amusement. All the way up the street I could hear the squealing of the rats.'

'Passed the lake in Northwick Park where Mrs Keiton drowned herself the other day, walking out from one of the council houses in Broad Campden after dark on one of the bitterest nights of a cold month.'

'During breakfast the rat-catcher mysteriously appeared with a spade and a brush and cleared our path of snow, and went again before we could pay him anything. He will never ask for money, too proud to do more than accept it when proffered, though he was not too proud to starve his wife to death.'

'The old man who sells the *News of the World* on Sunday mornings was found yesterday by his wife hanging dead; he was seventy-three and Greenall, our daily, says that he could no longer stand his wife's nagging.'

'All yesterday and today Martha Hedges has been moving from her cottage to the almshouses at the other end of the village, pushing her things in an old pram, very old and pink and jaunty. Polishing her pictures on the doorstep.'

'Charley Sykes, the Campden madman, who used to parade the village heavily bearded and in rags, talking and waving his stick, has been frozen to death in his cottage at Broad Campden. Nothing in the room but a broken chair, straw where he used to sleep, and a stink. He was a gentleman, the son of a doctor; his real name was Seitz, and he is said to have gone mad from overwork during his medical examination. He was a wonderfully handsome youth and there are photographs of him in flannels with a tennis racket. He is said to have been at St John's College, Oxford. He had some money but lived in absolute squalor and begged. Fred Hart put out sixpence for him every week. The Evesham police are said once to have tried to arrest him for begging, and the story goes that he flung two policemen over a hedge. He used to walk in and out of Evesham, nine miles each way, lurching along bent almost double. Once he is said to have made his way out to India to see his relations, but they would have nothing to do with him . . . He died in the upper room of his cottage, and to get him down they put the web with which they lower coffins into the ground round his shoulders and dragged him down head first, his legs bumping on the stairs. Then they crammed him into the coffin in the clothes he wore and nailed him down. According to Greenall the fleas jumped on them from his wrists. There were sixteen pairs of boots in the cottage.'

It seems astonishing to me today that, while I was making careful notes of the vivid life around me, I was content to pursue my romantic and derivative tale to its disastrous conclusion – to publication, to the sale of only 1,200 copies, and finally to a review in a popular paper which opened my eyes at last to the worthlessness of all the work I had done till then.

4

My three guaranteed years of security had been squandered. Thanks to Peter Fleming I was reviewing novels now in the *Spectator* every fortnight, but I was deep in debt to my publishers, a debt from which I was only freed by the war ten years later – I had even had to borrow an extra twenty-five pounds to pay my income tax. If *The Man Within* had shown promise, it was the brief promise of a dud rocket on Guy Fawkes night. It made no difference to me that the review which had opened my eyes to my fool's progress was by an author, Frank Swinnerton, for whom I had little respect – I knew the truth when I read it. There was nothing for me to do but dismantle all that elaborate scaffolding built from an older writer's blue print, write it off as apprentice work and start again at the beginning. Never again, I swore, would I read a novel of Conrad's – a vow I kept for more than a quarter of a century, until I found myself with *Heart of Darkness* in a small paddle boat travelling up a Congo tributary in 1959 from one leper colony to another. I had to begin again naked, and perhaps it was for that reason I chose an adventure story, imagining it might be easier to write, a mistake difficult to understand, since I had learnt with *The Name of Action* how hard it was to make physical action simple and exciting.

I wrote the book, to the music of Honegger's *Pacific 231* on my gramophone, with a sense of doom. It is always hard for me to reread an old book, but in the case of *Stamboul Train* it is almost impossible. The pages are too laden by the anxieties of the time and the sense of failure. It was not only the two previous novels that had failed: I had wasted time and effort on a life of Lord Rochester which Heinemann had without hesitation turned down, and I was too uncertain of myself to send it elsewhere. By the time I finished *Stamboul Train* the days of security had almost run out. Even my dreams were full of disquiet – I remember how in one I was condemned to prison for five years and I woke depressed by the thought that my wife would be over thirty when we lived with each other again. The dream proved to be the germ of my next novel, *It's a Battlefield*, but I didn't realize it then, for even before *Stamboul Train* was finished I had begun to plan its successor – a novel about spiritualism and incest, with only two main characters, a fraudulent spiritualist and his sister. The sister was to move through the corruption of her surroundings failing to see that the criminality of her beloved brother had any real importance. A little of the incestuous story must have sunk back into my unconscious to emerge again four years later in *England Made Me*.

The scenes for the book were to be set in Nottingham and London. Those two cities represented the real world to me: I had done with castles in Spain, and perhaps because my decision had been made at a deeper level than the conscious, I had a dream, which I found at least half encouraging. I dreamt that I received from Heinemann an advance copy of a new novel. It was printed on bad paper; it was badly bound with a bad title, and the novel was to be published at the derisive price of ninepence. The publisher obviously cared nothing for the book, but when I opened it I had immediately the sense of strong firm writing and was saddened at the thought that in such a poor format the novel would neither be reviewed nor bought.

On 4 August I noted in my diary, 'Sent off typescript to Heinemann. Is my position at its worst? Although I have been given till 15 September to pay the remainder of my income tax, I am to all intents minus about thirty pounds, with no guarantee of any money or employment after this month.' At the end of August my contract with Heinemann and Doubleday would be over. Nearly a fortnight passed without a word from Heinemann, and I noted, 'The suspense is becoming terrible,' and, when at last the letter arrived, 'I took it half way upstairs and opened it with fingers which really trembled'. It was strange what a few words of encouragement did for me. My financial situation was still the same: the unearned royalties on my previous books would absorb any small success *Stamboul Train* might achieve. Nonetheless hope was reborn and I noted the same day a new theme for a novel which was already ousting the story of the spiritualist: 'A large inclusive picture of a city, the connecting link the con-

152

viction of a man for the murder of a policeman. Is it politic to hang him? And the detectives go out through the city listening...'

One ominous day I took a ticket for London to discuss the future with Charles Evans and the representative of Doubleday, my American publisher. This was Mary Pritchett, who was later to be my agent in America and one of my greatest friends. But that day she seemed a dragon indeed. Nor was I very attached to her firm. Nelson Doubleday, a tall husky man, who had once served in Roosevelt's Rough Riders and who knew more about horses than about books, would descend on London once a year and summon his authors by telegram to see him at set hours at the Heinemann office. I had received a telegram the year before. I could ill afford the ticket, but I was his pensioner and I had to go. 'Siddown,' he said, and looked at me with gloomy resentment as though I were some underbred brute which a smart horse-dealer had swindled him into buying. He took out a handkerchief almost as huge as himself and blew his nose a number of times. 'Caught a cold coming over,' he said, and they were the only words he spoke to me. I took the next train back to Chipping Campden.

The interview with Evans and Mary Pritchett proceeded on its dreary course: accounts showing the disastrous sales of the last two books were before them: the typescript of *Stamboul Train* lay on the desk beside the accounts – the third book in the three-year contract which had now come to an end. No further advances would be due to me until another novel was completed. I waited hopelessly while an argument went on between Evans and Mary Pritchett, and then the meeting was quickly brought to a close. Heinemann, Evans said, would continue to pay me my three hundred pounds for one more year, but Doubleday would promise nothing beyond two further monthly payments, and in the meanwhile they would study the new manuscript. There were several conditions attached even to these payments – another contract for two books with all losses to be recovered by the publishers before any further royalties were paid. Only in the train back to Campden did I realize that I might have to write two novels more with no payment at all after the next year was over.

During the following two months, while I was still receiving payment from Doubleday, I had to find a job at all costs anywhere. Our country peace was over, and the nights held little sleep. I tried to engineer a return to *The Times* but received only Barrington-Ward's frozen response: I tried for half-time jobs on Sunday papers with no success. The *Catholic Herald* had advertised for a subeditor and again I spent the money for a ticket to London. The editor, a grey withered man who had made a name for himself as the strategical correspondent to the *Spectator*, received me with humiliating condescension. He asked for a little time to decide and I returned to the country full of hope. After two weeks he wrote asking me to come and see him again. This was certainly success, I thought, but, when I entered his room, he at once began to tell me how, with three novels to my name and my excellent experience on *The Times* behind me, he had come to the conclusion that I was too good for the job, I would never settle down. He was more condescending than ever and hardly disguised his pleasure in the interview – perhaps he hadn't liked my name appearing in the same number of the *Spectator* as his own. I had too much pride and too little spirit left to ask him to return my railway fare, and since then I have taken a biased view of Catholic journalism and Catholic humanity.

'I have been here before.' I noted in my diary the same symptoms which at sixteen used to drive me to London with my brother Raymond. They were the symptoms of a life with too little hope – then there had been frustrated love, now there was failure. 'My nerves horribly on edge; that feeling of lurking madness, of something swelling in the brain and wanting to burst; every sound, however small, made by anyone else, the clink of a plate or a fork, piercing the brain like a knife.' If there are recurrent themes in my novels it is perhaps only because there have been recurrent themes in my life. Failure seemed then to be one of them.

Events took an ironic turn and convinced me of the temporary nature of any possible success. *Stamboul Train* was chosen by the Book Society (which meant in those days a sale of 10,000 copies) and Doubleday's consented to renew payments for another year. My immediate anxieties seemed over when: 'My God! I don't know whether to laugh or cry. A telegram from Charles Evans at eleven to ring him immediately. I do so from a call-box in the square. J. B. Priestley threatens to bring a libel action if *Stamboul Train* is published.' (I heard later that he had read a review copy sent to the *Evening Standard*.) 'The character of Mr Savory he takes for his own.' Savory, a character in *Stamboul Train*, was described as a popular novelist. He was interviewed on the Orient Express by a sadistic woman journalist who tried to make a fool of him. J. H. Thomas, the politician, was in my mind when I gave him a touch of cockney, Baldwin when I gave him a pipe – after all a popular novelist is a bit of a politician. I had never met Mr Priestley and had been unable to read *The Good Companions* which had brought him immense popularity three years before.

My suggestion that we should fight the libel action was brushed aside. Evans made it clear to me that if Heinemann were going to lose an author, they would much prefer to lose me. Thirteen thousand copies of the book had already been printed and bound. Pages would have to be substituted, and I must share the cost. Alterations had to be made at once, on the spot, without reflection.

'Charles Evans then suggests alterations on the phone, deletion of "the modern Dickens" and of all references to Dickens as he says this will appease Priestley. I am to ring up again at three-thirty and hear the result. I would laugh if all my hopes did not rest on this book.

'Rang up at 3.30. References to Dickens, to a pipe and to "blunt fingers" all to come out. Objection to the line "sold a hundred thousand copies. Two hundred characters". I had to insert a new one, on the spot, in the telephone booth. The piece of dialogue: "You believe in Dickens, Chaucer, Charles Reade, that sort of thing?" to be altered. Shakespeare must go in, instead of Dickens. And the line "Dickens will live" has to be altered to "they will live".' It was almost as though Mr Priestley were defending Dickens rather than himself.

A child was on the way, and I had only twenty pounds in the bank. My mind shifted again towards the East, as it had done

155

when I left Oxford, and I wrote to an old Oxford friend to see whether he could fit me into his department of English at Chulankarana University near Bangkok. His favourable reply came just too late to save me from this career of writing. I had been turned back into the pen like a driven sheep by the temporary popular success of *Stamboul Train*. (How temporary it was may be judged by the fact I have already mentioned that the first printing of my first novel in 1929 was 2,500 copies and of my tenth, *The Power and the Glory*, in 1940 was 3,500.)

Twenty years later I visited my friend in Siam, as it was called then. He was still teaching in the department of English, and we smoked some opium pipes together in a little room which he had fitted up as a *fumerie* with a statue of Buddha and a couple of mattresses and a lacquer tray. At Oxford he had written poetry of great promise, but for long now he had given up any attempt to write. Unlike myself he had accepted the idea of failure and he had discovered in lack of ambition a kind of bleared happiness and an ironic amusement when he looked at his contemporaries who had found what people call success.

For a writer, I argued, success is always temporary, success is only a delayed failure. And it is incomplete. A writer's ambition is not satisfied like the business man's by a comfortable income, though he sometimes boasts of it like a *nouveau riche*. 'The reception of my *New Magdalen* was prodigious. I was forced to appear half way through the piece, as well as at the end. The acting took everyone by surprise, and the second night's enthusiasm quite equalled the first. We have really hit the mark. Ferrari translates it for Italy, Regnier has two theatres ready for me in Paris, and Lambe of Vienna has accepted it for his theatre.' Where is *The New Magdalen* now, and how many remember the name of its author?

The writer has the braggart's excuse. Knowing the unreality of his success he shouts to keep his courage up. There are faults in his work which he alone detects; even his unfavourable critics miss them, dwelling on obvious points which can be repaired, but like a skilled intuitive builder he can sniff out the dry rot in the beams. How seldom has he the courage to dismantle the whole house and start again.

The smell of opium is more agreeable than the smell of success. We were happy that long evening, as we passed the pipe to and fro and the small flame licked upwards towards the seed of opium and the shadow moved on Buddha's fat complacent face and we talked cheerfully of the past and analysed our differing failures without guilt or regret. Hadn't Buddha failed too? The starving, the sick and the mutilated dogs lay around his temple where the yellow-robed shaven priests picked their proud way.

'Another pipe? Do you remember that awful piece of verse you wrote at Oxford about eating a Lyons' chop?'

'Oh yes, I was in love . . .'

'That excuses a lot,' he said, 'at the age you were then.'

Graham Greene

WAYS OF ESCAPE

The second part of Greene's autobiography, which he began in
A Sort of Life.

From Haiti under Papa Doc, Vietnam in the last days of the
French, Kenya during the Mau Mau and Hollywood, to the
making of *The Third Man* in Vienna and his time in the British
Secret Service, Graham Greene writes exquisitely of people and
places, of faith, doubt, fear and of the craft of writing, as he
found himself repeatedly at 'the dangerous edge of things'.

'Marvellously rich' – William Trevor

DOCTOR FISCHER OF GENEVA OR THE BOMB PARTY

Doctor Fischer despises the human race. When the notorious
toothpaste millionaire decides to hold his own deadly version of
the Book of Revelations, Greene opens up a powerful vision of
the limitless greed of the rich; black comedy and painful satire
combine in a totally compelling novel.

'Manages to say more about love, hate, happiness, grief, immortality, greed and the disgustingly rich than most contemporary
English novels three times the length' – *The Times*

Also published

BRIGHTON ROCK   A BURNT-OUT CASE
COLLECTED ESSAYS   THE COMEDIANS
THE CONFIDENTIAL AGENT   THE END OF THE AFFAIR
ENGLAND MADE ME   A GUN FOR SALE
THE HEART OF THE MATTER   THE HONORARY CONSUL
THE HUMAN FACTOR   IT'S A BATTLEFIELD
IN SEARCH OF A CHARACTER   THE LAWLESS ROADS
JOURNEY WITHOUT MAPS   THE MAN WITHIN
LOSER TAKES ALL   MAY WE BORROW YOUR HUSBAND?
THE MINISTRY OF FEAR   OUR MAN IN HAVANA
THE POWER AND THE GLORY   THE QUIET AMERICAN
A SENSE OF REALITY   STAMBOUL TRAIN
THE THIRD MAN/THE FALLEN IDOL
TRAVELS WITH MY AUNT   TWENTY-ONE STORIES

Rather less than half of this book has appeared, though revised, cut and sometimes enlarged, in the introductions to the Collected Edition of my books published by The Bodley Head and William Heinemann and to *The Pleasure Dome* published by Secker and Warburg. Other portions have appeared in the *Sunday Times*, *The Times*, the *Sunday Telegraph*, the *Spectator*, the *Month*, the *London Magazine*, and *Life*. I must apologize to readers of *A Sort of Life* for a little overlapping between the end of that book and the beginning of this.

As my body continues on its journey,
my thoughts keep turning back and bury
themselves in days past.

— GUSTAVE FLAUBERT
to his mother, 23 November 1849

Preface

When I wrote a fragment of autobiography under the title
A Sort of Life I closed the record at the age of about twenty-
seven. I felt then that the future years belonged as much to others
as to myself. I couldn't infringe *their* copyright . . . They had a
right to privacy, and it was impossible to deal with my private
life without involving theirs. All the same I had tasted the
pleasure – often enough a sad pleasure – of remembering and so I
began a series of introductions to the Collected Edition of my
books, looking back on the circumstances in which the books
were conceived and written. They too were after all 'a sort of
life'.

I have added essays which I have written occasionally on
episodes in my life and on some of the troubled places in the
world where I have found myself involved for no good reason,
though I can see now that my travels, as much as the act of
writing, were ways of escape. As I have written elsewhere in
this book, 'Writing is a form of therapy; sometimes I wonder
how all those who do not write, compose or paint can manage
to escape the madness, the melancholia, the panic fear which is
inherent in the human situation.' Auden noted: 'Man needs
escape as he needs food and deep sleep.'

More rarely than might be supposed the places I visited
proved sources for my novels. I wasn't seeking sources, I stumbled
on them, though perhaps a writer's instinct may have been at
work when I bought my return ticket to Saigon or Port-au-
Prince or Asunción. So here is what I wrote of Haiti before I
thought of *The Comedians*, of Paraguay which was to form a
chapter in *Travels with my Aunt*. Yet the Emergency in Malaya
produced no novel, nor did the Mau Mau rebellion in Kenya.
Not even a short story emerged from the occasion when I was
deported by the American authorities from Puerto Rico or
from my experience of the Communist takeover in Prague in
1948. Poland in the Stalinist 1950s left the novelist's imagination

163

untouched, and yet and yet ... Politics since 1933 have taken an increasing place in my novels, and perhaps the Mau Mau prepared me for the more sinister Tontons Macoute and my apprehensions of ambush in Malaya lent an extra dimension to the fears which I sometimes experienced in Vietnam. I have included little from the articles I wrote on the French war there, for the American war made the earlier struggle seem a century away, and no one now can feel interest in such vanished characters as the Emperor Boa-Dai and Prince Buu-Loc.

Those parts of a life most beloved of columnists remain outside the scope of this book. The 'copyright' of others' lives I hope I have continued to observe.

Chapter 1

1

WHAT a long road it has been. Half a century has passed since I wrote *The Man Within*, my first novel to find a publisher. I was twenty-two years old when I began it and I was on sick leave from *The Times* after an operation for appendicitis. In the drawing-room of my parents' home at Berkhamsted there stood – or rather wobbled – one of those small writing bureaux with pigeonholes and little drawers which used to be thought suitable for women; the flap was just wide enough for my sheet of single-lined foolscap. Breakfast was over, and my mother was busy discussing a domestic problem with the parlourmaid. How 'period' such a title sounds today, and all those other household ranks – kitchenmaid, pantrymaid, nursemaid; I see myself now as a character in an historical novel writing the first words of an historical novel. If I am removed from him by fifty years, he was only removed by twice that time from his story of smugglers in the first decades of the nineteenth century.

Why has the opening line of that story stuck in my head when I have forgotten all the others I have written since? It is not a good line, for it has the ring of verse rather than prose; I have thought of changing it, but it would seem like a betrayal of my young self. 'He came over the top of the down as the last light failed and could almost have cried with relief at sight of the wood below.' I can hear my mother at that moment saying, 'If Miss Norah has the best spare room, we will have to put Mr . . .'

Perhaps the reason I remember the scene so clearly is that for me it was the last throw of the dice in a game I had practically lost. Two novels had been refused by every publisher I tried. If this book failed too I was determined to abandon the stupid ambition of becoming a writer. I would settle down to the safe and regular life of a sub-editor in Room 2 of *The Times* – in a year my probation would be over, I would rise to the minimum salary of nine guineas a week, and then I could just afford to marry. It was a career as settled as the Civil Service – no one was ever sacked from *The Times*, and in the end there would be a pension and I would receive a clock with a plaque carrying my name. As it happened I didn't have to wait so long for the clock – I got it a year later when I married, and for a long while after I had left *The Times* I felt a sense of guilt in front of the bold typeface on the mantelpiece which reminded me of the clock hanging over the main entrance in Queen Victoria Street. It always seemed to indicate that four in the afternoon was approaching and I ought to be on my way to join my companions in Room 2.

I hesitated some days before writing that opening sentence – it was a commitment. Hadn't I embarked twice before on what for months had seemed an interminable toil? It would be so much easier to resign myself, to give up all idea of escape. Why escape in those days? From what? I was happy on *The Times*.

I had finished my first novel when I was still at Oxford, after the unwise publication of a volume of verse, which is now an expensive curiosity for collectors. The subject, like so many first novels, was childhood and unhappiness. The first chapter described the hero's birth in an old country house. It seemed to me at the time a piece of rich evocative writing, and so it tried to be, but of the Jacobean rhythms of Walter de la Mare's prose rather than of personal experience. By a mistaken application of the Mendelian theory I told the story of a black child born of white parents – a throwback to some remote ancestor. (I hadn't then learned of my great-uncle Charles and the thirteen children he was said to have left behind him in St Kitts when he died of yellow fever at nineteen.) There followed in my novel a hushed-up childhood and a lonely colour-barred life at school, but to me even then the end seemed badly botched, and I can see that it was strangely optimistic for one of my temperament. I made the young man find a kind of content by joining a ship at Cardiff as a Negro deckhand, so escaping from the middle class and his sense of being an outsider. Escape again. I suspect that the word will chime from the title page on throughout this book.

A. D. Peters, a literary agent then new to the game, encouraged me to believe that the book was publishable. The months

166

passed, the tone of his letters changed from enthusiasm to cold second thoughts, finally hope died, but by that time a second novel was under way.

I had been reading Carlyle's *Life of John Sterling*, the only work of that great Scottish bore I have ever enjoyed. Carlyle provided the setting – Leicester Square in Victorian London, the haunt of Spanish refugees from the Carlist wars. Another young Englishman, anxious, like the black boy, to escape from his class, becomes involved in plots against the Spanish Government. Walter de la Mare (under the influence of Henry James) gave place to the later Conrad of *The Arrow of Gold* when he was writing under the same influence. Revolution and a Spanish setting – as a schoolboy I had envied the fate of Wilfred Ewart who had been shot accidentally during the Pancho Villa rising in Mexico. It had seemed to me a glamorous end in a glamorous country. Indeed my love affair with Spanish America and violent death only faded a little when I saw the *pistoleros* for myself years later during the voyage in Mexico which I described in *The Lawless Roads*.

I can't remember now what kind of fate overtook my hero who divided his time between the solid Belgravia house of his parents and the refugee dives of Soho. I know there was a love affair which depended heavily on that unbearable woman, Conrad's Doña Rita. I don't think he ever went nearer to Spain than Leicester Square, for I was paying a great deal of attention to unity and 'the point of view' after studying Percy Lubbock's admirable primer, *The Craft of Fiction*. I called the novel rather drably *The Episode* and that was all it proved to be. It never found a publisher – A. D. Peters even refused to handle it – and how grateful I was to him later.

So it was I began to plan the third novel, which I expected to be my last.

Lying in a general ward of Westminister Hospital, before returning to my parents' home to convalesce after the operation, I made a small jump back in time from the days of the Carlist refugees to the days of smugglers in Sussex. Now, if I ask myself why, I have no answer. Was it that I was half consciously aware I knew too little of the contemporary world to treat it? That the past was more accessible because it was contained in

167

books, such as the history of smuggling which I read in my hospital bed?

The Man Within had the temporary success that a first novel sometimes has through the charity of reviewers, and twenty years later a certain Mr Sidney Box made a highly coloured film of it. I had not sold him the rights – I had given them for a token payment to a documentary film dirctor with whom I had once worked on a propaganda film for what was then called Imperial Airways. He told me that with this book he had the chance of making his first feature film. Well, at least he made a profit from the resale to Mr Box, and Mr Box made his film with an extraordinary script which showed torture with branding irons as part of the nineteenth-century legal system. The film unlike the book did not suffer from youth or naïveté, and I received a letter from Istanbul written by a Turk who praised the picture for its daring homosexuality. Had I, he asked, devoted any other novels to this interesting subject? After the experience I added a clause to every film contract forbidding a resale to Mr Box. In a way I was hurt by this treachery to my first-born more than by the later treachery of Mr Joseph Mankiewicz when he made a film of *The Quiet American*. I was confident that the later book would survive the film, but *The Man Within* was a more feeble growth. If I had been a publisher's reader, which I became many years afterwards, I would have turned it down unhesitatingly. Yet a mystery remains. How could Aldous Huxley write of it so kindly in a letter to a friend, absurdly preferring it to Virginia Woolf's latest novel? Why did it bring me rather frightening friendships with two formidable characters, Lady Ottoline Morrell and Mrs Belloc Lowndes, and why did Jacques Maritain choose to publish it in France in a series which included Julien Green? I agreed at Maritain's request to delete a few lines from a sexual scene. To be censored by the French seemed to me then like an accolade.

I have another reason for remembering *L'Homme et Lui-Même*, as the novel was called in French. Writing a novel is a little like putting a message into a bottle and flinging it into the sea – unexpected friends or enemies retrieve it. My French translator, Denyse Clairouin, became both my friend and agent. In the days of the Stavisky riots we drove around Paris together looking

168

for trouble, but when the great trouble came and France fell, communication was impossible. It was only when the war was over I learned how she had worked in occupied France for the British Secret Service. In 1942 in Freetown, where I was working for the same service, I received news from London that a suspected spy, a Swiss businessman, was travelling to Lisbon in a Portuguese liner. While he queued up at the purser's for passport control, I sat in my one-man office typing out, as quickly as I could with one finger, the addresses in the notebook which he had been unwise enough to leave in his cabin. Suddenly, among all the names that meant nothing to me, I saw the name and address of Denyse. From that moment I feared for her safety, but it was not until the war was over that I learned she had died after torture in a German concentration camp. My mother's desk, a young man's sentimental story, a tin roof in Freetown and a German concentration camp . . . stages of a road which has proved very long.

2

My second and third novels, *The Name of Action* and *Rumour at Nightfall*, published in 1930 and 1931, can now be found, I am glad to think, only in secondhand bookshops at an exaggerated price, since some years after their publication I suppressed them. Both books are of a badness beyond the power of criticism properly to evoke – the prose flat and stilted and in the case of *Rumour at Nightfall* pretentious (the young writer had obviously been reading again and alas! admiring Conrad's worst novel, *The Arrow of Gold*), the characterization non-existent.

The main characters in a novel must necessarily have some kinship to the author, they come out of his body as a child comes from the womb, then the umbilical cord is cut, and they grow into independence. The more the author knows of his own character the more he can distance himself from his invented characters and the more room they have to grow in. With these early novels the cord has not been cut, and the author at twenty-six was as unreal to himself, in spite of psychoanalysis at sixteen, as Oliver Chant, the hero of *The Name of Action*, is to the reader. Chant is only a daydream in the mind of a young romantic author, for it takes years of brooding and of guilt, of self-criticism and of self-justification, to clear from the eyes the haze of hopes and dreams and false ambitions. I was trying to write my first political novel, knowing nothing of politics. I hope I did better many years later with *The Quiet American*, but how little I had learned of life and politics during three years in the sub-editors' room of *The Times*.

Even the setting of *The Name of Action* is fantasy. I imagined a dictator established in the city of Trier which I had visited soon after the French occupying force had abandoned the idea of forming an independent Palatinate state. The idealistic and wealthy Oliver Chant, contacted by exiles in London (an echo of my unpublished novel *The Episode*), goes to Trier to meet the leader of the opposition, a Jewish poet. He meets the dictator's wife in quite incredible circumstances and falls in love with her. He is invited improbably to the palace where he begins to develop a romantic admiration for the dictator. He sleeps with the dictator's wife who takes him out of boredom and lust and betrays the fact that her husband is impotent. When she refuses to leave her husband Chant tells the Jewish poet of the dictator's impotence. Guns, bought with Chant's money, are smuggled in barges from Coblenz, riots take place, the poet writes satirical songs about the dictator which are sung in the street. The book ends with Chant leaving Trier by train in charge of the defeated, wounded and unconscious dictator. What happened to the wife? It is only a matter of months since I drove myself to reread *The Name of Action* and I've already forgotten her fate, so little does she live or matter.

I can only wonder why the book was accepted for publication – I even received a congratulatory telegram from my publisher, Charles Evans of Heinemann, after he had read the typescript. Perhaps he was as innocent and romantic as his author. He once told me he had only once been sexually moved by a novel and that was by *Mademoiselle de Maupin*.

Here are examples of my style in those early days and my terrible misuse of simile and metaphor. Even the good can corrupt and perhaps I had been corrupted by much reading of the metaphysical poets. 'A revolver drooped like a parched flower to the pavement.' (I like to reverse this simile – 'A parched flower drooped like a revolver to the pavement.') 'The sound of far voices sprinkled over him like the seeds of a poppy bringing rest.' And here's a piece of pomposity which I had learned from Conrad at his worst: 'A clock relinquished its load of hours.'

In a book of 344 pages I can find only one redeeming scene – twelve pages of moderate suspense when the barge with its load of smuggled guns passes through the customs – and one redeeming character – the American arms-dealer who appears for eight pages and might well have earned a place in *The Quiet American* a quarter of a century later.

Rumour at Nightfall, the third published novel, began better than its predecessor and ended even more disastrously. I knew next to nothing of Spain where the story takes place (at sixteen I had spent one day between Vigo and Coruña), and all I knew of the Carlist war was drawn from Carlyle's *Life of John Sterling*. Again only one scene bears rereading. It is in the first chapter when an ageing tired colonel takes the place of a priest and extracts a confession from one of his men mortally wounded in an ambush – a scene which perhaps foreshadows the confessions of the American gangster in *The Power and the Glory*. As in *The Quiet American* the principal character Chase was a newspaper correspondent but unlike Fowler of that novel a most unrealistic one.

Rumour at Nightfall sold only twelve hundred copies (*The Man Within* had sold eight thousand). An unfavourable criticism by Frank Swinnerton opened my eyes to the defects of what I had believed to be true art, and so reality, blessed reality, broke through in the form of financial anxiety, the approaching birth of a child and, for I had left the paper after the success of *The Man Within*, the refusal of *The Times* to have a deserter back.

What do I find when I painfully reread the novel today? The author is too much concerned with style and the style is bad and derivative. A few years later I would be attacking Charles Morgan, like a reformed rake, for the sin I had abandoned. All is vague, shadowy, out of focus – there are no clear images, but the same extravagant similes and metaphors as in *The Name of Action*. 'The small drift of papers lay like winter between them, across the blown petals of the carpet.' There are far too many adjectives and too much explanation of motive, no trust in the reader's understanding, and overlong description.

171

The dialogue is ambiguous and dialogue in a novel as in a play should be a form of action, with the quickness of action. Here the dialogue has to be explained to the reader. I find 'he thought' ten times in ten pages. I am reminded of the young Stevenson teaching himself style by imitation – I was imitating badly a technique, the technique of 'the point of view'.

Perhaps all writers are superstitious. The hero of *The Name of Action* was called Chant, the two protagonists of *Rumour at Nightfall* were Chase and Crane. The books were failures and failure seemed to cling around the letter C. I abandoned C, I thought for ever, and a sense of doom descended on me when I named the chief character in *The Human Factor* Castle. I tried my best to give him another name, but there is a magic quality in names – to change the name is to change the character. Castle it had to be, but I went ahead with a sense of almost certain failure.

3

I had now published three novels of which the first had some success and the other two had deservedly failed, and I felt the desolate isolation of defeat, like a casualty who has been left behind and forgotten. The sudden arrival in 1931 down a muddy Gloucestershire lane of a Norwegian poet whom I didn't know from Adam seemed unaccountable, dreamlike and oddly encouraging. Like the appearance of three crows on a gate, Nordahl Grieg was an omen or a myth, and he remained a myth. Even his death was to prove legendary, so that none will be able to say with any certainty, 'In this place he died.' He was shot down in an air raid over Berlin in 1943.

I can remember with distinctness only three meetings. Each of our meetings was separated by a space of years from the next, yet I would not have hesitated to claim friendship with him – even a degree of intimacy. I was unable to read his books – for only one had been translated into English (in any case his poetry would have been untranslatable) – and so he struck me less as a fellow author with whom I must talk shop than as a friend I had grown up with, to whom I could speak and with whom I could argue about anything in the world.

I can't remember what we talked about that first time, when

he came 'to look me up', as he put it as sole explanation, in the cottage my wife Vivien and I had rented in the village of Chipping Campden, but I immediately felt caught up into his intimacy which seemed as impersonal – in the sense that I did not have to deserve it or work for it – as sunlight. The dreamlike atmosphere of his friendship remained: it was a matter of messages, warm and friendly and encouraging and critical, mostly in other people's letters. The only time I visited Norway he was away living in Leningrad, but the messages were there awaiting me. Nordahl Grieg, like a monarch, never lacked messengers.

I sometimes wonder whether he didn't also leave spells in far places which drew me there long afterwards. Why did I take a solitary holiday in Estonia in the thirties? Was it because I was following in his footsteps? And Moscow in the fifties? It was no longer any use then going to Room 313 in the Hotel Novo Moscowskaja, the address he had given me in case 'you one day suddenly find yourself in Moscow', his ghost had moved a long way on.

I have a letter which he wrote to me from Estonia with the sole address 'Poste Restante' and the year missing from the date as it always was, as though only the day of the month was important and the mere years could be left to look after themselves. 'I assure you that you before or later must come to Estonia, and please come now. It is a charming country, absolutely unspoilt, and the cheapest in the world. I am a very poor author, but here I can afford absolutely everything – a strange and marvellous feeling. If the weather is good, do let us hire a sailing boat and go for a week among the islands. The population there has scarcely seen a white man before, and for a few pieces of chocolate we could certainly buy what native girls we wanted to. Do come.'

But it was a long time before I could afford the fare, and by then Nordahl had entered his Russian period. Strange to think that it was the Russia of Stalin. Which of us now, in the days of Brezhnev, can stay for months in Moscow and borrow the flat of a poet? 'I have just returned to Moscow from the country ... What fun to meet you here! I am most likely to stay here the whole of May; but there is a vague possibility of me going to Tiflis and Caucasus (in that case perhaps you will come with

173

me?)' And in another letter: 'I have borrowed the flat of Boris Pilnyak who had written *Volga falls out in the Caspian Sea*. (Of course, all Russian writers call their books after some river, they are even worse than you English who always find some very exclusive quotation as a title), and here I am working in the strange bourgeois atmosphere (of blue lilacs and wooden houses) that is the Moscow summer ... I am sure you will like to live in Moscow, there is such an enormous mass of people – a vast multitude of races, hopes and disappointments. And your hatred to nature can easily be satisfied here, here is no nature for many hundred miles, only something flat and stupid under an idiotical sky. So come here for some months or more.' Any plan seemed possible for a few hours after I had read one of Nordahl's letters.

And then, with the shadows falling over Europe and only a few years left him before the raid over Berlin, back he went to Norway: 'I have just started a new, *very* left periodical to fight the rising wave of fascism and reaction in Norway. I have had the insolence to advertise you among my future contributors. Are you angry? If you forgive me for old days' sake, please then send me an article, something hair-risingly good ... My Moscow days are over. I have written a play – a violent attack on our 'neutrality' during the last war, which has caused very much bitterness. I am living in a ski-hut near Oslo in a forest. If you and your wife should like to come over, there will always be a room for you.'

How I wish I had borrowed, begged or stolen the necessary funds and replied to at least one of those messages – 'I arrive on Saturday.'

I suppose we may have met between 1931 and 1940, but I am not sure. Suddenly, instead of a message in a letter, he was a voice on the telephone. I was at the Ministry of Information by that time, in a silly useless job, the German invasion of Norway had begun, and here he was, just arrived from Narvik and war. His voice pulled me out of the great dead Bloomsbury building into his bedroom at the Charing Cross Hotel which was full of his countrymen, sitting about on the bed, the dressing-table, the floor, propped against the mantelpiece, discussing, planning, hoping while the telephone rang, with Narvik and disaster

174

just behind them and an immense confidence and the future all round them (a confidence you couldn't have found except in official handouts in the building I had left). And even in that setting I felt the old intimacy like sunlight; while everyone was talking plans, propaganda, future campaigns, Nordahl, making a private corner between bolster and bedpost, was talking of anything that seemed at the moment to matter – Marxism or the value of history or the Spanish war and Hemingway's new book, neglecting even the extraordinary adventure from which he had just emerged with the gold of the Bank of Norway. That I had to piece together while his cabinet in exile chattered around him.

Nordahl, waking one morning in Oslo to gunfire, had gone to his window and seen the German warships entering the fjord. He dressed and without so much as taking a spare pair of socks took to the mountains. There he encountered a military patrol and found himself recruited into the army without uniform or weapon as a private soldier. The patrol had with them in sacks the gold from the Bank of Norway and Nordahl was appointed to command a party to take it to Narvik, about five hundred miles by sea after a long journey through the mountains. I never heard the details of that journey – there were always too many other things for Nordahl to talk about – only the comedy of the ending.

He arrived safely at Narvik, a private soldier dressed as a fisherman, with his sacks of gold, and reported to a spick-and-span naval officer who turned out to be our mutual friend, the translator of *The Man Within*, Nils Lie. Nordahl was told to accompany the gold on an English destroyer to our shores, where the gold had to be delivered to the Bank of England. He argued that he wanted to stay in Norway to fight. Anyway what would the English think if they sent all that gold – Maria Theresa thalers and all – in the care of a private soldier? It wasn't suitable.

So they gave him some kind of commission – I forget what – and he left for England. From Harwich I think it was he took a train, and there his romantic nature took over and he pictured the scene at the Bank of England and his greeting by the Governor, but his arrival was not like that at all. Only one plainclothes

175

detective was waiting for him on the platform – of which station? – and they couldn't drive to the Bank of England without the clerk who had been sent to meet him. But the clerk had gone to find the station master because the ticket collector wouldn't let him past the barrier without a platform ticket and the clerk of the Bank of England absolutely refused to lower his dignity by buying one. So the detective and the poet waited there interminably with all the sacks of Norwegian gold until Nordahl got bored and left the detective alone with the gold and took a taxi to the Charing Cross Hotel.

After our meeting in the hotel Nordahl disappeared again from my view – I suppose he was busy getting into the RAF and afterwards I was away for fifteen months on a hopeless mission in West Africa, trying to get information out of the Vichy colonies. A few months before his death we met once more and spent a long evening with other Norwegian friends, an evening of which, because I never imagined it could be the last, I remember only talk and talk, then an air-raid siren and some gunfire, and talk again. There were always arguments where Nordahl was and never a trace of anger. He was the only man I have ever met with whom it was possible to disagree profoundly both on religion and politics and yet feel all the time the sense of goodwill and an open mind. He not only had goodwill himself, but he admitted goodwill in his opponent – he more than admitted it, he assumed it. In fact he had charity – of greater value than the gold of the National Bank, and to me he certainly brought a measure of hope in 1931, carrying it like a glass of akvavit down the muddy lane in Chipping Campden.

4

That year, 1931, for the first and last time in my life I deliberately set out to write a book to please, one which with luck might be made into a film. The devil looks after his own and in *Stamboul Train* I succeeded in both aims, though the film rights seemed at the time an unlikely dream, for before I had completed the book, Marlene Dietrich had appeared in *Shanghai Express*, the English had made *Rome Express*, and even the Russians had produced their railway film, *Turksib*. The film manufactured from my book by Twentieth Century-Fox came last and was far and away the worst, though not so bad as a later television production by the BBC.

I suppose the popular success of the film *Grand Hotel* gave me the idea of how to set about winning the jackpot, but as I had spent only twenty-four hours in Constantinople some years before, in the course of an Hellenic cruise, I had taken on a rather heavy assignment. I couldn't afford to leave the cottage in the Cotswolds and take a train to Istanbul. The best I could do was to buy a record of Honegger's *Pacific 231* which I hoped, when I played it daily, would take me far enough away from my thatched cottage, a Pekinese dog who suffered from hysteria, some barren apple trees, the muddy lane and a row of Cos lettuces.

Reluctantly, I also bought a third-class ticket as far as the German frontier. Beyond it, in those happy pre-Hitlerian days, a writer could obtain a free pass on the State Railways, so that I could travel on as far as Cologne which I knew already, having found myself there in 1923 in the ambiguous circumstances I have described in my account of my early years, *A Sort of Life*. The Honegger record helped me more than the trip from Calais to Cologne, and another record less obviously relevant played its part too – Delius's *Walk to the Paradise Garden*.

The reader will probably notice more details on this first stretch of the line than I had the confidence to include later, for as I sat at my third-class window I made notes all through the daylight hours, and you may be sure the allotments outside Bruges were just where I placed them in April 1931. Darkness had fallen on the Orient Express before Liège was reached, and it would be wrong for the reader to have any confidence in my report when he reaches the Yugoslav frontier at Subotica. (A few years ago when I made the whole journey to Istanbul it was night when I arrived at Subotica and I was too sleepy to check the details of my almost forgotten narrative.)

When the news came to me that the English Book Society had chosen *Stamboul Train*, I thought I was temporarily saved, and yet fate had still a flick of the tail in store, a threatened libel action from J. B. Priestley. Priestley, whom I had never met, had taken the character of Savory, in *Stamboul Train*, as a

177

portrait of himself – I had described Savory as a popular novelist in the manner of Dickens, and Priestley had recently published to enormous acclaim his novel *The Good Companions*, which led some reviewers to compare him with Dickens.

I was to learn in the years that followed how dangerous the libel laws could be to a writer. In this case Priestley, I am sure, really believed that this all-but-unknown writer was attacking him; he acted in good faith. The good faith of others was often more dubious. After the moderate success of *Stamboul Train* I began to be regarded as a monetary mark (no libel cases are ever brought against a failure). Between 1934 and 1938 one book, *Journey Without Maps*, had to be withdrawn and small damages paid to a doctor whom I didn't know even existed, twice I was threatened by libel actions for reviews written in the *Spectator*, and finally there was the case of Miss Shirley Temple who, aged nine, brought a libel action against me through Twentieth Century-Fox for a criticism of her film *Wee Willie Winkie* in the magazine *Night and Day*.

In those black days for authors – they ended with the war and a change in the libel laws – there was one firm of solicitors who went out of their way to incite actions for libel, checking the names of characters with the names in the London telephone directory. An acquaintance of mine was approached at the door of his flat by a solicitor's clerk who carried a novel which, he said, contained an undesirable character of the same name (the more uncommon the name the greater the danger, which was one reason why in my novel *The Comedians* I called my principal characters Brown, Jones and Smith). The solicitor's clerk told my friend that if he wished to institute proceedings his public-spirited firm would be glad to assist. There would be no expenses if the case were lost, but he assured my friend it was unlikely to reach the Courts. Unlikely indeed, for most publishers in those days had little zest for fighting. They were always prepared to cut their losses and make a small settlement. In the case of *Stamboul Train* about twenty pages had to be reprinted because of Priestley's threatened libel action, and Heinemann deducted the cost from my royalties, or rather added them to my increasing debt to the firm.

Well, one mustn't exaggerate the danger or complain too

much of it. There are professional risks in most trades – the girls who used in those halcyon days to put the gold leaf on our books had to drink their quota of milk each day as a protection, and what more suitable risk could I run than from obscure furtive characters, lurking on landings bowler-hatted, or cooped in the office-pen leafing through scenes of adultery or corruption? They might have emerged from my own pages.

There are, I think, a few points of academic interest in *Stamboul Train*. The young dancer Coral Musker had surely appeared at the Theatre Royal in Nottwich, like a character in a later book, Anne in *A Gun for Sale*, and I can detect in both books the influence of my early passion for playwrighting which has never quite died. In those days I thought in terms of a key scene – I would even chart its position on a sheet of paper before I began to write. 'Chapter 3. So-and-so comes alive.' Often these scenes consisted of isolating two characters – hiding in a railway shed in *Stamboul Train*, in an empty house in *A Gun for Sale*. It was as though I wanted to escape from the vast liquidity of the novel and to play out the most important situation on a narrow stage where I could direct every movement of my characters. A scene like that halts the progress of the novel with dramatic emphasis, just as in a film a close-up makes the moving picture momentarily pause. I can watch myself following this method even in so late a book as *The Comedians*. I had long abandoned that sheet of paper – otherwise perhaps I would have written on it, 'Scene: Cemetery. Jones and Brown come alive.' It might even be said that I reached the logical climax of the method in *The Honorary Consul* where almost the whole story is contained in the hut in which the kidnappers have hidden their victim.

More than forty years separate *Stamboul Train* from *The Honorary Consul*. Hitler had not yet come to power when *Stamboul Train* was written. It was a different world and a different author – an author still in his twenties. I am not sure that I detect much promise in his work, except in the character of Colonel Hartep, the Chief of Police, whom I suspect survived into the world of Aunt Augusta and *Travels with my Aunt*. And when I read the last chapter laid in Istanbul, and encounter the characters of Kalebdjian, a hotel clerk, and Mr Stein, a fraudulent businessman, presented with excellent brevity, the old writer can salute his young predecessor with a certain respect.

5

To go back far in time is always a reluctant return (as one approaches death one lives a step ahead, perhaps in a hurry to be gone). I began to write *It's a Battlefield* at a time of great financial anxiety. After the publication of my first novel my English and American publishers had guaranteed me six hundred pounds a year for three years which had enabled me to leave my safe job on *The Times* for the cottage at Chipping Campden, but in 1932 the three guaranteed years were nearly up, my second and third books had lost money, my fourth, *Stamboul Train*, was still in manuscript, and a biography which I had written of the poet, the Earl of Rochester, had been rejected; there was about twenty pounds left in the bank, and our first child was on the way.

I had kept a journal during that period, and I can read in it week after week the record of sleepless nights, of depression and my attempts again and again to find a job, on a Sunday newspaper, at a university in Bangkok. Little wonder that *It's a Battlefield* made slow progress* – I was also working on a long short story called *Brandon's Acre* which has disappeared even from my memory.

One gloomy day I took a ticket for London to discuss matters with Charles Evans, the head of Heinemann, and with the representative of Doubleday, my American publisher. Evans consented to renew my contract for a year, but Doubleday only for two months while they had time to study the manuscript of *Stamboul Train*. And there were heavy conditions – another two-book contract and any losses by the publishers had to be recovered before further royalties were paid. In other words I returned to our cottage in the country with two months'

---

*Another novel about spiritualism had been abandoned. I find the opening paragraphs in my journal: '"Pleased to meet you, Little Flower," said Mrs Partlett. "Can you tell us something of Summerland?"

'"Everything is very, very beautiful," the high imperfect child's voice spoke through the dark. "There is music everywhere."'

security, and the prospect of having to write two more novels after *Stamboul Train* without any payment at all. *Stamboul Train* saved us, but only at the very last moment. (There is another thing which my journal shows to counterbalance the sleepless nights – the courage and understanding of my wife who never complained of this dangerous cul-de-sac into which I had led her from the safe easy highroad we had been travelling while I remained on *The Times*.)

It seems to me now almost an act of self-destruction to have embarked on *It's a Battlefield* at this particular moment. I had no illusions that it could prove popular; indeed it remains the least read of all my books, although certain passages remain in my own memory (the interview between Milly and the murdered policeman's widow; Conrad's last pursuit of the Assistant Commissioner, his revolver loaded only with blanks).

The subject, I remember, was suggested by a dream, the fruit of anxiety-ridden weeks, in which I had been condemned to death for murder, and I find a piece of rough verse written down in a diary I kept then which suggests that the opening of the novel was already coming to mind.

> This the analysis of blood-stain –
>   'on woollen beret of a common make';
> the experts complain
>   that the fingers left no mark
>
> On the park chair
>   or the young breast;
> microscopic stare
>   at uncertain past,
>
> Grass inspected, note-book entry,
>   'torn bodice and lace';
> Over the body the solitary sentry
>   of her certain peace.

I have seldom had the courage to reread a book of mine more than once, and that immediately after publication when I check it for misprints and for small changes which I ought to have made in manuscript, typescript or proof, so that I may have a marked copy ready for another edition if one is ever required. I broke this rule with *It's a Battlefield* because two passages remained obstinately wrong with the book. The most important was an episode, quite unrelated to the main theme – the injustice of men's justice – when the Assistant Commissioner accompanies a detective superintendent to effect the arrest of a trunk-murderer in Paddington. It was monstrously unlikely behaviour for an Assistant Commissioner, and so when, six years after the first publication in 1934, I set about revising the book for a paper-covered edition, I cut the whole scene out. But when the shorter version of the book was published and I read it through yet again, I realized that, unlikely as the episode had been, it was an essential one. Without the mad murderer of the Salvation Army the battlefield of the title lacked the sense of violence and confusion. The metaphor became a political and not an ironic one.

The other scene which has always worried me, with which I could only tinker, altering phrases and cutting wherever possible, is the meeting of a Communist Party branch attended by Mr Surrogate, an intellectual member. I had only once in my life attended a large Communist meeting, and that was in Paris in 1923, at a time when I held for four weeks a Party card at Oxford, and this experience was totally insufficient as a basis for a scene which now to me lacks authenticity.

I have seldom employed living models in a novel except for very minor characters, but in *It's a Battlefield* I was aware of Lady Ottoline Morrell's presence in the background of Lady Caroline; my idea of Middleton Murry, whom I did not personally know, was responsible in small part for Mr Surrogate, and my uncle Graham Greene, who had been Secretary of the Admiralty under Mr Churchill during the First World War, lent a little of his stiff inhibited bachelor integrity to the character of the Assistant Commissioner. My uncle though had had no experience of the Far East – that was to be mine nearly twenty years later, a curious foreshadowing.

If the reception of this book, which added to my failure in the eyes of my publishers, did not discourage me, it was for three reasons: the best review I had yet earned came from V. S. Pritchett, a kind phrase from Ezra Pound, and some words of praise from Ford Madox Ford. What did it matter after that, the opinion of the popular reviewers or the indifference of readers?

I had received my spurs. I still think the last sixty pages are as successful as anything I have written since.

6

I have always had a soft spot in my heart for my fifth published novel, *England Made Me* (a feeling which has not been shared by the general public), yet of the circumstances of its composition I can remember very little. I think of those years between 1933 and 1937 as the middle years for my generation, clouded by the Depression in England, which cast a shadow on this book, and by the rise of Hitler. It was impossible in those days not to be committed, and it is hard to recall the details of one private life as the enormous battlefield was prepared around us.

When the story came to me, when Anthony and Kate, the twins in the novel, clamoured for attention, and their incestuous situation (which was yet to contain no incestuous act) for exploration, I knew nothing at all of Sweden. I think it is the only occasion when I have deliberately chosen an unknown country as a background and then visited it, like a camera-team, to take the necessary stills. (Many years later I visited the Belgian Congo for something of the same purpose, but the Congo was a geographical term invented by the white colonists – I already knew Negro Africa, in Sierra Leone, Nigeria, Kenya, the hinterland of Liberia.)

The photographs I brought back from Sweden were, I think, reasonably accurate, reasonably representative, and yet, now that I know Stockholm well in winter, spring, summer and autumn, I am a little afraid when I come to reread the book. That midsummer festival at Saltsjö-Duvnäs, a New Year's night when lead was melted over the fire to tell the future and the piece I threw in the pan formed a perfect question mark – such impressions are not to be found here, nor the swans gathering on the ice outside the Grand Hotel, the taste of akvavit in the Theatre Grill, the lakes of Dalecarlia, nor that island in the archipelago from which in that later time I would row every morning to fetch water for cooking and where a lavatory seat stood like a surrealist object all alone in a mosquito-loud glade. These impressions are Sweden to me now, and it might be as distressing to reread this novel as an ancient letter containing some superficial critical estimate of a woman whom twenty years later one had grown to love.

I have few memories of that visit with my younger brother Hugh in August 1934; the clearest, because they have not been overlaid by the later memories, are attached to the speckless miniature liner which brought us up the canal from Gothenburg to Stockholm (and which I imagined falsely would prove a background for the novel), of waking to the soft summer brilliance of midnight and the silver of the birches going by, almost within reach of my hands, and the chickens pecking on the bank. I remember that my brother and I carried on a harmless flirtation with two English visitors of sixteen and twenty; we went for walks in separate pairs when the boat stopped at a lock, and once, for some inexplicable reason, considerable alarm arose because my brother and the younger girl had not returned to the little liner at the proper time, and the mother – an intellectual lady who frequently won literary competitions in the Liberal weekly *Time & Tide* – was convinced that both had been drowned in the canal. One evening in Stockholm, on the borders of the lake, my companion of the canal slapped my face in almost the same circumstances as those in which Loo slapped Anthony's in my story, for I had told her that I believed she was a virgin. Afterwards we sat decorously enough in Skansen, Stockholm's park, among the grey rocks and the silver trees. (Her reaction was the only characteristic she had in common with Loo.) But August is not the best time of year to see Stockholm for the first time – what with the heat and the humidity, and the extreme formality of one dinner which we attended at Saltsjöbaden, we decided to move on to Oslo. I am amazed now at my temerity in laying the scene of a novel in a city of which I knew so little.

Would I have written the book any better now when I can easily find in my memories a model for Krogh, the industrialist, who so obstinately at that time refused to come alive? I doubt it. In most of my books, however well I might know the scene, there is one lay figure who obstinately refuses to live, who is there only for the sake of the story – Krogh in *England Made Me*, the barmaid in *Brighton Rock*, Wilson in *The Heart of the Matter*, Smythe in *The End of the Affair*, the journalist Parkinson in *A*

Burnt-Out Case. The sad truth is that a story hasn't room for more than a limited number of created characters. One more successful creation and like an overloaded boat the story lists. This was the unexpected danger I encountered in *England Made Me*.

I was quite satisfied with my portrait of Anthony. Hadn't I lived with him closely over many years? He was an idealized portrait of my eldest brother, Herbert, and I had myself shared many of Anthony's experiences. I had known Annette, the young tart whom Anthony loved. I had walked up those forbidding stairs and found with the same emotion the notices – 'No milk this morning', 'Gone out. Be back at —' (no hour which would ever be recorded on the dial of my watch). I was satisfied too with Kate, Anthony's sister, who seems to me the woman I have drawn better than any other, with the possible exception of Sarah in *The End of the Affair*. Anthony and Kate were the heart of the book; Krogh was only there to manipulate their story, and the others, Loo, Hall, Hammarsten, Young Andersson were background figures; no one else was needed. Then suddenly the boat listed because Minty stepped on board.

He was entirely unexpected when he emerged from the pre-conscious – this remittance man who woke up one morning in his Stockholm lodgings watched by a spider under a tooth glass – a late-comer at the end of Part Two. I suppose, for the purposes of Anthony's story, I had required, as a minor figure, some fellow outsider who would recognize – as only a fellow countryman can – the fraudulent element in Anthony, who could detect the falsity of the old Harrovian tie, but I had no intention of introducing into the story a sly pathetic Anglo-Catholic; a humble follower, perhaps, of Sir John Betjeman, who would steal all the scenes in which he played a part and have the last word, robbing even Kate of her curtain at Anthony's funeral. Oh yes, I resented Minty, and yet I couldn't keep him down.

The subject – apart from the economic background of the thirties and that sense of capitalism staggering from crisis to crisis – was simple and unpolitical, a brother and sister in the confusion of incestuous love. I found it odd to read once in a monthly review an article on my early novels in which a critic *disinterred* this theme. He wrote of the ambiguity of the subject, how the author himself feared or was even perhaps unaware of the nature of the passion between brother and sister. He quoted examples to show how the dialogue between the two broke suddenly at a dangerous moment into irrelevancies – I was shirking the true nature of my subject, so he wrote.

How dangerous it is for a critic to have no technical awareness of the novel. Surely the great prefaces of Henry James have marked one novelist's route indelibly – the route of 'the point of view'. There was no ambiguity in *my* mind; the ambiguity was in the minds of Kate and Anthony whom I had chosen for my 'points of view'. They were continually on the edge of self-discovery, but some self-protective instinct warded off, with false or incomplete memories and irrelevancies, the moment of discovery. Kate was nearer to knowledge than Anthony and both used their superficial sexual loves, Kate with Krogh and Anthony with Loo, to evade the real right thing. The cowardly evasions were not mine; they belonged to the doomed pair.

7

A friendship can be among the most important events in a life, and a way of escape, just as much as writing or travel, from the everyday routine, the sense of failure, the fear of the future. Certainly my meeting with Herbert Read was an important event in my life. He was the most gentle man I have ever known, but it was a gentleness which had been tested in the worst experience of his generation. The young officer, who gained the Military Cross and a DSO in action on the Western Front, had carried with him to all that mud and death Robert Bridges's anthology *The Spirit of Man*, Plato's *Republic* and *Don Quixote*. Nothing had changed in him. It was the same man twenty years later who could come into a room full of people and you wouldn't notice his coming – you noticed only that the whole atmosphere of a discussion had quietly altered, that even the relations of one guest with another had changed. No one any longer would be talking for effect, and when you looked round for an explanation there he was – complete honesty born of complete experience had entered the room and unobtrusively taken a chair.

It is typical of Herbert Read's character that I cannot remember where or how we first met. I think it must have been in 1935, the year when his only novel, *The Green Child*, was published, a novel which I would put among the great poems of this century along with David Jones's *In Parenthesis*. I was already an ardent admirer of *English Prose Style*, which should be compulsory reading for any would-be writer, of his *Wordsworth* – no one had ever written so revealingly of Wordsworth, or so self-revealingly – and of *The Innocent Eye*, the account of his childhood on a Yorkshire farm, one of the best autobiographies in our language.

T. S. Eliot and Herbert Read were the two great figures of my young manhood (they meant more to me than Joyce, and as for Pound he was somehow always a very long way off – an explorer of whose survival at any particular moment one could never be quite certain). I had not the courage to approach Eliot or Read myself. What interest could they feel for a young and unsuccessful novelist? So it must have been chance which led to my first encounter with Read, and I was proud, surprised and a little daunted when I received a letter from him inviting me to dinner. 'Eliot is coming, but no one else, and everything very informal.' To me it was a little like receiving an invitation from Coleridge – 'Wordsworth is coming, but no one else.' He gave me very clear directions with a small map that looked like the sketch of a trench system on the Western Front torn from that young officer's pad, and then for a moment the countryman, the author of *The Innocent Eye*, peeped out. 'The Mall is what I call a "ginnel", a narrow passage through a double gate.' And I felt nearer to Yorkshire than to Belsize Park.

Two years later when I became part-editor of the weekly magazine *Night and Day* I had the temerity, perhaps because I had gained more confidence in myself, to ask the author of *Art Now* to write for me regular reviews of detective stories and he promptly accepted. (At that dinner with Eliot we had talked of Arsène Lupin – a subject which always helped Eliot to unbutton – perhaps for a moment it made him feel safe from ladies going to and fro talking of Michelangelo.) Our new relationship was celebrated by a verse in red ink which accompanied the first review.

> Shall it be Graham or be Greene?
> There's nothing betwixt or between.
> Shall it be Graham or be Greene?
> Neither is Christian or intime,
> But one is milk the other cream.
> So Graham let it be, not Greene.

I would like one day to see those reviews republished, so different are they from the stock image of Herbert Read, the intellectual. The first, on 8 July 1937, contained a devastating and deserved criticism of Dorothy L. Sayers's *Busman's Honeymoon*. Later he was unfriendly to Peter Cheyney, but had a charitable word for Agatha Christie. I really believe he enjoyed writing these reviews more than that long series of art books which hid from so many eyes his real genius as a poet, literary critic and autobiographer. He knew I didn't care very much for them and he never resented it; even when I put my feelings into print he only wrote: 'You did make my bread and butter look pretty stale, but then it is . . .' His reviews in *Night and Day*, I like to think, were a holiday to him, and his humour streamed suddenly and volcanically out. He quoted hilariously from second-rate authors who had certainly not learnt the lessons of *English Prose Style*.

'Maynard poured some more coffee and broke the narcissistic shell of another egg.' We have always found our eggs distinctly indifferent to their own appearance.

Alas that *Night and Day* died at the end of 1937, for on 4 November of that year, in an essay called 'Life without a Shoehorn', Herbert Read made his début as a comic writer under the name of James Murgatroyd. I seem to have objected to the pseudonym which was at first simply Murgatroyd, a name I thought more suitable to a character of Wodehouse. He wrote firmly back: 'In defence of Murgatroyd. It is a perfectly real name, and if I had been born in the West instead of the North Riding it might easily have been my own name. Would it do if I gave him a Christian name as well, say James? In any case, I refuse to be called Bertram Meade. I once knew a man in the Ministry of Labour called that, and that is what it sounds like. I want something funny, and something vaguely evocative of something square and squat with protruding amphibian eyes; something weary and patient, like a frog in a drought. If it can wait until Tuesday, I will try and think of an alternative. But if I am to go on with the creature, he must have an inspiring name – like Murgatroyd.'

So Murgatroyd it was. He was planning a series. If he had completed it, we might have had a worthy successor to *The Diary of a Nobody*. Is it possible that a few of these essays remain among his papers?

I write of trivial matters, but when one loves a man, as I loved him, it is the small things which others may have forgotten or not known which first come to mind before the great enduring achievements, *The Green Child*, *Wordsworth*, *The End of a War*, *The Contrary Experience*, and that essay on Vauvenargues in which he suddenly speaks of the ruling passion that links these autobiographies with a steel thread: the search for glory. 'Glory is now a discredited word, and it will be difficult to re-establish it. It has been spoilt by a too close association with military grandeur; it has been confused with fame and ambition. But true glory is a private and discreet virtue, and is only fully realized in solitariness.' He had known military glory: from the danger and squalor of the front line he was able to write in a private letter: 'If I were free today, I'm almost sure I should be compelled by every impulse within me to join this adventure,' but when, on 11 November 1918, as a bell in Canterbury pealed for victory and with heart numb and mind dismayed, he turned to the fields 'and walked away from all human contacts', it was towards glory that he walked, glory 'realized in solitariness' and finally achieved in his last years among the hills and moors, within hearing of the millstream of his childhood, the setting of *The Innocent Eye*.

Nothing became him better than his terribly painful end – the young man in France would have suffered less from gas or shell-burst, but courage in facing agony and death had not diminished in the fifty years that had passed, and the deep sense of glory which he had first felt as a lonely boy in the streets of Leeds was maintained through the savage suffering at the end. He looked at death with the same clear, shrewd, gentle eyes he turned on a friend. In the last months of his life he had been planning, after yet one more operation, to go and stay awhile in a small cottage which I had come to possess in Anacapri, and he wrote to me more frequently and intimately during that last period than ever before. 'I am haunted by the thought of Freud and did you read Jones's life of him? I have exactly the same condition in the same place ... I don't think I worry about my own remaining years – it is only the thought of leaving Ludo alone, though there again I could comfort myself with the thought that we have such devoted children.' Then suddenly the last letter came, the last he ever wrote, to say that he must abandon the idea of Anacapri – 'I had built up the Lourdes spirit and there was going to be a miraculous cure.'

The reference to Lourdes from this most Christian of unbelievers came as no surprise. Hadn't he written in the autobiographies of another essential aspect of his idea of glory? 'At certain moments the individual is carried beyond his rational self, on to another ethical plane, where his actions are judged by new standards. The impulse which moves him to irrational action I have called the sense of glory.'

To Gayle on our future
Feb. 1992

1

THE further back we research the past, the more the 'documents in the case' accumulate and the more reluctant we feel to open their pages, to disturb the dust. To a stranger they would appear innocuous enough – a diary in pencil, an African's letter scribbled probably by a public letter-writer according to a recognized formula, a scrap of indecipherable writing found in a Vai hut – but one is never certain what vivid memory may not revive, and the longer life goes on the more surely one finds that old memories will be painful, and hung around with associations, like the cobwebs in a room whose occupant left many years ago 'under a cloud'. And yet in 1935 I rashly proposed to make memory the very subject of my next book, *Journey Without Maps*, for forty-five years ago I could play happily enough even with the darkest and furthest memories of childhood – they were not so dark or so distant as they seem to me today.

It was a period when 'young authors' were inclined to make uncomfortable journeys in search of bizarre material – Peter Fleming to Brazil and Manchuria, Evelyn Waugh to British Guiana and Ethiopia. Europe seemed to have the whole future; Europe could wait. In 1940 it was a shock to realize that the door to Europe was closed – perhaps for ever – and that I had more memories of Mexico and Liberia than of France. As for Italy, one night in Naples had been for me the sum.

We were a generation brought up on adventure stories who had missed the enormous disillusionment of the First World War, so we went looking for adventure, much as in the summer of 1940 I used to spend Saturday nights in Southend, looking for an air raid, with little thought that in a few months I should have my fill of them in London day and night.

I had never been out of Europe; I had not very often been outside England, and to choose Liberia and to involve my cousin Barbara, a twenty-three-year-old girl, in the adventure was, to say the least, rash. My invitation to her can only be excused because I had drunk too much champagne at my brother Hugh's wedding, and I never expected her to accept. I did my best afterwards to discourage her. I sent her a League of Nations report on conditions in the interior, on the unchecked diseases, on Colonel Davis's savage campaign against the Kru tribes and on President King's private export of slaves to Fernando Po. The report had rendered me nervous, and Sir Harry Johnston's account of his travels in the interior, his endless difficulties with carriers, whom he could only take from village to village, made me realize that perhaps Liberia was a tough venture for a young man who had never been further than Athens on an Hellenic cruise. I felt the need of a companion, but I panicked, when the champagne had worn off, at my choice.

Luckily for me my cousin appeared unmoved by the reading material I sent her, for she proved as good a companion as the circumstances allowed, and I shudder to think of the quarrels I would have had with a companion of the same sex after exhaustion had set in, all the arguments, the indecisions ... My cousin left all decisions to me and never criticized me when I made the wrong one, and because of the difference of sex we were both forced to control our irritated nerves. Towards the end we would lapse into long silences, but they were infinitely preferable to raised voices. Only in one thing did she disappoint me – she wrote a book. However, her generosity was apparent even there, for she waited several years, until my own book had appeared (and disappeared, for it was suppressed almost immediately by the threat of the libel action from the unknown doctor) before she published her *Land Benighted*. I hadn't even realized that she was making notes, I was so busy on my own.

It had seemed simple, before I set out, to write a travel book, but when I returned and was faced with my material I had a moment of despair and wished to abandon the project. A diary written in pencil with increasing fatigue and running to less than eighty quarto pages of a loose-leaf notebook, the piece of paper on which I kept the accounts of my carriers' advances (the headman had usually drawn ninepence, most of the others threepence at a time only), a few illiterate notes from Mr Wordsworth, the District Commissioner of Tapee-Ta, and from Colonel Elwood Davis, the Commander of the Liberian Frontier Force, some political literature from Monrovia, a selection of Liberian newspapers, a few Buzie swords and musical instruments long lost (they seemed so valuable then), a number of photographs taken with an old vest-pocket Kodak, and memories, memories chiefly of rats, of frustration, and of a deeper boredom on the long forest trek than I had ever experienced before – how was I, out of all this, to make a book? But I had already spent on the journey the three hundred and fifty pounds which my publishers had advanced to me, and I could earn no more until the book was written.

The problem to be solved was mainly a problem of form. I was haunted by the awful tedium of A to Z. This book could not be written in the manner of a European tour; there was no architecture to describe, no famous statuary; nor was it a political book in the sense that Gide's *Voyage au Congo* was political, nor a book of adventure like those of Peter Fleming – if this was an adventure it was only a subjective adventure, three months of virtual silence, of 'being out of touch'. This thought gave me a clue to the form I needed. The account of a journey – a slow footsore journey into an interior literally unknown – was only of interest if it paralleled another journey. It would lose the triviality of a personal travel diary only if it became more completely personal. It is a disadvantage to have an 'I' who is not a fictional figure, and the only way to deal with 'I' was to make him an abstraction. To all intents I eliminated my companion of the journey and supported the uneventful record with memories, dreams, word-associations: if the book in one sense became more personal, the journey became more general – if Jung is to be believed we share our dreams. It was not when I come to think of it a very new form for me. The idea of A to Z has always scared me, like the thought in childhood of the long summer term, and I have always broken the continuity of a story with the memories of my chief character, just as I was now to break the continuity of the journey with the memories of 'I'.

More than forty years have passed since I wrote the book and I cannot bring myself to reread it as a whole (the last time I read it through was in 1945 after I had returned from my wartime sojourn in shabby Freetown, when I wrote a preface for a new edition to mark a change of attitude). It has occurred to me now to make a small psychological experiment and to see how one particular experience, recorded in my diary, was changed when I came to write the book, and how it appeared to a third party, my cousin – three parties because surely 'I' the diarist and 'I' the writer were distinct persons.

Towards the end of the journey, between Ganta and the sea, I became ill. I had seldom walked for less than fifteen miles in a day, and I was unused to the climate – stiflingly hot during the hours of sun and sometimes at night in a native hut cold enough for two blankets. I was forced to press on because the rains were threatening and if they broke central Liberia would become impassable. My cousin did not realize the need of haste and thought these forced marches were a form of nerves connected with my sickness. One night on arriving at a village I collapsed.

This is what I find in my diary:

A long tiring day to Zigi's Town. Started at 6.45. Took eight and a half hours solid trek. Ducks on a pond. My temperature up and went to bed. It went up a bit more at bedtime and I sweated all night naked between the blankets. Took violent dose for my stomach. A thunderstorm. Shadow on the mosquito-net, the dim hurricane lamp, the empty whisky bottle on the chop box.

Not much there, less really than in the briefer record next day: 'Last tin of biscuits, last tin of milk, last piece of bread.'

With Barbara's permission I print now what my cousin made of that unpleasant night.

Graham was tottering as we got to Zigi's Town; he was staggering as though he was a little drunk. He could get no rest from the carriers while he was up, for they came to him as usual with all their troubles, but I managed to persuade him to go to bed. I took his temperature and it was very high. I gave him plenty of whisky and Epsom salts, and covered him with blankets, hoping that I was doing the right thing.

I had supper by myself while the thunder roared; and the boys served me with grave faces. The same thought was in all our minds. Graham would die. I never doubted it for a minute. He looked like a dead man already. The stormy atmosphere made my head ache and the men quarrelsome. I could hear them snapping at each other, but I left them alone.

I took Graham's temperature again, and it had gone up. I felt quite calm at the thought of Graham's death. To my own horror I felt unemotional about it. My mind kept telling me that I was really very upset, but actually I was so tired that though I could concentrate easily on the practical side of it all, I was incapable of feeling anything. I worked out quietly how I would have my cousin buried, how I would go down to the coast, to whom I would send telegrams. I had no fear of going on alone, for I realized by this time that with Amedoo I would be perfectly safe. Only one thing worried me in the most extraordinary way. Graham was a Catholic, and into my muddled, weary brain came the thought that I ought to burn candles for him if he died. I could not remember why I should burn candles, but I felt vaguely that his soul would find no peace if I could not do that for him. All night I was troubled by this thought. It seemed to me desperately important.

It was a pleasant little village. I walked through it, enjoying, as I always did, the friendliness of the natives. Laminah and Mark came with me, but I told them I was not in the mood to talk, and with graceful understanding they immediately dropped ten yards behind me, giving me the feeling that I was alone and yet showing me that they were there to protect me. Amedoo stayed within hearing distance of Graham. They were doing their best to try to make me understand that whatever happened, they would never forget that they had given their word in Freetown that they would protect us to the end of the journey. It was only that evening in Zigi's Town that I realized how much I cared for our boys, and what valuable and loyal friends they were.

The storm broke and I hurried back to my hut as the rains came down. It was a big hut with two rooms, and before I went to bed I went and had another look at Graham. He was in a restless doze, muttering to himself, and soaked in perspiration.

To my great surprise Graham was not dead in the morning. I was quite amazed, and gazed at him for some moments without speaking. I went into his room expecting to see him either delirious or gasping out his last few breaths, and I found him up and dressed. He looked terrible. A kind of horrid death's head grinned at me. His cheeks had sunk in, there were black smudges under his eyes, and his scrubby beard added nothing of beauty to the general rather seedy effect. His expression, however, was more normal, for the uncanny harsh light that had glowed in his eyes the day before had disappeared. I took his temperature and it was very subnormal.

'We must go on quickly,' he said. 'I'm all right again.'

'Won't you rest just one day?' I asked.

'No,' said Graham impatiently. 'We must get down to the coast.'

The coast. My cousin was craving to get down to the coast as a pilgrim might crave to get to a holy city.

I went out and got hold of the boys and told them to find out how far it was to Grand Bassa. Tommy, I thought, might know, or perhaps the chief.

'Two days,' said Mark.

'Two weeks,' said Laminah.

'Oh, my God,' I said.

I asked the headman, 'How far Grand Bassa? Ask chief.'

He gave his lovely vague smile, and said softly, 'Too far.' And all round me like an angry chorus carriers echoed, 'Too far, too far.'

I must admit that my cousin's account is more in keeping with an adventure story than my few lines in pencil, for the absurd journey, which seemed so boring at the time, was in retrospect an adventure for a man of thirty-one who had never been in Africa before and a girl of twenty-three. And how did the second reflective 'I' recount this crisis of the journey? I find to my surprise, for now I have few memories of that night, that 'I' shared his cousin's fear. Here is the passage from my book:

I remember nothing of the trek to Zigi's Town and very little of the succeeding days. I was so exhausted that I couldn't write more than a few lines in my diary: I hope never to be so tired again. I retain an impression of continuous forest, occasional hills emerging above the bush so that we could catch a glimpse on either side of the great whale-backed forests driving to the sea. Outside Zigi's Town there was a stream trickling down the slope and a few ducks with a curiously English air about them. I remember trying to sit down, but immediately having to deal with the town chief over food for the carriers, trying to sit down again and rising to look for threepenny-bits* the cook needed for buying a chicken, trying to sit down and being forced to stand up again to dress a carrier's sores. I couldn't stand any more of it; I swallowed two tablespoons of Epsom in a cup of strong tea (we had finished our tinned milk long ago) and left my cousin to deal with anything else that turned up. My temperature was high. I swallowed twenty grains of quinine with a glass of whisky, took off my clothes, wrapped myself in blankets under the mosquito-net and tried to sleep.

A thunderstorm came up. It was the third storm we'd had in a few days; there wasn't any time to lose if we were to reach the Coast, and I lay in the dark as scared as I have ever been. There were no rats, at any

---

*All our money was in threepenny-bits because the Liberian carriers recognized no higher currency. They also demanded Queen Victoria's head on the pieces. The only smaller change were Liberian 'irons' – strips of metal.

196

rate, but I caught a jigger under my toe when I crawled out to dry myself. I was sweating as if I had influenza; I couldn't keep dry for more than fifteen seconds. The hurricane lamp I left burning low on an up-ended chop box and beside it an old whisky bottle full of warm filtered water. I kept remembering Van Gogh at Bolahun burnt out with fever. He said you had to lie up for at least a week: there wasn't any danger in malaria if you lay up long enough; but I couldn't bear the thought of staying a week here, another seven days away from Grand Bassa. Malaria or not, I'd got to go on next day and I was afraid.

The fever would not let me sleep at all, but by the early morning it was sweated out of me. My temperature was a long way below normal, but the worst boredom of the trek for the time being was over. I had made a discovery during the night which interested me. I had discovered in myself a passionate interest in living. I had always assumed before, as a matter of course, that death was desirable.

It seemed that night an important discovery. It was like a conversion, and I had never experienced a conversion before. (I had not been converted to a religious faith. I had been convinced by specific arguments in the probability of its creed.) If the experience had not been so new to me, I should have known that conversions don't last, or if they last at all it is only as a little sediment at the bottom of the brain. Perhaps the sediment has value, the memory of a conversion may have some force in an emergency; I may be able to strengthen myself with the intellectual idea that once in Zigi's Town I had been completely convinced of the beauty and desirability of the mere act of living.

Did I learn the lesson of Zigi's Town? I doubt it.

It used to be a habit with Victorian novelists to give brief résumés of the future fate of their minor characters. I can do little in that way and the little I can do is not very cheering – no happy marriages or births. Six years later, back in wartime Freetown, I one day encountered Laminah – he was no longer 'a small boy' in shorts wearing a woollen cap with a scarlet bobble on it. War had brought him prosperity and dignity. I had already searched in vain for traces of Amedoo, my impeccable headboy, who had made the journey possible, but it was about the old cook I inquired first, whose name I could never remember, whom I saw only as a figure in a long white robe that slowly disintegrated as he strode through the bush, kitchen knife in hand. He must be very old indeed, I thought, by now, if still alive. 'Old cook,' Laminah replied, rocking with laughter at the irony of life, 'old cook, he fine, but Amedoo he dead.'

Another character is dead too: the mysterious German whom the District Commissioner of Kailahun on the Sierra Leone border mistook for a messenger from Liberia come to guide us to Bolahun.

It was a long while before anyone thought of asking whether he was the Liberian messenger. He wasn't, the messenger had disappeared from Kailahun, the stranger was a German. He wanted a bed; he had dropped in to Kailahun as casually as if it were a German village where he would be sure to find an inn. He had a bland secretive innocence; he had come from the Republic and he was going back to the Republic; he gave no indication of why he had come or why he was going or what he was doing in Africa at all.

I took him for a prospector, but it turned out later that he was concerned with nothing so material as gold or diamonds. He was just learning. He sat back in his chair, seeming to pay no attention to anyone; when he was asked a question, he gave a tiny laugh (you thought: I have asked something very foolish, very superficial), and gave no answer until later, when you had forgotten the question. He was young in spite of his beard; he had an aristocratic air in spite of his beachcomber's dress, and he was wiser than any of us. He was the only one who knew exactly what it was he wished to learn, who knew the exact extent of his ignorance. He could speak Mende; he was picking up Buzie; and he had a few words of Pelle: it took time.

Years were to pass before I learned his fate and the news arrived as ambiguously as he had done. It was 1955 and I was sitting up late in a hotel room in Cracow drinking with a Polish novelist and talking with caution. Gomulka had not yet come to power – it was still a Stalinist Poland. I knew nobody in Cracow except the novelist. We were both taken aback by a rap on the door and the same notion of the secret police came to both our minds. The man who came in was an obvious German. He looked from one to another of us and asked, 'Mr Greene?'

'Yes?'

'You knew my brother,' he said, 'in Liberia.'

I searched my memory in vain. 'He walked with you to Bolahun.'

Then I remembered and asked his whereabouts now. 'He was killed in 1943 on the Russian front.'

Politeness forced me, unwilling though I was, to ask the stranger to join us over my flask of whisky; since I had visited Auschwitz and seen those long halls filled with women's hair and children's toys and old suitcases marked with the names and addresses of the dead, all the economy of a German murder camp, I had no desire to sit at a table with a German in Poland. My companion, who had been a Polish officer and afterwards a member of the underground army, cared for the German's company even less than I. And he proved as ambiguous as his brother. We had been that day to Zakopane, I told him, and he remarked on the beauty of the place, 'where I stayed for two or three years during the war', as casually as an Englishman might speak of his residence in Switzerland. My companion and I were both aware that it was not often that a German soldier stationed in Poland stayed so long in one place, but there were other employments than the army for Germans at that period . . .

I asked, 'Why have you come back?'

'I am painting pictures,' he said.

2

Four and a half years of watching films several times a week . . . I can hardly believe in that life of the distant thirties now, a way of life which I adopted quite voluntarily from a sense of fun. More than four hundred films – and I suppose there would have been many, many more if I had not suffered during the same period from other obsessions – four novels had to be written, not to speak of a travel book which took me away for months to Mexico, far from the Pleasure Dome – all those Empires and Odeons of a luxury and an extravagance which we shall never see again. How, I find myself wondering, could I possibly have written all those film reviews? And yet I remember opening the envelopes, which contained the gilded cards of invitation for the morning press performances (mornings when I should have been struggling with other work), with a sense of curiosity and anticipation. Those films were an escape – escape from that hellish problem of construction in Chapter Six, from the secondary character who obstinately refused to come alive, escape for an hour and a half from the melancholy which falls inexorably round the novelist when he has lived for too many months on end in his private world.

The idea of reviewing films came to me at a cocktail party after the dangerous third martini. I was talking to Derek Verschoyle, the Literary Editor of the *Spectator*. The *Spectator* had hitherto neglected films and I suggested to him I should fill the gap – I thought in the unlikely event of his accepting my offer it might be fun for two or three weeks. I never imagined it would remain fun for four and a half years and only end in a different world, a world at war. Until I came to reread the notices the other day I thought they abruptly ended with my review of *Young Mr Lincoln*. If there is something a little absentminded about that review, it is because, just as I began to write it on the morning of 3 September 1939, the first air-raid siren of the war sounded and I laid the review aside so as to make notes from my high Hampstead lodging on the destruction of London below. 'Woman passes with dog on lead,' I noted, 'and pauses by lamp-post.' Then the all-clear sounded and I returned to Henry Fonda.

Those were not the first film reviews I wrote. At Oxford I had appointed myself film critic of the *Oxford Outlook*, a literary magazine which appeared once a term and which I edited. *Warning Shadows*, *Brumes d'Automne*, *The Student of Prague* – these are the silent films of the twenties of which I can remember whole scenes still. I was a passionate reader of *Close Up* which was edited by Kenneth Macpherson and Bryher and published from a *château* in Switzerland. Marc Allégret was the Paris Correspondent and Pudovkin contributed articles on montage. I was horrified by the arrival of 'talkies' (it seemed the end of film as an art form), just as later I regarded colour with justifiable suspicion. 'Technicolor,' I wrote in 1935, 'plays havoc with the women's faces; they all, young and old, have the same healthy weather-beaten skins.' Curiously enough it was a detective story with Chester Morris which converted me to the talkies – for the first time in that picture I was aware of *selected* sounds; until then every shoe had squeaked and every door-handle had creaked. I notice that the forgotten film *Becky Sharp* gave me even a certain hope for colour.

Rereading those reviews of more than forty years ago I find many prejudices which are modified now only by the sense of nostalgia. I had distinct reservations about Greta Garbo whom

I compared to a beautiful Arab mare, and Hitchcock's 'inadequate sense of reality' irritated me and still does – how inexcusably he spoilt *The Thirty-Nine Steps*. I still believe I was right (whatever Monsieur Truffaut may say) when I wrote: 'His films consist of a series of small "amusing" melodramatic situations: the murderer's button dropped on the baccarat board; the strangled organist's hands prolonging the notes in the empty church ... very perfunctorily he builds up to these tricky situations (paying no attention on the way to inconsistencies, loose ends, psychological absurdities) and then drops them: they mean nothing: they lead to nothing.'

The thirties too were a period of 'respectable' film biographies – Rhodes, Zola, Pasteur, Parnell and the like – and of historical romances which only came to a certain comic life in the hands of Cecil B. de Mille (Richard Coeur de Lion was married to Berengaria according to the rites of the Anglican Church). I preferred the Westerns, the crime films, the farces, the frankly commercial, and I am glad to see that in reviewing one of these forgotten commercial films I gave a warm welcome to a new star, Ingrid Bergman – 'What star before has made her first appearance on the international screen with a highlight gleaming on her nose-tip?'

There were dangers, I was to discover, in film-reviewing. On one occasion I opened a letter to find a piece of shit enclosed. I have always – though probably incorrectly – believed that it was a piece of aristocratic shit, for I had made cruel fun a little while before of a certain French marquis who had made a documentary film in which he played a rather heroic role. Thirty years later in Paris at a dinner of the *haute bourgeoisie* I sat opposite him and was charmed by his conversation. I longed to ask him the truth, but I was daunted by the furniture. Then, of course, there was the Shirley Temple libel action. The review of *Wee Willie Winkie* which set Twentieth Century-Fox alight cannot be found here for obvious reasons. I kept on my bathroom wall, until a bomb removed the wall, the statement of claim – that I had accused Twentieth Century-Fox of 'procuring' Miss Temple 'for immoral purposes' (I had suggested that she had a certain adroit coquetry which appealed to middle-aged men). Lord Hewart, the Lord Chief Justice, sent the papers in the case to the Director of Public Prosecutions, so that ever since that time I have been traceable on the files of Scotland Yard. The case appeared before the King's Bench on 22 March 1938, with myself *in absentia*, and on 23 May 1938, the following account of the hearing appeared among the Law Reports of *The Times*. I was at the time in Mexico on a writing assignment. It is perhaps worth mentioning in connection with the 'beastly publication' that *Night and Day* boasted Elizabeth Bowen as theatre critic, Evelyn Waugh as chief book reviewer, Osbert Lancaster as art critic, and Hugh Casson as architectural critic, not to speak of such regular contributors as Herbert Read, Hugh Kingsmill and Malcolm Muggeridge.

The case appeared as follows in *The Times* Law Reports:

HIGH COURT OF JUSTICE
King's Bench Division

Libel on Miss Shirley Temple: 'A Gross Outrage'
Temple and Others *v.* Night and Day Magazines,
Limited, and Others
Before the Lord Chief Justice

A settlement was announced of this libel action which was brought by Miss Shirley Jane Temple, the child actress (by Mr Roy Simmonds, her next friend), Twentieth Century-Fox Film Corporation, of New York, and Twentieth Century-Fox Film Company, Limited, of Berners Street, W., against Night and Day Magazines, Limited, and Mr Graham Greene, of St Martin's Lane, W.C., Hazell, Watson and Viney, Limited, printers, of Long Acre, W.C., and Messrs Chatto and Windus, publishers, of Chandos Street, W.C., in respect of an article written by Mr Greene and published in the issue of the magazine *Night and Day* dated October 28, 1937.

Sir Patrick Hastings, KC, and Mr G. O. Slade appeared for the plaintiffs; Mr Valentine Holmes for all the defendants except Hazell, Watson and Viney, Limited, who were represented by Mr Theobald Mathew.

Sir Patrick Hastings, in announcing the settlement, by which it was agreed that Miss Shirley Temple was to receive £2,000, the film corporation £1,000 and the film company £500, stated that the first defendants were the proprietors of the magazine *Night and Day*, which was published in London. It was only right to say that the two last defendants, the printers and publishers, were firms of the utmost respectability and highest reputation, and were innocently responsible in the matter.

The plaintiff, Miss Shirley Temple, a child of nine years, has a world-wide reputation as an artist in films. The two plaintiff companies produced her in a film called *Wee Willie Winkie*, based on Rudyard Kipling's story.

On October 28 last year Night and Day Magazines, Limited, published an article written by Mr Graham Greene. In his (counsel's) view it was one of the most horrible libels that one could well imagine. Obviously he would not read it all – it was better that he should not – but a glance at the statement of claim, where a poster was set out, was quite sufficient to show the nature of the libel written about this child.

This beastly publication, said counsel, was written, and it was right to say that every respectable distributor in London refused to be a party to selling it. Notwithstanding that, the magazine company, with the object no doubt of increasing the sale, proceeded to advertise the fact that it had been banned.

Shirley Temple was an American and lived in America. If she had been in England and the publication in America it would have been right for the American Courts to have taken notice of it. It was equally right that, the position being reversed, her friends in America should know that the Courts here took notice of such a publication.

SHOULD NOT BE TREATED LIGHTLY

Money was no object in this case. The child had a very large income and the two film companies were wealthy concerns. It was realized, however, that the matter should not be treated lightly. The defendants had paid the film companies £1,000 and £500 respectively, and that money would be disposed of in a charitable way. With regard to the child, she would be paid £2,000. There would also be an order for the taxation of costs.

In any view, said counsel, it was such a beastly libel to have written that if it had been a question of money it would have been difficult to say what would be an appropriate amount to arrive at.

Miss Shirley Temple probably knew nothing of the article, and it was undesirable that she should be brought to England to fight the action. In his (counsel's) opinion the settlement was a proper one in the circumstances.

Mr Valentine Holmes informed his Lordship that the magazine *Night and Day* had ceased publication. He desired, on behalf of his clients, to express the deepest apology to Miss Temple for the pain which certainly would have been caused to her by the article if she had read it. He also apologized to the two film companies for the suggestion that they would produce and distribute a film of the character indicated by the article. There was no justification for the criticism of the film,

203

which, his clients instructed him, was one which anybody could take their children to see. He also apologized on behalf of Mr Graham Greene. So far as the publishers of the magazine were concerned, they did not see the article before publication.

His Lordship – Who is the author of this article?

Mr Holmes – Mr Graham Greene.

His Lordship – Is he within the jurisdiction?

Mr Holmes – I am afraid I do not know, my Lord.

Mr Theobald Mathew, on behalf of the printers, said that they recognized that the article was one which ought never to have been published. The fact that the film had already been licensed for universal exhibition refuted the charges which had been made in the article. The printers welcomed the opportunity of making any amends in their power.

His Lordship – Can you tell me where Mr Greene is?

Mr Mathew – I have no information on the subject.

His Lordship – This libel is simply a gross outrage, and I will take care to see that suitable attention is directed to it. In the meantime I assent to the settlement on the terms which have been disclosed, and the record will be withdrawn.

From film-reviewing it was only a small step to scriptwriting. That also was a danger, but a necessary one as I now had a wife and two children to support and I remained in debt to my publishers until the war came. I had persistently attacked the films made by Alexander Korda and perhaps he became curious to meet his enemy. He asked my agent to bring me to Denham Film Studios and when we were alone he asked if I had any film story in mind. I had none, so I began to improvise a thriller – early morning on Platform 1 at Paddington, the platform empty, except for one man who is waiting for the last train from Wales. From below his raincoat a trickle of blood forms a pool on the platform.

'Yes? And then?'

'It would take too long to tell you the whole plot – and the idea needs a lot more working out.'

I left Denham half an hour later to work for eight weeks on what seemed an extravagant salary, and the worst and least successful of Korda's productions thus began (all I can remember is the title, *The Green Cockatoo*). So too began our friendship which endured and deepened till his death, in spite of my reviews which remained unfavourable. There was never a man who bore less malice, and I think of him with affection – even love – as the only film producer I have ever known with whom I could spend days and nights of conversation without so much as mentioning the cinema. Years later, after the war was over, I wrote two screenplays for Korda and Carol Reed, *The Fallen Idol* and *The Third Man*, and I hope they atoned a little for the prentice scripts.

If I had remained a film critic, the brief comic experience which I had then of Hollywood might have been of lasting value to me, for I learned at first hand what a director may have to endure at the hands of a producer. (One of the difficult tasks of a critic is to assign his praise or blame to the right quarter.)

David Selznick, famous for having produced one of the world's top-grossing films, *Gone with the Wind*, held the American rights in *The Third Man* and, by the terms of the contract with Korda, the director was bound to consult him about the script sixty days before shooting began. So Carol Reed, who was directing the film, and I journeyed west. Our first meeting with Selznick at La Jolla in California promised badly, and the dialogue remains as fresh in my mind as the day when it was spoken. After a brief greeting he got down to serious discussion. He said, 'I don't like the title.'

'No? We thought . . .'

'Listen, boys, who the hell is going to a film called *The Third Man*?'

'Well,' I said, 'it's a simple title. It's easily remembered.'

Selznick shook his head reproachfully. 'You can do better than that, Graham,' he said, using my Christian name with a readiness I was not prepared for. 'You are a writer. A good writer. I'm no writer, but you are. Now what we want – it's not right, mind you, of course it's not right, I'm not saying it's right, but then I'm no writer and you are, what we want is something like *Night in Vienna*, a title which will bring them in.'

'Graham and I will think about it,' Carol Reed interrupted with haste. It was a phrase I was to hear Reed frequently repeat, for the Korda contract had omitted to state that the director was under any obligation to accept Selznick's advice. Reed during the days that followed, like an admirable stonewaller, blocked every ball.

We passed on to Selznick's view of the story.

'It won't do, boys,' he said, 'it won't do. It's sheer buggery.'

'Buggery?'

'It's what you learn in your English schools.'

'I don't understand.'

'This guy comes to Vienna looking for his friend. He finds his friend's dead. Right? Why doesn't he go home then?'

After all the months of writing, his destructive view of the whole venture left me speechless. He shook his grey head at me. 'It's just buggery, boy.'

I began weakly to argue. I said, 'But this character – he has a motive of revenge. He has been beaten up by a military policeman.' I played a last card. 'Within twenty-four hours he's in love with Harry Lime's girl.'

Selznick shook his head sadly. 'Why didn't he go home before that?'

That, I think, was the end of the first day's conference. Selznick removed to Hollywood and we followed him – to a luxurious suite in Santa Monica, once the home of Hearst's film-star mistress. During the conference which followed I remember there were times when there seemed to be a kind of grim reason in Selznick's criticisms – surely here perhaps there *was* a fault in 'continuity', I hadn't properly 'established' this or that. (I would forget momentarily the lesson which I had learned as a film critic – that to 'establish' something is almost invariably wrong and that 'continuity' is often the enemy of life. Jean Cocteau has even argued that the mistakes of continuity belong to the unconscious poetry of a film.) A secretary sat by Selznick's side with her pencil poised. When I was on the point of agreement Carol Reed would quickly interrupt – 'Graham and I will think about it.'

There was one conference which I remember in particular because it was the last before we were due to return to England. The secretary had made forty pages of notes by this time, but she had been unable to record one definite concession on our side. The conference began as usual about 10.30 p.m. and finished after 4 a.m. Always by the time we reached Santa Monica dawn would be touching the Pacific.

'There's something I don't understand in this script, Graham.

206

Why the hell does Harry Lime . . .?' He described some extraordinary action on Lime's part.

'But he doesn't,' I said.

Selznick looked at me for a moment in silent amazement. 'Christ, boys,' he said, 'I'm thinking of a different script.'

He lay down on his sofa and crunched a benzedrine. In ten minutes he was as fresh as ever, unlike ourselves.

I look back on David Selznick now with affection. The forty pages of notes remained unopened in Reed's files, and since the film has proved a success, I suspect Selznick forgot that the criticisms had ever been made. Indeed, when next I was in New York he invited me to lunch to discuss a project. He said, 'Graham, I've got a great idea for a film. It's just made for you.'

I had been careful on this occasion not to take a third martini.

'The life of St Mary Magdalene,' he said.

'I'm sorry,' I said, 'no. It's not really in my line.'

He didn't try to argue. 'I have another idea,' he said. 'It will appeal to you as a Catholic. You know how next year they have what's called the Holy Year in Rome. Well, I want to make a picture called *The Unholy Year*. It will show all the commercial rackets that go on, the crooks . . .'

'An interesting notion,' I said.

'We'll shoot it in the Vatican.'

'I doubt if they will give you permission for that.'

'Oh sure they will,' he said. 'You see, we'll write in one Good Character.'

(I am reminded by this story of another memorable lunch in a suite at the Dorchester when Sam Zimbalist asked me if I would revise the last part of a script which had been prepared for a remake of *Ben Hur*. 'You see,' he said, 'we find a kind of anticlimax after the Crucifixion.')

Those indeed were the days. I little knew that the reign of Kubla Khan was nearly over and that the Pleasure Dome would soon be converted into an enormous bingo hall, which would provide quite other dreams to housewives than had the Odeons and the Empires. I had regretted the silent films when the talkies moved in and I had regretted black and white when Technicolor washed across the screen. So today, watching the latest soft-porn film, I sometimes long for those dead thirties, for

207

Cecil B. de Mille and his Crusaders, for the days when almost anything was likely to happen.

3

I had been temporarily saved from the danger of destitution by *Stamboul Train*, but I had squandered my reserves by writing *It's a Battlefield* which in spite of the praise from Ezra Pound and V. S. Pritchett remained almost unread. Second to it in public indifference came *England Made Me*. It was urgently necessary to repeat, if I could somehow manage it, the success of my first 'thriller', but the decision was not, all the same, entirely a question of money. I have always enjoyed reading melodrama, and I enjoy writing it. An early hero of mine was John Buchan, but when I re-opened his books I found I could no longer get the same pleasure from the adventures of Richard Hannay. More than the dialogue and the situation had dated: the moral climate was no longer that of my boyhood. Patriotism had lost its appeal, even for a schoolboy, at Passchendaele, and the Empire brought first to mind the Beaverbrook Crusader, while it was difficult, during the years of the Depression, to believe in the high purposes of the City of London or of the British Constitution. The hunger-marchers seemed more real than the politicians. It was no longer a Buchan world. The hunted man of *A Gun for Sale*,* which I now began to write, was Raven not Hannay; a man out to revenge himself for all the dirty tricks of life, not to save his country.

The subject: I cannot remember now the name or nature of the commission which in the thirties inquired into the private manufacture and sale of armaments. Did I attend some of the hearings because I was already writing *A Gun for Sale* or did the idea come to me after attending them? My chief memory of the hearings is the politeness and feebleness of the cross-examination. Some great firms were concerned and over and over again counsel found that essential papers were missing or had not been brought to court. A search of course would be made . . . there was a relaxed air of *mañana*. About the same time some-

* In the U.S.A. the title was *This Gun for Hire*, my American publisher being a stickler for accuracy.

body had written the life of Sir Basil Zaharoff, a more plausible villain for those days than the man in Buchan's *The Thirty-Nine Steps* who could 'hood his eyes like a hawk'. Sir Marcus in *A Gun for Sale* is, of course, not Sir Basil, but the family resemblance is plain. I had not met Sir Marcus's agent Mr Davis nor did I ever meet him, but after the book was written I did, for the only time in my life, encounter a former traveller in armaments. No one could have been less like Mr Davis.

I was one of two passengers on a small plane flying from Riga to Tallinn, then the capital of the independent Estonian Republic. (I was there for no reason except escape to somewhere new.) I happened to be reading a novel of Henry James and when I glanced at my fellow passenger I saw that he too was absorbing James in the same small Macmillan edition. In the thirties it was more rare than it is today to find a fellow devotee of James. Our eyes went to each other's books and we immediately struck up an acquaintance.

He was a man considerably older than myself and he was serving as British Consul at Tallinn. Since he was not very busy and a bachelor – indeed he struck me as a man rather scared of women – we spent a good deal of time together during those periods when I was not vainly searching for a brothel which had been run by the same family in the same house for three hundred years – a picturesque feature of the little capital on no account to be missed, according to my informant, Baroness Budberg, though, alas, I failed to find it. (When I asked the help of a waiter in Tallinn's most elegant hotel, patronized by the Diplomatic Corps, he was puzzled by my antiquarian interest. 'But there is nothing of that kind which we cannot arrange for you here,' he said.)

My new friend had travelled in armaments – for Beardmore I think – after the First World War. He was surely unique among armaments salesmen, for I doubt if any of his colleagues could have claimed to be a former Anglican clergyman. When the Great War started he became an army chaplain. Before it ended he was converted to Catholicism and was about to be received into the Roman Church by the Archbishop of Zagreb when an Austrian air raid interrupted things and the Archbishop fled to the cellar. When the war was over his conversion was consummated, and he was left without a job. For want of anything better he became an armaments salesman. He was a very gentle, very solitary man, in whom James might well have discovered a character, in spite of his bizarre past (James would have wrapped it in folds of ambiguity) – someone a little like Ralph Touchett in *The Portrait of a Lady*, the novel I was reading in the plane from Riga. He received something like six hundred pounds a year as Consul, but in those days the cost of living in Tallinn was extraordinarily low. He had a little flat in the capital, with a daily woman to look after it, and a small wooden dacha in the country, and he was still able to leave half his income in England with his mother. For a fortnight, thanks to Henry James, we were close friends. Afterwards? I never knew what happened. He must have lost his home when the Russians moved in. It seemed hardly a danger in those days – our eyes were on Germany.

Out of the blue, more than thirty years later, I received a letter from him. He had remembered our mutual interest in James and now that he had reached the age of eighty he wished to pass on to me his first editions – thus crowning one of the most pleasant chance encounters of my life.

The greater part of *A Gun for Sale* takes place in Nottwich, which I later used again as a background for my play *The Potting Shed*. Nottwich, of course, is Nottingham where, as I have recounted in *A Sort of Life*, I lived for three winter months with a mongrel terrier, working in the evenings as a trainee on the *Nottingham Journal*. I don't know why a certain wry love of Nottingham lodged in my imagination rather as a love of Freetown was to do later. It was the furthest north I had ever been, the first strange city in which I had made a home, alone, without friends.

The main character in the novel, Raven the killer, seems to me now a first sketch for Pinkie in *Brighton Rock*. He is a Pinkie who has aged but not grown up. The Pinkies are the real Peter Pans – doomed to be juvenile for a lifetime. They have something of a fallen angel about them, a morality which once belonged to another place. The outlaw of justice always keeps in his heart the sense of justice outraged – *his* crimes have an excuse and yet he is pursued by the Others. The Others have committed worse crimes and flourish. The world is full of Others who wear the masks of Success, of a Happy Family. Whatever crime he may be driven to commit the child who doesn't grow up remains the great champion of justice. 'An eye for an eye.' 'Give them a dose of their own medicine.' As children we have all suffered punishments for faults we have not committed, but the wound has soon healed. With Raven and Pinkie the wound never heals.

If Raven is an older Pinkie, Mather I can imagine to have been trained as a police officer under the Assistant Commissioner of *It's a Battlefield*; a little of his superior's sober temperament has rubbed off on him. He is not, like the Assistant Commissioner, a born bachelor, but I think in time he must have proved a little too square for Anne Crowder with her indiscriminate passion for love.

What can I say of the other characters? Doctor Yogel has something of a certain police doctor near Blackfriars to whom I once went in my youth, terrified that I might be suffering from what used to be called by an ironic euphemism a social disease; he told me not to eat tomatoes, an instruction which I have obeyed to this day. His dingy rooms on the top of a tenement block and his abrupt furtive manner remained a memory which I think contributed to the sketch of Doctor Yogel.

There are certain scenes I like in this book. For example I am a little proud of the air-raid practice in Nottwich which enabled Raven to enter the offices of Sir Marcus. I wrote the scene in 1935 and the National Government had certainly not reached that point of preparation, though such a practice would have been plausible enough four years later. I like too the character of Acky, the unfrocked clergyman, and of his wife – the two old evil characters joined to each other by a selfless love. I had not chosen an Anglican clergyman for the part with any ill intent – I doubted at the time whether such purity of love would seem plausible in a married and excommunicated Catholic priest. I was to draw one later in *The Power and the Glory*, Father José, but as a man I prefer poor Acky. He was not the kind of sinner who has the makings of a saint. His sense of guilt led only to innumerable letters to his bishop, of self-justification or accusation ... He belongs to the same world of wounds and guilt as Raven and Pinkie.

Brighton Rock I began in 1937 as a detective story and continued, I am sometimes tempted to think, as an error of judgement. Until I published this novel I had like any other novelist been sometimes praised for a success, and sometimes condemned with good enough reason as I fumbled at my craft, but now I was discovered to be – detestable term! – a Catholic writer. Catholics began to treat some of my faults too kindly, as though I were a member of a clan and could not be disowned, while some non-Catholic critics seemed to consider that my faith gave me an unfair advantage in some way over my contemporaries. I had become a Catholic in 1926, and all my books, except for the one lamentable volume of verse at Oxford, had been written as a Catholic, but no one had noticed the faith to which I belonged before the publication of *Brighton Rock*. Even today some critics (and critics as a class are seldom more careful of their facts than journalists) refer to the novels written *after* my conversion, making a distinction between the earlier and the later books.

Many times since *Brighton Rock* I have been forced to declare myself not a Catholic writer but a writer who happens to be a Catholic. Newman wrote the last word on 'Catholic literature' in *The Idea of a University*:

I say, from the nature of the case, if Literature is to be made a study of human nature, you cannot have a Christian Literature. It is a contradiction in terms to attempt a sinless literature of sinful man. You may gather together something very great and high, something higher than any Literature ever was; and when you have done so, you will find that it is not Literature at all.

Nevertheless it is true to say that by 1937 the time was ripe for me to use Catholic characters. It takes longer to familiarize oneself with a region of the mind than with a country, but the ideas of my Catholic characters, even their Catholic ideas, were not necessarily mine.

More than ten years had passed since I was received into the Church. At that time I had not been emotionally moved, but only intellectually convinced; I was in the habit of formally practising my religion, going to Mass every Sunday and to Confession perhaps once a month, and in my spare time I read a good deal of theology – sometimes with fascination, sometimes with repulsion, nearly always with interest.

I was still not earning enough with my books to make a living for my family (after the success of my first novel and the spurious temporary sale of *Stamboul Train* each novel added a small quota to the debt I owed my publisher), but reviewing films regularly for the *Spectator* and novels once a fortnight, I could make ends meet. I had recently had two strokes of good fortune, and these enabled me to see a little way ahead – I had received a contract from Korda to write my second film script (and a terrible one it was, based on Galsworthy's short story *The First and Last* – Laurence Olivier and Vivien Leigh, who had much to forgive me, suffered together in the leading parts), and for six months I had acted as joint editor with John Marks of the weekly *Night and Day*. My professional life and my religion were contained in quite separate compartments, and I had no ambition to bring them together. It was 'clumsy life again at her stupid work' which did that; on the one side the socialist persecution of religion in Mexico, and on the other General Franco's attack on Republican Spain, inextricably involved religion in contemporary life.

I think it was under those two influences – and the backward and forward sway of my sympathies – that I began to examine more closely the effect of faith on action. Catholicism was no longer primarily symbolic, a ceremony at an altar with the correct canonical number of candles, with the women in my Chelsea congregation wearing their best hats, nor was it a philosophical page in Father D'Arcy's *Nature of Belief*. It was closer now to death in the afternoon.

A restlessness set in then which has never quite been allayed: a desire to be a spectator of history, history in which I found I was concerned myself. I tried to fly into Bilbao from Toulouse, for my sympathies were more engaged by the Catholic struggle against Franco than with the competing sectarians in Madrid. I carried a letter of recommendation from the Basque Delegation in London to a small café owner in Toulouse who had been breaking the blockade of Bilbao with a two-seater plane. I found him shaving in a corner of his café at six in the morning and handed him the Delegation's dignified letter sealed with scarlet wax, but no amount of official sealing wax would induce him to fly his plane again into Bilbao – Franco's guns on his last flight had proved themselves too accurate for his comfort. With Mexico I was more fortunate, an advance payment for a book on the religious persecution enabled me to leave for Tabasco and Chiapas where the persecution was continuing well away from the tourist areas, and it was in Mexico that I corrected the proofs of *Brighton Rock*.

It was in Mexico too that I discovered some emotional belief, among the empty and ruined churches from which the priests had been excluded, at the secret Masses of Las Casas celebrated without the Sanctus bell, among the swaggering *pistoleros*, but probably emotion had been astir before that, or how was it that a book which I had intended to be a simple detective story should have involved a discussion, too obvious and open for a novel, of the distinction between good-and-evil and right-and-wrong and the mystery of 'the appalling strangeness of the mercy of God' – a mystery that was to be the subject of three more of my novels? The first fifty pages of *Brighton Rock* are all that remain of the detective story; they would irritate me, if I dared to look at them now, for I know I ought to have had the strength of mind to remove them, and to start the story again – however difficult the revisions might have proved – with what is now called Part Two. 'A lost thing could I never find, nor a broken thing mend.'

Some critics have referred to a strange violent 'seedy' region of the mind (why did I ever popularize that last adjective?) which they call Greeneland, and I have sometimes wondered whether they go round the world blinkered. 'This is Indo-China,' I want to exclaim, 'this is Mexico, this is Sierra Leone carefully and accurately described. I have been a newspaper correspondent as well as a novelist. I assure you that the dead child lay in the ditch in just that attitude. In the canal of Phat Diem the bodies stuck out of the water ... ' But I know that argument is useless. They won't believe the world they haven't noticed is like that.

However, the setting of *Brighton Rock* may in part belong to an imaginary geographic region. Though Nelson Place has been

214

cleared away since the war, and the Brighton race gangs were to all intents quashed for ever as a serious menace at Lewes Assizes a little before the date of my novel, and even Sherry's dance hall has vanished, they certainly did exist; there *was* a real slum called Nelson Place, and a man was kidnapped on Brighton front in a broad daylight of the thirties, though not in the same circumstances as Hale, and his body was found somewhere out towards the Downs flung from a car. Colleoni, the gang leader, had his real prototype who had retired by 1938 and lived a gracious Catholic life in one of the Brighton crescents, although I found his name was still law when I demanded entrance by virtue of it to a little London nightclub called The Nest behind Regent Street. (I was later reminded of him when I watched the handsome white-haired American gangster, one of Lucky Luciano's men, spending the quiet evening of his days between the piazza of Capri and the smart bathing pool of the Canzone del Mare restaurant at Marina Piccola.)

All the same I must plead guilty to manufacturing this Brighton of mine as I never manufactured Mexico or Indo-China. There were no living models for these gangsters, nor for the barmaid who so obstinately refused to come alive. I had spent only one night in the company of someone who could have belonged to Pinkie's gang – a man from the Wandsworth dog-tracks whose face had been carved because he was suspected of grassing to the bogies after a killing at the stadium. (He taught me the only professional slang I knew, but one cannot learn a language in one night however long.)

The Brighton authorities proved a little sensitive to the picture I had drawn of their city, and it must have galled them to see my book unwittingly advertised at every sweetstall – 'Buy Brighton Rock' – but the popular success of the book was much more limited than they realized. About eight thousand copies were sold at the time and just lifted me out of debt to my publishers.

Would they have resented the novel even more deeply if they had known that for me to describe Brighton was really a labour of love, not hate? No city before the war, not London, Paris or Oxford, had such a hold on my affections. I knew it first as a child of six when I was sent with an aunt to convalesce after some illness – jaundice, I think. It was then I saw my first film, a silent one of course, and the story captured me for ever: *Sophie of Kravonia*, Anthony Hope's tale of a kitchenmaid who became a queen. When the kitchenmaid rode with her army through the mountains to attack the rebel general who had tried to wrest the throne from her dying husband, her march was accompanied by one old lady on a piano, but the tock-tock-tock of the untuned wires stayed in my memory when other melodies faded, and so has the grey riding habit of the young queen. The Balkans since then have always been to me Kravonia – the area of infinite possibility – and it was through the mountains of Kravonia that I drove many summers later and not through the Carpathians of my atlas. That was the kind of book I always wanted to write: the high romantic tale, capturing us in youth with hopes that prove illusions, to which we return again in age in order to escape the sad reality. *Brighton Rock* was a very poor substitute for Kravonia, like all my books, and yet perhaps it is one of the best I ever wrote.

Why did I exclude so much of the Brighton I really knew from this imaginary Brighton? I had every intention of describing it, but it was as though my characters had taken the Brighton *I* knew into their own consciousness and transformed the whole picture (I have never again felt so much the victim of my inventions). Perhaps their Brighton did exist, but of mine only one character remained, poor hopeless Mr Prewitt, the lawyer, watching with sad envy 'the little typists go by carrying their little cases' (I think no one has remarked the echo of Beatrix Potter in that phrase). It was Mr Prewitt with a difference who had spoken to me one December night more than ten years earlier in a shelter on the sea-front with the thin phosphorescent line of the surf smoothed back by a frosty wind: 'Do you know who I am?' the voice sadly inquired, but I hadn't even seen in the darkness that the shelter had another occupant. 'I'm Old Moore,' it said, naming that anonymous astrologer whose predictions still appear every year. It added, 'I live alone in a basement. I bake my own bread,' and then, humbly, because I hadn't taken its meaning, 'The Almanac, you know, I write the Almanac.'

Chapter 3

1

IT IS a curious experience to read an account of one's own past written by – whom? Surely not by myself. The self of forty years ago is not the self of today and I read my own book, *The Lawless Roads*, as a stranger would. So many incidents in my story have been buried completely in my subconscious: so many I now recall only faintly like moments in a novel which I once read when I was young. And yet *The Lawless Roads* is not a novel, only a personal impression of a small part of Mexico at a particular time, the spring of 1938, shortly after the country had suffered at the hands of President Calles – in the name of revolution – the fiercest persecution of religion anywhere since the reign of Elizabeth. In Tabasco and Chiapas the persecution lingered on. These are all facts, I tell myself. These things really happened to me – in 1937–8 – or at least to that long-dead man who bore the same names on his passport as I do.

Mexico too has changed, though perhaps not in essentials – not in the cruelties, injustices and violence. All successful revolutions, however idealistic, probably betray themselves in time, but the Mexican revolution was phoney from the start. I went back to Mexico City more than a dozen years ago on my way to Havana and drove around the new suburb for the rich built on lava – the most expensive house of all belonged to the Chief of Police. That was a Mexico I could recognize, as I could recognize the extreme poverty a few streets away from the American hotels and the tourist shops. The Mexican Government made a hypocritical pretence of supporting Cuba by allowing a Cubana service between Mexico City and Havana, but it was a one-way service. If you went out it was very hard indeed to get a transit visa to return. This was one method used then to reduce the numbers of American students illegally visiting Cuba – to return to the States they would have to make an expensive round trip via Madrid. There was another inducement not to go. As one passed Immigration a camera flashed – the photograph of every passenger travelling to Havana ended on the CIA or FBI files. With difficulty and much argument I obtained from the Mexican Embassy in Havana a tourist visa for my return through Mexico City, but it was valid for forty-eight hours. The return plane contained only about twenty-four passengers, but it took me three hours to get through Customs and Immigration. (The customs officer made a very diligent search between the leaves of *David Copperfield*.) This was how the Mexican revolutionary government made a pretence of supporting Castro with one hand and helped the United States authorities with the other. During my brief stay a Mexican friend told me, over an evening drink, 'There is nothing you need to change in your book. All is the same.'

I had not meant to write more than this one book, commissioned by a publisher, on the religious persecution. I had no idea, even after I had returned home, that a novel, *The Power and the Glory*, would emerge from my experiences. The proofs of *Brighton Rock*, while I was away in Mexico, had occupied my thoughts, and perhaps the Franco volunteers on the German ship I took back to Europe began a train of ideas which ended in *The Confidential Agent*. Now, of course, when I reread *The Lawless Roads*, I can easily detect many of the characters in *The Power and the Glory*. The old Scotsman, Dr Roberto Fitzpatrick, whom I met in Villahermosa, with his cherished scorpion in a little glass bottle, was the kind of treasure trove that falls to the lucky traveller. In recounting the story of his own life he told me of the kindly disreputable Padre Rey of Panamá with his wife and daughter and the mice – not a scorpion – which he kept in a glass lamp. So it was that the doctor put me on the track of Father José in my novel; perhaps he even showed me the road to Panamá which I was to postpone visiting for nearly forty years, and then was amply rewarded. Above all he presented me with my subject: the protagonist of *The Power and the Glory*. 'I asked about the priest in Chiapas who had fled. "Oh," he said, "he was just what we call a whisky priest." He had taken one of his sons to be baptized but the priest was drunk and would insist on naming the child Brigitta. "He was little loss, poor man."'

But long before the drunken priest another character had

come on board my awful boat in Frontera where my story was to open – the dentist I called Mr Tench, who made his living with gold fillings even in that abandoned little port. In fact he was American and not English. He was married to a Mexican woman, who was some relation to the State Governor, and he came on board to flee from his wife and children. He took refuge in my hotel in Villahermosa – I don't think there was another – but after a few days his family ambushed him in the corridor. I remember him always wearing an old yachting cap, even at meals which he would interrupt if a bone or a piece of gristle stuck in his throat by vomiting promptly and skilfully upon the floor. He would take swigs out of a bottle of olive oil for the sake of his health. His character needed no 'touching up'. He was as complete in *The Lawless Roads* as he was in *The Power and the Glory*, and as I read on I encounter more and more characters whom I have forgotten, who beckon to me from the pages and say ironically, 'And did you really believe you had invented me?' Here is the amiable corrupt Chief of Police in Villahermosa, and in the village of Yajalon I encountered 'a mestizo with curly sideburns and two yellow fangs at either end of his mouth. He had an awful hilarity and an inane laugh which showed the empty gums. He wore a white tennis shirt open at the front and he scratched himself underneath it.' After a week of his company I would find it impossible to abandon him for ever, and so he became the Judas of my story. And the Lehrs – the kindly Lutheran couple – they didn't belong to my imagination, for here they are giving shelter to a tired traveller in the same fashion as they did to the whisky priest. Of invented characters how very few seem to remain apart from the two protagonists, the priest and the Lieutenant of Police; when I came to write I was handing out alternative destinies to real people whom I had encountered on my journey.

It was a journey I wouldn't like to take today. I rode from Yajalon through the Chiapas mountains for three days on a mule, not knowing I was following the footsteps of my whisky priest in his escape from the lieutenant, before I came finally to the city of Las Casas, spread out under the mountains at the end of the mule-track. In Tabasco all the churches had been destroyed. Here they were still standing, and even open, but no priest was allowed to enter them, and because it was Holy Week bizarre services were celebrated by the Indians from the hills who tried to remember what they had been taught – scraps of strangely pronounced Latin and odd uncanonical gestures. Perhaps I was even less happy in this city than I had been in Villahermosa, for the place was full of swaggering *pistoleros* – any of whom might have been a model for my Chief of Police – and it was impossible to sit in the plaza at evening without being insulted, or to order a drink in a cantina without being refused, for by this time diplomatic relations with England had been broken because of the nationalization of the oil companies.

So it is that the material of a novel accumulates, without the author's knowledge, not always easily, not always without fatigue or pain or even fear.

I think *The Power and the Glory* is the only novel I have written to a thesis: in *The Heart of the Matter* Wilson sat on a balcony in Freetown watching Scobie pass by in the street long before I was aware of Scobie's problem – his corruption by pity. But I had always, even when I was a schoolboy, listened with impatience to the scandalous stories of tourists concerning the priests they had encountered in remote Latin villages (this priest had a mistress, another was constantly drunk), for I had been adequately taught in my Protestant history books what Catholics believed; I could distinguish even then between the man and his office. Now, many years later, as a Catholic in Mexico, I read and listened to stories of corruption which were said to have justified the persecution of the Church under Calles and under his successor and rival Cardenas, but I had also observed for myself how courage and the sense of responsibility had revived with persecution – I had seen the devotion of peasants praying in the priestless churches and I had attended Masses in upper rooms where the Sanctus bell could not sound for fear of the police. I had not found the idealism or integrity of the Lieutenant of *The Power and the Glory* among the police and *pistoleros* I had actually encountered – I had to invent him as a counter to the failed priest: the idealistic police officer who stifled life from the best possible motives: the drunken priest who continued to pass life on.

The book gave me more satisfaction than any other I had written, but it waited nearly ten years for success. In England the first edition was one of 3,500 copies – a printing one thousand larger than that of my first novel eleven years before – and it crept out a month or so before Hitler invaded the Low Countries; in the United States it was published under the difficult and misleading title of *The Labyrinthine Ways* chosen by the publishers (selling, I think, two thousand copies). After the war was over its success in France, due to François Mauriac's generous introduction, brought danger from two fronts, Hollywood and the Vatican. A pious film called *The Fugitive*, which I could never bring myself to see, was made by John Ford who gave all the integrity to the priest and the corruption to the Lieutenant (he was even made the father of the priest's child), while the success of the novel in French Catholic circles caused what we now call a backlash, so that it was twice delated to Rome by French bishops. Some ten years after publication the Cardinal Archbishop of Westminster read me a letter from the Holy Office condemning my novel because it was 'paradoxical' and 'dealt with extraordinary circumstances'. The price of liberty, even within a Church, is eternal vigilance, but I wonder whether any of the totalitarian states, whether of the right or of the left, with which the Church of Rome is often compared, would have treated me as gently when I refused to revise the book on the casuistical ground that the copyright was in the hands of my publishers. There was no public condemnation, and the affair was allowed to drop into the peaceful oblivion which the Church wisely reserves for unimportant issues. Years later, when I met Pope Paul VI, he mentioned that he had read the book. I told him that it had been condemned by the Holy Office.

'Who condemned it?'

'Cardinal Pissardo.'

He repeated the name with a wry smile and added, 'Mr Greene, some parts of your books are certain to offend some Catholics, but you should pay no attention to that.'

2

It amazes me to think that in those early days I could usually write a novel in nine months – but six weeks ... *The Confidential Agent* was written in six weeks in 1938 after my return from Mexico. The Spanish Civil War furnished the background, but it was the Munich Agreement which provided the urgency. At that time, when trenches were being dug on London commons, when our children were evacuated carrying gas masks in little cardboard containers to strange homes in the country, many of us joined a mysterious organization called the Officers' Emergency Reserve which advertised for professional men, journalists, bankers, God knows what ... When I write 'mysterious' I only mean that the reserve was mysterious in its motives like the forces of nature. The emergency but not the reserve passed; the trenches were left uncompleted; the children returned, but many of us were left with the uneasy sense that when war came – as undoubtedly it would in a matter of months or years – we would find ourselves caught up into the army a day, a week, after war was declared, leaving our families without support.

I was struggling through *The Power and the Glory*, but there was no money in the book as far as I could foresee. Certainly my wife and two children would not be able to live on one un-saleable book, while I satisfied my conscience in the army.

So I determined to write another 'entertainment' as quickly as possible in the mornings, while I ground on slowly with *The Power and the Glory* in the afternoons. To create a proper atmosphere for work, free from telephone calls and the cries of children, I took a studio in Mecklenburg Square – a lovely eighteenth-century square in those days, but most of it, including my studio, was blown to pieces two years later.

Now that I had my place of work I lacked only an idea. The opening scene between two rival agents on the cross-channel steamer – I called them D and L because I did not wish to localise their conflict – was all I had in mind, and a certain vague am-bition to create something legendary out of a contemporary thriller: the hunted man who becomes in turn the hunter, the peaceful man who turns at bay, the man who has learned to love justice by suffering injustice. But what the legend was to be about in modern terms I had no idea.

I fell back for the first and last time in my life on benzedrine. For six weeks I started each day with a tablet, and renewed the dose at midday. Each day I sat down to work with no idea of what turn the plot might take and each morning I wrote, with the automatism of a planchette, two thousand words instead of my usual stint of five hundred words. In the afternoons *The Power and the Glory* proceeded towards its end at the same leaden pace unaffected by the sprightly young thing who was so quickly overtaking it.

The Confidential Agent is one of the few books of mine which I have cared to reread – perhaps because it is not really one of mine. It was as though I were ghosting for another man. D, the chivalrous agent and professor of Romance literature, is not really one of my characters, nor is Forbes, born Furtstein, the equally chivalrous lover. The book moved rapidly because I was not struggling with my own technical problems: I was to all intents ghosting a novel by an old writer who was to die a little before the studio in which I had worked was blown out of existence. All I can say as excuse, and in gratitude to an honoured shade, is that *The Confidential Agent* is a better thriller than Ford Madox Ford wrote himself when he attempted the genre in *Vive Le Roy*.

I was forcing the pace and I suffered for it. Six weeks of a benzedrine breakfast diet left my nerves in shreds and my wife suffered the result. At five o'clock I would return home with a shaking hand, a depression which fell with the regularity of a tropical rain, ready to find offence in anything and to give offence for no cause. For long after the six weeks were over, I had to continue with smaller and smaller doses to break the habit. The career of writing has its own curious forms of hell. Sometimes looking back I think that those benzedrine weeks were more responsible than the separation of war and my own infidelities for breaking our marriage.

The anxiety that had driven me to write so fast had an ironic end. I was summoned to a draft board for the Emergency Reserve during the winter of 1939 – it had taken a few weeks of phoney war before the authorities had reached the letter G. The days of the shaking hand were over and I was passed A for health and went in to see the Board, consisting of a major-general and two colonels. They were obviously puzzled by their brief and knew as little as I did what the reserve of untrained officers was intended to do. 'How do you *visualize* yourself?'

223

the general asked with a certain pathos. I muttered something about the original advertisement for the reserve having mentioned journalists among the categories of men required. I had once been a journalist.

'Yes, yes,' the general said with a complete lack of interest, 'but how do you *see* yourself?'

All three watched with anxiety. I was aware of their bated breath, and I felt some sympathy for what they had endured day by day from all my fellow reservists ranging from Ab to Go. I believe they dreaded the thought that once again they were to suffer that word 'Intelligence'. They leaned a little forward in their chairs and I had the impression they were holding out to me, in the desperation of their boredom, a deck of cards with one card marked. I decided to help them. I took the marked card and said, 'I suppose . . . the Infantry.'

One of the colonels gave a sigh of relief and the general said with unmistakable pleasure, 'I don't think we need ask Mr Greene any more questions, do you?'

I had so evidently pleased them that I thought I could safely make a small request. I only needed a few more months to complete *The Power and the Glory*. Could my call-up be postponed for those few months?

The general positively beamed. Of course I should have those precious months – 'Shall we say until June? Try and keep fit, though, Mr Greene, in the meanwhile. What I mean is . . .' (I could see him searching for the *mot juste*) 'I mean sometimes when you want to take a bus, walk instead.' Strange to think that it was in that world the Commandos were born.

As it turned out the Infantry were not to find themselves burdened with my inefficiency. Why, even at school I had to be left out of important parades because I failed to master the fixing of a bayonet, and in 1941 the commandant of an intelligence course had to abandon the idea that I would ever be able to learn to ride a motorcycle after I had damaged two. An intelligence course? Yes, it had not proved so easy to escape in war the many-armed embrace of Intelligence.

There are certain things I like in *The Confidential Agent*: for example the predicament of the agent with scruples, who is not trusted by his own party and who realizes that his party is right not to trust him. In this case it was the predicament of a Communist (though D did not in fact possess a Party card). A writer who is a Catholic cannot help having a certain sympathy for any faith which is sincerely held and I was glad when more than twenty years later Kim Philby quoted this novel when explaining his attitude to Stalinism. It seemed to indicate that I had not been far wrong, although at the period I wrote I knew nothing of intelligence work.

There are other moments which seem to belong to a period much later: surely the delinquent gang of Woolhampton who helped D to sabotage the mine and their fathers' jobs just for the fun of the thing belongs to the postwar period and so too does the awful hotel of Southcrawl called The Lido, which with its organized fun resembled the Butlin's holiday camp at Clacton where many years later the artist Edward Ardizzone and I spent two extraordinary days before we packed secretly and fled from the red blazers of the prefects in the dining-halls, which were loyally called Gloucester and Kent after the two royal dukes, and the grey sea which no one visited. Mr Forbes of my story had had the idea long before Mr Butlin. 'We are advertising it as a cruise on land. Organized games with a secretary. Concerts. A gymnasium. Young people encouraged – no reception clerk looking down his nose at the new Woolworth's ring.' Swimming pools too and when D asks about the sea, Mr Forbes dismisses it in the true Butlin manner. 'That's not heated.'

This is a flippant example of what hardly bears too much thought. Dunne has written in *An Experiment with Time* of dreams which draw their symbols from the future as well as the past. Is it possible that a novelist may do the same, since so much of his work comes from the same source as dreams? It is a disquieting idea. Was Zola, when he wrote of the imprisoned miners dying of poisoned air, drawing something from a 'memory' of his own death, smothered with fumes from his coke stove? Perhaps it's just as well for an author not to reread the books he has written. There may be too many hints from an unhappy future. Why in 1938 did I write of D listening to a radio talk on the Problem of Indo-China? (Was there any such problem then serious enough to reach the English radio?) Six years were to pass before the French war in Vietnam began and eight more before the problem of Indo-China became vivid to me as I stood, scared motionless, beside the canal filled with Viet Minh bodies near the cathedral of Phat Diem.

Chapter 4

1

IN THE winter of 1941 I found myself on a small Elder-Dempster cargo-ship in the North Atlantic, part of a slow convoy bound by a roundabout route for West Africa. I had been recruited into the Secret Service, commonly known as MI6 or SIS, by my sister Elisabeth. Only after recruitment did I realize the meaning of all those parties, given by a mysterious Mr Smith, to which I had been invited in London where, in spite of the blitz and the rationing, there seemed no lack of liquor and where everybody seemed to know each other. I was being vetted. I was also of course vetted by Scotland Yard who turned up traces of the Shirley Temple case.

During the voyage I finished writing a short book called *British Dramatists* between the watches of the day – one aeroplane watch and one submarine watch. Ten days out of Belfast we reached the latitude of Land's End, having gone north nearly to Iceland, and at that rate the West African coast seemed very far away. I had brought with me a steel trunk full of books, but they would have to last me until my leave which might be two years off, so I read what I could find in the ship's library.

One of these books was by Michael Innes – an author whom I didn't then know. I had never cared much for English detective stories. With all their carefully documented references to Bradshaw's timetable or to the technique of campanology or to the geography – complete with plan – of a country house, I found them lacking in realism. There were too many suspects and the criminal never belonged to what used to be called the criminal class.

Outside the criminal class sexual passion and avarice seemed the most likely motives for murder; but the English detective writer was debarred by his audience of the perpetually immature – an adjective which does not preclude a university professor here or there – from dealing realistically with sexual passion, so he was apt to involve his readers in a story of forged wills, disinheritance, avaricious heirs, and of course railway timetables.

Michael Innes's book provided a surprising and welcome change. It was a detective story both fantastic and funny.

Lying at night in my bunk with a half-hope that a warning siren – so many short blasts, so many long – would prelude a return to England (submarines only seemed a real menace to those going home on leave), I developed the ambition to write a funny and fantastic thriller myself. If Innes could do it, why not I? Perhaps it was the circumstances of the time – December 1941, Japan had just struck at Pearl Harbor, the German armies were smashing their way towards Moscow – we listened every night to the news on the steward's radio – that made the plot I chose for *The Ministry of Fear* seem to me a funny one: a man acquitted of the murder of his wife by a jury (though he knows his own guilt) who finds himself pursued for a murder of which he is entirely innocent but which he believes he has committed. It sounds a bit complicated told like that, and long before I finished the book I realized the story was not after all very funny, though it might have other merits.

It was not written in the easiest of circumstances. After three months of 'training' in Lagos I had found myself master of a one-man office in Freetown (and after four months or so of a secretary). I do not think I can have begun the book in Lagos where my days were spent coding and decoding in an office and my nights were passed with a colleague in a disused police bungalow on a mosquito-haunted creek. To cheer ourselves we used to hunt cockroaches by the light of electric torches, marking in pencil on the walls one point for a certain death, half a point if the roach had been washed down the lavatory bowl. I described this pursuit later in *The Heart of the Matter*. Greeneland perhaps: I can only say it is the land in which I have passed much of my life.

My house in Freetown stood on the flats below Hill Station, the European quarter, opposite a transport camp of the Nigerian Regiment which attracted flies and vultures. The house had been built by a Syrian and was remarkable for having a staircase and a first floor in this land of bungalows. It had been condemned by the medical officer of health, but houses were not easily obtainable now that the Army, the Navy and the Air Force had moved into Freetown. When the rains came I realized why it had been condemned: the ground on which it stood became a swamp. Between it and the sea stretched a few acres of scrub used as a public lavatory by the African inhabitants of the slum houses close by.

At six in the morning I would get up and have breakfast. The kitchen equipment was limited and once I was roused by the cries of my cook (who later went off his head completely); he was chasing my steward with a hatchet because the boy had borrowed the empty sardine tin in which the cook was accustomed to fry my morning egg. Life was very different from the blitzed London of my story, but it is often easier to describe something from a long way off.

At seven I would take my little Morris car and drive into Freetown, do my shopping at the stores – PZ or Oliphant's – and collect my telegrams at the police station to which I was fictitiously attached by my cover employment of CID Special Branch. They arrived in a code unintelligible to the police and were handed me by the Commissioner, a man at the end of his middle years, to whom I became greatly attached. Then I would drive home and decode the telegrams and reply to them as best I could, write my reports or rearrange the reports of others into an acceptable form – work was over by lunchtime, unless an urgent telegram arrived or a convoy had brought a bag to be opened and dealt with.

By the end of lunch in the full humid heat of the day I would take a siesta, my sleep disturbed by the heavy movements of the vultures on the iron roof above my head (I have seen as many as six perched up there, like old broken umbrellas). When one of them took off or landed it was as though a thief were trying to break through the iron roof. At four thirty I would have tea, then take a solitary walk along an abandoned railway track once used by European officials, halfway up the slopes below Hill Station. There was a wide view of the huge Freetown bay where sometimes the *Queen Mary* would be lying at anchor as though she had been hijacked from the North Atlantic, and the old *Edinburgh Castle* – now a naval depot ship – lay rotting on a reef of empty bottles. As the sun began to set, the laterite paths turned the colour of a rose. It was the hour and the place I liked best.

When dusk began to fall it was time to turn home; I write 'home' for as one year ebbed away the house on the swamp where I lived alone really became home. I had to take my bath before night dropped suddenly at six, for that was the rat-hour. I had constructed a covered way between the house and the kitchen and this provided a bridge for the invaders. Once, a little late at six thirty, I found a rat making its toilet on the rim of the bath (the rats were always punctual) and I never bathed as late again. At night I would be woken under my mosquito-net by the rats swinging on the bedroom curtains. Perhaps all this may have helped to rob *The Ministry of Fear* of what I intended to be care-free humour, and yet I can swear that in those first six months I was a happy man – I was in a land I loved. Kipling wrote: 'We've only one virginity to lose, And where we lost it there our hearts will be.' In the nineteenth century the American, Henry James, took the long voyage to Europe and lost his heart once and for all to Italy. 'No one who has ever loved Rome as Rome could be loved in youth wants to stop loving her.' At thirty-one in Liberia I had lost my heart to West Africa.

There was not much time, however, for writing a novel. Into what hours did I manage to wedge my writing? Between tea and the walk along the railway track? Between the six o'clock whisky and dinner? Certainly the evening whisky did not take me long. I had the civilian ration of one bottle a month, with two bottles of gin and six bottles of beer. After a painful period of deprivation, I was able, with the help of the Air Force Intelligence officer, to obtain a few extra bottles of Canadian Club which no one in the Air Force seemed to like, and with the aid of an RNVR officer, who once a month took his little anti-submarine patrol boat to Bissau in Portuguese Guinea to fetch the Consul's mail, I would obtain demijohns of excellent Portuguese wine, red and white – tasting all the better because no duty had been paid. Gin remained a problem. One type of Canadian gin became the subject of an Admiralty order, so dangerous it proved to be. All bottles had to be dumped overboard, adding to the reef on which the *Edinburgh Castle* rested.

When the book was somehow finished . . . but I have to pause again on the word 'somehow' which leaves out all those inter-ruptions that come flooding so vividly back. One interruption was always welcome – a trip into the interior. A little narrow-gauge line ran up to Pendembu near the Liberian and the French Guinea borders – I had taken it years ago when I was about to begin the long walk described in *Journey Without Maps* and nothing at all had changed after seven years: one took one's 'boy', one's own supply of tinned food, one's own chair, one's own bed, even one's own oil-lamp to hang on a hook in the compartment when dark fell. The little train stopped for the night at Bo, where there was a Government rest-house, and thence chugged laboriously uphill to Pendembu. At Pendembu there was a rest-house, not very well maintained by the local chief, so I preferred to take my evening meal on the railway line, my camp table set up on the track. I got into trouble about the expenses of these trips, but not in the way that might be supposed. I was in the habit of charging five shillings a day, the proper Colonial Office rate, which was supposed to represent the difference in price between buying tinned food and market food – the railway and the rest-houses were free. I received a severe telegram in code from London pointing out that the proper charge for an officer in my position was three guineas a day when he was away from his station, to cover the cost of hotels. 'Please adjust accordingly and confirm.' I obeyed with alacrity. I opened my office safe and transferred some forty pounds in notes to my own pocket, then telegraphed back in code that all was now in order.

There were less agreeable interruptions: my relations with my senior officer in Lagos two thousand miles away were very strained. We had disliked each other on sight. He was a professional. I was an amateur. A note of sarcasm crept into my reports, even into my cables. I feel sorry now for the poor man, who had to deal at the last stage of his career with a writer. He was a sick man, totally unacquainted with Africa: how sick I did not realize then, and I learned later that he would keep the Freetown bag unopened on his desk for days in fear of the contents. Once he tried to discipline me by cutting off my funds, which he was supposed to send me once a month in cash by bags from Lagos, but I borrowed from the Police Commissioner, so that harassment failed. Finally we came to open war – I had a rendezvous at Kailahun on the Liberian border and he sent me a telegram forbidding me to leave Freetown because of the imminent arrival of a Portuguese liner. Portuguese ships from Angola had all to be searched for industrial diamonds and illicit correspondence, but this was no affair of mine, the job belonged to the Commissioner, who represented MI5. After some inner debate I obeyed, wrote, as it proved, an accurate report to London of the unfortunate events which would ensue from my not keeping the rendezvous and resigned. My resignation was not accepted. I had to stay on another six months, but I was freed at last from the control of Lagos. Perhaps the sense of freedom helped the novel on.

All the same I wonder how I ever finished the book. The title *The Ministry of Fear* I took from a poem by Wordsworth (Arnold's selection of his poems was one of the volumes I had brought with me from England), and the novel was bought unseen by an American film company on the strength of Wordsworth's title. Then came the problem of sending the manuscript home. In Freetown it was impossible to forget the menace of submarines – it was part of our everyday life; the reason why so many wives stayed throughout their husbands' tours, the reason why I had no refrigerator – it had been lost on the way out. So, having finished the book, I began the weary task of typing it out with one finger after dinner, and I was lucky to finish it before the scurry of the North African landings affected even my remote coast with cables at all hours.

I have written little here about the novel itself though it is my favourite among what I called then my 'entertainments' to distinguish them from more serious novels. I wish now that the espionage element had been less fantastically handled, though I think Mr Prentice of the Special Branch is real enough – I knew him under another name in my own organization when I was his pupil. The scenes in the mental clinic are to my mind the best in the novel, and it was surprising to me that Fritz Lang, the old director of *M* and *The Spy*, omitted them altogether from his film version of the book, thus making the whole story meaningless.

I think too the atmosphere of the blitz is well conveyed. The three flares which Rowe saw come 'sailing slowly, beautifully, down, clusters of spangles off a Christmas tree', I had

232

watched myself, flattened up against the wall of Maple's store on the night of the great raid of 16 April 1941, some months before I left for Africa.

In those days London had been a cluster of villages – one hardly ever wandered to distant places like Hampstead, Knightsbridge, Chelsea, though some people would go for a quiet weekend to St John's Wood. My own village was bounded on the south by New Oxford Street, on the north by Euston Road, on the east by Gordon Square, on the west by Gower Street. The author of *The Napoleon of Notting Hill* would have loved those days, and so in a sense did I and my fellow wardens at our post under the School of Tropical Medicine in Gower Street. While I wrote *The Ministry of Fear* far away in West Africa a little of the love crept, I think, into the book. I find it too in the fragment of a journal which I kept during the blitz. I called it *The Londoners*.

LONDON 1940–1941

They got into the bus at Golders Green after the pantomime: a dyed blonde woman in the late forties and her older husband, with the relics of histrionic good looks. The old wrinkled tortoise skin and the heavy-lidded eyes might have belonged to a Forbes-Robertson – somebody who had played *Hamlet* too often. Now he was tired, very tired, and the vulgar woman he had married nagged and bullied and insulted him all the time in the public bus, and he made no reply but 'Yes, dear,' 'No, dear.' He hadn't noticed or understood anything in the pantomime, and this was her excuse to bait him. Slowly a whole wartime life emerged. They lived in a hotel and had nowhere to sit without having to buy drinks. So after the pantomime they were going to the 'flicks' for an hour, and after the flicks, dinner, and after dinner, bed in the big steel-built reinforced hotel. And the next day, just the same again.

The man sat in an alcove of the London Library with his back to the room facing a window. With both hands he held his handkerchief tightly distended in front of him against the light, and ruffled it. This went on and on – the regular ruffling of

233

the handkerchief. I watched him for five minutes: there was nothing eccentric in his appearance: he might have been looking at a watermark.

From *The Times* Personal Column

BLACK OUT. Carry a white Pekinese. Lovely puppies from 2 guineas. Goad, 23 Overbury Avenue, Beckenham (Bec. 1860)

The Times remains itself.

COMFORTABLE WORDS

Mr Churchill ended his speech on Sunday night with the last two verses of a poem by Arthur Hugh Clough. A Latin version of the whole poem, printed on another page of this issue, shows not only the scholarly art of the translator but also the success with which Clough's English poetry passes the severe test of being turned into Latin.

Old Clements is an Alsatian who has been a waiter at the Salisbury in St Martin's Lane for thirty years – broken by a brief spell in the French army near Verdun from which one leg has never recovered. When his boss died he asked old C on his deathbed to keep his eye on the pub and his son – who is now in the army. The other night Clements, who lives in Kilburn, was walking home with three other waiters. Planes were over and no buses were running. A lorry pulled up beside them and Clements put his hand up for a lift. At that moment a gun on the lorry went off. 'Oh my,' old Clements said, 'you never heard such noises. Boom – whizz – oomph. We jumped in the air. Even my old leg jumped that high. Boom – whizz – oomph. We came down flat on our faces and then it drove on down the road and stopped. Whizz – boom – oomph. Oh my, we were scared. We thought it was a lorry and then whizz – boom – oomph. I jumped up in the air so high. "Oh, mother," I said when I got home, "have you any whisky in the house?" "Why, daddy," she said, "you look bad," and I told her – whizz – boom – oomph.' He was laughing all the time, dressed to go out in his worn-out brown suit and his old soft hat and a walking stick under his arm. But as usual there was an alert on.

'If we grumble at sickness, God won't grant us death.' – *War and Peace.*

234

Charlie Wix is the heroic raconteur of No. 1 Post under the School of Tropical Medicine in Gower Street. He was once, I think, a waiter, but his chief occupation seems to have been giving evidence in divorce cases. He refers to himself in his elaborate anecdotes about high explosives and delayed action bombs and the crassness of the Chief Warden, as 'Charlie Wix'. 'Then Charlie Wix arrives . . .' One sentence in a long description of a land-mine incident at the corner of Oxford Street and Tottenham Court Road: '"Mr Wix," 'e says, "what 'ave you done with the bodies?"' There had been trouble because bodies were sent off in a dust-cart instead of an ambulance.

Of another occasion when a St Pancras post arrived first and there was a lot of confusion and too many cooks (it was in Ridgmount Gardens): 'Mr Lewin wouldn't open 'is mouth. 'E was *disgusted* with the incident.'

Of a foreigner in Windmill Street. 'Didn't speak 'ardly a word of English. There was a DA [Delayed Action Bomb] outside, an' I had to clear the house. So I went up. He was in bed. "Out," I says to him. "Out." 'E didn't take any action, didn't understand. "Bomb," I said, "bomb." "Blimey," 'e said, an' jumped out.'

Below Mallard's, Store Street, there is a nightly little group round an oil stove at one end of the shelter warming bricks – a middle-aged man,* a Scots girl with a sharp tongue who claims to work at Fortnum & Mason and dislikes wardens** on principle – particularly Charlie Wix – and sometimes an unshaven man in a bowler hat. A gipsy-like effect round their fire. They are there, raid or no raid. She put up a board in pokerwork at the foot of her bunk: 'Wild Scottish bull dog at large. Wardens beware.' Which reminds me that on the occasion of the first bad raid, Lewin and Wix were on duty outside Mallard's when there was a crash on the pavement. 'Shrapnel,' Lewin

* Later note. This man died suddenly one night when alone with the girl. Another warden, David Low, the secondhand bookseller, and I should have been inspecting the shelter at the time, but all was quiet and we didn't go down. We were caught out badly by this death.
**A skin-deep dislike. Later she would offer us sweets and be quite ready to make us 'at home'.

said, dragging Wix into cover, but it turned out to be a Watney quart bottle someone had thrown at them.

The extraordinary nervousness of the police who disappear from the streets during a bad raid. The noisy night in Coptic Street and the policeman who mistook a new heavy gun for a land-mine. 'Went off just behind me. Shook me up.' He dived into a pub and out again a few minutes later when the gun went off again, he couldn't keep still. That was the night when the coils of wire – part of a new defence weapon – descended on Heinemann's at 99 Great Russell Street, and in Store Street, which was closed to traffic till next morning.*

One of the wardens called L was once in the Army. He entered it at eighteen, his height being then five foot three inches, and he put on seven inches. He went to Egypt. His father was the captain of a P & O liner, and L hadn't seen him for two years when he heard that he would be at Aden. He had a week's leave at Suez but couldn't get any conveyance, so he walked the ninety miles along the Red Sea, and had one day left at the end of it. He was a little disappointed. He had remembered his father as a big man. When he reached the ship there was a man in civilian clothes and a major hanging over the rail. The man in civilian clothes looked at him and said, 'Of course I'm sorry for the poor devils, but there ought to be a rule excluding them from the first class.' That was his father. L's uniform had five days' dust and the blood from an accident at gun-stations the day before he left. The major, when he learned who it was, insisted that they should all have a drink together in the saloon. L had never had a short drink before and asked for the first thing his eye saw on the list – Benedictine. His father and the major tossed down whiskies, and L tried to toss down his Benedictine . . . A kindly weak ugly face with a broken nose from boxing.

The shelter at 25 Bedford Square – with two Chinamen in one room and three old ladies in another.

---

*Later note. A lot of this wire came down on Heal's store, marked with Heal's name: they had been concerned in the manufacture.

The land-mine night: the body, laid out in Tottenham Court Road, which three fire engines passed over. Another man was laid bleeding on a door in the road to escape glass. Wix put a fur coat over him from a shop window. The ambulance was too full to take him. When Wix came back some time later, he had been removed to the pavement – 'just the sort of thing a policeman would do' – and a thief was going through his pockets. Wix rescued his notecase, and then could find nobody who would consent to take charge of it. At last next day he took it to University College Hospital. The man was a Turk with a whole string of names. 'Is Mr So-and-so-and-so here?' he asked a nurse. 'He *was* here,' she said. 'Would you like to see him? He's in the mortuary.'

A little man with a Home Guard button lunching with a friend at the Orange Tree in Euston Road. A copy of Wedgewood's ponderous and banal anthology *Forever Freedom* by his plate. 'Young So-and-so,' he said, 'seems wrapped up in that girl of his.'

'Where did he find her?' his friend asked glumly.

'Don't know. Can't get him alone to ask him.'

He was apparently a fire-watcher, and that night was going to watch at his office with the bosses, who always played bridge. But they were much better players than himself. '"Do you play the Culbertson game?" they asked me the first time. Knocked me silly. I'd never heard of it. Always play my own game.'

Overheard in the Duke of Grafton on April Fool's Day. The executive of some works fulfilling Air Force contracts was talking. Apparently he was below ground that morning with two workmen when they phoned down: 'Haven't you heard the Alert? The fire-watcher ought to be up,' and up on the roof the fire-watcher went and stayed there in the biting east wind from nine till ten, when somebody told him it was April Fool's Day. 'Now you might say we lost one man's work for an hour – but it was worth it for the merriment it caused. Made everything go smoother.'

Basil Dean took Ernest Bevin and myself on a lightning tour of the ENSA entertainments round Aldershot. Bevin innocently on the spree, talking excitedly – 'I'm Mr Bevin' –

to the dimmest of ENSA leading ladies. Very likeable, very un-selfconscious. He told us a story of Churchill announcing to the Cabinet the Lofoten Raid. 'I've got interesting news for you, gentlemen. We've been making a little excursion – to the Lofoten Islands. We've brought back quite a lot of things, including some Quislings. Mark my words' – turning to Duff Cooper – 'Quislings, Mr Minister of Information. Call them Quislings – not Quisling-ites, or you'll be starting a religious movement.' Bevin sleeps at the Strand Palace.

After dinner – with champagne – at the Anchor, Liphook, we drove back between twelve and one. It was interesting and beautiful to see, from the outside, the London guns playing.

The Great Blitz of Wednesday, 16 April

This was the worst raid Central London had ever experienced.
The sirens which usually don't go before ten went at nine. I was drinking with Dorothy Glover, in the Horsehoe. We went out and tried to get dinner. Corner House full, Frascati's closed. Victor's closed. At the York Minster the chef was about to go home. Ended in the Czardas in Dean Street. Sitting next the plate-glass windows we felt apprehensive. By ten it was obvious that this was a real blitz. Bomb bursts – perhaps the ones in Piccadilly – shook the restaurant. Left at ten thirty and walked back to Gower Mews. Wished I had my steel helmet. Changed, and went out with D, who was fire-watching. Standing on the roof of a garage we saw the flares come slowly floating down, dribbling their flames: they drift like great yellow peonies.

At midnight reported at the post and went out on the north side. At a quarter to two nothing had happened in the district, and I planned to sign off at two thirty. Then the flares came down again right on top of us, as the Pole, Miss S (of Bourne & Hollingsworth) and I stood in Tottenham Court Road at the corner of Alfred Place. A white southern light: we cast long shadows and the flares came down from west to east across Charlotte Street. Then a few minutes later, without the warning of a whistle, there was a huge detonation. We only had time to get on our haunches and the shop window showered down on our helmets.

Ran down Alfred Place. A light shone out in a top flat at the corner of Ridgmount Gardens: we shouted at it and ran on – the windows must have been blasted. Then confusion. Gower Street on both sides seemed ravaged. Never realized the parachute bomb had fallen behind on the Victoria Club in Malet Street where 350 Canadian soldiers were sleeping. Women bleeding from cuts on the face in dressing-gowns said there was someone hurt on the top floor above RADA. Two other wardens and a police-man – we ran up four littered flights. Girl on the floor. Bleeding. Stained pyjamas. Her hip hurt. Only room for one man to lift her at a time. Very heavy. Took her over for two flights, but she had to be changed three times. In pain, but she apolo-gized for being heavy. Stretcher party came and took her away from the ground floor. All down Gower Street they came out in their doorways – many unhurt, but so many bleeding in a super-ficial way in squalid pyjamas grey with debris dust. These were the casualties of glass.

Confusion. Not enough stretcher parties. Went back to post and the blackout boards blew out and we went down on the floor. Out again to find something to do. That was the odd difficulty.

Jacobs had become Incident Officer with a blue light beside him at the corner of Gower Street and Keppel Street. This was indeed local and domestic war like something out of *The Napoleon of Notting Hill*. Ordered round to the Victoria Club.

All stretcher men and no wardens visible. What are a warden's duties? The lectures no longer seemed clear. Soldiers still coming out in grey blood-smeared pyjamas: pavements littered by glass and some were barefooted. Everybody suddenly seemed to have cleared from the front. A soldier came out and said there was a man trapped on the stairs. We took a stretcher and went in. On one side a twenty-foot drop into what seemed the foundations of the building. One wished that things would stop: *this* was our incident, but the guns and bombs just went on. Came on what was apparently a body: only the head and shoulders visible and a clot of blood by the head. Quiet and slumped and just a peaceful part of the rubble. 'Is this him?' 'No. He's a goner.' But another stretcher party seemed to be working out of sight on the stairs. My companion couldn't

239

find what he was looking for, so we had to make do with the corpse. (Perhaps it wasn't a corpse.) Time went very slowly and I wanted to get out: the whole place seemed to be held together with wishful thinking. Shouted for stretcher-bearers and at last got them: lighted their way out with the body. Outside there seemed to be flames all round the shop. Then another stick of three bombs came whistling down and we lay on the pavement – a sailor on top of me: broken glass cut my hand which bled a great deal – so I went back to have it dressed at the post under the School of Tropical Medicine.

A street accident is horrible and fortuitous, but all this belonged to human nature.

As I was having my hand dressed another stick of three came down. Down again on the floor of the post. At the first the windows blew in. One really thought that this was the end, but it wasn't exactly frightening – one had ceased to believe in the possibility of surviving the night. Began an Act of Contrition. Then it was over. Went out again.

Dallas, the big white factory in Ridgmount Gardens, was ablaze. Behind every window on every floor a wall of flame blowing up. Not much more than an hour had passed since the first bomb in our area. It seemed a long while.

One forgets the progression of small incidents. A man fetched me to a friend in a house opposite Dallas – a large fat foreigner. One foot was crushed and bloody, and he was the only person I saw that night whose nerve had gone. He was whimpering and crying to be taken to hospital. But what a weight he was. We crossed hands and got him to the corner of Gower Street, Then we had to rest in spite of his cries. It was broad daylight at three fifteen from the flares. Jacobs and Lewin, the Deputy Chief Warden, came up. Jacobs said, 'You must stop there. There are people more injured than you,' but the man began to cry and moan. His friend had slipped away, so Lewin began to help me with him towards the Ministry of Information, which had become a temporary dressing station.* But we gave out

*The Ministry was also a beacon guiding German planes towards King's Cross and St Pancras Stations. Hardly a night passed without the blackout being ignored, and in my area we suffered for it. I wrote a letter to the *Spectator* with the title 'Bloomsbury Lighthouse'. I signed it prudently again in Keppel Street and he fetched a soldier to help. All the time we waited the man leaned his weight on me and moaned to be taken to hospital. An awful journey into the basement of the M of I, the passage cluttered with Ministry people. It turned out later that the man had internal injuries and fought the doctor who tried to give him morphia.

Out again, after three minutes spent in what had seemed a lovely solid secure building. The fire brigade had still not come for Dallas (it didn't come for three hours), and Jacobs sent me with a message to the post. Going down the iron steps into the well round the building I heard another bomb coming down. Crouched and heard it fall well away.

Out again, and a soldier fetched me. An old man in a basement in Gower Street. The back wall had been blown out, exposing Dallas and the flames, but he didn't want to stir. He was reasonable and didn't make a fuss. A daughter helped him with his clothes. He was old and white-bearded and very concerned about waistcoats. Just out of hospital with a tube in his bladder, told he would never walk again. He was worried about the tube – not nice for people to see it hanging out, but he forgot it walking across Gower Street, he was so delighted at having proved the hospital wrong.

Called in at the shelter in Gower Mews where Dorothy acted as shelter warden. She was very cheerful, but glad to see me. A warden had told her that he had seen me in the Victoria Club. 'I think he was all right. He was covered in blood, but I don't think it was his blood.'

That was really all there was to remember: the raid died away, and at five, while I was counting stretcher cases from Warwick House and forgetting to take the number of the ambulance, 'raiders past' went. It turned out that there had been another parachute bomb at the end of Bloomsbury Street, and on my own beat and not reported at the time an HE on the Jewish Girls' Club in Alfred Place behind Dallas (many days later

'Air Raid Warden' for a policeman visited our post and demanded the name of the writer. No one informed on me and afterwards the lights were dimmed, but I wonder on what charge under what regulation I would have been brought to court.

they were still getting out the bodies – more than thirty killed)*
and another taking away the side of the Embassy Cinema in
Torrington Place. A house gutted opposite the *Spectator* in
Gower Street, and part of Maple's burnt out.

Other people's stories: a girl from my post was told that a
man was trapped on the top floor of a building. She went up
and found him pinioned but not badly hurt. Two soldiers stood
in the room doing nothing – just laughing.

Father Gervase Mathew, the Byzantine historian. He was
called out twice – to the Aperitif restaurant in Jermyn Street
and to a gun emplacement in Hyde Park – which was hit by a
parachute bomb – to give a conditional absolution. The soldier
in Hyde Park when he asked if there were any Catholics said,
'I'm a Catholic, Father. Haven't been to Mass for forty years,
but I'm one.'

A young priest – a friend of GM – was called to a wrecked
public house where the landlord, his wife and daughter, all
Catholics, were trapped. He cleared the way to a billiard table,
got under it, and was then near enough to them to hear their
confessions. A voice above his head suddenly asked, 'Who's
that?' and he heard himself making the odd statement, 'I am a
Catholic priest and I am under the billiard table hearing confessions.' 'Stay where you are a moment, Father,' the voice
said, 'and hear mine too.' It was a rescue-party man.

Looking back, it is the squalor of the night, the purgatorial
throng of men and women in dirty torn pyjamas with little blood
splashes standing in doorways, which remains. These were
disquieting because they supplied images for what one day would
probably happen to oneself.

I had to take a train later that morning to Oxford where I
had promised to talk to the Newman Society, but I hadn't
time to shave. At Oxford I went into a chemist and asked for
a packet of razor blades. He glared at me in fury. 'Don't you
know there's a war on?' he asked.

*For days afterwards there was the sweet smell of corruption in Store
Street.

Evelyn Waugh once wrote to me that the only excuse he could offer for *Brideshead Revisited* was 'spam, blackouts and Nissen huts'. I feel much the same towards *The Heart of the Matter*, though my excuse might be different – 'swamps, rain and a mad cook' – for our two wars were very different.

In the six years that separated the end of *The Power and the Glory* from the start of *The Heart of the Matter* my writing had become rusty with disuse and misuse (the misuse included the innumerable telegrams and reports from Freetown in Sierra Leone to my headquarters in London). I began the book soon after the war was over in 1946, three years after I had closed my small office and burnt my files and code-books. For reasons of security I had been unable to keep a proper diary in West Africa, but looking at the few random notes which survive I seem to have been already, between telegrams and reports, playing with the idea of a novel – though not the novel I eventually wrote.

There had been a chance encounter during one of my journeys up-country with a Father B whom I have now completely forgotten, though I must have been remembering him when I wrote in *The Heart of the Matter* of Father Clay whom Scobie met when he went out to Bamba to inquire into young Pemberton's suicide. 'Poor little red-headed north country boy neglected by his fellows,' I read in my notebook. 'His account of the black-water fever. "I walk up and down here."' (These were Father Clay's very words.) '£38 in cash at the Mission when he arrived, but a £28 bill. Apparently no interests. 6 year tour – 3½ done. The old raincoat over a dirty white shirt.'

I had no idea of Major Scobie in those days. It was the young north country priest who grew in my imagination, so that I find a few lines in faded pencil beginning his story.

If I were a writer, I would be tempted to turn this into a novel. I imagine this is what writers feel – the haunting presence of an individual whom they wish to understand. But I haven't the time or the skill for such work and all I have been able to do is to gather the impressions that this man made on others who knew him, the documents as it were in the case of Father —. I am afraid a character can hardly emerge from such a collection as this. In the reviews I have read novelists are praised or blamed for their success or failure in creating a character, but such characters usually seem to bear about the same relation to life as the pictures in this country that you see painted on the mud walls of the native huts. A train is represented by a row of rectangles, each rectangle balanced on two circles. So a 'character' is simplified by the novelist: the contradictions you find in human beings are pared or explained away. The result is Art – which is arrangement and simplification for the purpose of conveying a mental condition. This book cannot pretend to be art because the compiler has left in all the contradictions: its only purpose is to present as truthfully as possible an enigma, though I daresay it is an enigma common to most of us if every man had his own case-book.

'My name is . . . I am a line-agent for . . .'

The name and the firm were never filled in and the novel went no further. It was just another object abandoned on the Coast like the old guns on Bunce Island in Sierra Leone River. I am glad to put this small memorial to what might well have been a better book than *The Heart of the Matter*.

Looking through my old notebook I find stray incidents and characters which could have been included in my novel; they formed part of the routine life of an SIS representative in Freetown, and some of them may have found a hole or corner in the book which came to be written – but I don't want to search for them now.

The German agent's letters. The list of ships which have called. Tell so-and-so he's too optimistic when he says no ships can call here. The touch of pacifism: 'What would Livingstone have said?'

Who was that agent? Forgotten as deeply as Father B.

The small brown kid dead in the middle of the road between the shops, and the vulture hopping round, hopping back towards the gutter when cars came by.

The suitcase of the suspect – the squalor and intimacy of a man's suitcase.

The funeral party going home outside – I had thought it was a wedding. The crowd of women in bright native dress wearing a kind of black apron and overshirt. The trombone players going Dum, dum, dum, and the women making little dancing steps and posturing and shouting to the soldiers in the camp as they went by. All a little tipsy. At the house young men were kicking a football. The last mourners seem sedate and sombre, carrying handkerchiefs. One woman in white European dress walking alone.

My boy's brother's dying. Of gonorrhoea. My boy too has had g. 'Cured now.' 'Injections?' 'No.' He makes an expressive gesture with his hands. 'Doctor throw it out.' His stilted walk with buttocks projecting and the smell of drink. 'You drink if you see your brother – own father, own mother – lying on bed, not seeing you. You drink to keep water out of eyes.' He cannot yet tell his brother's wife. If people know he's dying they'll all come in and steal his things. All night he's going to have a party at his brother's, drinking so that water doesn't come out of his eyes, and quietly checking on his brother's belongings and getting his small brother to write them down. Next morning he tells me with interest that there are two sewing machines – but his brother isn't dead yet.

This must have been my first unsatisfactory 'boy', a Mende, the one my mad cook had tried to kill with a hatchet. I thankfully lost the boy when he went to prison for perjury, an offence beyond his comprehension, though I had him defended before the absurd bewigged English judge by the best black lawyer in Freetown. I was a little unfortunate with the law. My cook was later accused of taking money for witchcraft and not fulfilling his promise. I found my house deserted one night when I returned from a long trek, with no one to cook me an evening meal. The cook, I learnt from a neighbour, was in prison. When I visited him there I couldn't bear to see him in his grim cell. I got in touch, but it wasn't easy in wartime, with a Vichy district commissioner across the border in French Guinea and had him returned to his native village where he would end his days well looked after, at liberty except for an iron ring round his ankle to show that he had been afflicted by God.

The letter to the African agitator in his internment who has married again. In England he seems to have had relations with an ardent humanitarian Englishwoman who financed him. The letter is from an African in the Gower Street – Gray's Inn district. First about letting him have collars left at the laundry. Reference to the agitator's new romance. 'Oh, she will be jealous when she hears the news. You are a real heart-breaker.' The photo of the heart-breaker on the files. The respectable humanitarian names chiming in the right places – Victor Gollancz, Ethel Mannin . . .

The Court Messenger at Yengema (the headquarters of the diamond mines) with his senseless face and his bandy legs suffering from ju-ju. (He had to be sent back to his native village to be treated by a witch doctor.)

The mammas in the market wrapping up their fruit and vegetables in confidential telegrams from the secretariat files.

The Commissioner back subdued from a hanging. 'I can't eat meat for a week after a hanging.'

There was another event which I couldn't put down in the notebook and which sickened me – the interrogation of a young Scandinavian seaman from Buenos Aires who was suspected of being a German agent. I knew from a report about the girl he had loved in Buenos Aires – a prostitute probably, but he was really in love in his romantic way. If he came clean he could go back to her, I told him, if he wouldn't speak he would be interned for the duration of the war. 'And how long do you think she'll stay faithful to you?' It was a police job, an MI5 job again. I was angry that I had been landed with it. It was a form of dirty work for which I had not been engaged. I gave up the interrogation prematurely, without result, hating myself. He may even have been innocent. To hell, I thought then, with MI5.

My experiences in Sierra Leone were rich enough, but I have never been satisfied with what I made of them. My critics have complained, perhaps with justice, that 'I laid it on too thick', but the material *was* thick. The real fault, as I have written, lay in the rustiness of my long inaction. What I was engaged in through those war years was not genuine action – it was an escape from reality and responsibility. To a novelist his novel is the only reality and his only responsibility. Like the man suffering from ju-ju I had to go back to my proper region to be cured.

In 1946 I felt myself at a loss. How had I in the past found the progressions from one scene to another? How confine the narrative to one point of view, or at most two? A dozen such technical questions tormented me as they had never done before the war when the solution had always come quickly. Work was not made easier because the booby-traps I had heedlessly planted in my private life were blowing up in turn. I had always thought that war would bring death as a solution in one form or another, in the blitz, in a submarined ship, in Africa with a dose of black-water, but here I was alive, the carrier of unhappiness to people I loved, taking up the old profession of brothel-child. So perhaps what I really dislike in the book is the memory of personal anguish. As Scott Fitzgerald wrote, 'A writer's temperament is continually making him do things he can never repair.' I was even contemplating one night the first move to suicide when I was interrupted in that game by the arrival at ten in the evening of a telegram (I had never known they delivered telegrams so late) from someone whom I had made suffer and who now felt anxious about my safety.

But long before that point of despair was reached I had found myself so out of practice and out of confidence that I couldn't for months get the character Wilson off his balcony in the hotel from which he was watching Scobie, the Commissioner of Police, pass down the wide unpaved street. To get him off the balcony meant making a decision. Two very different novels began on the same balcony with the same character, and I had to choose which one to write.

One was the novel I wrote; the other was to have been an 'entertainment'. I had long been haunted by the possibility of a crime story in which the criminal was known to the reader, but the detective was carefully hidden, disguised by false clues which would lead the reader astray until the climax. The story was to be told from the point of view of the criminal, and the detective would necessarily be some kind of undercover agent. MI5 was the obvious organization to use, and the character Wilson is the unsatisfactory relic of the entertainment, for when I left Wilson on the balcony and joined Scobie I plumped for the novel.

It was to prove a book more popular with the public, even with the critics, than with the author. The scales to me seem too heavily weighted, the plot overloaded, the religious scruples of Scobie too extreme. I had meant the story of Scobie to enlarge a theme which I had touched on in *The Ministry of Fear*, the disastrous effect on human beings of pity as distinct from compassion. I had written in *The Ministry of Fear*: 'Pity is cruel. Pity destroys. Love isn't safe when pity's prowling round.' The character of Scobie was intended to show that pity can be the expression of an almost monstrous pride. But I found the effect on readers was quite different. To them Scobie was exonerated, Scobie was 'a good man', he was hunted to his doom by the harshness of his wife.

Here was a technical fault rather than a psychological one. Louise Scobie is mainly seen through the eyes of Scobie, and we have no chance of revising our opinion of her. Helen, the girl whom Scobie loves, gains an unfair advantage. In the original draft of the novel a scene was played between Mrs Scobie and Wilson, the MI5 agent who is in love with her, on their evening walk along the abandoned railway track below Hill Station. This put Mrs Scobie's character in a more favourable light, for the scene had to be represented through the eyes of Wilson, but this scene – so I thought when I was preparing the novel for publication – broke Scobie's point of view prematurely; the drive of the narrative appeared to slacken. By eliminating it I thought I gained intensity and impetus, but I had sacrificed tone. In later editions I reinserted the passage.

Maybe I am too harsh to the book, wearied as I have been by reiterated arguments in Catholic journals on Scobie's salvation or damnation. I was not so stupid as to believe that this could ever be an issue in a novel. Besides I have small belief in the doctrine of eternal punishment (it was Scobie's belief not mine). Suicide was Scobie's inevitable end; the particular motive of his suicide, to save even God from himself, was the final twist of the screw of his inordinate pride. Perhaps Scobie should have been a subject for a cruel comedy rather than for tragedy . . .

All this said there are pages in *The Heart of the Matter* (and one character, Yusef) for which I care, descriptions of Freetown and the interior of Sierra Leone which bring back many happy months and some unhappy ones. The Portuguese liners with their smuggled letters and smuggled diamonds were very much a part of the odd life I led there in 1942–3. Scobie was based on nothing but my own unconscious. He had nothing to do with my Commissioner of Police, whose friendship was the human thing I valued most during fifteen rather lonely months. Nor was Wilson – who obstinately refused to come alive – based on any of the MI5 agents who trailed – in two cases disastrously – down the West African coast in those days.

'Those days' – I am glad to have had them; my love of Africa deepened there, in particular for what is called, the whole world over, the Coast, this world of tin roofs, of vultures clanging down, of laterite paths turning rose in the evening light. My cook who went to prison for witchcraft, my steward who was sentenced unjustly for perjury, the boy from the bush who arrived with no recommendation from anyone and took charge of me as faithfully as Ali did of Scobie, refusing the bribes offered by the representative of another secret service, S O E, to leave my employ – were they just inhabitants of Greeneland? As well tell a man in love with a woman that she is only a figment of his imagination.

Chapter 5

1

MY film story, *The Third Man*, was never written to be read but only to be seen. The story, like many love affairs, started at a dinner table and continued with headaches in many places: Vienna, Venice, Ravello, London, Santa Monica.

Most novelists, I suppose, carry round in their heads or in their notebooks the first idea for stories that have never come to be written. Sometimes one may turn them over after many years and think regretfully they would have been good once, in a time now dead. So it was that long before, on the flap of an envelope, I had written an opening paragraph: 'I had paid my last farewell to Harry a week ago, when his coffin was lowered into the frozen February ground, so that it was with incredulity that I saw him pass by, without a sign of recognition, among the host of strangers in the Strand.' I, like my hero, had not the least inkling of an explanation, so when Alexander Korda over dinner asked me to write a film for Carol Reed – to follow our *Fallen Idol* which I had adapted from my short story 'The Basement Room' a year before – I had nothing more to offer him except this paragraph, though what Korda really wanted was a film about the Four-Power occupation of Vienna. In 1948 Vienna was still divided into American, Russian, French and British zones, while the Inner City was administered by each Power in turn for a month and patrolled day and night by groups of four soldiers drawn from the Four Powers. It was this complex situation which Korda wanted put on film, but he was prepared all the same to let me pursue the tracks of Harry. So to Vienna I went.

For me it is impossible to write a film play without first writing a story. A film depends on more than plot; it depends on a certain measure of characterization, on mood and atmosphere, and these seem impossible to capture for the first time in the dull shorthand of a conventional treatment. I must have the sense of more material than I need to draw on (though the full-length novel usually contains too much). *The Third Man*, therefore, though never intended for publication, had to start as a story rather than as a treatment before I began working on what seemed the interminable transformations from one screenplay to another.

On the continuity and the story-line Carol Reed and I worked closely together when I came back with him to Vienna to write the screenplay, covering miles of carpet a day, acting scenes at each other. (It's a curious fact that you cannot work out a continuity at a desk – you have to move with your characters.) No third ever joined our conferences, not even Korda himself; so much value lies in the cut and thrust of argument between two people. To the novelist, of course, his novel is the best he can do with a particular subject; he cannot help resenting many of the changes necessary for turning it into a film play; but *The Third Man* was never intended to be more than the raw material for a picture. The reader will notice many differences between the story and the film, and he should not imagine these changes were forced on an unwilling author: as likely as not they were suggested by the author. The film in fact is better than the story because it is in this case the finished state of the story.

Some of these changes have obvious superficial reasons. The choice of an American instead of an English star involved a number of alterations – the most important, Harry had to become American too. Joseph Cotten quite reasonably objected to my choice of name, Rollo in the story, which to his American ear apparently involved homosexuality. I wanted the name none the less to be an absurd one, and the name Holly occurred to me when I remembered that figure of fun, the nineteenth-century American poet Thomas Holley Chivers.

One of the few major disputes between Carol Reed and myself concerned the ending, and he was proved triumphantly right. I held the view that an entertainment of this kind was too light an affair to carry the weight of an unhappy ending. Reed on his side felt that my ending – indeterminate as it was, with no words spoken, Holly joining the girl in silence and walking away with her from the cemetery where her lover Harry was buried – would strike the audience who had just seen Harry's death and burial as unpleasantly cynical. I was only half convinced: I was

251

afraid few people would wait in their seats during the girl's long walk from the graveside towards Holly, and the others would leave the cinema under the impression that the ending was still going to be as conventional as my suggested ending of boy joining girl. I had not given enough credit to the mastery of Reed's direction, and at that stage, of course, we neither of us anticipated Reed's discovery of Anton Karas, the zither player. All I had indicated in my treatment was a kind of signature tune connected with Lime.

The episode in the treatment of the Russians kidnapping Anna (a perfectly plausible incident in Vienna in those days) was eliminated at a fairly late stage. It was not satisfactorily tied into the screenplay, and it threatened to turn the film into a propagandist picture. We had no desire to move people's political emotions; we wanted to entertain them, to frighten them a little, even to make them laugh.

Reality in fact was to be only the background to a fairy tale, though the story of the penicillin racket was based on a grim truth, all the more grim because so many of the traffickers were innocent, unlike Lime. A surgeon I knew took two friends to see the film. He was surprised to find them subdued and depressed by the picture which he had enjoyed. They told him that at the end of the war, when they were with the Royal Air Force in Vienna, they had both sold penicillin. The consequences of their petty larceny had never occurred to them till they saw the film and the scene in the children's hospital where watered penicillin had been used.

When Carol Reed came with me to Vienna to see the scenes which I described in the treatment I was embarrassed to find that between winter and spring Vienna had completely changed. The blackmarket restaurants, where in February one was lucky to find a few bones described as oxtail, were now serving legal if frugal meals. The ruins had been cleared away from in front of the Café Mozart which I had christened 'Old Vienna'. Over and over again I found myself saying to Carol Reed, 'But I assure you Vienna was really like that – three months ago.'

It had proved difficult to find my story – Harry's phoney funeral was the only scrap of plot I had to cling to. All that came as the days too rapidly passed were bits of photogenic background; the shabby Oriental nightclub, the officers' bar at Sacher's (somehow Korda had managed to fix me a room in the hotel, which was reserved for officers), the little dressing-rooms which formed a kind of interior village in the old Josefstadt Theatre (Anna was eventually to work there), the enormous cemetery where electric drills were needed to pierce the ground that February. I had allowed myself not more than two weeks in Vienna before meeting a friend in Italy where I intended to write the story, but what story? There were three days left and I had no story, not even the storyteller, Colonel Calloway, whom I see now always in my mind with the features of Trevor Howard.

On the penultimate day I had the good fortune to lunch with a young British Intelligence officer (the future Duke of St Albans) – my wartime connection with the SIS used to bring me useful dividends in those days. He described how when he first took over in Vienna he demanded from the Austrian authorities a list of the Viennese police. A section of the list was marked 'Underground Police'.

'Get rid of these men,' he ordered, 'things have changed now,' but a month later he found the 'underground' police were still on the list. He repeated his order with anger, and it was then explained to him that the 'underground police' were not secret police, but police who literally worked underground along the enormous system of sewers. There were no Allied zones in the sewers, the entrances were dotted throughout the city disguised as advertisement kiosks, and for some inexplicable reason the Russians refused to allow them to be locked. Agents could pass uncontrolled from any zone to another. After lunch we dressed in heavy boots and macintoshes and took a walk below the city. The main sewer was like a great tidal river, and as sweet smelling. At lunch the officer had told me of the penicillin racket, and now, along the sewers, the whole story took shape. The researches I had made into the functioning of the Four-Power occupation, my visit to an old servant of my mother's in the Russian zone, the long evenings of solitary drinking in the Oriental, none of them was wasted. I had my film.

My last evening I gave dinner to my friend, Elizabeth Bowen, who had come to Vienna to lecture at the British Institute, as a guest of the British Council. I took her afterwards to the Oriental.

I don't think she had ever been in so seedy a nightclub before. I said, 'They will be raiding this place at midnight.'

'How do you know?'

'I have my contacts.'

Exactly at the stroke of twelve, as I had asked my friend to arrange, a British sergeant came clattering down the stairs, followed by a Russian, a French and an American military policeman. The place was in half-darkness, but without hesitation (I had described her with care) he strode across the cellar and demanded to see Elizabeth's passport. She looked at me with respect – the British Council had not given her so dramatic an evening. Next day I was on my way to Italy. All was over except the writing.

2

The view of an outsider at a revolution is an odd and slanting one, rather like a pretentious camera-angle; he may sometimes even be unaware that anything is happening around him at all. I remember in the thirties, when I came back from my holiday in Estonia to spend a few days with my brother Hugh, who was the *Daily Telegraph* correspondent in Nazi Berlin, I had to change trains at Riga, at midnight. There were two hours to kill and so I took to the streets around Central Station and the Post Office: I was charmed by the old droshky drivers with Tolstoy beards asleep over their bony horses, and by the prostitutes who might well have been plying their trade in Victorian London. They stood at street corners and, when the young foreigner passed, they raised a skirt just far enough to disclose an elegant ankle and the beginning of a well-shaped calf. When I arrived at breakfast time in Berlin my brother met me. 'What about Riga,' he asked me, 'and the revolution?'

'Revolution?'

'There was a military *coup d'état* at midnight. The Post Office has been taken and the Central Station. There are machine-guns at every corner.'

It was true, it must have been true, I read it afterwards in the *Telegraph*, but I had seen only the old droshky drivers and the Victorian tarts.

The only way to keep my rendezvous in Rome in 1948 and begin my screenplay was to fly from Vienna by way of Prague. I thought I would take the opportunity to stay a few days and see my two publishers – one, a Social Democrat, published what I called my 'entertainments', the other, a Catholic, had published *The Power and the Glory*. On the evening I left Vienna there were rumours of a Communist takeover, but I was more concerned about the heavy snow which delayed the plane for hours from taking off. There were two English correspondents travelling on the same plane, one belonged to an agency and the other to the BBC. They told me they were on their way to report the revolution.

'Revolution?'

I remembered how years ago in Riga . . .

'Have you booked a room?' one of them asked.

'No. I didn't think it necessary at this time of year.'

'Hotels are always full,' the other said with professional knowledge, 'when there's a revolution.'

'I've been recommended the Ambassador.'

'We are sharing a room there. It was the last one they had. Better stick to us.'

The snow fell thicker and thicker and the plane was very late. It was well after midnight when we landed and none of us had eaten since lunch. Food seemed even more important than a bed, but at least, I thought, there would be no difficulty about food at an international hotel. How wrong I was. There was no bed, but that was quickly solved. There was a sofa in the correspondents' room – I could have that, and now, at one thirty in the morning, surely some simple nourishing food . . . 'I am sorry,' the porter said, 'but the restaurant is closed. *All* the restaurants in Prague are closed.'

'A sandwich,' I suggested desperately.

'I regret . . .'

Then the porter's heart relented. 'Perhaps,' he said, 'there is a way. In the basement we are holding a servants' ball. There will be refreshments. If you would care to try . . . they may allow you . . .'

In the basement we found that we were not the only ones in search of food. The Venezuelan Ambassador was there dancing ponderously with the fat cook, and there were other members of the Diplomatic Corps. A nice chambermaid made room for us at her table and pointed out the celebrities – 'That is the First Secretary from the Uruguayan Embassy – that is the valet from the third floor – that is Josef – he is in charge of the pastry – someone from the Central Bank, I don't know what he does.' If this was really a revolution it seemed to me not so bad. The band played, everyone was happy, the beer flowed. After my third glass I thought of Wordsworth – 'Bliss was it in that dawn to be alive.' The ambassador returned to our table with the cook. He put his arm round her stout waist and squeezed gently and persistently. As far as I could make out – but I was getting down to my sausage and potatoes – he was asking her to promise him that next time he came to the restaurant upstairs she would make sure he had a really large oversized schnitzel. He pressed her with one hand and gestured with the other – 'just that thick'.

Who could have foretold on that fantastic night the Slansky trial, all the Stalin horrors, the brief spring, and then Dubček and Smrkovsky dragged as prisoners to Moscow? Twenty-one years later, in February 1969, I came back: the Russian troops were in occupation and I had a meeting one morning before breakfast with Smrkovsky, already a tired sick man with cancer of the bone. I asked him, 'In the West we have an impression that perhaps Kosygin was more sympathetic than Brezhnev to your case. Is that true?' He said, 'The three men, Brezhnev, Kosygin and Suslov, came into the room together and sat down opposite us. I could see no difference at all between Brezhnev and Kosygin. There was one moment when I imagined that I could detect in Suslov's eyes a hint of sympathy, but he spoke exactly like the others.' It seemed to me I was much more than twenty-one years away from the servants' ball.

That night in 1948 I didn't sleep very well. It was not the fault of the sofa, but I was anxious to observe two special correspondents in action during a revolution. A lot of noise and singing began early in the streets, but at half past eight neither of the two men had begun to stir. I didn't want to wake them, although I was impatient to go outside. At last about nine thirty one correspondent aroused himself to go as far as the bathroom: the other moved sleepily across to the telephone, trailing his dressing-gown cord, and dialled the number of his stringer. 'Anything happening? No? Well, then I'll look in later. About eleven? I was up terribly late last night.' He looked a little puzzled when he saw that I was already getting dressed. 'Going out?' he asked. 'You might come and tell us if you see anything interesting.' To be a special correspondent was not after all to belong to a very dynamic profession.

In the streets there were processions and red flags and shouting. I walked at random, confused by the Czech street names, until I saw a building marked British Information Office and I went in to try and borrow or buy a map. When I came out I was aware of being followed. I turned down one street and then another: the thin man in a dark suit and a respectable hat followed. At last I paused and let him overtake me. He said, 'Please. If you will turn left here.' We went into a small quiet street and left the processions behind. I was a little worried by his furtive air.

'You are British?'

'Yes.'

'Will you do something for me? It is very important. The fate of my poor country is at stake.'

He really talked like that, like a character in a bad film.

'What can I do?'

'You have to see your ambassador and tell him. I explain myself badly.' At intervals when someone appeared in the street he would stop talking until whoever it was had passed well out of hearing. He said, 'I must tell you. I am an inventor and I have invented a parachute which can be guided for fifty kilometres after the drop. I gave my invention to the Ministry of Defence, but now these people who are taking charge, they will hand over my plans to the Russians. You see how important this is for your country as well as my own.'

He was very convincing in spite of the melodrama. I began to imagine how an army might be guided through the sky . . . the Channel no obstacle . . . I asked him to give me his name and he wrote it on a scrap of paper. In my mind I was already half-way to the Embassy, but caution made me ask him another question. 'Have you invented anything else?'

He replied promptly, with enthusiasm, 'I have made a machine for building walls. That too I will give to the British Government. It builds a wall one foot every second.' With a sense of disappointment I decided that it would be better not to go to the Embassy.

Nothing during the week I stayed in Prague lived up to the happiness of the servants' ball or even the fantasy of the parachutes. Already the bitter humour of defeat was circulating – mainly jokes about the weight of the fat wife of Gottwald, the Communist leader.

I visited my Catholic publisher twice, and the second time there was an armed sentry at the foot of his stair. His vigil was in our minds as we drank slivovitz (my publisher was soon to vanish into prison for ten years).

I was taken out by a Communist literary agent to the castle which had been allocated to the Union of Writers. There was only one writer to be seen: he was up a ladder in the library picking out a volume of the *Encyclopaedia Britannica*. 'Our chief authority on Shakespeare,' I was told over tea in a magnificent drawing-room hung with chandeliers. The authority mentioned *Hamlet* and the literary agent kicked him sharply on the ankle under the table. 'Mr Greene hasn't come all this way to hear you talk about Shakespeare,' he said. I began to realize that to be alive in this dawn was not necessarily bliss.

In a bookshop in the old town I was handed a note. Someone would guide me to see a Catholic deputy who was in hiding. I thought he needed help to escape and I brought a variety of currencies in my pocket, but he explained he did not require such help – he had merely thought the situation would interest me because I had written *The Power and the Glory*.

One day the novelist Egon Hostovsky who was employed in the Ministry of Foreign Affairs came and sat on my bed – I had obtained a room by this time – and told me how that afternoon Masaryk, the Minister, had said good-bye to his staff. He wept as he told the story and between us we finished my whisky. A few days later Masaryk was dead.

I was glad to take my plane to Rome. There were no passengers except myself and a young married couple. The husband was Prince Schwarzenburg and he had been appointed Minister to the Vatican by the former government. I noticed that they had a lot of luggage with them, and I was not surprised to hear a few weeks later of the prince's defection.

Just before the plane left a loudspeaker called me back to the immigration officer who demanded to see my passport again. I wondered whether after all I would be able to keep my rendezvous in Rome. I remembered the armed sentry at my publisher's office, Hostovsky weeping on my bed and the deputy hidden in a tortuous street of the old city, waiting for the right number of rings at the door that indicated a friend. The officer examined my passport closely. He said, 'This passport is valid for two visits. This is your first visit. You can come again,' but it was twenty-one years before I returned and then the Russians were there without the help of parachutes.

3

In Italy I wrote the treatment of *The Third Man*, but more important for the future I found the small house in Anacapri where all my later books were to be at least in part written. (I am proud now to be an honorary citizen of that little town of five thousand inhabitants.)

Writing a novel does not become easier with practice. The slow discovery by a novelist of his individual method can be exciting, but a moment comes in middle age when he feels that he no longer controls his method; he has become its prisoner. Then a long period of ennui sets in: it seems to him he has done everything before. He is more afraid to read his favourable critics than his unfavourable, for with terrible patience they unroll before his eyes the unchanging pattern of the carpet. If he has depended a great deal on his unconscious, on his ability to forget even his own books when they are once on the public shelves, the critics remind him – this theme originated ten years ago, that simile which came so unthinkingly to his pen a few weeks back was used nearly twenty years ago in a passage where . . .

I had tried to escape from my prison by writing for the films, but *The Third Man* only beckoned me into another and more luxurious prison. Before I returned to what I considered my proper job I read *Great Expectations*. I had never before found

Dickens a very sympathetic writer, but now I was captivated by the apparent ease with which he used the first person. Here seemed an escape from the pattern, a method I had not tried. The first person had always offered an obvious technical advantage – the chosen point of view was insured against any temptation to deviate, 'I' could only observe what 'I' observed (though Proust cheated shamelessly) – but when I sometimes encountered the use of the first person in the novels of Somerset Maugham and his imitators, I always thought it a little too easy and dry, too close to clumsy human speech, colourless . . .

Dry and colourless perhaps it was, but easy, no. Many a time I regretted pursuing 'I' along his dismal road and contemplated beginning *The End of the Affair* all over again with Bendrix, my leading character, seen from outside in the third person. I had never previously had to struggle so hard to lend the narrative interest. For example how could I vary the all-important 'tone' when it was one character who was always commenting? The tone had been set on the first page by Bendrix – 'This is a record of hate far more than of love' – and I dreaded to see the whole book smoked dry like a fish with his hatred. Dickens had somehow miraculously varied his tone, but when I tried to analyse his success, I felt like a colour-blind man trying intellectually to distinguish one colour from another. For my book there were only two shades of the same colour – obsessive love and obsessive hate; Mr Parkis, the private detective, and his boy were my attempt to introduce two more tones, the humorous and the pathetic.

The book began to come to life in December 1948 in a bedroom of the Hotel Palma in Capri before I moved to my cottage. I have always imagined it was influenced by the book I was reading at the time, a selection from Baron von Hügel, in particular by passages from his study of St Catherine of Genoa. I have a habit of marking the books I read, and yet I can find no passage marked on St Catherine which has any relevance. But in another essay of von Hügel's I come on this underlined: 'The purification and slow constitution of the Individual into a Person, by means of the Thing-element, the apparently blind Determinism of Natural Law and Natural Happenings . . . Nothing can be more certain than that we must admit and place this undeniable, increasingly obtrusive, element and power *somewhere* in our lives: if we will not own it as a means, it will grip us as our end.'

Nothing could have been further from von Hügel's meaning than the story which now began to itch at my mind – of a man who was to be driven and overwhelmed by the accumulation of natural coincidences, until he broke and began to accept the incredible – the possibility of a God. Alas! It was an intention I betrayed. There is much that I like in the book – it seems to me more simply and clearly written than its predecessors and ingeniously constructed to avoid the tedium of the time sequence (I had learned something from my continual rereadings of that remarkable novel *The Good Soldier* by Ford Madox Ford), but until I reached the final part I did not realize the formidable problem I had set myself.

Sarah, the chief character, was dead, the book should have continued at least as long after her death as before, and yet, like her lover, Bendrix, I found I had no great appetite to continue now she was gone beyond recall and only a philosophic theme was left behind. I began to hurry to the end, and although, in the last part, there are scenes, especially those which express the growth of tenderness between Bendrix and Sarah's husband, which seem to me successful enough, I realized too late how I had been cheating – cheating myself, cheating the reader, cheating Baron von Hügel. The incident of the atheist Smythe's strawberry mark (apparently cured by Sarah after her death) should have had no place in the book; every so-called miracle, like the curing of Parkis's boy, ought to have had a completely natural explanation. The coincidences should have continued over the years, battering the mind of Bendrix, forcing on him a reluctant doubt of his own atheism. The last pages would have remained much as they were written (indeed I very much like the last pages), but I had spurred myself too quickly to the end.

So it was in a later edition I tried to return nearer to my original intention. Smythe's strawberry mark gave place to a disease of the skin which might have had a nervous origin and be susceptible to faith healing.

An episode in the book which many of my critics have disliked is the discovery that Sarah had been secretly baptized

261

a Catholic by her mother when she was a child. It seems to the agnostic reader – with whom I increasingly sympathize – to introduce the notion of magic. But if we are to believe in some power infinitely above us in capacity and knowledge, magic does inevitably form part of our belief – or rather magic is the term we use for the mysterious and the inexplicable – like the stigmata of Padre Pio which I watched from a few feet away as he said Mass one early morning in his monastery in South Italy.

The episode of Sarah's secret baptism I drew from the life of Roger Casement. The Catholic chaplain of Casement's prison, to whom he had applied for reception into the Church, found after inquiries that he had been secretly baptized when he was a child. We are not necessarily in the realm of 'magic' here or coincidence – we may be in the region of Dunne's *Experiment with Time*.

The End of the Affair was a greater success with readers than with critics. I felt such doubt of it that I sent the typescript to my friend Edward Sackville-West and asked his advice. Should I put the book in a drawer and forget it? He answered me frankly that he didn't care for the novel but none the less I should publish – we ought to have the vitality of the Victorians who never hesitated to publish the bad as well as the good. So publish I did. I was much comforted by words of praise from William Faulkner, and I was later grateful for the two years' practice I had had in the use of the first person or I might have been afraid to use it in *The Quiet American*, a novel which imperatively demanded it, and which is, technically at least, perhaps a more successful book.

Chapter 6

1

THE fifties were for me a period of great unrest. It was with some intuition that Pius XII told the then Bishop Heenan that he had been reading *The End of the Affair* (strange reading for a pope) and said to him, 'I think this man is in trouble. If he ever comes to you, you must help him.' (Needless to say, I never went to Heenan.)

I was in that mood for escape which comes, I suppose, to most men in middle life, though with me it arrived early, even in childhood – escape from boredom, escape from depression. If I had been a bank clerk, I would have dreamed of betraying my trust and absconding to South America.

> God bless the thoughtful islands
> Where never warrants come;
> God bless the just Republics
> That give a man a home.

Kipling's poem has always appealed to me. But I had no employer from whom to escape – only myself, and the only trust I could betray was the trust of those who loved me. I asked a psychiatrist friend to arrange for an electric-shock treatment, but he refused. I seemed to be finding my way the long road back to Berkhamsted Common, where as a boy I had played at Russian roulette to escape an unhappy love.

In *The End of the Affair* I had described a lover who was so afraid that love would end one day that he tried to hasten the end and get the pain over. Yet there was no unhappy love affair to escape this time: I was happy in love. There are difficulties, of course, even in a love affair, but the chief difficulty was my own manic-depressive temperament. So it was that in the fifties I found myself tempting the end to come like Bendrix, but it was the end of life I was seeking, not the end of love. I hadn't the courage for suicide, but it became a habit with me to visit troubled places, not to seek material for novels but to regain the sense of insecurity which I had enjoyed in the three blitzes on London – 1951, three months of travel in Malaya during the Emergency as a correspondent of *Life*; 1951–1955, four winters in Vietnam reporting the French war for the *Sunday Times* and *Figaro*; 1953, in Kenya reporting the Mau Mau outbreak for the *Sunday Times*; 1956, a few weeks in Stalinist Poland, though there the only insecurity I felt was when I had to pass a gold watch to a musician on the turn of a staircase so as to give him the means of escape to the West (but he didn't want to escape and I let him keep the watch); 1958, the furthest escape of all (I don't mean geographically), to a leper colony in the last days of the Belgian Congo.

Malaya was the first of my escapes.

A cloud of moral disapprobation hung over Malaya in 1951 – how heavily I only realized later when I went on to Indo-China. To the Englishman war is a departure from the normal, like passion. To the Frenchman war is just a part of human life: it can be pleasant or unpleasant, like adultery. '*La vie sportive*' – that is how a French commandant described to me his life on a small landing craft in the delta south of Saigon, hunting for Viet Minh guerrillas in the narrow channels, within easy mortar-fire from either bank.

One must be fair. It is partly a question of geography. Malaya is nearer the Equator; it steams away under the almost daily rainfall, sapping the energy of tired, over-worked men, too few for the jobs that the Emergency produced: too few directors of labour, too few planters. Apart from the planters and the officials belonging to the Malayan Civil Service, most men were here on a short-term basis: in their minds they were already on that boat going home. If the Emergency were over (like the French in Indo-China the Government did not officially call it a war), release might come sooner. But the war (to call it by the right name) showed no sign of ever reaching a climax. While the whole world became excited over whether war was on or off in Korea, the forgotten war in Malaya dragged on. There was the daily drip of casualties: four hundred civilians had been killed in the first eleven months of 1950, one guerrilla camp destroyed, three guerrillas shot and six escaped. The war was like a mist: it pervaded everything; it sapped the spirits; it wouldn't clear. It certainly wasn't *la vie sportive*.

Of all civilians in Malaya the rubber planter was in the position of greatest danger. One aim of the Communist commandos was to ruin the country economically, to make it a territory not worth while maintaining, and the wealth of Malaya was chiefly tin and rubber. A tin mine compared to a rubber estate was relatively easy to defend, and so the main attack was directed against the planter. Who was the planter?

I had an idea before I went to Malaya, an idea picked up from an unsympathetic Press, of a group of men, the harsh overseers of great capitalist enterprises, intransigent, unconstructive exploiters of native labour, drinking stengah after stengah in the local club, probably in the Somerset Maugham manner making love to each other's wives. But before I had stayed long in Malaya I learned that there was no such thing as the Planter – there was only X or Y.

Take X. He lived with his wife in a small house of two floors surrounded by barbed wire, the ground lit at night by searchlights as far as the first trees. He was a man of late middle age, a former prisoner of the Japanese, who should have been looking forward to the final, easier, more prosperous years. He was a great hunter, and much more of his time ought to have been given to his work as a game warden (for elephants had to be contended with as well as Communists, and of his plantation one block about the size of Trafalgar Square had been devastated by them as though by bombs – not a tree left standing).

But the life that remained for him was very different – if one could call life this slow approach of inevitable violence. He had no assistant, for his assistant had been murdered on the estate some months before, and he could not get another. Night and day the telephone rang at half-hour intervals from the nearest village to make sure the line had not been cut. He was ambushed once only a mile from his house but shot his way out and saved his wounded companions. A short while before I came to stay, Communists had come into the estate to question his tappers about his movements (his assistant had made the mistake of visiting the blocks of the estate in regular order at a regular time). When he moved outside the wire, if only to the estate office a hundred yards away, he carried a Sten gun over his arm, an automatic pistol on his hip and two hand grenades at his

265

belt. A man of great courage, vitality, and a kind of buccaneering kindliness, he would not contemplate retirement – he was in the front line for life and there was no expectation of peace but death. The closest to peace was an occasional visit to relatively safe, bureaucratic Kuala Lumpur, the capital.

One could hardly be surprised if he drank a brandy and ginger ale for breakfast instead of coffee. 'Dutch courage,' he said to me, pushing the starter of the little inadequately armoured car, setting off for a round of the estate or moving slowly out at the blind corner past which the road to the village ran and where one day, from the jungle opposite, a Sten gun would almost certainly open fire. In the village a glass of warm beer with the ambiguous Chinese shopkeeper, surrounded by Chinese candles and chests of tea, who bought his cheap rubber and acted as his banker (paying out ten thousand Malay dollars at sight) – and probably reported his movements to the guerrillas. Then a pink gin or two at the rest-house, where the army officers lived, before he drove back along the lonely two-mile stretch, slowed down at the turn before that jungle wall, ten seconds of stretched nerves, and then the false security of the rubber plantation, where death was just as likely to happen but where at least you could see it coming from some way between the grey monotonous uniform trunks. One morning he and I were half an hour late in returning, and his wife waited with the anger of love for the sound of the engine, until he was safely back in the prison of wire. That night the radio announced the murder of three more planters.

Or take B, who was another civilian doing his peace-time job in the atmosphere of emergency. He was not a planter but a traffic superintendent at an important railway junction, where the East Coast Railway joins the line that runs from Kuala Lumpur to Singapore: a big broad man with an unexpected taste for books, a sensitivity in human relations (all his assistants were Indian) and a patience I never saw impaired. He looked like a sergeant major and behaved like a doctor.

The East Coast Railway ended in the state of Pahang. The Japanese had destroyed the farther reaches of the line and this section was being laid down again – with rather mixed feelings, for already it was impossible to maintain safe service on the line that existed. The night mail on the southern Singapore line had been abandoned altogether; on the East Coast line eight engines were out of commission, and I don't know how many freight cars. In one year there were forty-nine derailments on the whole system. As with the casualties among planters, most armies would find it hard to maintain their morale at this percentage of loss. A railway notice in each compartment conveyed in English, Malay, Tamil and Chinese the ordinariness of the situation:

WARNING: TERRORISM
IN THE EVENT OF FIRING ON THE LINESIDE
PASSENGERS ARE ADVISED TO LIE ON THE FLOOR AND
IN NO CIRCUMSTANCES SHOULD THEY LEAVE THE TRAIN

I spent a few days with B in the January rains. His house faced the inevitable jungle a hundred yards away; barbed wire, a police sentry, the sense of constriction. Then the rains came, the worst for twenty-five years. To bandits was added the problem of floods, washouts, landslides. One had a sense of unfairness, as when a serious incident occurred during the blitz on London in one's own civil defence area, and then the raids just went on instead of ending there. God, one felt, should allot each man one problem at a time.

Here is the schedule of the two allies, the Communists and nature, for a couple of days. The first move was nature's.

Friday, 10 a.m. One landslide on the southern line to Singapore. The morning mail train from Kuala Lumpur however had just got through, so nature had to move again. 2 p.m. Two more landslides to the south. By this time the breakdown train with a guard of troops was off to try to clear the line for the next morning's train.

At intervals through the night I could hear the telephone ringing – I was reminded of the planter's house. At 1 a.m. on Saturday the power plant was flooded and electricity failed. At 2.15 a.m. the Communists emerged from the jungle and derailed the breakdown train. At 4 a.m. the junction was completely cut off by road and the East Coast line was cut by floods. By breakfast time the water supply had failed – an odd discomfort in the pouring rain. Even the station a quarter of a mile away must now be reached by wading. To the north a new landslide had taken place.

In the evening we waded through to the station and sat in the little refreshment room by the light of candles while the messages came in. Even the signal boxes were lit only dimly by oil lamps; figures disappeared in the dark of the long platform, and the whole obscure station and its wet acres had a strangely Victorian air as though electricity had not yet come into use. At 6 p.m. there was a washout to the south, and another landslide to the north. At 8.45 p.m. an East Coast train was derailed – by floods this time, not Communists. All the labour of the little town had to be called in to load freight cars with ballast by the light of lamps, but was there enough labour, enough ballast, enough freight cars? And at intervals the big patient man padded away back to his glass, laughing at the wet, the cold, the enemy, and waited unruffled for the next telegram of disaster. One talks in terms of soldiers and civilians, but there was never a better soldier than B. This campaign was as serious as the long plodding search in the jungle, his troops were ambushed by floods as well as commandos, and like a good officer he was loved by his men. So often in Kuala Lumpur I found myself thinking: if only government officials could work as these men, X and B, worked, but perhaps you do not find courage where there is no danger, and love, too, may be a product of active war.

The nature of this war had been little understood abroad. It was not a nationalist war; ninety-five per cent of the enemy combatants were Chinese and of the few Malays in the jungle the greater part were Indonesian terrorists. I visited Kelantan, a state where the Malays are in an overwhelming majority, and it was like visiting a foreign land. Here was peace: you could walk at will unarmed; no need for convoys on the road; there was an air of happiness and content; the clothes were brighter; even the sun seemed to shine more brightly because the jungle had, literally, receded. How tired I had become of that dark green hostile wall: the jungle was no longer neutral.

Our British consciences could be clear – we were not holding down the Malays against their will; we were fighting with them against Communism and its Chinese adherents, and it was a more serious war than the use in the Press of the word 'bandit'

268

suggested. Bandits could not year after year survive the hard jungle life as these men did: a few thousand bandits could not continue to operate against a hundred thousand armed Malayan police and twenty-five thousand British, Gurkha and Malay troops. These men were the commandos of Communism, organized like a Russian division, with their political branches, their educational branches, their political commissars, their tireless and industrious intelligence service. No one knew where their GHQ lay – perhaps in one of the cities, Singapore, Kuala Lumpur, perhaps even in the old and relatively peaceful city of Malacca – but the leader was known. He had fought the Japanese bravely in World War II and marched in the Victory Parade in London.

One had to spend at least a few days in the Malayan jungle to realize its difficulties and its tediums. A far denser jungle than that of Burma, it restricted movement to less than a mile an hour. Visibility was sometimes twenty feet. Almost every day water poured down upon it, making the steep slippery slopes of the innumerable hills a cruel effort to climb. One was never dry and at night one was never in quiet – the ugly din of insects came between the newcomer and sleep. When you paused for a halt on the march you could see the leeches make for your boots – thin matchsticks looping with blind purpose across the wet leaves, later to swell into fat grey slugs if they found an opening in your clothing. And always there was the jungle stench – the heavy odour of decaying vegetation. It clung to your clothes. When you came out, your friends would avoid you until you had bathed and changed.

There were many British units operating in Malaya – the Royal Fusiliers, the Royal Marines, the Worcestershires, the Seaforth Highlanders, to name only a few – and if I take my example from the Gurkha Rifles it is only because they were hospitable enough to have me with them on one of their smallest routine operations in Pahang. The enemy, however, did distinguish between the Gurkhas and its other opponents. A captured intelligence report exhibited a rather unfair contempt for the Malay Regiment. British troops were described as courageous but noisy – they could be heard coming a long way off – while the Gurkhas were ferocious and silent.

The Gurkha is a mercenary. His vocation is to kill his official enemy, and perhaps because he has a genuine vocation he is extremely tractable. There was no woman trouble with the Gurkhas – they carried with them to their cantonments a happy, domesticated life of wives and children. In return for their pay the Gurkhas gave their British Officers absolute loyalty, and their officers returned them a quality of love you would not find in any other unit. Officers of the British regiments complained that their colleagues in the Gurkhas never stopped talking of their men. Their men were their passion.

A Gurkha patrol worked by the compass, and not by paths. It moved as the crow flies. The RAF had bombed a certain area and two hundred Communist commandos were believed to be milling around somewhere within those particular map squares. One Gurkha platoon of fourteen men under a British officer was considered a sufficiently strong reconnaissance. The patrol struck straight out from camp through the kitchen quarters, through the thin belt of rubber, into the jungle. Only nine miles separated us from our objective, the main road on the other side of the block of jungle, but it took two and a half days of walking and two nights to get there. We had started late and we began to camp after five hours' march. When our position was plotted we had penetrated rather more than three miles. There had been an interminable succession of five-hundred-foot hills, the slippery laterite slopes set at an angle of almost forty-five degrees. Even the Gurkhas sometimes slipped and fell as they tried to hold themselves up by the branches of trees, the rubber soles of their jungle boots taking no grip in the mud and slime of leaves.

Experience had justified this arduous compass trail. If, like the British troops, you patrolled by paths, you avoided the worst hills, which sometimes rose in this area to two thousand feet, and you never had to carve your way through the under-growth, but you were staking all on finding tracks on the one path you followed. The Gurkha technique meant that in the course of a day you cut across many paths in your search for signs of the enemy; a newly broken bamboo with the juice still wet might be the only indication.

The march was halted by four thirty to allow time for camp to be made before dark. First the sentry posts were chosen, then with their *kukris* (that wonderful all-purpose weapon) boughs were cut, shelters made for the men in pairs with one ground sheet stretched overhead to keep out the night rains and one laid on the bed of branches and leaves, a clearing hacked out for the radio with its aerial tossed up to a height of a hundred feet. Darkness had begun to fall when the *kukri* became a can opener. In a can about $9 \times 4 \times 3$ inches was the Gurkha ration – rice, raisins, curry powder, tea, sugar and a little spirit lamp with hard fuel for cooking. The small flames glowed like nursery night-lights in the dark. My companion, Major Cheers, stood upright listening, but not for Communists. He whispered, 'There is one bird I always listen for – at dark and at dawn. There it is. Like a bell. Do you hear it?' I could hear nothing but the clamour of the jungle barnyard. At six in the morning he was standing by our bed in the new mud of the night's downpour. 'There. Do you hear it?' he whispered. 'Like a bell.'

And so after two and a half days' heavy marching and scrambling, with no result but the discovery of two abandoned camps, we emerged nine miles from where we started – two little buttons could be added to the map in the operations room, that was all; no sign even of the air strike except an empty shell and a landslide that might have been caused by rain; a routine patrol, routine leeches, routine fatigue and routine stench.

But we could bathe and change, while for the Communist troops in their wet green prison there was no change.

And so to keep the spirits up they had lectures, courses in Marxism, the hectographed *Lenin News* and the *Red Star*, meetings for self-criticism. What an odd, naïve contrast it was to the remorseless terrorism. One could build up a picture of this life from captured documents, in which one learned of Lee Kheng who is 'not hygienic enough'; of Ah Chye who 'possesses the friendly group spirit'; of Lau Beng who is a little lazy, slipshod in his studies and 'not too agreeable' in his behaviour (he is sometimes 'fearful of the situation' and his comrades regard him as 'rather immature').

Love is treated with a stern sympathy (the jungle troops include many women). One learned from a captured copy of the *Lenin News* that male and female comrades who were not married were forbidden to stay together, but in special cases permission might be obtained from the higher authorities. 'We do not prohibit anybody making love. But such love must be proper. Once love is established, one should report it to the organization and the exact circumstances. The matter will have to undergo the organization's investigation, then both parties will be informed in accordance with the resolution.' Questions are set for discussion.

1. Why is the love of Communists a serious instinct?
2. What is the proper view of love?
3. Are the present few kinds of improper love still appearing in our area?
4. Under what circumstances are they appearing?
5. What is the cause?
6. What is our attitude towards love?
7. How are we to overcome improper love? How deal with it?

It is strange to think of such questions written in that script running backwards in a beautiful formal pattern that seems to the uninstructed eye nearly unchanged since it was made by the brush of the poet Mei Sheng when, more than two thousand years ago, he wrote of love (as translated by Ezra Pound):

> Blue, blue, is the grass about the river
> And the willows have overfilled the close garden.
> And within, the mistress, in the midmost
> of her youth,
> White, white of face, hesitates, passing the door.
> Slender, she puts forth a slender hand . . .

One cannot picture this slow, dreary Malayan conflict without the strange contrasts. A patrol finds a lone guerrilla apparently engaged in a literary exercise – hectographed sentences in which he had to spot and correct mistakes. A planter and his wife have driven into the Kuala Lumpur Club to a Scottish dinner, with 'Scotch Broth, Salmon Frae the Dee, A Wee Bit Haggis, Champit Tatties and Bashed Neeps, Moor O'Dinnet Special, Sugar Peas and Roast Potatoes, Balmoral Sundae.' Had they reached that wee bit haggis when the news was brought them that their two-year-old daughter had been shot by Chinese Communists at point-blank range? 'The Party has resolved the question of love.'

This was the work of the Chinese commandos, but you could

not measure the enemy's strength only by the fighters who emerged from the jungle to shoot up a car or a patrol, to murder a planter, to derail a train. Their strength was estimated at between three and five thousand. In this dense country one numbered casualties on the fingers of the hand – the death of ten Communists was a major victory – and they had no difficulty in acquiring new members. Their real strength lay in the unarmed combatants of the ground organization known as the Min Yuen. Here we are on speculative ground, but it is unlikely that this organization ran into less than six figures. Its main responsibility was supply, but it was employed also for intelligence, propaganda and liaison work, and it was responsible – perhaps that was its chief success – for the suspicion which rose everywhere like the mist from the saturated Malayan soil. Don't mention on the telephone what time you are leaving – the operator may be a member of the Min Yuen. Don't talk about your movements in front of your waiter or your room boy. Do you remember that young resettlement officer they killed last month? He told his Chinese taxi girl where he was going next day.

In Malaya the real successes might never be recognized, and defeat was in the minds of men. You could not win the Malayan war by military force: with the jungle against you, you could only contain the enemy until other measures succeeded.

The most important weapon was starvation. No one could subsist on the jungle, and any large cultivated area would be spotted sooner or later by air reconnaissance. The main sources of the terrorists' food supply were the Chinese squatter areas – patches of unauthorized cultivation on the edge of the jungle. The squatters were not necessarily Communist sympathizers, though it was hard to see what they could possibly lose by a Communist victory. But who of us would refuse food to a terrorist at the point of a bayonet? These squatters were being brought together into new villages which could be surrounded with wire and properly policed. The old huts were burned. The squatters were provided with building materials or houses, a small sum of money and a legal tenure of their new land.

It was a formidable task. There were about four hundred thousand squatters to settle; there was a shortage of wire and transport; there was a shortage of police for guarding the settlement and of proper arms for the police. There was sometimes a defeatism on the part of European officers. A Communist military patrol on one occasion passed unchallenged through a wired-in village, both gates wide open, at two in the morning. The European officer, when this was reported to him, shrugged the affair off. What difference did it make? You couldn't keep the Communists out with a bit of wire. This was defeat in the mind.

None the less the resettlement was a turn of the screw of discomfort. I sometimes felt a measure of compassion for these men, struck from the air, hunted however ineffectively by patrols, bled by the leeches, with insufficient food and medicines, their success measured in a resettlement officer or a planter killed, a bus burned, a patrol ambushed and a Sten gun captured. The nights are very long in the jungle. By six it is dark except for the shine of phosphorescent leaves: by midnight the rain will be falling down on yesterday's soaked leaves, and long after the storm is over the rain will continue to drip from the reservoirs of foliage. There will be nearly twelve hours of virtual darkness, and even Marx must have palled.

2

It was quite by chance that I fell in love with Indo-China; nothing was further from my thoughts on my first visit than that I would one day set a novel there. An old friend of the war years, Trevor Wilson, was then our Consul in Hanoi, where another war had long been in progress almost ignored by the British Press, which took their reports from Reuter's, or in the case of The Times from Paris. So after Malaya I stopped off in Vietnam to see my friend, without any idea that all my winters would be spent there for several years to come. I had found Malaya, apart from the Emergency, as dull as a beautiful woman can sometimes be. People used to say to me, 'You should have seen this country in peace-time,' and I wanted to reply, 'But all that interests me here is your war.' Peace-time Malaya would surely have been no more interesting than a round of British clubs, of pink gins, of little scandals waiting for a Maugham to record them.

But in Indo-China I drained a magic potion, a loving-cup which I have shared since with many retired *colons* and officers of the Foreign Legion whose eyes light up at the mention of Saigon and Hanoi.

The spell was first cast, I think, by the tall elegant girls in white silk trousers, by the pewter evening light on flat paddy fields, where the water-buffaloes trudged fetlock-deep with a slow primeval gait, by the French perfumeries in the rue Catina, the Chinese gambling houses in Cholon, above all by that feeling of exhilaration which a measure of danger brings to the visitor with a return ticket: the restaurants wired against grenades, the watch-towers striding along the roads of the southern delta with their odd reminders of insecurity: '*Si vous êtes arrêtés ou attaqués en cours de route, prévenez le chef du premier poste important.*' (This brought to mind the notice in the cool style typical of British Railways hung in the compartments of the little train that ambled along the track from Singapore to Kuala Lumpur.)

I stayed little more than a fortnight on that occasion, and I crammed to the limit 'the unforgiving minute'. Hanoi is as far from Saigon as London is from Rome, but I succeeded, besides staying in those cities, in paying the first of many visits in the southern delta to the strange religious sect, the Caodaists, whose saints include Victor Hugo, Christ, Buddha and Sun Yat-sen, and to the little medieval state established in the marshes of Bentre by the young half-caste, Colonel Leroy, who read de Tocqueville and struck, with the suddenness and cruelty of a tiger, at the Communists in his region. Not so many years ago he had been a small child riding a water-buffalo in the rice fields – now he was all but a king. I was glad years later to write a preface to his autobiography in which he did not attempt to hide the tiger's face behind the smile – a rather small return since he had probably saved my life. It was in 1955, when the French were evacuating the north and I was waiting in Saigon for permission to enter Hanoi, now in the hands of the Viet Minh. To pass the time I thought I would call on the 'general' of one of the original sects who fought their private wars in the south. I received a telephone call from Leroy asking me to come to him at his Saigon office. A Frenchman was there whom he introduced as the public relations officer of 'the general'. The general, he told me, had received my message and would be glad to see me at his headquarters for lunch. However it would be better if I did not accept. The general had called for his files and he had found that three years before I had described him in *Paris-Match* as a former trishaw driver. This was libellous. He had never been a trishaw driver. He had been a bus conductor. Knowing that I was a friend of Leroy, the Frenchman had come to warn me that the general, though he would show me every courtesy at lunch, would make sure that an accident happened to me on the road back to Saigon.

I was anxious on this first visit in 1951 to pay a visit to Phat Diem, one of the two Prince Bishoprics of the north (the other, Bui-Chu, I knew some years later, and there I would have reached the end of my road if a mine had not been detected buried in the track at a point my jeep was about to pass). The two bishops, like the Caodaist Pope, were allies rather than subjects of the French, and maintained small private armies. On this first occasion I was still basking in the favour of General de Lattre and he had put a little Morane plane at my disposal. He had expected me to fly round in it to his own outposts on what were mistakenly called the lines of Hanoi: instead I went with Trevor Wilson to look at the little army of Phat Diem's bishop. On the way back the plane was shot at well within the fictional lines and I made the mistake of mentioning the incident to the general at dinner that night. He was not amused. That evening our relations began to cool – an inconvenience to me, but a disaster to my friend.

The change was not immediately noticeable. I was the general's honoured guest in Hanoi; he presented me with a shoulder-flash of the First French Army, which he commanded at the fall of Strasbourg, and he brought me with him to a reunion of his old comrades. A few months before, all French families had been evacuated from Hanoi, the fall of the city was regarded as imminent, there was the demoralization of defeat. De Lattre had changed all that. In those days the general was able to cast a spell; I heard him tell his old comrades, 'I am returning now to Saigon, but I am leaving with you my wife as a symbol that France will never, never leave Hanoi.'

It was the high summer of his success. It was impossible to imagine then that in little more than a year he would be dying of cancer in Paris, in the sadness of defeat, and that in less than four years I would be taking tea with President Ho Chi Minh in Hanoi.

I went back to England determined to return, but still unaware that I would find the subject for a novel in Vietnam. *Life* had been satisfied with my article on Malaya, so they agreed to send me to Vietnam the next autumn (they did not like the article I wrote there, but they generously allowed me to publish it in *Paris-Match*: I suspect my ambivalent attitude to the war was already perceptible – my admiration for the French army, my admiration for their enemies, and my doubt of any final value in the war).

When I returned some eight months later in October 1951, the changes were startling. De Lattre had lost his only son, ambushed with a Vietnamese battalion in the region of Phat Diem, and he was an altered man. His rhetoric of hope was wearing painfully thin; his colonels were openly critical of him, even to a foreigner. They were tired of his continual references to his own sacrifice – others had sacrificed their sons too and had not been able to fly the bodies home for a Paris funeral. The general had always suffered from a certain anglophobia and, in spite of the deep piety of his wife, he was highly suspicious of Catholicism. Now in a strange sick manner he linked the death of his son with my visit to Phat Diem and the fact that both Trevor Wilson and I were Catholics. He had shifted on to us, in his poor guilt-ridden mind, the reponsibility for his son's death (he had sent his son to join a Vietnamese battalion to break up his relationship with a Vietnamese girl who was a former mistress of the Emperor). He reported to the Foreign Office that Trevor Wilson, who had been decorated for his services to France during the war, was no longer *persona grata*. Trevor was thrown out of Indo-China, and the Foreign Office lost a remarkable Consul and the French a great friend of their country. He was already gone when I returned to Hanoi, but he was allowed to come back for two weeks to pack up his effects.

In the meanwhile I found myself under the supervision of the Sûreté, in the person of a gentleman who I used to call

277

Monsieur Dupont. Alas, poor Monsieur Dupont, what anxieties the two of us caused him when we were again temporarily together. We used to meet him at night in the Café de la Paix in Hanoi and tell him our movements and plans for the morrow and drink *vermouth-cassis* and play *quatre cent vingt-et-un* at which Trevor Wilson consistently threw the winning dice.

Monsieur Dupont had a rather weak head. He would return home to his wife always a little the worse for wear, so that domestic trouble was added to his official trouble, for his wife refused to believe that his light and innocent tippling was all in the cause of duty. On one sad occasion he accompanied Trevor Wilson to Haiphong where Trevor wanted to say good-bye to his friends. Trevor had a passion for unfamiliar bath-houses and he stopped Monsieur Dupont's official car at the beginning of town, attracted by a board advertising a Chinese bath. Monsieur Dupont took the cubicle next to his, as he was bound in duty to do, but a Chinese bath includes an intimate Chinese massage and Monsieur Dupont's heart was too weak to stand it. He passed out and had to be revived by a lot of whisky to which he was equally unaccustomed. The next-tmorning his *gueule de bois* had to be cured with a dose of Fernet Branca, which he had never drunk before. (I am sure he considered that internal spirit was part of the spy's plot.) To add to all these worries he had lost track of me. I was in forbidden Phat Diem with the martial bishop.

I spread the story that I was writing a *roman policier* about Indo-China and the title I had chosen in French was *Voilà, Monsieur Dupont*, and so of an evening, sitting on the pavement, outside the Café de la Paix, while the troops passed, and the lovely drifting Tonkinoises, I would watch the approach of nervous dutiful Monsieur Dupont, his eyes lifted towards mine like a dog's, waiting for the next 'tease'.

The surveillance had started before Trevor's arrival. A few days after I reached Hanoi, Monsieur Dupont came to call. He brought with him two of my books in French editions, and I signed them and drank a glass of lemonade with him. The next day Monsieur Dupont arrived with another book – a *dédicace* to his wife was required – and the next day he brought yet others, for his friends. He had cleared every bookshop in Hanoi, as I found when I tried to get a few copies to give away myself. After that we dropped the pretence and arranged the evening meetings, but it was odd how often in my daily strolls Monsieur Dupont would crop up: in a café where I was drinking, in a shop where I was buying some soap, in a long dull street along which I was walking only for the sake of exercise. We became genuinely fond of each other, and after Trevor's departure he began to feel for me a paternal responsibility. I was smoking then a little opium two or three times a week, and he would plead with me earnestly that this night at least I would go home quietly to bed after the game of *quatre cent vingt-et-un*.

The crisis of suspicion had come when an unsigned telegram was delivered to me in which Trevor announced his imminent arrival from Paris. It was his eccentric economy never unnecessarily to sign a telegram, but obviously to the censorship this was a deliberate attempt to deceive. I guessed matters were coming to a head when I received, through the head of the Sûreté in Vietnam, a command to have lunch with the general. De Lattre was leaving for Paris the next day.

At lunch nothing was said. The guest of honour was a Swiss representative of the Red Cross who was trying to arrange an exchange of prisoners; I sat next to Mr Tam, the head of the Vietnamese police, a man with a reputation for savagery since he had lost a wife, a son and a finger by enemy action. When lunch was over (it was the first occasion when I had seen de Lattre quiet at his own table) the general came to me. '*Ah, le pauvre Graham Greene*,' he had been unable to speak to me, I must come to his cocktail party that evening, and stay on to dinner. So back I went.

The cocktail party went on and on – it was de Lattre's farewell to Hanoi: there were rumours he would not return, and that the recent empty victory of Hoa Binh was the fairing he had expensively bought to take back with him to Paris. At last everybody left except the generals and colonels who were staying for dinner. There was some singing by a soldiers' choir, and General de Lattre sat on the sofa holding his wife's hand. If I had known he was a dying man perhaps I would have perceived in him again the hero I had met a year before. Now he seemed only the general whose speeches were too long, whose magic had faded, whom his

279

colonels criticized – a dying flame looks as if it had never been anything but smoke.

At ten o'clock the singing stopped and the general turned to me. 'And now, Graham Greene, why are you here?' His broken English had an abrupt boastful quality he did not intend. I said, 'I have told you already. I am writing an article for *Life*.'

'I understand,' he said, while the two-starred generals, Linarés and Salan and Cogny, sat on the edges of their chairs pretending not to listen, 'that you are a member of the British Secret Service.'

I laughed.

'I understand you were in the Intelligence Service in the war. For three years.'

I explained to the general that under National Service we did not pick our job – nor continue it when the war was over.

'I understand that no one ever leaves the British Secret Service.'

'That may be true of the Deuxième Bureau,' I said, 'it is not true with us.' A servant announced dinner.

I sat next to the general and we talked polite small talk. Madame de Lattre eyed me sternly – I had disturbed the peace of a sick man whom she loved, on his last night in Hanoi, the scene of his triumph and his failure. Even though I was unaware how sick he was, I felt a meanness in myself. He deserved better company.

When we rose from the table I asked if I might see him alone. He told me to stay till the others had gone and at half past one in the morning he sent for me to his study. Madame de Lattre bade me a cold goodnight. Hadn't her husband enough to worry about?

I had prepared in my mind what I thought was a clear narration, which included even the amount I was being paid by *Life* for my article. He heard me out and then expressed his satisfaction with some grandiloquence (but that was his way). 'I have told the Sûreté, Graham Greene is my friend. I do not believe what you say about him. Then they come again and tell me you have been here or there and I say, I do not believe. Graham Greene is my friend. And then again they come . . .' He shook hands warmly, saying how glad he was to know that all was a mistake, but next day, before he left for Paris, his misgivings returned. I had received yet another dubious telegram, again unsigned – this time from my literary agent in Paris. 'Your friend will arrive on Thursday. Dorothy under instruction from Philip.'

The last sentence referred to my friend, Dorothy Glover, the illustrator of my children's books, who had decided to become a Catholic, and Philip was Father Philip Caraman, the well-known London Jesuit, but it was obvious what the Sûreté made of it. 'I knew he was a spy,' de Lattre told one of his staff, before boarding his plane. 'Why should anyone come to this war for four hundred dollars?' I had forgotten how uncertain his English was – he had mislaid a zero.

I never wrote *Voilà, Monsieur Dupont*; instead the moment for *The Quiet American* struck as I was driving back to Saigon after spending the night with Colonel Leroy. Less than a year ago, when we had toured together his watery kingdom, it was in an armoured boat with guns trained on the bank, but now as night fell we moved gently along the rivers in an unarmed barge furnished, not with guns, but with gramophones and dancing girls. He had built at Bentre a lake with a pagoda in imitation of the one at Hanoi, the night was full of strange cries from the zoo he had started for his people, and we dined on the island in the lake and the colonel poured brandy down the throats of the girls to make the party go and played the Harry Lime theme of *The Third Man* on a gramophone in my honour.

I shared a room that night with an American attached to an economic aid mission – the members were assumed by the French, probably correctly, to belong to the CIA. My companion bore no resemblance at all to Pyle, the quiet American of my story – he was a man of greater intelligence and of less innocence, but he lectured me all the long drive back to Saigon on the necessity of finding a 'third force in Vietnam'. I had never before come so close to the great American dream which was to bedevil affairs in the East as it was to do in Algeria.

The only leader discernible for the 'third force' was the self-styled General Thé. At the time of my first visit to the Caodaists he had been a colonel in the army of the Caodaist Pope – a force of twenty thousand men which theoretically fought on the French side. They had their own munitions factory in the Holy See at Tay Ninh; they supplemented what small arms they could squeeze out of the French with mortars made from the exhaust pipes of old cars. An ingenious people – it was difficult not to suspect their type of ingenuity in the bicycle bombs which went off in Saigon the following year. The time-bombs were concealed in plastic containers made in the shape of bicycle pumps and the bicycles were left in the parks outside the ministries and propped against walls ... A bicycle arouses no attention in Saigon. It is as much a bicycle city as Copenhagen.

Between my two visits General Thé (he had promoted himself) had deserted from the Caodaist army with a few hundred men and was now installed on the Holy Mountain, outside Tay Ninh. He had declared war on both the French and the Communists. When my novel was eventually noticed in the *New Yorker* the reviewer condemned me for accusing my 'best friends' (the Americans) of murder since I had attributed to them the responsibility for the great explosion – far worse than the trivial bicycle bombs – in the main square of Saigon when many people lost their lives. But what are the facts, of which the reviewer needless to say was ignorant? The *Life* photographer at the moment of the explosion was so well placed that he was able to take an astonishing and horrifying photograph which showed the body of a trishaw driver still upright after his legs had been blown off. This photograph was reproduced in an American propaganda magazine published in Manila over the title 'The work of Ho Chi Minh', although General Thé had promptly and proudly claimed the bomb as his own. Who had supplied the material to a bandit who was fighting French, Caodaists and Communists?

There was certainly evidence of contacts between the American services and General Thé. A jeep with the bodies of two American women was found by a French rubber planter on the route to the sacred mountain – presumably they had been killed by the Viet Minh, but what were they doing on the plantation? The bodies were promptly collected by the American Embassy, and nothing more was heard of the incident. Not a word appeared in the Press. An American consul was arrested late at night on the bridge to Dakow (where Pyle in my novel lost his life) carrying plastic bombs in his car. Again the incident was hushed up for diplomatic reasons.

So the subject of *The Quiet American* came to me, during that talk of a 'third force' on the road through the delta, and my characters quickly followed, all but one of them from the unconscious. The exception was Granger, the American newspaper correspondent. The press conference in Hanoi where he figures was recorded almost word for word in my journal at the time.

Perhaps there is more direct *reportage* in *The Quiet American* than in any other novel I have written. I had determined to employ again the experience I had gained with *The End of the Affair* in the use of the first person and the time-shift, and my choice of a journalist as the 'I' seemed to me to justify the use of *reportage*. The press conference is not the only example of direct reporting. I was in the dive-bomber (the pilot had broken an order of General de Lattre by taking me) which attacked the Viet Minh post and I was on the patrol of the Foreign Legion paras outside Phat Diem. I still retain the sharp image of the dead child couched in the ditch beside his dead mother. The very neatness of their bullet wounds made their death more disturbing than the indiscriminate massacre in the canals around.

I went back to Indo-China for the fourth and last time in 1955 after the defeat of the French in the north, and with some difficulty I reached Hanoi – a sad city, abandoned by the French, where I drank the last bottle of beer left in the café which I used to frequent with Monsieur Dupont. I was feeling very ill and tired and depressed. I sympathized with the victors, but I sympathized with the French too. The French classics were yet on view in a small secondhand bookshop which Monsieur Dupont had rifled a few years back, but a hundred years of French civilization had fled with the Catholic peasants to the south. The Metropole Hotel where I used to stay was in the hands of the International Commission. Viet Minh sentries stood outside the building where de Lattre had made his promise, 'I leave you my wife as a symbol that France will never, never . . .' •

Day after day passed while I tried to bully my way into the presence of Ho Chi Minh. It was the period of the *crachin* and my spirits sank with the thin day-long drizzle of warm rain. I told my contacts I could wait no longer – tomorrow I would return to what was left of French territory in the north.

I don't know why my blackmail succeeded, but I was summoned suddenly to take tea with Ho Chi Minh, and now I felt too ill for the meeting. There was only one thing to be done. I went back to an old Chinese chemist's shop in the rue des Voiles which I had visited the year before. The owner, it was said, was 'the Happiest Man in the World'. There I was able to smoke a few pipes of opium while the mah-jong pieces rattled like gravel on a beach. I had a passionate desire for the impossible – a bottle of Eno's. A messenger was dispatched and before the pipes were finished I received the impossible. I had drunk the last bottle of beer in Hanoi. Was this the last bottle of Eno's? Anyway the Eno's and the pipes took away the sickness and the inertia and gave me the energy to meet Ho Chi Minh at tea.

Of those four winters which I passed in Indo-China opium has left the happiest memory, and as it played an important part in the life of Fowler, my character in *The Quiet American*, I add a few memories from my journal concerning it, for I am reluctant to leave Indo-China for ever with only a novel to remember it by.

31 December 1953. Saigon

One of the interests of far places is 'the friend of friends': some quality has attracted somebody you know, will it also attract yourself? This evening such a one came to see me, a naval doctor. After a whisky in my room, I drove round Saigon with him, on the back of his motorcycle, to a couple of opium *fumeries*. The first was a cheap one, on the first floor over a tiny school where pupils were prepared for '*le certificat et le brevet*'. The proprietor was smoking himself: a *malade imaginaire* dehydrated by his sixty pipes a day. A young girl asleep, and a young boy. Opium should not be for the young, but as the Chinese believe for the middle-aged and the old. Pipes here cost 10 piastres each (say 2s.). Then we went on to a more elegant establishment – *Chez Pola*. Here one reserves the room and can bring a companion. A great Chinese umbrella over the big circular bed. A bookshelf full of books beside the bed – it was odd to find two of my own novels in a *fumerie: Le Ministère de la Peur*, and *Rocher de Brighton*. I wrote a *dédicace* in each of them. Here the pipes cost 30 piastres.

My experience of opium began in October 1951 when I was in Haiphong on the way to the Baie d'Along. A French official took me after dinner to a small apartment in a back street – I could smell the opium as I came up the stairs. It was like the first sight of a beautiful woman with whom one realizes that a relationship is possible: somebody whose memory will not be dimmed by a night's sleep.

The madame decided that as I was a *débutant* I must have only four pipes, and so I am grateful to her that my first experience was delightful and not spoiled by the nausea of over-smoking. The *ambiance* won my heart at once – the hard couch, the leather pillow like a brick – these stand for a certain austerity, the athleticism of pleasure, while the small lamp glowing on the face of the pipe-maker, as he kneads his little ball of brown gum over the flame until it bubbles and alters shape like a dream, the dimmed lights, the little chaste cups of unsweetened green tea, these stand for the '*luxe et volupté*'.

Each pipe from the moment the needle plunges the little ball home and the bowl is reversed over the flame lasts no more than a quarter of a minute – the true inhaler can draw a whole pipeful into his lungs in one long inhalation. After two pipes I felt a certain drowsiness, after four my mind felt alert and calm – unhappiness and fear of the future became like something dimly remembered which I had thought important once. I, who feel shy at exhibiting the grossness of my French, found myself reciting a poem of Baudelaire to my companion, that beautiful poem of escape, *Invitation au Voyage*. When I got home that night I experienced for the first time the white night of opium. One lies relaxed and wakeful, not wanting sleep. We dread wakefulness when our thoughts are disturbed, but in this state one is calm – it would be wrong even to say that one is happy – happiness disturbs the pulse. And then suddenly without warning one sleeps. Never has one slept so deeply a whole night-long sleep, and then the waking and the luminous dial of the clock showing that twenty minutes of so-called real time have gone by. Again the calm lying awake, again the deep brief all-night sleep. Once in Saigon after smoking I went to bed at 1.30 and had to rise again at 4.00 to catch a bomber to Hanoi, but in those less-than-three hours I slept all tiredness away.

Not that night, but many nights later, I had a curiously vivid dream. One does not dream as a rule after smoking, though sometimes one wakes with panic terror; one dreams, they say, during disintoxication, like de Quincey, when the mind and the body are at war. I dreamed that in some intellectual discussion I made the remark, 'It would have been interesting if at the birth of Our Lord there had been present someone who saw nothing at all,' and then, in the way that dreams have, I was that man. The shepherds were kneeling in prayer, the Wise Men were offering their gifts (I can still see in memory the shoulder and red-brown robe of one of them – the Ethiopian), but they were praying to, offering gifts to, nothing – a blank wall. I was puzzled and disturbed. I thought, 'If they are offering to nothing, they know what they are about, so I will

285

offer to nothing too,' and putting my hand in my pocket I found a gold piece with which I had intended to buy myself a woman in Bethlehem. Years later I was reading one of the gospels and recognized the scene at which I had been an onlooker. 'So they were offering their gifts to the mother of God,' I thought. 'Well, I brought that gold piece to Bethlehem to give to a woman, and it seems I gave it to a woman after all.'

10 January 1954. Hanoi

With French friends to the Chinese quarter of Hanoi. We called first for our Chinese friend living over his warehouse of dried medicines from Hong Kong – bales and bales and bales of brittle quackery. The family were all gathered in one upper room with the dog and the cat – husband and wife, daughters, grandparents, cousins. After a cup of tea we paid a visit to a relative – variously known as Serpent Head and the Happiest Man in the World. All these Chinese houses have little frontage, but run back a long way from the street. The Happiest Man in the World sat there between the narrow walls like a tunnel, in thin pyjamas – he never troubled to dress. He was rich and he had inherited the business from his father before it was necessary for him to work and when his sons were already old enough to do the work for him. He was like a piece of dried medicine himself, skeletonized by opium. In the background the mah-jong players built their walls, demolished, reshuffled. They didn't even have to look at the pieces they drew, they could tell the design by a touch of the finger. The game made a noise like a stormy tide turning the shingle on a beach. I smoked two pipes as an apéritif, and after dinner at the New Pagoda returned and smoked five more.

11 January 1954. Hanoi

Dinner with French friends and afterwards smoked six pipes. Gunfire and the heavy sound of helicopters low over the roofs bringing the wounded from – somewhere. The nearer you are to war, the less you know what is happening. The daily paper in Hanoi prints less than the daily paper in Saigon, and that prints less than the papers in Paris. The noise of the helicopters had an odd effect on opium smoking. It drowned the soft bubble of the wax over the flame, and because the pipe was silent, the opium seemed to lose a great deal of its perfume, in the way that a cigarette loses taste in the open air.

12 January 1954. Vientiane

Up early to catch a military plane to Vientiane, the administrative capital of Laos. The plane was a freighter with no seats. I sat on a packing case and was glad to arrive.

After lunch I made a rapid tour of Vientiane. Apart from one pagoda and the long sands of the Mekong river, it is an uninteresting town consisting only of two real streets, one European restaurant, a club, the usual grubby market where apart from food there is only the debris of civilization – withered tubes of toothpaste, shop-soiled soaps, pots and pans from the Bon Marché. Fishes were small and expensive and covered with flies. There were little packets of dyed sweets and sickly cakes made out of rice coloured mauve and pink. The fortune-maker of Vientiane was a man with a small site let out as a bicycle park – hundreds of bicycles at 2 piastres a time (say 20 centimes). When he had paid for his concession he was likely to make 600 piastres a day profit (say 6,000 francs). But in Eastern countries there are always wheels within wheels, and it was probable that the concessionaire was only the ghost for one of the princes.

Sometimes one wonders why one bothers to travel, to come eight thousand miles to find only Vientiane at the end of the road, and yet there is a curious satisfaction later, when one reads in England the war communiqués and the familiar names start from the page – Nam Dinh, Vientiane, Luang Prabang – looking so important temporarily on a newspaper page as though part of history, to remember them in terms of mauve rice cakes, the rat crossing the restaurant floor as it did tonight until it was chased away behind the bar. Places in history, one learns, are not so important.

After dinner to the house of Mr X, a Eurasian and a habitual smoker. Thinned by his pipes, with bony wrists and ankles and the arms of a small boy, Mr X was a charming and melancholy companion. He spoke beautifully clear French, peering down at his needle through steel-rimmed spectacles. His house was a hovel too small for him to find room for his wife and child whom he had left in Phnom Penh. There was nothing to do in the evening – the cinima showed only the oldest films, and there was really nothing to do all day either, but wait outside the government office where he was employed on small errands. A palm tree was his bookcase and he would slip his book or his newspaper into the crevices of the trunk when summoned into the house. Once I needed some wrapping paper and he went to the palm tree to see whether he had any saved. His opium was excellent, pure Laos opium, and he prepared the pipes admirably. Soon his French employers would be packing up in Laos, he would go to France, he would have no more opium – all the ease of life would vanish but he was incapable of considering the future. His sad amused Asiatic face peered down at the pipe while his bony fingers kneaded and warmed the brown seed of contentment, and he spoke musically and precisely like a don on the types and years of opium – the opium of Laos, Yunan, Szechuan,

Istanbul, Benares – ah, Benares, that was a kind to remember over the years.*

13 January 1954

On again to Luang Prabang. Where Vientiane has two streets Luang Prabang has one, some shops, a tiny modest royal palace (the King is as poor as the state) and opposite the palace a steep hill crowned by a pagoda which contains – so it is believed – the giant footprint of Buddha. Little side streets run down to the Mekong, here full of water. There is a sense of trees, temples, small quiet homes, river and peace. One can see the whole town in half an hour's walk, and one could live here, one feels, for weeks, working, walking, sleeping, if the Viet Minh were not on their way down from the mountains. We determined, tomorrow before returning, to take a boat up the Mekong to the grotto and the statue of Buddha which protects Luang Prabang from her enemies. There is more atmosphere of prayer in a pagoda than in most churches. The features of Buddha cannot be sentimentalized like the features of Christ, there are no hideous pictures on the wall, no stations of the Cross, no straining after unfelt agonies. I found myself praying to Buddha as always when I enter a pagoda, for now surely he is among our saints and his intercession will be as powerful as the Little Flower's – perhaps more powerful here among a race akin to his own.

After dinner I was very tired, but five pipes of inferior opium – bitter with dross – smoked in a chauffeur's house made me feel fresh again. It was a house on piles and at the end of the long narrow veranda, screened from the dark and the mosquitoes, a small son knelt at a table doing his lessons while his mother squatted beside him. The soft recitation of his lesson accompanied the murmur and the bubble of the pipe.

16 January 1954. Saigon

Laos remained careless Laos till the end. I was worried by the late arrival of the car and only just caught the plane which left the airfield at 7.00 in the dark. Two stops on the way to Saigon. I got in about 12.30. Why is it that Saigon is always so good to come back to? I remember on my first journey to Africa, when I walked across Liberia, I used to dream of the delights of a hot bath, a good meal, a comfortable bed. I wanted to go straight from the African hut with the rats

*A connoisseur would say 'The No. 1 Xieng Khouang opium of Laos' when referring to the best opium from this country. (As, for instance, rubber from Malaya is described as No. 1 r.s.s.) Xieng Khouang is a province to the north-east of Vientiane where the best opium is grown.

running down the wall at night to some luxury hotel in Europe and enjoy the contrast. In fact one never satisfactorily found the contrast – either in Liberia or later in Mexico. Civilization was always broken to one slowly: the trader's establishment at Grand Bassa was a great deal better than the jungle, the Consulate at Monrovia was better than the tradesman's house, the cargo boat was an approach to civilization, by the time one reached England the contrast had been completely lost. Here in Indo-China one does capture the contrast: Vientiane is a century away from Saigon.

18 January 1954

After drinking with M and D of the Sûreté and a dinner with a number of people from the Legation, I returned early to the hotel in order to meet a police commissioner (half-caste) and two Vietnamese plainclothes men who were going to take me on a tour of Saigon's night side. Our first *fumerie* was in the *paillote* district – a district of thatched houses in a bad state of repair. In a small yard off the main street one found a complete village life – there was a café, a restaurant, a brothel, a *fumerie*. We climbed up a wooden ladder to an attic immediately under the thatch. The sloping roof was too low to stand upright, so that one could only crawl from the ladder on to one of the two big double mattresses spread on the floor covered with a clean white sheet. A cook was fetched and a girl, an attractive, dirty, slightly squint-eyed girl, who had obviously been summoned for my private pleasure. The police commissioner said, 'There is a saying that a pipe prepared by a woman is more sweet.' In fact the girl only went through the motions of warming the opium bead for a moment before handing it over to the expert cook. Not knowing how many *fumeries* the night would produce I smoked only two pipes, and after the first pipe the Vietnamese police scrambled discreetly down the ladder so that I could make use of the double bed. This I had no wish to do. If there had been no other reason it would still have been difficult to concentrate on pleasure, with the three Vietnamese police officers at the bottom of the ladder, a few feet away, listening and drinking cups of tea. My only word of Vietnamese was 'No,' and the girl's only word of English was 'OK,' and it became a polite struggle between the two phrases.

At the bottom of the ladder I had a cup of tea with the police officers and the very beautiful madame who had the calm face of a young nun. I tried to explain to the Vietnamese commissioner that my interest tonight was in *ambiance* only. This dampened the spirits of the party.

I asked them whether they could show me a more elegant brothel and they drove at once towards the outskirts of the city. It was now about one o'clock in the morning. We stopped by a small wayside café and entered. Immediately inside the door there was a large bed with a tumble of girls on it and one man emerging from the flurry. I caught sight of a face, a sleeve, a foot. We went through to the café and drank orangeade. The madame reminded me of the old Javanese bawd in *South Pacific*. When we left the man on the bed had gone and a couple of Americans sat among the girls, waiting for their pipes. One was bearded and gold-spectacled and looked like a professor and the other was wearing shorts. The night was very mosquitoey and he must have been bitten almost beyond endurance. Perhaps this made his temper short. He seemed to think we had come in to close the place and resented me.

After the loud angry voices of the Americans, the bearded face and the fat knees, it was a change to enter a Chinese *fumerie* in Cholon. Here in this place of bare wooden shelves were quiet and courtesy. The price of pipes – one price for small pipes and one price for large pipes – hung on the wall. I had never seen this before in a *fumerie*. I smoked two pipes only and the Chinese proprietor refused to allow me to pay. He said I was the first European to smoke there and that he would not take my money. It was 2.30 and I went home to bed. I had disappointed my Vietnamese companions. In the night I woke dispirited by the faults of the play I was writing, *The Potting Shed*, and tried unsuccessfully to revise it in my mind.

20 January 1954. Phnom Penh

After dinner my host and I drove to the centre of Phnom Penh and parked the car. I signalled to a rickshaw driver, putting my thumb in my mouth and making a gesture rather like a long nose. This is always understood to mean that one wants to smoke. He led us to a rather dreary yard off the rue A —. There were a lot of dustbins, a rat moved among them, and a few people lay under shabby mosquito-nets. Upstairs on the first floor, off a balcony, was the *fumerie*. It was fairly full and the trousers were hanging like banners in a cathedral nave. I had eight pipes and a distinguished looking man in underpants helped to translate my wishes. He was apparently a teacher of English.

9 February 1954. Saigon

After dinner at the Arc-en-Ciel, to the *fumerie* opposite the Casino above the school. I had only five pipes, but that night was very dopey. First I had a nightmare, then I was haunted by squares – architectural squares which reminded me of Angkor, equal distances, etc., and then mathematical squares – people's income, etc., square after square after square which seemed to go on all night. At last I woke and when I slept again I had a strange complete dream such as I have experienced only after opium. I was coming down the steps of a club in St James's Street and on the steps I met the Devil who was wearing a tweed motoring coat and a deerstalker cap. He had long black Edwardian moustaches. In the street a girl, with whom I was apparently living, was waiting for me in a car. The Devil stopped me and asked whether I would like to have a year to live again or to skip a year and see what would be happening to me two years from now. I told him I had no wish to live over any year again and I would like to have a glimpse of two years ahead. Immediately the Devil vanished and I was holding in my hands a letter. I opened the letter – it was from some girl whom I knew only slightly. It was a very tender letter, and a letter of farewell. Obviously during that missing year we had reached a relationship which she was now ending. Looking down at the woman in the car I thought, 'I must not show her the letter, for how absurd it would be if she were to be jealous of a girl whom I don't yet know.' I went into my room (I was no longer in the club) and tore the letter into small pieces, but at the bottom of the envelope were some beads which must have had a sentimental significance. I was unwilling to destroy these and opening a drawer put them in and locked the drawer. As I did so it suddenly occurred to me, 'In two years' time I shall be doing just this, opening a drawer, putting away the beads, and finding the beads are already in the drawer.' Then I woke.

There remains another memory which I find it difficult to dispel, the doom-laden twenty-fours I spent in Dien Bien Phu in January 1954. Nine years later when I was asked by the *Sunday Times* to write on 'a decisive battle of my choice', it was Dien Bien Phu that came straightway to my mind.

Fifteen Decisive Battles of the World – Sir Edward Creasy gave that classic title to his book in 1851, but it is doubtful whether any battle listed there was more decisive than Dien Bien Phu in 1954. Even Sedan, which came too late for Creasy, was only an episode in Franco-German relations, decisive for the moment in a provincial dispute, but the decision was to be reversed in 1918, and that decision again in 1940.

Dien Bien Phu, however, was a defeat for more than the French army. The battle marked virtually the end of any hope the Western Powers might have entertained that they could dominate the East. The French with Cartesian clarity accepted the verdict. So, too, to a lesser extent, did the British: the independence of Malaya, whether the Malays like to think it or not, was won for them when the Communist forces of General Giap, an ex-geography professor of Hanoi University, defeated the forces of General Navarre, ex-cavalry officer, ex-Deuxième Bureau chief, at Dien Bien Phu. (That young Americans were still to die in Vietnam only shows that it takes time for the echoes even of a total defeat to encircle the globe.)

The battle itself, the heroic stand of Colonel de Castries' men while the conference of the Powers at Geneva dragged along, through the debates on Korea, towards the second item on the agenda – Indo-China – every speech in Switzerland punctuated by deaths in that valley in Tonkin – has been described many times. Courage will always find a chronicler, but what remains a mystery to this day is why the battle was ever fought at all, why twelve battalions of the French army were committed to the defence of an armed camp situated in a hopeless geographical terrain—hopeless for defence and hopeless for the second objective, since the camp was intended to be the base of offensive operations. (For this purpose a squadron of ten tanks was assembled there, the components dropped by parachute.)

A commission of inquiry was appointed in Paris after the defeat, but no conclusion was ever reached. A battle of words followed the carnage. Monsieur Laniel, who was Prime Minister when the decision was taken to fight at Dien Bien Phu, published his memoirs, which attacked the strategy and conduct of General Navarre, and General Navarre published his memoirs attacking M. Laniel and the politicians of Paris. M. Laniel's book was called *Le Drame Indo-Chinois* and General Navarre's *Agonie de l'Indo-Chine*, a difference in title which represents the difference between the war as seen in Paris and the war as seen in Hanoi.

For the future historian the difference between the titles will seem smaller than the contradictions in the works themselves. Accusations are bandied back and forth between the politician who had never visited the scene of the war and the general who had known it only for a matter of months when the great error was made.

The war, which had begun in September 1946, was, in 1953, reaching a period for the troops not so much of exhaustion as of cynicism and dogged pride – they believed in no solution but were not prepared for any surrender. In the southern delta around Saigon it had been for a long while a war of ambush and attrition – in Saigon itself of sudden attacks by hand-grenades and bombs; in the north, in Tonkin, the French defence against the Viet Minh depended on the so-called lines of Hanoi established by General de Lattre. The lines were not real lines; Viet Minh regiments would appear out of the rice-fields in sudden attacks close to Hanoi itself before they vanished again into the mud. I was witness of one such attack at Phat Diem, and in Bui Chu, well within the lines, sleep was disturbed by mortar-fire until dawn. While it was the avowed purpose of the High Command to commit the Viet Minh to a major action, it became evident with the French evacuation of Hoa Binh, which de Lattre had taken with the loss, it was popularly believed, of one man, that General Giap was no less anxious to commit the French army, on ground of his own choosing.

Salan succeeded de Lattre, and Navarre succeeded Salan, and every year the number of officers killed was equal to a whole class at Saint-Cyr (the war was a drain mainly on French officers, for National Service troops were not employed in Indo-China on the excuse that this was not a war, but a police action). Something somewhere had to give, and what gave was French intelligence in both senses of the word.

There is a bit of a schoolmaster in an intelligence officer; he imbibes information at second hand and passes it on too often as gospel truth. Giap being an ex-professor, it was thought suitable perhaps to send against him another schoolmaster, but Giap was better acquainted with his subject – the geography of his own northern country.

The French for years had been acutely sensitive to the Communist menace to the kingdom of Laos on their flank. The little umbrageous royal capital of Luang Prabang, on the banks of the Mekong, consisting mainly of Buddhist temples, was threatened every campaigning season by Viet Minh guerrilla regiments, but I doubt whether the threat was ever as serious as the French supposed. Ho Chi Minh can hardly have been anxious to add a Buddhist to a Catholic problem in the north, and Luang Prabang remained inviolate. But the threat served its purpose. The French left their 'lines'.

In November 1953, six parachute battalions dropped on Dien Bien Phu, a plateau ten miles by five, surrounded by thickly wooded hills, all in the hands of the enemy. When I visited the camp for twenty-four hours in January 1954, the huge logistic task had been accomplished; the airstrip was guarded by strongpoints on small hills, there were trenches, underground dug-outs, and miles and miles and miles of wire. (General Navarre wrote with <u>Maginot pride</u> of his wire.) The number of battalions had been doubled, the tanks assembled, the threat to Luang Prabang had been contained, if such a threat really existed, but at what a cost.

It is easy to have hindsight, but what impressed me as I flew in on a transport plane from Hanoi, three hundred kilometres away, over mountains impassable to a mechanized force, was the vulnerability and the isolation of the camp. It could be reinforced – or evacuated – only by air, except by the route to Laos, and as we came down towards the landing-strip I was uneasily conscious of flying only a few hundred feet above the invisible enemy.

General Navarre writes with naïveté and pathos, 'There was not one civil or military authority who visited the camp (French or foreign ministers, French chiefs of staff, American generals) who was not struck by the strength of the defences . . . To my knowledge no one expressed any doubt before the attack about the possibilities of resistance.' Is anyone more isolated from human contact than a commander-in-chief?

One scene of evil augury comes back to my mind. We were drinking Colonel de Castries' excellent wine at lunch in the mess, and the colonel, who had the nervy histrionic features of an old-time actor, overheard the commandant of his artillery discussing with another officer the evacuation of the French post of Na-San during the last campaigning season. De Castries struck his fist on the table and cried out with a kind of Shakespearian hysteria, 'Be silent. I will not have Na-San mentioned in this mess. Na-San was a defensive post. This is an offensive one.' There was an uneasy silence until de Castries' second-in-command asked me whether I had seen Claudel's *Christophe Colombe* as I passed through Paris. (The officer who had mentioned Na-San was to shoot himself during the siege.)

After lunch, as I walked round the intricate entrenchments, I asked an officer, 'What did the colonel mean? An offensive post?' He waved at the surrounding hills: 'We should need a thousand mules – not a squadron of tanks – to take the offensive.'

M. Laniel writes of the unreal optimism which preceded the attack. In Hanoi optimism may have prevailed, but not in the camp itself. The defences were out of range of mortar fire from the surrounding hills, but not an officer doubted that heavy guns were on the way from the Chinese frontier (guns elaborately camouflaged, trundled in by bicycle along almost impassable ways by thousands of coolies – a feat more brilliant than the construction of the camp). Any night they expected a bombardment to open. It was no novelist's imagination which felt the atmosphere heavy with doom, for these men were aware of what they resembled – sitting ducks.

In the meanwhile, before the bombardment opened, the wives and sweethearts of officers visited them in the camp by transport plane for a few daylight hours: ardent little scenes took place in dug-outs – it was pathetic and forgivable, even though it was not war. The native contingents, too, had their wives – more permanently – with them, and it was a moving sight to see a woman suckling her baby beside a sentry under waiting hills. It wasn't war, it wasn't optimism – it was the last chance.

The Viet Minh had chosen the ground for their battle by their menace to Laos. M. Laniel wrote that it would have been better to have lost Laos for the moment than to have lost both Laos and the French army, and he put the blame on the military command. General Navarre in return accused the French Government of insisting at all costs on the defence of Laos.

All reason for the establishment of the camp seems to disappear in the debate – somebody somewhere misunderstood, and passing the buck became after the battle a new form of logistics. Only the Viet Minh dispositions make sense, though even there a mystery remains. With their artillery alone the Communists could have forced the surrender of Dien Bien Phu. A man cannot be evacuated by parachute, and the airstrip was out of action a few days after the assault began.

A heavy fog, curiously not mentioned by either General Navarre or M. Laniel, filled the cup among the hills every night around ten, and it did not lift again before eleven in the morning. (How impatiently I waited for it to lift after my night in a dug-out.) During that period parachute supplies were impossible and it was equally impossible for planes from Hanoi to spot the enemy's guns. Under these circumstances why inflict on one's own army twenty thousand casualties by direct assault?

But the Great Powers had decided to negotiate, the Conference of Geneva had opened in the last week of April with Korea first on the agenda, and individual lives were not considered important. It was preferable as propaganda for General Giap to capture the post by direct assault during the course of the Geneva Conference. The assault began on 13 March 1954, and Dien Bien Phu fell on 7 May, the day before the delegates turned at last from the question of Korea to the question of Indo-China.

But General Giap could not be confident that the politicians of the West, who showed a certain guilt towards the defenders of Dien Bien Phu while they were discussing at such length the problem of Korea, would have continued to talk long enough to give him time to reduce Dien Bien Phu by artillery alone.

So the battle had to be fought with the maximum of human suffering and loss. M. Mendès-France, who had succeeded M. Laniel, needed his excuse for surrendering the north of Vietnam just as General Giap needed his spectacular victory by frontal assault before the forum of the Powers to commit Britain and America to a division of the country.

> The Sinister Spirit sneered:
> 'It had to be!'
> And again the Spirit of Pity
> whispered, 'Why?'

3

It was 1953 – between my winter visits to Vietnam – and from the window of the room in which I was writing my report on the Mau Mau rebellion, I was aware first, as always in Kenya, of the huge expanse of sky and the terraces of cloud. Never was there a land so wrapped in air; for in Kikuyuland one lives on a mountain-top, with Nairobi at over five thousand feet and this mission in the Kikuyu Reserve two thousand feet higher yet.

Two miles ahead of me across the Chania River was the Mau-Mau-ridden Fort Hall Reserve from which attackers had come to the mission a year before; fifteen miles behind me was the scene of the Lari massacre, where 150 wives and children of the Kikuyu Home Guard were hacked to death; and six miles away I could see the forested slopes of the Aberdares, the stamping ground of the chief enemy, 'General' Dedan Kimathi. Outside, the red dust rose in little tornadoes, and the maize crackled like light continuous rain.

In moments of depression I sometimes wondered why I had bothered to come so far to be still so distant from the heart of the conflict. In Indo-China, even in Malaya, there was something approaching a front line; I could feel myself sharing to a small extent in the battle. Here the war was secret: it would happen the day after I left or the day before I arrived. It was a private African war which could be hidden so easily from white eyes, just as seventeen strangled bodies lay for weeks unnoticed in a squatters' village on the outskirts of Nairobi, a mile from the highway and the houses of officials.

But if I was still far from the real stage, I was also far from the theatre gallery in London where I could hear only the voices of my fellow 'gods' telling how the play would end and how it should have been written. What seemed plausible there seemed complacent here, and ignorant.

'Where is the man of courage who will see that so long as able men like Kenyatta or Kimathi are excluded from effective political power . . . ?' The voice droned on in the London theatre gallery. From there you could not see the group of burnt huts, the charred corpse of a woman, the body robbed of its entrails, the child cut in two halves across the waist, the officer found still living by the roadside with his lower jaw sliced off, a hand and foot severed. For that, here, was the political power of Kimathi, the power of the panga.

At best I had come down from the gallery to the front of the circle and could see a little more – not of what the play was about but of the movements and moods of the players: I could begin to understand that in this small area of Kenya it was unreasonable to expect people to talk reasonably. There was too much bewilderment and too much fear.

The 1950s had seen the triumph of guerrilla tactics: Indo-China, Malaya, the Central Province of Kenya. At the moment when the weapons of war had increased immeasurably in power and efficiency, the ill-armed guerrilla depending on surprise, mobility and the nature of his native ground had exhibited the limitations of the armament factory. The day of the Lee-Enfield and the Maxim gun were more favourable to the European than those of the dive-bomber and the Bren. (We may yet find this a happy augury in our own troubled future.)

Along the roads out of Saigon I had seen the return of the watch-tower and the border castle, and Kenya too had gone back to the bamboo tower, the wall of pointed thorns, the stakes slanting in the ditch; what we call civilization – for want of a more accurate name – was on the defensive. The offensive was in the hands of the homemade gun and the steel panga. The Victorians had so taught us the idea of progress that we found it disquieting to go back in time. The world had been going in a particular way, and now it was going in another. The prophets had proved more wrong than the witch-doctors – even the prophets of the London School of Economics.

The liberal administrator – from governor to agricultural officer – had been honestly planning a land in which the position of the African would gradually, very gradually, improve, soil erosion would be stopped, new industries would be established, land-hunger be appeased. The day of colour prejudice would run its course: already the old conservative settler was dying out, and the task of ensuring justice between European, African and Asian was becoming a little easier. A common roll of electors and universal suffrage was still, of course, an impracticable dream – the liberal is never hasty – but perhaps one day the only bar would be a cultural one. Quite happily the administrator would administrate himself out of existence.

As for the settler, he had established that peculiarly English dream of a 'home from home' whether it was the rough farmhouse of the old settler, still lit by oil lamps, though surrounded by sixty thousand acres of his own ranching land, or the finely built traditional country house with a touch of Regency.

The Englishman, in those days, liked to be sentimental about the African: he admired the Masai because of their physical beauty, their indifference to civilization (which removed a competitor), and because like Venice they were doomed to extinction ('only born to bloom and drop'). But the Kikuyu were perhaps too close to ourselves. They were naturally a democracy (it was the Government which had forcibly substituted chiefs for the Councils of Elders), they believed in God, even their discontent had European parallels, and their passionate belief in their few lost acres around Fort Hall had something in common with the laments after 1870 for the lost land of Alsace. The half-affectionate nickname, 'the Kukes', was a measure of our limited acceptance. They were sometimes compared to the Jews because of their commercial astuteness, but the Jews are a deeply religious people and so too are the Kikuyu.

When the revolt came, it was to the English colonist like a revolt of the domestic staff. The Kikuyu were not savage, they made good clerks and stewards. It was as though Jeeves had taken to the jungle. Even worse, Jeeves had been seen crawling through an arch to drink on his knees from a banana-trough of blood; Jeeves had transfixed a sheep's eye with seven kie-apple thorns; Jeeves had had sexual connection with a goat; Jeeves had sworn, however unwillingly, to kill Bertie Wooster 'or this oath will kill me and all my seed will die'.

Only missionaries gave unheeded warnings two years before the outbreak of violence; perhaps love is really not so blind as superiority. A belief in God leaves you nearer to the aberrations of paganism than an interest in wattle-clearing or artificial insemination, and the celibate priest in a lonely mission in the Reserve praying daily to the Mother of God was closer to those dark assemblies around the naked woman and the dead goat.

A touch of hysteria was natural enough when the surprise came. Polo-players rode off into the forest carrying their polo sticks on the search for Mau Mau hide-outs; demonstrators, after the murder of a family, pushed aside African police at Government House; there were exaggerated demands that all Kikuyu should be returned to the Reserve, and more than sixty thousand squatters drifted back (twenty thousand by compulsion) from the Rift Valley, leaving the farmers without labour and the Reserve overcrowded and short of food. At a moment when the Kikuyu were dying in hundreds and Europeans only in tens, there were cries of 'Send them back and let the loyal prove their loyalty and the disloyal get back into the forest with the Mau Mau.'

To me who had known Malaya, the settler at first seemed unduly susceptible to the idea of violent death. (Not only the settler: I have seen a judge trying a case in a tin hut at a police station surrounded by barbed wire and watch-towers, with two armed askaris sitting in the court, who yet found it necessary to place on the table before him a revolver covered by his wig – it was a warm day.) In Malaya there had been no demonstrations at Government House and the risks of death were far worse – in the state of Pahang alone, one-tenth of the planters lost their lives in the first three years.

But I had only to stay a while in the countryside and I became aware of how this smaller conflict could prey worse on the nerves. I might smile at the tiny revolver-holster in crocodile, as becoming to a pretty girl as a Dior fashion, at the notice on the hotel board at Nyeri, '12-bore shotgun, lady wishes to exchange for 16-bore,' but stay a while in a lonely farm on the edge of the Aberdare or Kenya forest and you would see the other side.

It is not only that human nature fears bullets less than steel (the photographs of a trunk from which the head has been severed remain long in memory), but that night is more the time of unreason than day. In Malaya it was the days which were dangerous – the morning inspection of the plantation, the ride into town between the walls of jungle: but at night one slept behind barbed wire; one's Malay houseboy was on the same side; there was a Malayan guard who would at least sound the alarm. One's enemy was better armed and trained, but he was more comprehensible. In Kenya the settler was often his only guard, he was well aware that his houseboy had taken the Mau Mau oath and any day might be required to help kill his employer, he had to depend for safety on a flimsy lock to his bedroom door, the revolver by his bed and the vigilance of his dog, and the night inevitably seems longer than the day and full of the creaks of wood and the trottings of a scavenger. I remember one night in the Highlands at a kindly settler's. He couldn't find the key to my room which was separated from the rest of the house. He was afraid it might have been stolen for the Mau

Mau, so, as I had no revolver, he lent me a young boxer. During the night there was the sound of a gunshot and the dog spent the rest of the night awake pointing at the door, ready to spring.

In yet another way the hard lot of the Malayan planter was to be preferred. His stake in the country was thirty years' service and a pension at the end of it. He was a salaried employee who would one day make his home in England (perhaps for that reason Malaya is more free from the hideous architecture of nostalgia). The Kenya planter on the other hand had sunk his capital in the land. Many hardly regarded themselves as English: even a certain bitterness crept into the voice of the second generation: 'England isn't my home. This is my home.'

Not all were rich men: the eccentric days of Happy Valley, of bright young people and free exchangeable love, had been over long ago – only a few haggard relics of Happy Valley remained.

Most farmers had a hard enough struggle without Mau Mau. Locusts came down from Abyssinia to destroy the maize. There were rinderpest, necrosis of the tongue, quarter evil, wireworm, fluke. Foot and mouth, common and uncontrollable, ran through the herds and weakened their resistance; even the puff adder sniped a few head every year. Now the margin of profit was threatened by the emergency. The Mau Mau stole and slashed, the best labour disappeared.

Fear of ruin was to most farmers worse than the fear of death, for their whole life had to be lived here. This was their burial ground. They had been settled, in some parts of Kenya, a third as long as the Kikuyu. In England they would be exiles.

1953 had been a bad year for drought; often there was not enough labour left to gather the pyrethrum crop – a harvest which cannot be delayed – or to dip the cattle with sufficient regularity. In some areas the Government had ordered all maize to be destroyed within three miles of the forest to prevent it falling into Mau Mau hands (the farmer was promised an *ex gratia* payment, but was reasonably anxious about the what and the when). In the ranching areas near Mount Kenya, where 'General China', one of the three Mau Mau leaders, carried on his war for food, the farmer was ordered to *boma* his cattle near

301

his home, but this might mean that they starved on exhausted pastures.

Under these circumstances I was sometimes amazed that the liberal settler was as common as I found him: the young man who recognized that the White Highlands could not remain white for ever and that unused land would one day have to be sequestered: the old veteran who said: 'Those who don't love the African had better get out of here. It's not the country for them.'

I have written of the farmer, but there was another type of settler who brought less good to his new country. You could see him drinking beer in the lounge of the New Stanley Hotel in Nairobi with all the arrogance of Brighton Pier: the day-tripper had found himself four thousand miles from home with black servants to command. Perhaps he worked in one of the big stores and was the more determined after shopping hours to assert himself by being served in his turn. He helped to give the Kenya Police Reserve an ambiguous name; no doubt in his gun-happy 'cops and robbers' romanticism he contributed some of the 460 revolvers and guns which had been lost and stolen during the rebellion.

It was one of the great problems here to convince the Africans that the white, too, was an individual – and that Europeans might be pagan or Christian.

What a strange divided country it was, even this small section of Kenya which one may call Kikuyuland, divided by geography and divided psychologically. The flat, parched acres of the ranchland to the north were no more different from the rolling Wiltshire landscapes and the Kentish lanes twenty miles away and two thousand feet down than were the minds of the whites from each other. The farmer everywhere would talk to you of the slowness of Government, of emergency regulations lying on a desk in Whitehall where the tempo of life goes with the regularity of the bus service outside. Every evening the local radio gave out the long list of violent crimes in Nairobi, and the criticism of the police increased. Periodically came the cry for more summary justice.

The long delays of Kenyatta's trial, which could hardly reach any conclusion through the maze of technicalities for two years at least, the drawn-out mass trials of those concerned in the

302

Lari massacre, were an irritation to worn nerves. Men and women living in the dangerous regions imagined that the speed of justice had been slowed down by inefficiency in gathering evidence – hardly a single blood-stained panga or shirt was unearthed by the police after Lari – by a lack of urgency in Nairobi and a lack of imagination. (There was something a little pedantic and absurd in the wooden shed like an outside lavatory at Githenguri, where the Lari trials were held, marked in chalk 'Judge's Chambers'.)

Some argued that, as the Mau Mau had declared war on their own tribesmen, their own tribesmen might be allowed to try them, and certainly it could be argued that it would be better for a wild African justice to prevail than for British justice to alter the strict requirements of evidence. There are occasions when Pilate's gesture might well be imitated.

But if the settlers were united in their irritation at Colonial Office government, the irritation was returned. Even though the extreme conservative farmers were dying out they could not avoid all responsibility for what had occurred. You were more likely to hear about them from other farmers than to meet them, but somewhere among the parched uplands or the wooded valleys there must have existed that archetypal figure who would slap his servant's face if he replied to him in English.

If emergency regulations remained too long in Whitehall, they were too often ignored when they had been issued. Farmers, for example, were asked, for their own protection and the protection of their neighbours, to group their squatter labour into villages, but in one district this was ignored by one of the leading farmers, and no action was taken by the local Police Reserve, who were themselves settlers. 'We can't enforce that on old So-and-so' was too often the comment on a regulation.

On both sides strange fairy stories were half-believed – by Government, that in certain circumstances the farmers might go into armed rebellion; by farmers, that Government and Army plotted some political solution of the Mau Mau struggle, some form of self-government with equal rights for Europeans, Africans, Asiatics.

The nightmare of the common electoral roll disturbed the

Mau-Mau-haunted sleep. For it was a land of rumour and division – the rumours came in by car with the neighbour from thirty miles away, rumours slipped along the red greasy roads and got bogged down in districts where the denial never turned up for supper: rumours of mass surrenders, of white Mau Mau leaders in the forest, of European desertions. If these were believed by Europeans, in what fantastic world of fantasy did the African live? 'We are bewildered,' an English-speaking Kikuyu said to me, 'and we are afraid. A knock on the door at night. Is it the Mau Mau, the Home Guard, or the police? They all treat us like enemies.' Europe seemed to have come to the Kikuyu Reserve, for nearly all Europe since 1933 has known that momentary stoppage of the heart at the sound of brakes, footsteps, a knock.

Sometimes one felt surprised that the Kikuyu tribe had not all taken to the forest, for the man who was called a loyal Kikuyu too often gained no friend, while if he became a Mau Mau he had one enemy less. Only in the forest, under the three 'Generals' – Dedan Kimathi, Stanley Methengi, and 'China' – did he know for good or ill where he stood.

Dedan Kimathi, a former clerk in the King's African Rifles, was believed to be the chief leader of the forest gangs. He worked in the bamboo forest of the Aberdares, 'China' on the slopes of Mount Kenya. The total numbers were variously estimated, but it is quite possible that the hard core of fighters did not number five hundred men. Added to these were the food carriers and the camp-followers, and the fringe of frightened men who had taken a Mau Mau oath and believed themselves to be bound by it as long as life lasted – houseboys, farmhands, even clerks – these could be called upon at need to help in an elimination.

Perhaps ninety per cent of the Kikuyu tribe had taken the first oath, but the oaths varied in degree until they reached a stage of elaborate and literally bestial obscenity. These last oaths were believed by Europeans to leave the initiate forever doomed, uncleansable, outside his tribe, just as the atrocities at Auschwitz and Belsen put certain Germans for ever outside the pale. It is difficult not to believe that these oaths had been thought out by a mind erudite, complex and trained in anthropology. The leaders in the forest war were simpler men.

We know a little of 'General' Kimathi and his naïve vanity. He was fond of writing letters, to police officers, district officers, even to the Press (signed sometimes 'Askari of the Liberation'). They varied from absurd claims to be head of a Defence Council covering the whole of Africa, from touches of pathetic vanity when he referred to his tours of Africa and Palestine (who knows the satisfaction he may have got from such unlikely dreams cooped up with his followers in the caves and hide-outs of the Aberdare mountains?), to moments of moving simplicity which recall the last letters of Sacco and Vanzetti. *'I am explaining clearly that there is no Mau Mau but the poor man is the Mau Mau and if so, it is only Mau Mau which can finish Mau Mau, and not bombs and other weapons.'*

Who can say that he had no reason to be vain, when you consider that this African clerk now found himself confronted by three British generals, five British regular battalions, six battalions of the King's African Rifles, a battalion of the Kenya Regiment, a squadron of bombers, twelve thousand regular and reserve police, not to speak of eighteen thousand Home Guard of his own tribe? (He was helped of course by his terrain: the altitude of ten thousand feet difficult for sustained operations, the depth and obscurity of the bamboo forest, even by the wild game – elephant, leopard, rhinoceros – who took their toll on the nerves of the young National Service men fresh from the cinemas of Margate or Folkestone.)

It would be easier to draw Kimathi as a heroic figure if we could put out of our minds those bestial ceremonies with the living sheep and the dead goat and the naked woman, or the pictures of mutilated bodies, the white farmer lying hacked wide open in his bath, and the little Ruck boy cut to pieces on his bed beside the toy railway track. Heroes should behave like heroes, and then how easily they would win our allegiance. For over and over again one was moved by the simplicity and pathos of this savage enemy.

Here are the contents of a young Mau Mau's box when he was arrested. How far it seems from that world of the three oaths which he had taken, the compulsory circumcision of an eighteen-year-old girl at which he had stood on guard. One essay in English, illustrated by chalk drawings, of the differences between a straight and curved bird's beak; an essay on the pollination of plants; a third on the difference between an ostrich's and an eagle's claw; a *simi* – the two-edged knife so often used by the Mau Mau; a Scottish hymn book; a Boy Scout belt; a dictation of fifty words, with forty-nine mistakes; three years' accumulation of letters from a Kikuyu girl, and a careful copy of Hamlet's speech, 'To be or not to be.'

> The oppressor's wrong, the proud man's contumely,
> The pangs of disprised love, the law's delay,
> The insolence of office . . .

It would be romantic to read into this copy more than a school exercise, and yet who knows? A missionary told me that the works of Shakespeare and of the author of the Biggles books were the only forms of imaginative literature to which he had found his pupils attracted.

And if it would be easy to paint the Mau Mau leaders and followers in too heroic and simple a light, so it would be easy to darken the character of their opponents; for neither the trigger-happy East African Rifles, the European Police nor the Home Guard came out of the struggle unstained. Perhaps, I thought, the worst problems of the future will be the blood feuds surviving the shooting war. In this case the Mau Mau leaders showed a kind of savage statesmanship, for wherever possible they tried to involve the relatives of the murdered in the crime. Both the sister and mother of Chief James, who was killed by ambush in the Fort Hall Reserve, were implicated. The terror of the oath broke down the bond of blood.

The Home Guard – sometimes armed with nothing better than a spear or a bow – knew the interminable memory of his tribe, and his occasional heroism was more remarkable than his occasional cowardice. Prudence recommended that he should do nothing, but when once his stand had been taken and his spear dipped he had to exact what he could, while he could. Even granted that in this conflict he was likely to prove to be on the successful side, who was going to guarantee his safety in the years of so-called peace when his weapons would have been taken away from him?

Little wonder that fear sometimes drove him to undiscriminating violence and sometimes to cowardice. There were cases where cattle had been driven away from a *boma* next door to a Home Guard post without a shot being fired. 'It's your cattle we want, not your lives.'

Because they and their families were under the threat of death it was natural for them to feather the moment's nest. The repentant Mau Mau oath-taker, the stranger who had fled into the Reserve, gave him his opportunity. The newcomer had been compelled to take the oath; now he hoped to be cleansed from it at a tribal ceremony and settle again, as in the old days, with the past dead and buried, herd his cattle and grow his maize and bananas, grow old in peace, but very soon he found that *this* past would never be allowed to die.

The cleansing ceremony had cost him two shillings, but afterwards a confession was required (if he had nothing to confess it was best to invent something – the name of the oath administrator, the names of the askaris who stood on guard outside the hut; unfortunate for some of these if several inventions tallied). The confession was taken down by the Home Guard and presented to a Council of Elders who must be entertained, and for this twenty shillings perhaps would be required of him.

Worse still his name was now on a list; he could be made the scapegoat for any crime that happened in his district. Next time the Home Guard on their nocturnal patrol visited his *shamba*, perhaps a hundred shillings would be needed to buy them off. If he was beaten by the loyal Home Guard, who would defend an ex-Mau Mau?

The Home Guard increased his own danger with every exaction and always at the back of his mind was the fear of the future. He, too, like the oath-breakers of the fourth degree, had separated himself; he had the praise of the white men and the official chiefs and headmen, but white men have short memories, they do not harbour blood feuds, and officials change.

He listened to the Indian radio. Pamphlets from Indian sources told him that the great Indian Nehru was once in a British prison and now ruled his country. In the forest the Mau Mau fighter dreamed of a Messiah's return and in the Reserve the Home Guard had his terrified nightmare of That Man, Kenyatta.

When Jomo Kenyatta won his first appeal on a technicality, depression lay over the Kikuyu Reserve; there was no man except the Mau Mau fighter who did not dread his return. Better than several battalions of British troops, I thought then, would be the announcement by the Kenyan Government that, whatever the result of Kenyatta's appeal, expedience dictated that he should never be allowed to live in Kenya.

The guilt or innocence of Kenyatta was not involved. The world is wide enough and it was for the good of Kenya that one man should finish his life outside its borders. One decisive and spectacular act such as this, I thought, might cure the worst ill from which Kenya suffered – the sense of indecision.

Indecision ruled the Government before the Emergency and it ruled the Emergency because it is part of the modern mind. We have lost the power of clear action because we have lost the ability to believe.

Even a surrender offer addressed to the gang leaders was so drafted that it could be explained away as meaning little at all. Badly timed – for offers of surrender terms should surely come after successes and not reversals – it seemed to mean little more than, 'Come in, waving your green branches, and if you have been implicated in murder you will be tried by all the usual processes of law and hanged; otherwise you can trust to our justice and merely fill our overloaded prisons.' That was not the intention, but between the thought and the act had fallen the shadow of indecision – how would the loyal Kikuyu who had lost wives and children regard an amnesty, how would the settler when he remembered the murder of the Ruck family?

Indecision is not understood by the African mind. It irritates him in the smallest details of his life. How often was the complaint made by a Kikuyu that one year he was told his wattle-trees had to be grown nine feet apart, another year seventeen feet, and then again nine, that one year the terracing of his sloping acres had to be done one way, another year differently? The idea of truth developing through trial and error is alien to the African – one may say that he is nearer to the Catholic with his deposit of faith than he is to the scientific inquirer. His own tribal framework with its elaborate customs gave him a sense of the unchanging; the European had broken that up and had so far given little in return.

The Protestant missionaries offered him rites apt to vary with each individual missionary, just as agricultural policy varied with every agricultural officer. The Government offered schools free from what idealists considered the excrescences of religious teaching and it was the African who brought religious teaching back in a strange and garbled form into the independent schools founded by Jomo Kenyatta after the Protestant missionaries had refused to allow the girls in their schools to be circumcized in the tribal fashion.

For the Kikuyu – you can tell it even in the grim sad ritual of the oath – is deeply religious. It is not the European who brought God to Africa; too often he had driven Him out. 'Of course we believe in God,' a Kikuyu said to a priest of my acquaintance. 'Everybody does. Don't we say, "God" when we cut our finger?'

In the Fort Hall Reserve I was being guided to a Home Guard post by a young Kikuyu, the son of a chief condemned to death by Mau Mau. 'Where is your revolver?' he asked me. I told him I didn't possess one. 'Ah,' he said, 'I see you trust in the kindness of God.'

A priest said to me: 'They ask unanswerable questions. They say to me: "Didn't God make a land for each people to live in, black and white, and didn't he put the sea between us so that we shouldn't interfere with each other?"'

It is impossible not to love these people when you don't fear them. They have a vivid and direct imagery; when they talk of the soul it is as if they saw it – the soul goes up this way and down that and they can report its progress.

A Kikuyu was condemned to death for being found in possession of gelignite. He had had it for many years he said, for medical purposes; and the judge believed his story and while formally sentencing him indicated the likelihood of a reprieve. A priest visited his wife to comfort her with the news of his probable safety. 'I hope you are right, Father,' she said. 'My soul is like a clock that goes round and round, but if he dies it will stop right there for ever,' and she showed him the hour of twelve.

There was one odd thing about the condemned Mau Mau.

Nine out of ten became Catholics in the condemned cell when hope was over. Perhaps it was the personality of one Irish priest who began instructing them as soon as they had been sentenced and spent the last night in the cell with them. The Attorney-General walking round the prison one night in Nyeri saw a white man squatting on the floor of the condemned cell with three Africans sitting round him. It was the Father.

At Nyeri there was an attempted prison break from the condemned cell; troops cordoned the cell: tear-gas was used, and at last the prisoners made their final conditions. They would die quietly if the priest would come in to them: they wanted beer and baptism.

'They die like angels,' this priest said to me. 'I don't often see Europeans die so well.' When so many hundred times you have had to descend into the pit below the gallows to give the last rites to the broken-necked carrion lying there, each body becomes the body of an individual. You are in a different world from the courtroom at Githenguri with the rows of numbered black figures from which justice – with often insufficient means – tries to separate what we call the guilty from what we call the innocent.

British justice was not a sufficient gift to the Kikuyu people to win them for the future. There is an English axiom that justice should not only be done, but that it should be seen to be done. That condition was almost impossible under the Emergency. Nor was a progressive agricultural policy enough nor a secular education. To take the place of the lost tribal discipline the Kikuyu sought another discipline, and other sacraments in place of their own tribal sacrifices.

For good or ill the future of the Kikuyu seemed to me then to depend on religion – either they would be won by the Christianity of the priest in the execution pit or by the strange faith of Kenyatta's independent schools where they were taught that there was a white God and a white Bible and every text had a secret meaning which the African was not expected to notice. 'Eyes have you and see not' – this means, their teachers said, that you cannot see what these white people and their white God intend for you and your children, while the black God lay in hiding like the Mau Mau in the bamboo forest.

My stay in Kenya brought me unexpectedly in contact with a friend whom I had known since I left Oxford. How little we change. We are pursued through life by our shadow which caricatures us but which only our friends notice. We are too close to pay it any attention, even when it quite outrageously plays the clown, exaggerating our height in the evening and dwarfing us at the midday hour. And then there are those lines stamped on the left hand ... I wonder whether, if our tracks about the globe were visible at one glance from a god's point of view, they would not have the same designs as they have on the palm. In my case perhaps African rivers run down below the thumb, and a skirmish in Indo-China lies where the cross is formed below the mount of Venus.

These are thoughts which rise whenever my old friend Robert Scott comes to mind. He was one of my greatest friends at Oxford, but I lost touch with him completely for nearly thirty years. One day I arrived in Nairobi to report the Mau Mau rebellion and forty-eight hours later a message was left at my hotel that the High Commissioner for East Africa wished to see me at his office. He was sending his car and his secretary.

In the car I asked his secretary the High Commissioner's name. 'Sir Robert Scott.' The last time I had heard of Robert he was a Colonial Secretary in Palestine. Scott is a common name. It seemed unlikely that this was my old friend.

'Sir Robert has asked me to show you straight in.'

It was indeed Robert. He sat in the enormous gleaming room completely unchanged, Gaelic, dark, brooding, somehow nervous, behind his great bare desk, fingering a pipe. At Oxford he had always fingered a pipe as though it kept him by a finger's breadth in touch with reality, because the odd thing about this heavy blunt figure, who always seemed to speak with some reluctance, after a long pondering, with a gruff Scottish accent, was that at any moment he was liable to take flight into the irrelevant, irrational world of fantasy.

'Robert!' I exclaimed.

It was as if we had been whirled simultaneously into that Oxford past. At Balliol I had sometimes teased him mercilessly.

Coming from a Scottish university, he seemed much older than I was, and his pipe gave him in my eyes an air of bogus wisdom against which I reacted. A puff was the excuse for a long laconic silence. If I hadn't teased him I might have been in danger of accepting him as an authority on life, and that would have been rash indeed.

For instance there had been the affair of the young barmaid of the Lamb and Flag in St Giles's whom we all agreed resembled in her strange beauty the Egyptian Queen Nefertiti. What quantities of beer we drank in order to speak a few words with her. We were too young and scared to proceed further, and more than a month of one summer passed before I realized how the slow pipe-smoking wiseacre Robert had succeeded beyond any of us. He was regularly taking her out on her day off in a punt on the Isis and reading her translations from Ronsard. His own translations, for like myself he wrote verse in those days – very traditional verse, but unlike me he was lucky enough not to find a publisher. They might not have done well for his future in the Colonial Office, and anyway who would need a publisher when he had Nefertiti as an audience?

One evening he came to see me. He was even more laconic than usual and puffed a great deal at his pipe. He wanted my advice, he said, and that surprised me, for it had usually been his part to give advice. Apparently Nefertiti had threatened to write to the Dean of Balliol and complain of his conduct.

'What have you done to her?'

'Nothing.'

'Perhaps that's why she's complaining.'

Nevertheless the danger was serious. The Dean, known as 'Sligger', was not a man to sympathize with a heterosexual dilemma. I was at a loss what to advise.

'I have thought of a plan,' Robert said.

'What?'

'I'll invite her to tea, and while she's coming up the stairs I'll lean over the banisters and empty a glass of water on her.'

'But, Robert . . . surely that will only make things worse.'

'I can think of nothing else,' he said sadly.

A few weeks later he called on me again. 'It worked,' he said.

'What worked?'

312

'The glass of water.'

I looked at him in amazement. A douche of cold water ...
no more Ronsard ... it seemed to me he must have tapped some
deep source of irrational Celtic wisdom. The Lamb and Flag
lost a group of customers, but there was no complaint to the
Dean.

I remember another illustration of his strange irrationality,
which was never apparent in the rather pedestrian essays he
read aloud at tutorials (we had the same tutor, Kenneth Bell,
who was often impatient with the slow impeccable logic of Scott's
prose leading to a judgement which condemned once again the
errors of Henry VIII or the frivolity of the Young Pretender).
A number of us in a manic mood had decided to enliven the
little town of Wallingford. I chose to go as an artist drawing
souls in the marketplace at sixpence a time. The future father of
the House of Commons, Robin Turton, was one of us, but I
can't remember what part he played, though I think he was
dressed in an officer's uniform of some foreign power. Robert,
who could already boast grey hairs, went as a middle-aged
clergyman who was hunting for a runaway wife. He called at the
rectory and took tea with the sympathetic wife of the rector in
her husband's absence. She urged him to be generous and forgive,
and after tea they prayed together. As we returned to Oxford he
added a detail to his story. 'When she went out of the room to
find her prayer book I left a bunch of bananas in the grand
piano.'

'Bananas? What on earth for?'

'It seemed the right thing to do.'

Now in Nairobi the High Commissioner looked nervously
at me over the great bare desk. Was he too thinking back into
that absurd past? He asked me to stay with him. He had a house
on the outskirts of Nairobi. 'Scotch baronial,' he said shyly,
perhaps afraid that I would laugh.

But I had hired a car with an African driver and was leaving
next day for the Kikuyu Reserve. 'I'll be coming back in a week
or two,' I promised.

It was nearly a month before I returned to Nairobi and rang
up the High Commissioner's office.

'Sir Robert is not at the office,' I was told. 'He is not well.'

313

'Nothing serious, I hope?'

'He will not be back at work for some days,' I was told guardedly, but an hour later his secretary rang me at the hotel and I was told that Sir Robert would like me to go to dinner. A car would be sent for me.

The house – I'm not sure that it was not called Abbotsford – was certainly Scotch baronial, singularly out of place in Africa, though not perhaps in Nairobi. My voice when I called 'Boy!' was hushed and lost in a great stony hall and nobody came. It was like the opening of a Hammer film. At last I heard Robert's voice faintly calling to me from above to come up. A door stood open and I went in. Robert lay in bed propped on two pillows. He fingered his pipe nervously.

'What's wrong, Robert?'

'I've had an accident.'

Again there was that apprehensive look as though he expected me to laugh.

'What happened?'

'I slipped in my bath.'

'You haven't broken your hip?'

'I sat down on the soap dish,' he said.

I wish I could convey that slow Scottish accent which could make putting bananas into a grand piano seem reasonable, even banal. He said, 'The soap dish broke. I was badly cut and I called for my boy. He came in, and when he saw the blood he thought it was a Mau Mau outrage so he ran away.'

He paused, perhaps waiting for the laugh which now I suppressed easily because I was no longer young.

'I got to a telephone,' he said, 'and asked for a doctor. But when he came there was a power cut – or it may have been the Mau Mau. He had to put in twelve stitches by the light of an electric torch.' He finished his story and looked at me with relief – I hadn't laughed.

'Poor Robert,' I said, but I was thinking of young Robert bending over the banisters and pouring water on Nefertiti's head, praying with the rector's wife in Wallingford – life that begins absurdly will go on absurdly to the end. The lines don't alter on the palm.

It was the last time I spent with him. A few years later I

314

had a Christmas card from Mauritius where he had been appointed Governor and lived in a beautiful old colonial house with, I imagined, eighteenth-century cannon on the lawn. He invited me to stay, but I never went, and I regret it now, for who knows what bizarre event might have occurred there?

Sir Robert Scott died years ago. I have reached the age when one outlives friends more easily than memories of them and, as I write, another incident returns to mind – that occasion outside Berkhamsted Town Hall when he wore a heavy moustache and appeared as Rudyard Kipling making an appeal for the Boy Scout movement and a retired admiral called Loder-Symonds took the chair until he noticed that something seemed somehow to be wrong ... I don't think the Colonial Office ever realized how strange a servant they had enlisted.

Chapter 7

1

IT WAS, I think, in 1954 that I was deported from Puerto Rico, an occasion I shall always remember with pleasure. Life is not rich in comedy; one has to cherish what there is of it and savour it during the bad days.

Under the McCarran Act I had become a prohibited immigrant to the United States. At the age of nineteen for the fun of the thing I had joined the Communist Party in Oxford as a probationary member and during my short stay with them contributed four sixpenny stamps monthly to the Party's funds. These facts had not, as one might have imagined, been cleverly unearthed by the CIA. I had disclosed them rather naïvely myself, for I trusted the First Secretary of the American Embassy in Brussels, where I happened to be for a debate with François Mauriac, and he had told me that the State Department were anxious for cases which would expose the absurdity of the Act. So I mentioned my past to a *Time* correspondent.

The plastic curtain fell immediately and was not lifted again until John Kennedy was President. If I wished to visit the United States I had to get special permission from the Attorney General in Washington – this took as a rule about three weeks and my stay was limited to four. I had to inform the authorities on which planes I would arrive and leave, and mysterious letters and numbers were inscribed on my temporary visa which always ensured a long delay at Immigration. I rather enjoyed the game – it provided an admirable excuse when I wanted to refuse invitations from my publisher. The first time I found it a little inconvenient was in 1954.

I had been staying in Haiti (then a relatively happy country) with my friends Peter Brook and Truman Capote and I wanted to return to England by the quickest possible route. This was by Delta Airlines to San Juan in Puerto Rico, on to New York by a connecting Pan American plane and thence by BOAC to London. I went to see the American Ambassador in Port-au-Prince and explained my problem. Could he grant me a transit visa without all the delay of applying to the Attorney General? He was sympathetic, but he told me no. What I could do, however – and he assured me it was quite legal – was transit without a visa if I had no objection to being locked in a room at the airports in San Juan and New York.

I had no objections, but I had a strong instinct his plan wouldn't work as easily as all that.

My plane arrived in San Juan about nine thirty in the evening and my connection left two hours later. A large flushed man in a khaki uniform with a surly manner took one look at my passport and the mysterious figures.

'Ever been a member of the Communist Party?'

'Yes. For four weeks at the age of nineteen.' It was my blithe formula.

He told me to get out of the queue and wait till he had time to deal with me. His tone was not friendly, and I felt sure now that my journey was going to be an unconventional one. With a sense of exhilaration I sat down to read an adventure of Jeeves and Bertie Wooster. How dull a flight can be when the only delays are occasioned by 'mechanical faults' or 'late arrival of incoming plane'. Here, at long last, was something different.

Nearly an hour passed and then the Immigration man summoned me abruptly to follow him into a small office. Closing the door he leaned his heavy weight against it as though he expected me to make a bolt for freedom. On the other side of the table sat his senior officer, a man in his forties with a charming and intelligent manner, who offered me a seat. He said, 'I'm afraid we can't let you go on.'

I told him what the American Ambassador had said, but ambassadors cut no ice at all with Immigration.

'We'll put you on a plane back to Haiti in the morning.'

I said, 'If you'd lock me in the bar I could have a drink. I'm rather thirsty.'

The surly man resented the politeness of his superior. He wanted to put me back in my proper place. 'This'll be a dry airport for you, buddy,' he said.

All the same it was not to be a dry city. His officer was more accommodating. 'If you give us your word of honour not to escape you can spend the night at a hotel in San Juan.'

317

'I have no dollars,' I said, though that was not strictly true.
'Uncle Sam will pay,' he said.

He summoned two plainclothes men to take me to a hotel, and as we drove into the city they explained they would sleep in the next room to mine and would wake me at six thirty to take me to the airport. I smiled to myself at my recent knowledge that I had no visa to return to Haiti. American citizens did not require a visa, so no one had thought of that, but I wasn't going to enlighten them yet.

We became friendly on the drive and I invited the two officers to drink whisky with me in the bar of the hotel. We had one round and then a second – I could be as generous as I liked at Uncle Sam's expense. Presently one of the officers said, 'Seems a pity he shouldn't see anything of San Juan.'

'Let's drive him around a bit,' the other said.

I didn't see very much of the city, the streets were dark and few people were still about – once a man with a bloodstained bandage staggered into our headlights – but I saw a lot of bars. At one thirty in the morning one of my companions was finding it difficult to balance on two feet, and I suggested it was time for bed – if I really had to be up by six thirty.

In the morning we hardly talked on the way to the airport – one of the detectives was suffering from a bad hangover. We advanced in an official group towards the desk of Delta Airlines, and the more sober showed his badge. 'You are to put this gentleman on the flight to Haiti.'

It was then I played my joker. 'I have no visa for Haiti,' I said. I couldn't have timed it better.

'We can't take him without a visa,' the Delta official said.

'What time does the Haitian Embassy open?'

'Ten thirty.'

'We'll take him downtown to get his visa and you'll have to put him on the next plane.'

'I'm on my way to England,' I said, 'I don't want to go to Haiti and I'm not going to ask for a visa.'

The confusion was complete and leaving them to sort it out I strolled to the telegraph office in the airport hall where I sent a telegram to Reuter's in London: 'Am being deported to Haiti by

American authorities in Puerto Rico. For background ring my secretary at such and such a number.' It was one of the rare occasions when I welcomed a little publicity. On my return to the Delta desk I found they had sorted matters out – or so they believed. The Delta official would telegraph to his manager in Port-au-Prince to get permission from the Haitians to let me land. I thought it as well to make no more trouble for the moment, and I was escorted between the two detectives like a VIP to the boarding steps. We took off a little late.

I had only just undone my belt when the captain settled down beside me. 'Been in a bit of trouble?' he asked with sympathy.

I told him what had happened.

'Ah,' he said, 'I was a Communist myself once.'

He told me his story. He had been an actor in Hollywood and had been blacklisted. So he had become a pilot for Delta. I wondered how all the blue-haired women on the plane would have reacted to the knowledge that their pilot had been a Communist.

I said, 'You go on to Havana, don't you?'

'Yes, and then to Miami.'

'Do you mind if I stay with you as far as Havana?'

'I'll be glad to have you,' he said.

When we came in to land at Port-au-Prince I could see the Delta manager pacing the tarmac. During my two weeks in Haiti I had met him several times and had taken an irrational dislike to him. Now when I came down the ladder he stormed towards me.

'You've caused the hell of a lot of trouble,' he said. 'I've had to go to the Foreign Ministry here and persuade them to let you spend the night. Then we shall send you to Jamaica.'

For the first time I was irritated – after all I had passed a very short night. I said, 'I'm not a bloody parcel and you are not sending me anywhere.'

'Huh?'

'I'm going on in this plane to Havana.'

'You aren't going anywhere in my plane.'

The captain had joined us. He said, 'I'm taking this gentleman to Havana in *my* plane.'

It was fine socialist theatre: the good Communist confronted the bad capitalist, and in the socialist theatre the issue is never in doubt. The manager turned disagreeably away.

After we had taken off for Havana the air hostess began to distribute coloured cards. 'What are they?' I asked.

'Transit cards for passengers to Miami.'

'Can I have one?'

She gave me a card. I thought that it might in some way prove useful, even though as a British subject I could land in Havana in those days without a visa.

After we landed at Havana the blue-haired women who were bound for Miami streamed through Immigration showing their transit cards. It seemed quicker to get through Immigration that way, so I showed the transit card too. Then I took a taxi to a hotel I knew in the old town and after a hot bath went to bed. It had been a tiring trip and I was soon asleep.

A telephone woke me.

'Who's there?'

'Is that Mr Greene?'

'Yes.'

'This is the *New York Times*. We've received a Reuter's message about your being deported from Puerto Rico.'

'Yes, I was.'

'The message said to Haiti, but we found you'd gone on to Havana.'

'Yes. I like it better here.'

'We've been trying all the big hotels and I never thought of this one.'

'I like this one the best.'

After his call I tried to sleep again, but the telephone rang and rang and I found myself having to make the same conversation. This time it was with the local correspondent of the *Daily Telegraph*. He got my confirmation of the Reuter's message. Then he said, 'Perhaps I ought to warn you.'

'What about?'

'I spoke to the Immigration authorities here when I was trying to trace you. They were quite surprised. They say you never passed Immigration. They are looking for you everywhere.'

They never found me. The police were not very efficient in the days of Batista.

2

The End of the Affair had appeared in 1951 – now it was 1955 and I had just finished *The Quiet American*. The mood of escape was still there, but this time it took me no further than to Monte Carlo, to live luxuriously for a few weeks in the Hôtel de Paris (chargeable as an expense to my income tax), to work long hours at the Casino tables (my losses I considered might be fairly chargeable too), and to write what I hoped would prove an amusing, agreeably sentimental *novella* – something which neither my friends nor my enemies would expect. It was to be called *Loser Takes All*. A reputation is like a death mask. I wanted to smash the mask.

I followed a strict routine – breakfast in bed, work till eleven, an hour in the *cuisine* of the Casino before lunch, a siesta, two more hours in the *cuisine*, dinner, and then a period of sustained work in the *Salle Privée* from nine till midnight. I never discovered a system, but I didn't lose. At the end of my stay I had made a profit of four pounds – an ignoble figure which I hastened to lose *en plein* before catching my plane. They had been happy days.

For the first time – and I think the last – I drew a principal character from the life. Dreuther, the business tycoon in *Loser Takes All*, is undeniably Alexander Korda, and the story remains important to me because it is soaked in memories of Alex, a man whom I loved. I have even used scraps of his dialogue. I can still remember him saying to me, in that hesitant Hungarian accent, which lent a sense of considered wisdom to his lightest words, what Dreuther said in my book to Bertram, the accountant who is going to marry and whom he promises a honeymoon on his yacht at Monte Carlo, 'My dear boy, it is not easy to lose a good woman. If one must marry it is better to marry a bad woman.'

He even provided me with the plot of *Loser Takes All*. I was on holiday in Anacapri with a very dear friend when we received a telegram inviting us both to join him in Athens for a cruise in his yacht, the *Elsewhere*. The *Elsewhere*, so romantically named, was *his* way of escape, from film scripts and directors and the

321

Prudential Insurance Company. At first she had been a rather incomplete escape – the *Elsewhere* was kept in the old port of Antibes, which I can see now from my window as I write; she was on a sort of tether there that allowed him to go ashore daily to telephone his office – from Monte Carlo, from Portofino, from Calvi, but as the years passed she was allowed to wander loose – in one small Greek island where we were weather-bound on the way to Istanbul (which we never reached) there was not even a post office. He was really at last elsewhere, happy and carefree. He could talk about pictures, the poetry of Baudelaire the theatre – anything but films. We had an unspoken pact to change the subject quickly if anybody on board spoke of films.

This trip in Greek waters to which we had been invited was the first time, I think, when he let the *Elsewhere* loose. The rendezvous was the Hôtel Grande Bretagne, but when we arrived there was no *Elsewhere* and no Korda and no message. The hotel knew nothing of his coming.

Those were still the days of strict currency regulations and we had very little money with us and the Grande Bretagne was a very expensive hotel. The first day we were alone we were extravagant but waking a second morning with no news of the boat, we had to be careful . . . which meant being more extravagant: all our meals in the hotel rather than in a cheap café; in place of a taxi an expensive hotel car which could be put on the bill. I still remember the severe price for a picnic lunch provided by the hotel – we ate it over the Corinth Canal in hope of seeing the *Elsewhere* below us making her way to Athens.

Well, Alex like Dreuther did eventually turn up in time to pay our 'honeymoon' bill, and the story of *Loser Takes All* had been born over the retsina wine of the anxious picnic lunch. I even sold the film rights, and the film proved a disaster of miscasting, with a middle-aged actress as the twenty-year-old heroine, a romantic Italian star as the unromantic English accountant, and Robert Morley playing Robert Morley. Over the casting Alex had his little revenge (he must certainly have recognized himself as Dreuther) by refusing permission for Alec Guinness, who was under contract to him, to play the part. All the same I don't think he was offended by the portrait, which was drawn with some of the deep affection I felt for him.

322

In spite of the Hungarian accent it mustn't be thought that Alex was monotonously wise. He had strange and endearing lapses. Only a foreigner could have plunged so deeply in that disastrous costume drama – was it even shown? – *Bonnie Prince Charlie*. It was often better not to take his advice when it came to films. I remember the only script conference Carol Reed and I had with him before starting work on our film, *The Fallen Idol*, the adaptation of my short story about a child and a butler called 'The Basement Room'. Alex wanted me to change the butler into a chauffeur 'because children are so interested in mechanics, Graham. And then, you see, you open the film at London airport and the parents are going away by plane and the little boy is very interested in the engine of the car . . .' I objected. 'How many films begin with a plane leaving an airport or arriving at one?' He wasn't convinced, but he let us have our way.

His human wisdom was always greater than his film wisdom. The fifties were for me a period of great happiness and great torment – manic depression reached its height in that decade, and I remember there was one more than usually suicidal suggestion – I forget what – which I had put up to a Sunday newspaper. He spoke to me on the telephone. 'My dear boy, this is so foolish what you plan. Come with me to Antibes. You are bored. All right. We will go on the *Elsewhere*.' How he penetrated my life. It was he who had taken me for the first time to Monte Carlo, and so it was that my character Brown in *The Comedians* was born in that city. I knew Antibes first with him, and now it seems possible that I shall end my days there.

Was it on that voyage in the *Elsewhere*, with two American couples as a fine cover, that he confided to me how he had obtained for both of us a currency allowance of some size from British Intelligence because we were going to photograph the length of the Yugoslav coastline? He was back playing with lenses as he hadn't played for years – not since *The Six Wives of Henry VIII* and *Rembrandt*. He had helped the Secret Service during the war and he had a childlike delight now in spying all down the Adriatic coast without the knowledge of his American guests who, I think, would not have been prepared for that kind of holiday.

This was his mischievous side. Like Dreuther in the Hôtel de

Paris, he liked to play an old sailor in a T-shirt and a battered yachting cap with a white stubble on his chin. One night in Naples, in a waterfront bar frequented by GIs, he persuaded the barman and the American soldiers standing around that Coca-Cola rendered men impotent – my word would have carried no weight with them, nor a film producer's, but from this old seadog who had learnt his wisdom 'on the seven seas' . . .

A sad wisdom it was too: I remember him saying to me, 'When my friends and I were young in Hungary, we all dreamed of being poets. And what did we become? We became politicians and advertisement men and film producers.'

3

I was flying from Warsaw to Brussels in an Aeroflot plane. The ancient editor-in-chief of *L'Humanité* was also leaving Warsaw: they put flowers on him as you put flowers on a tomb. The smooth managerial types stood around and kissed the nicotine-yellow cheeks, and then they shovelled him on board the plane. One pushed from behind, another tugged from in front, another took the hat off his long white locks, another caught his flowers: the Communist editor-in-chief went aboard. It was 1956. Stalin was dead, but in Poland Stalinism still survived.

The passenger who sat beside me was young with a grey puffy face, and, when he took off his hat, I saw he had a shaven skull: he too had been seen off, and by his country's representative, who had succeeded after seven years in fishing him out of a Polish prison where he was serving fifteen years for espionage. He wouldn't talk, for another of his countrymen still lay in the same jail, but he ate, how he ate. There was more thick bread than anything else in our meal, but his tray was empty before I had eaten more than one sandwich, so he cleared my tray as well and emptied my briefcase of all the biscuits and chocolates and sandwiches with which kind friends in Poland had stuffed it. The night before he had eaten two kilogrammes of sausage, he told me, but he hadn't been able to sleep a wink in the comfortable Embassy bed.

Monsieur Cachin, the editor, dozed in his seat out of touch with the problems of *L'Humanité*, and I couldn't help smiling when I thought of all the readers who have asked me why I sometimes write thrillers, as though a writer chooses his subject instead of the subject choosing him. Our whole planet since the war has swung into the fog-belt of melodrama, and, perhaps, if one doesn't ask questions, one can escape the knowledge of the route we are on. A venerable old man with long white hair and long white moustaches says goodbye to his warm-hearted friends, who present him with flowers, and after life's fitful fever he sleeps well: a young man, as young men should, has a healthy appetite. The world is still the world our fathers knew.

It might even have been possible to so regard Poland. In Warsaw the Old Town had risen like a phoenix: when I stood in the main square I found it almost impossible to believe that a few years past there had been nothing there but a heap of rubble. Every house had been faithfully reconstructed: each bit of moulding was exactly as it had been.

At first I was inclined to praise the poetic sense of the Communist Government. Hitler had said Warsaw was to be erased, and here it stood again: the fifteenth- and sixteenth-century houses, the little *apotheke*, the old café. Faced with an eliminated town and the terrible problems of housing one would have expected a Communist government to rear great tenement flats with perhaps another Palace of Art and Culture, nearly (but not quite, for the Poles have taste) as hideous as the gift palace from Moscow that shoots up its useless tiers like a gangster's wedding-cake in the centre of the city. Poetic, imaginative, a little 'reactionary', how charming to be able to praise a Communist government for these qualities.

But then a doubt niggled at the brain. The Old Town was destroyed in the insurrection of 1944, one of the bravest and foolhardiest episodes in all Polish history, when men armed with homemade grenades and a few pistols held out for two months against a German army already on the spot, seeing their city destroyed house by house rather than surrender, while the Russian generals halted their advance to allow Hitler time to eliminate these men and women who had wanted to liberate themselves. Officially the insurrection never took place, there is no record of it – so I was told – in the Museum of War, and soon there will not even be any broken bricks to show that the Old

325

Town had once been destroyed. We know how Trotsky has been excluded from the history of the Revolution. Perhaps history has to be rewritten architecturally too.

A blinkered traveller can certainly find much that seems unchanged. The wide grey windy square of Cracow with its stone market colonnade full of toys and gay peasants' clothes and the apple-women sitting in black shawls by the piles of bright apples: in Czestochowa the trumpets wail as the silver curtain descends at the last Mass over the most convincing portrait ever painted of Our Lady, with the Swedish lance-thrust in her cheek – 'Help of the half-defeated' Belloc wrote: the old streets of Lublin: the little fifteenth-century wooden church at Dembo with the relics of Sobieski in a vestry hardly larger than a confessional box: the humour and lightheartedness of Warsaw (let us give the Communist Government the credit for being the source of so much humour; it was they who prevented for some while the publication of the dogma of the Assumption because they thought the date of the feast – which had been celebrated since the ninth century – was somehow connected with the defeat of the Russians by Pilsudski after the First World War).

In the countryside there are still native craftsmen carving wooden saints and Stations of the Cross as though Byzantium had not fallen to the Turks: at a wedding in snowy Zakopane the carriages wait, the drivers in the tight trousers of the Tatra mountains, while the Inviters to the Feast ride to and fro in their bright jackets, and the bride is drawn from the church by two men and the bridegroom by two girls who hold his arms, and the singing begins as the carriages wheel away.

The traditional storytellers still fix you with an Ancient Mariner's eye, and little touches of modernity only give life to the old fables. When we picked our way through the freezing mud of one village an old man told me his tale of how he had visited the United States, where a Mr Frick possessed two piles of gold and silver so large it would have taken twelve men to shift them. A friend of the storyteller had been invited to go and see the piles, but when he got there, Mr Frick commanded him to add twenty-five dollars in gold and twenty-five dollars in silver to each pile. Oh, he had been properly caught, his friend had been. But when the old man was invited to see the piles, he got the better of Mr Frick, telling him, through his interpreter, 'If there were seven million fools in the world, you could climb to heaven on your piles of gold and silver.'

In the same way it would have been possible to pass through Poland, as it was possible for many tourists to pass through Mexico in the 1930s, and see no sign of tension between Church and State. But the State has learned wisdom since the experience of Mexico, and here in Poland, where the Church really represented the country, the Communist had to tread with care. The Church represented the nation against Russia in the days of the Tsar, it represented the nation against Hitler, and now it represents the nation, in the eyes of the nation, far more than the group of men who rule it in the interests of Russia.

Even the workers in Nowa Huta, the industrial city built out of nothing in three years on the plain outside Cracow, filled the churches – not always for religious motives, but as a little gesture of independence where the opportunities for independence were few. Nevertheless the number of communicants (and a man will not go to Communion as a political act) had grown enormously. It is only since the Revolution that the Pole, I believe, has changed his habit of only communicating on certain major feast days.

But in 1956 when you turned the stone the position was not so happy.

The old independent Catholic Press was dead. *Tygodnik Powszechny*, a Catholic weekly, whose circulation ran into six figures, was closed down because the editor refused to prejudge one of those clerical trials in which the Government unwisely indulged before it realized the strength of Catholic feeling. For some months there ceased to be a Catholic Press, but this, too, did not suit the Government, who needed the façade of religious toleration. *Tygodnik* was started again, though no member of the old staff consented to work for it, and it was put into the hands of the Pax movement. It was Pax who had invited me to visit Poland as their guest – a guest, I'm afraid, who bit the hand that fed him.

The Pax movement is perhaps the most ambiguous feature of Polish life and it still goes on though its founder, Boleslaw Piasecki, is dead. In 1956 he was still very much alive. Before the war he had been a nationalist and anti-Semite; during the war he was a partisan leader who fought with great courage against both the Germans and the Russians (he lost his first wife in the Warsaw insurrection). He was captured by the Russians and was condemned to death. However, he was spared and taken to Moscow, whence to the astonishment of the Poles he returned to Warsaw with permission to start the Pax publishing firm and the Pax movement which formed a keystone of the so-called Clerical Lay Catholic National Front Activists.

Pax in those days (I don't know how it is today) was a cadre consisting of only about 350 members, all laymen, and round that cadre, which reminded one a little of the Communist Party, there were a great many fellow-travellers – many of genuine sincerity – including several thousand priests. Their ostensible aim was to support the social and economic changes in Poland – many of which were both necessary and admirable – and to prove, as it were, the 'progressiveness' of Catholicism.

They were allowed to publish a certain number of books from the West and one can give a great deal of praise to this activity, though the Catechism which has been printed in hundreds of thousands contains phrases of political significance unknown to our 'penny' version.

The opponents of Pax (who were the vast majority of Catholics in Poland) claimed that the movement was Russian-inspired and was a clever attempt to divide the Church. One uses the past tense; for, if that was the intention of the Pax leaders, they dismally failed. Pax had very little importance in the Catholic life of Poland. Conventions were held: a Vicar-General appeared once on a platform, priests with humourless and uneasy faces helped to fill the big halls in Cracow and Warsaw: visiting Viet Minh priests (as the Eastern custom is) clapped delightedly their own speeches, and Piasecki orated on the subject of the aggressive Atlantic Powers in true Marxist terms. But the Church went on without them, and congregations preferred to go for Mass or confession to the churches which were served by a priest who was not an Activist.

It is easy for us to condemn them. We have no Auschwitz to remember. A girl of Pax who entertained me to dinner had a prison number tattooed upon her arm. A visitor to my hotel room pointed at the ceiling with a smile and suggested that on such a beautiful day we should take a walk. The Swedish Ambassador, an interesting and cultured man, had a fancy after our lunches together for walks in the park, for only in the park could we talk freely. The British Ambassador took a different line. I was astonished by the freedom of his speech between four walls. He explained that technicians came every four weeks to check them. He spoke, I reported later in London, like the madame of a brothel who assures the client that her girls are safe because they are 'inspected' by a doctor once a week.

The crucial question which I found no followers of Pax ready to answer with directness or simplicity was: 'Where is your point of resistance? At what point will you warn the Government that if they go further you will cease your collaboration and close down your presses? You exist. Therefore you must be of value. Therefore you have the possibility of blackmail.'

My relations with Mr Piasecki were ambiguous. I was met on arrival by a distinguished novelist who immediately I got off the plane hustled me away from Warsaw, to Cracow, Katowice, Czestochowa. During our travels he told me that I had been invited to Lublin's Catholic university on a certain day. He warned me that when we returned to Warsaw and I met the head of Pax, Piasecki would ask me to alter the date of my visit so that he could accompany me to Lublin. 'This you must refuse,' he said. 'The only date possible for you is the one arranged.'

Sure enough when I visited the Pax office Piasecki, after he had ordered two half-pint glasses of brandy for us (it was eleven in the morning) suggested that he would like to visit Lublin with me, but the date . . . The date was the only one I could manage, I told him.

The explanation came when I arrived at Lublin. The English department of the University had the right every year to present a play in English. It was usually a play of Shakespeare and performed in costume in the great hall of the University. This year they had chosen to perform Eliot's *Murder in the Cathedral*, so costumes were forbidden and the great hall not available. In the small room at their disposal there was little space for an audience. The actors were more numerous than the watchers. What the authorities had not realized was the effectiveness of this play, at this moment in time, in modern dress, and the way the words of the chorus struck home. 'Where is our Archbishop?' The

Archbishop of Poland, of course, was under house arrest. In the crowded little cloakroom after the performance a girl's hand pushed a letter into my pocket. It was addressed to her fiancé in England.

I returned for a last meeting one evening with Mr Piasecki in the elegant house he had all to himself on the outskirts of Warsaw. How few people in those days still possessed a house. An old lady – an Englishwoman who had spent the war years in Poland – had been summoned as an interpreter. She looked a little scared as we sat and drank our apéritifs – half-pint glasses of neat whisky this time instead of brandy – and she only spoke when she was spoken to and that was rarely because with the excellent wine over dinner we got on well enough in French. After dinner she was dismissed and we sat till one in the morning over the wine. No wonder I remember little of what we talked about, but I think from his uncertain steps when he led me to his car, Mr Piasecki would have remembered even less. I had been advised in England to carry with me a bottle of olive oil and always to take a spoonful before I went out of an evening, but I found I could manage quite well without.

Sitting in the plane next day, beside the hungry ex-prisoner wolfing the thick Polish sandwiches, I was glad I had refused to carry with me the tape recorder too big to fit into anything smaller than an overcoat pocket which had been pressed on me in England, and no one had noticed me passing the gold watch at the turn of the staircase.

Chapter 8

1

IT WAS in the fifties that I began to write plays which were produced. Like the Mau Mau and the wars in Malaya and Vietnam, the theatre offered me novelty, an escape from the everyday.

When a novelist has produced a play for the first time in middle age, it is natural to assume he has come rather late to the theatre. I feel certain I would have regarded with suspicion the publication of a Terence Rattigan first novel, if there had ever been one. To put up with the disappointments and the difficulties, the false starts and false curtains, the stubborn intransigence of a method which depends for communication on dialogue alone, an apprentice needs to have a passion for his work, but can we believe in a passion which has only declared itself at the eleventh hour?

So this is an apology for a latecomer to the theatre – but I am a latecomer, I want to add, only to actual production. My life as a writer is littered with discarded plays, as it is littered with discarded novels. I cannot count the number of plays which preceded *The Living Room*. I do know, however, that the first to be accepted, though not produced, was written at the age of sixteen. I have described that disappointing affair in *A Sort of Life*. Not for nearly twenty years did I seriously attempt another play.

My first attempt, a comedy based on one of the frequent kidnapping incidents which took place in Japanese-occupied Manchuria before the last war, never reached the second act. I was pleased enough with the first: the scene a draughty railway station on the Manchurian border: the characters a Japanese officer always busy at his typewriter, a correspondent of the *Daily Mail*, a paper which had embarrassed the authorities by offering a large reward for the return of the kidnapped (there were no currency problems in those happy old-world days), the British Consul, a Chinese go-between, the anxious husband, and last the kidnapped couple – the wife and a young employee who had been taken by the bandits while riding at a local race-club. The husband's anxiety was less for his wife's safety than for his own marital security, since the victims, according to the Press, had been bound together by the wrists for the last fortnight, night and day. I liked my first act. There seemed to me a freshness and authenticity in the setting, the action marched, but alas! when I came to time it, the first act only lasted for eighteen minutes and a half. It was to be a play in two acts, and the second act was to be a little shorter than the first . . . I abandoned the play with reluctance.

Length has always bedevilled me. My early novels as a rule fell a long way below those seventy-five thousand words which publishers used to consider a minimum length. Just before we were to start rehearsing *The Living Room* (a play written off-and-on over three years, which I had sent to Donald Albery under the mistaken impression that he was a theatrical management – however, he became one in order to produce the play), we received an authoritative timing of one hour and a quarter. There was general despondency – for it was impossible to enlarge the play. However my own timing of one hour and three-quarters after all proved more correct and by raising the curtain a little late, by imperceptibly (to those in the bar) increasing the interval beyond a quarter of an hour, it was possible to pass the minimum two hours which to a theatrical management remain as necessary as seventy-five thousand words once were to a publisher.

Thanks to Dorothy Tutin and Eric Portman, and Peter Glenville, the director, *The Living Room* was a success, but to me it was more than a success. I needed a rest from novels. I disliked the drudgery of film writing. I had discovered what was in effect a new drink just at that period when life seemed to have been going on for far too many years. At the end of this first experience of the theatre I found myself writing with an excitement which I still feel:

The novelist works alone: he is lucky if there is one other human being with whom he can discuss a problem or try out a difficult passage. Even the screen writer in my fortunate experience works with only one other man, the director, but so soon as the shooting script is completed he is excluded from the act of creation. Unless a crisis arises in the studio and the director needs his presence to rewrite a scene, the author is a forgotten man who emerges again, a bewildered figure watching the rough cut, clearing his throat nervously at new lines that are not his, feeling a sense of guilt because he is the only spectator who remembers what happened once – like a man who has witnessed a crime and is afraid to speak, an accomplice after the fact. There had been, of course, moments of great interest in learning the new craft of film writing, but so often the excitement of creation was confined to the preliminary idea, sketched at a dinner table, and lost again in the many rewritings, the first, second and third treatment, the first, second and third script. The screen is not there – like the page of foolscap – on which to test an idea; nor is there a stage from which the author can hear his lines brought to life or exhibited in their deadness. When the lines are at last spoken on the studio-floor the author is not there to criticize and alter. Another hand (earning, I suppose, a smaller salary and perhaps more easily controlled by the director) plays with his work. My own experience of screen writing has been fortunate and happy, and yet with what relief I have gone back afterwards to that one-man business, to the privacy of a room in which I bear the full responsibility for failure.

But – the fact remains – one must try every drink once. I had imagined that to write a play and to write a film would be very similar: the author, even though he could not be excluded from rehearsals, would be an unwelcome stranger lurking ashamed in the studio. A film studio – when you are allowed to penetrate it – has the callow comradeship of a great factory: signs, lights, clappers, cranes, and behind all the façade of Christian names (the union must be kept happy), the hierarchy of canvas chairs. I had not anticipated the warmth, the amusement, and comradeship of the theatre. Above all I had not realized that the act of creation, as with the novel, would continue for long after the first draft of the play was completed, that it would extend through rehearsals and through the opening weeks of the tour. It is for the act of creation that one lives, and after the author has returned from tour, how empty the hours are, the telephone rings seldom – couldn't we have delayed launching a little longer for the sake of the fun? I suppose that every author feels this, and that is why he writes another play.

There had been the excitement of acceptance, the excitement and frustrations of casting, the grim interest of auditions when every line became more leaden, the first reading with the complete cast, the conferences and changes over coffee, the delight of working with players interested not only in their own parts but in the play as a whole (a film actor is hardly aware of what happens when he is not on the set), nearly a dozen lively informed intelligences criticizing and suggesting. But this becomes a fading memory as the lights go out on the first audience who are probably not either lively or informed, who have

333

not worked on the play morning, afternoon and evening for many weeks, who don't know yet what the play is about and whose response is therefore conditioned by the momentary effect and not by the mood of the last curtain. Then one uncovers the unexpected laughs in the wrong places, the laughs legitimate but over strong, the coughs that indicate a failure in tension. For a night the writer may be discouraged, but how fascinating it is, when he has cut out this line here or altered that action there, to return the next night to the theatre and see – as with the novel he can never see – the effect of his changes, the laugh killed, the laugh modified, the apparent improvement in the epidemic of colds.

One newcomer at any rate was very happy in the theatre, in the deserted stalls at rehearsals, at the note-takings on the stage after performances, in the corridors and bars and dressing-rooms: the theatre even brought certain bizarre experiences which the cinema had never offered: a struggle on an Edinburgh hotel floor at two in the morning with a breeder of prize bulls, a long session with a stranger whose gratifying response to the play, I found too late, had been conditioned by his stay in four different lunatic asylums from the last of which he had temporarily escaped (our conversation in the hotel lounge was cut short by the arrival of the warders) – these, I suppose, are the everyday experiences of going on tour.

I had tried a new drink: I had liked the flavour. How I wished my glass was not empty and that it was not time to go.

So I approached the bar again to order another drink. Too soon perhaps after the first. No play was pressing on me from the unconscious. I deliberately took one of my abandoned novels (I had written a few thousand words of it in 1946) and fabricated *The Potting Shed*. I am fond of the first act – that is about all I can say. The material proved intractable. I was to make a better attempt, in my own opinion, to draw a 'hollow man' in *A Burnt-Out Case*. The intractability of the last act showed itself during the production in America where I rewrote the last scene unsatisfactorily against time, at rehearsals; then with the London production I went back with equal dissatisfaction to the original. I think my main objection to the play was the old Aristotelian lack of unity – five scenes and three sets. I have met many a director who has told me: 'Write what you like, in as many scenes as you like. Treat a play as loosely as a film. It is my job to find a way of putting it upon the stage.' But I don't want a producer's play – I want an author's play, and anyway there is a fascination in unity,

334

in trying to work in what Wordsworth called 'the sonnet's narrow room'.

The strain of writing a novel, which keeps the author confined for a period of years with his depressive self, is extreme, and I have always sought relief in entertainments – melodrama and farce are both expressions of a manic mood. So with my third play, *The Complaisant Lover*, I sought my usual escape – only to find as I reached the final curtain that the depressive mood had contributed almost as much as the manic to the piece. Perhaps that was why I had so full a sense of enjoyment in the writing. I have never worked with less feeling of conflict between two moods, and perhaps I can be forgiven for defending the play, out of gratitude. It arrived suddenly one spring day in the country at the turn of a road and it moved with dreamlike quickness – four months at most – towards birth. Later, when my fourth play, *Carving a Statue*, was struggling with all the accustomed difficulties to be born, I regretted the twilight sleep of that spring and summer; all the more when the new birth proved to be an abortion. Never before have I known a play so tormenting to write or so fatiguing in production as *Carving a Statue*. I was glad to see the end of it, and to that extent I was grateful to the reviewers who may have accelerated the end. At the age of sixty there was no reason to work, except to earn a living or to have 'fun'. This play was never fun and I earn my living in another field.

All the same the faults the reviewers found in it were curiously different from the faults I find, which are harder faults to defend, and I may be forgiven perhaps for not pointing them out. I was accused of overloading the play with symbols, but I have never cared greatly for the symbolic and I can detect no symbols in this play; sometimes there is an association of ideas which perhaps the reviewers mistook for the symbolic – the accurate use of words is difficult, as I know from my own experience as a theatre reviewer, when one writes against time.

I remember that when my film *The Third Man* had its little hour of success a rather learned reviewer expounded its symbolism with even less excuse in a monthly paper. The surname of Harry Lime he connected with a passage about the lime tree in Sir James Frazer's *The Golden Bough*. The 'Christian' name of the principal character – Holly – was obviously, he wrote, closely connected with Christmas – paganism and Christianity were thus joined in a symbolic dance. The truth of the matter is, I wanted for my 'villain' a name natural and yet disagreeable, and to me 'Lime' represented the quicklime in which murderers were said to be buried. An association of ideas, not, as the reviewer claimed, a symbol. As for Holly, it was because my first choice of name, Rollo, had not met with the approval of Joseph Cotten. So much for symbols.

Other reviewers, because the word God frequently crops up, thought that *Carving a Statue* contained that dreaded thing, 'theology'. Theology is the only form of philosophy which I enjoy reading and if one of these reviewers had ever opened a work of theology, he would have quickly realized there was nothing theological in this play.

What was it about then? I have always believed that farce and tragedy are far more closely allied than comedy and tragedy. *Carving a Statue* was to me a game played with the same extremes of mood as *The Complaisant Lover*. The first act is, almost completely, farce: the sculptor was based on Benjamin Robert Haydon, who was obsessed – to the sacrifice of any personal life – by the desire to do great Biblical subjects, already, even in his day, out of fashion. You cannot read the diaries of Haydon without realizing that he had a true daemon and yet he had no talent at all – surely a farcical character, though he came to a tragic end. In my story, as I intended it, the artist lost even his tragic end – no Tom Thumb was capable of shattering permanently his dream and driving him to the saving bullet. He had a greater capacity to recover than poor Haydon. Alas! The principal actor saw the play quite differently from me. He believed he was playing Ibsen.

I thought then that I would never write another play. I told myself it was not worth the candle. I was wrong, of course: *The Return of A. J. Raffles* was put on by the Royal Shakespeare Company and I found again the pleasure of rehearsing, and I am writing these words in the interval between yet more rehearsals of a farce called *For Whom the Bell Chimes*. The fate of the play is not important – the fun of testing the spoken word, of cutting and altering and transforming, of working with a group, of escaping solitude is everything.

336

Soon after the war ended, my friend Alberto Cavalcanti, the Brazilian director, asked me to write a film for him. I thought I would write a Secret Service comedy based on what I had learned from my work in 1943–4 of German Abwehr activity in Portugal. I had returned from Freetown – and my futile efforts to run agents into the Vichy colonies – and been appointed to Kim Philby's sub-section of our Secret Service, which dealt with counter-espionage in the Iberian peninsula. My responsibility was Portugal. There those Abwehr officers who had not been sub-orned already by our own service spent much of their time send-ing home completely erroneous reports based on information received from imaginary agents. It was a paying game, especially when expenses and bonuses were added to the cypher's salary, and a safe one. The fortunes of the German Government were now in decline, and it is wonderful how the conception of honour alters in the atmosphere of defeat.

I had sometimes thought, in dealing with Portugal, of how easily in West Africa I could have played a similar game, if I had not been content with my modest salary. I had learned that nothing pleased the services at home more than the addition of a card to their intelligence files. For example there was a report on a Vichy airfield in French Guinea – the agent was illiterate and could not count over ten (the number of his fingers and thumbs); nor did he know any of the points of the compass except the east (he was Mohammedan). A building on the airfield which he said housed an army tank was, I believed from other evidence, a store for old boots. I had emphasized the agent's disqualifications, so that I was surprised when I earned a rating for his report of 'most valuable'. There was no rival organization in the field, except SOE, with whose reports mine could be compared, and I had no more belief in SOE reports than in my own – they prob-ably came from the same source. Somebody in an office in London had been enabled to add a line or two to an otherwise blank card – that seemed the only explanation.

So it was that experiences in my little shack in Freetown recalled in a more comfortable room off St James's gave me the idea of what twelve years later in 1958 became *Our Man in Havana*.

The first version written in the forties was an outline on a single sheet of paper. The story was laid in 1938, in Tallinn, the capital of Estonia, a reasonable enough setting for espionage. The English agent had nothing at this stage in the story to do with vacuum cleaners, and it was the extravagance of his wife and not his daughter which led him to cheat his service. He was a more besotted character than Wormold in *Our Man in Havana* and less innocent. As the 1939 war approached, his enemies, like Wormold's, began to treat him seriously – the local police too. The incident of the misused micro-photographs was already in this draft. Cavalcanti, before we started work, thought it necessary to get clearance from the censor, and he was told that no certificate could be issued to a film that made fun of the Secret Service. At least that was the story he told me. Perhaps he invented an excuse because he was not enamoured of the subject.

The story remained at the back of my mind, submitting itself to the wide criticism of the pre-conscious. In the meanwhile I had visited Havana several times in the early fifties. I enjoyed the *louche* atmosphere of Batista's city and I never stayed long enough to be aware of the sad political background of arbitrary imprisonment and torture. I came there ('in search of pleasure for my punishment', Wilfred Scawen Blunt wrote) for the sake of the Floridita restaurant (famous for daiquiris and Morro crabs), for the brothel life, the roulette in every hotel, the fruit-machines spilling out jackpots of silver dollars, the Shanghai Theatre where for one dollar twenty-five cents one could see a nude cabaret of extreme obscenity with the bluest of blue films in the intervals. (There was a pornographic bookshop in the foyer for young Cubans who were bored by the cabaret.) Suddenly it struck me that here in this extraordinary city, where every vice was permissible and every trade possible, lay the true background for my comedy. I realized I had been planning the wrong situation and placing it at the wrong period. The shadows in 1938 of the war to come had been too dark for comedy; the reader could feel no sympathy for a man who was cheating his country in Hitler's day for the sake of an extravagant wife. But in fantastic Havana, among the absurdities of the Cold War (for who can accept the survival of Western capitalism as a great cause?) there was a situation allowably comic, all the more if I changed the wife into a daughter.

Strangely enough, as I planned my fantastic comedy, I learned for the first time some of the realities of Batista's Cuba. I had hitherto met no Cubans. I had never travelled into the interior. Now, while the story was emerging, I set about curing a little of my ignorance. I made Cuban friends, I took a car and travelled with a driver around the country. He was a superstitious man and my education began on the first day when he ran over and killed a chicken. It was then he initiated me into the symbols of the lottery – we had killed a chicken, we must buy such and such a number. This was the substitute for hope in hopeless Cuba.

Destiny had produced this driver in a typically Cuban manner. I had employed him some two or three years before for a few days in Havana. I was with a friend and on our last afternoon we thought of trying out a novelty – we had been to the Shanghai, we had watched without much interest Superman's performance with a mulatto girl (as uninspiring as a dutiful husband's), we had lost a little at roulette, we had fed at the Floridita, smoked marijuana, and seen a lesbian performance at the Blue Moon. So now we asked our driver if he could provide us with a little cocaine. Nothing apparently was easier. He stopped at a newsagent's and came back with a screw of paper containing some white powder – the price was the equivalent of five shillings which struck me as suspiciously cheap.

We lay on our bed and sniffed and sniffed. Once or twice we sneezed.

'Do you feel anything?'

'Nothing at all.'

We sniffed again.

'No lift?'

'No lift.'

I was of a more suspicious nature than my companion and I was soon convinced that we had been sold – at what now appeared an exorbitant price – a little boracic powder. Next morning I told the driver so. He denied it. The years passed.

When I came back to Havana in 1957 I looked for him in all the quarters where drivers congregated; I left messages for him without effect; I turned down many volunteers, for Castro's nocturnal bombs were frightening away the tourists and there was much unemployment. The man I remembered might be a swindler, but he had been a good guide to the shadier parts of Havana, and I had no desire for a dull and honest man to be my daily companion on this long trip. One night, when I had decided to wait no longer, I went to the Shanghai Theatre. When I came out into the dingy street I saw a number of taxis drawn up. A driver advanced towards me. 'I have to apologize humbly, señor. You had reason. It *was* boracic powder. Three years ago I was deceived too. The accursed newspaper seller. A swindler, señor. I trusted him. I give you back the five shillings . . .' In the course of the tour which followed he made a better profit than he had lost. Every hotel, every restaurant, every cantina paid him his commission. I never saw him on my next two visits to the island. Perhaps he was able to retire on his gains.

There was one place in Cuba to which we were unable to drive – Santiago, the second city of the island. This was now the military headquarters in the operations against Fidel Castro who made periodic sorties from the mountains with his handful of men. It was the beginning of the heroic period. The Oriente Province, almost to the last man, woman and child (I say child advisedly), was on the side of Fidel. There were military road-blocks all round the capital of Oriente and every foreigner arriving by private car was suspect. An unofficial curfew began at 9 p.m. dangerous to ignore, there were arbitrary arrests, and often when day broke a man's body would be found hanging from a lamp-post. That was a lucky victim. One building had an unsavoury reputation because of the screams which could be heard in the street outside, and after Santiago had fallen to Fidel a cache of mutilated bodies was found in the country outside the city bounds.

Not long before, the United States Ambassador, who had the disagreeable task of supporting Batista, had visited Santiago to be received by the mayor. An impromptu demonstration by the women of Santiago was organized with the lightning speed that a regime of terror induces. There was no class differentiation. This was still the period of national revolt. Middle-class women and peasants joined in singing Cuban patriotic songs to the American

340

Ambassador who watched from the balcony of the town hall. The military ordered the women to disperse. They refused. The officer in command had fire-hoses turned on them, and the Ambassador, to his honour, broke up the party. He was not going to stand there, he said, and watch women assaulted. For this he was later rebuked by John Foster Dulles: he had committed a breach of neutrality. There was to be no Day of Pigs during Batista's reign of terror. In the eyes of the United States Government terror was not terror unless it came from the left. Later at a diplomatic cocktail party in Havana I referred to the American Ambassador's protest while I was talking to the Spanish Ambassador. 'It was most undiplomatic,' he said.

'What would you have done?'

'I would have turned my back.'

The only way to go to Santiago was by plane. The night before I left I was at a late party with some Cuban friends. They were all of the middle class and all supporters of Fidel (though at least one of them has now left Cuba). One young woman there had been arrested by Batista's notorious police chief, Captain Ventura, and beaten. Another girl claimed that she was a courier for Fidel. She was going by the same plane as myself and she asked me to take in my suitcase a few sweaters and heavy socks badly needed by the men in the mountains. In Santiago the heat was tropical. There was a Customs examination at the airport, and it was easier for a foreigner to explain away the winter clothes. She was anxious for me to meet Fidel's representatives in Santiago – the genuine ones, she said, for the place was full of Batista's spies, especially the hotel where I would be staying.

Thus began a comedy of errors as absurd as anything I described later in *Our Man in Havana*. The next morning the correspondent of *Time* called on me. His paper had instructed him to accompany me to Santiago to give me any aid I wanted. I wanted no aid, but his paper obviously thought that I might supply a paragraph of news in one way or another. I had to get hold of the girl to warn her that I would not be alone. Unfortunately I did not know her name or her address, nor was my host of the previous night better informed. However he drove me to the airport and while I waited in the bar he watched by the entrance. Eventually he came back with the instruction that I was not to recognize her – she would telephone me in the morning at my hotel.

The hotel stood at the corner of the little main square of Santiago: on one side was the cathedral, its wall lined by shops. A couple of taxis and a horse-cab looked as if they had given up all hope of custom. Nobody came to Santiago now, except presumably the spies against whom I had been warned. The night was hot and humid; it was nearly the hour of the unofficial curfew, and the hotel clerk made no pretence of welcoming strangers. The taxis soon packed up and went, the square cleared of people, a squad of soldiers went by, a man in a dirty white drill suit rocked himself backwards and forwards in a chair in the hall, making a small draught in the mosquitoey evening. I was reminded of Villahermosa during the persecution in Tabasco. The smell of a police station lay over the city. I was back in what my critics imagine to be Greeneland.

While I was having breakfast next morning there was a knock on my door – it was the *Time* correspondent accompanied by a middle-aged man in a smart gabardine suit with a businessman's smile. He was introduced as Castro's public relations man in Santiago – he seemed a world away from the guerrillas in the mountains outside. I was embarrassed, for at any moment I expected the telephone to ring. I tried to persuade him to call a little later, when I was dressed. He went on talking. Then the telephone rang.

By this time I was so convinced of the danger of 'spies' that I asked Mr X and the correspondent of *Time* to leave my room while I answered the telephone. They went reluctantly. My caller was the girl, who asked me to come to a certain number in Calle San Francisco. Mr X returned to the room. He told me he was convinced I had been contacted by a Batista agent. None of his organization would have been so reckless . . . He demanded to know what had been said to me on the telephone.

I was irritated. I had never asked to be involved. I indicated that so far as I was concerned he might himself be a Batista agent. It was an impasse, and he left.

Now my problem was to find the street. I felt afraid even to consult the hotel clerk. I went into the square and sat down in one of the two forlorn taxis. Before I had time to speak to the

driver a Negro, flashily dressed, took the seat beside him. 'I
speak British. I show you where you want to go.' If any man was
a British informer, I thought, this was the one.

'Oh,' I said vaguely, 'I want to see the city, the points of
interest' – and off we went, down the hill to the port, up the hill
to the memorial to the American marines killed in the Spanish-
American war, the town hall . . . I could see myself landed back
at the hotel again, unless I found an excuse.

'You have an old church, San Francisco?' I asked. If such a
church existed surely it would be in the street of that name.

The guess proved correct: there was an old church and it was
in the street I wanted. I told my guide that I would find my own
way back to the hotel – I wanted to pray. Soon my stroll in the
cloisters was interrupted by a priest, unfriendly and suspicious: I
could hardly explain to him that all I wanted was a little time for
my taxi and my Negro to disappear from sight.

After that began a walk up Calle San Francisco in the hot
noon sun. The street was as long as Oxford Street and the
number I wanted was at the further end. I had only covered half
the distance when a car drew up at my side. It was Mr X and the
Time correspondent.

'We have been searching for you everywhere,' Mr X said
reproachfully.

I tried to think of an explanation of why I should be walking
up this interminable street in the hot sun.

'It is OK,' Mr X said. 'Completely OK. I find my own
organization has contacted you,' so I finished the journey in
comfort, in the car.

At the house, which was owned by a wealthy bourgeois family
of Santiago, were the courier from Havana, her mother, a priest
and a young man who was having his hair dyed by a barber. The
young man was a lawyer called Armando Hart who later became
Minister of Education in Castro's Government and then the
Second Secretary of the Communist Party in Cuba. A few days
before he had made his escape from the Law Courts in Havana
while he was being taken under military escort to trial. There was
a long line of the accused – a soldier at each end. Hart knew the
exact point beside the lavatory where the corridor turned and
where momentarily he would be out of sight of the soldier in

343

front and the soldier behind. He slipped into the lavatory and out of the window; his friends were waiting in the street outside. His absence was not noted until his name was read out in court.

His wife, now known to all Latin America as Haidée Santamaria, was with him in the house, a young haggard woman who looked in those days as if she had been battered into fanaticism by events outside her control. Before she married Hart she had been affianced to another young Fidelista. He was captured after the unsuccessful attack on the Moncada barracks in Santiago in 1953 and she was taken to the prison to be shown his blinded and castrated corpse. (I remembered that story when the wife of the Spanish Ambassador spoke to me of Batista's social charm.)

That was past history. All they were concerned with now were the jet planes which the British were preparing to sell to Batista – they were better informed than the British Government in this house in Calle San Francisco, for when, after my return to England, a Labour MP at my request asked a question on the subject, he was assured by the Foreign Secretary, Selwyn Lloyd, that no arms at all were being sold to Batista. Yet some months later, a week or two before Castro entered Havana, the Foreign Secretary admitted that an export licence for some out-of-date planes had been granted. At the time he had granted the licence he had no information – so he said – that a civil war was in progress in Cuba.

For one observer there was already in Santiago plenty of evidence of civil war. The night after my arrival three sisters, aged between eight and ten, were seized from their home by soldiers in the middle of the night. Their father had fled from Santiago and joined Castro in the mountains, so they were taken in their night clothes to the military barracks as hostages.

Next morning I saw the revolution of the children. The news had reached the schools. In the secondary schools the children made their own decision – they left their schools and went on the streets. The news spread. To the infants' schools came the parents and took away their children. The streets were full of them. The shops began to put up their shutters in expectation of the worst. The army gave way and released the three little girls. They could not turn fire-hoses on the children in the streets as they had turned them on their mothers or hang them from lamp-posts as

344

they would have hanged their fathers. What seemed strange to me was that no report of the children's revolt ever appeared in *Time* – yet their correspondent was there in the city with me. But perhaps Henry Luce had not yet made up his mind between Castro and Batista.

And the British Government? The civil war was still invisible as far as the Foreign Office was concerned. But by the time of my next visit to Havana – the very time when the export licence for planes was granted – the civil war was sufficiently in evidence to confine me to Havana. Not even by plane could I visit Santiago. Indeed I was unable to travel more than a hundred kilometres from Havana – no taxi-driver would accept the risk of ambush, for not even the main roads were secure. By that time I had finished *Our Man in Havana*. I had no regrets. It seemed to me that either the Foreign Office or the Intelligence Service had amply merited a little ridicule.

Alas, the book did me little good with the new rulers in Havana. In poking fun at the British Secret Service, I had minimized the terror of Batista's rule. I had not wanted too black a background for a light-hearted comedy, but those who had suffered during the years of dictatorship could hardly be expected to appreciate that my real subject was the absurdity of the British agent and not the justice of a revolution, nor did my aesthetic reasons for changing a savage Captain Ventura into a cynical Captain Segura appeal to them.

A postscript to history: Captain Ventura escaped from Cuba to the Dominican Republic by holding up his own President at the point of a gun. Batista intended to leave him behind like the last drop in a glass, a sacrifice to the gods. But Ventura arrived on the airfield at Havana and forced Batista to disgorge some of his baggage to make room for him. They must have made an uneasy couple, those two, in the hotel in Ciudad Trujillo, where Ventura spent long hours playing the fruit-machines.

Enough of Cuban politics. The British agent Wormold in *Our Man in Havana* has no origin that I can recognize, but the elegant Hawthorne owes a little, in his more imaginative flights, to an officer in the same service who was at one time my chief. C's black monocle too was not imaginary, though his fashion of cooking from his bed by telephone belongs to his famous predecessor Admiral Sinclair. I was told the story by Sinclair's niece who had to obey the phone.

Poor Doctor Hasselbacher, who suffers death by being Wormold's notional recruit, came into my life on another island. Baron Schacht, a friend of Norman Douglas, had a tiny apartment above a restaurant in Capri. A big sad gentleman, he had lived there in poverty ever since the end of the First World War in which he served as an officer in the uhlans. He used to be tormented by the smell of cooking from the restaurant below, for he had an enormous appetite and no means to assuage it. He lived mainly on pasta and herbs gathered on Monte Solaro. In the early fifties the Adenauer Government suddenly recognized his existence and granted him a small pension. It was the end of him. He was a generous man and suddenly he found himself able to return hospitality. One August evening, after a long swim and too much wine, he suffered a stroke and was found dead at his bedside. I arrived on the island next day and joined the little procession which followed the coffin to the Protestant cemetery. The police wished to seal up his rooms with all their contents, but after some argument I obtained permission to put his *pickelhaube* helmet and his white uhlan gloves on the coffin. He had loved his uniform, and like Hasselbacher, every year on the Kaiser's birthday he would put on his uniform and drink to the emperor's memory (I don't know how he got into his breastplate, for the years had not dealt lightly with his figure). Like Hasselbacher too he had a photograph hanging in his tiny hall which showed the Kaiser on a white horse inspecting a troop of uhlans, and I remember Baron Schacht saying to me, years before Hasselbacher made the same comment: 'It was all so peaceful.'

3

I went to the Belgian Congo in January 1959 with a new novel already beginning to form in my head by way of a situation – a stranger who turns up in a remote leper settlement for no apparent reason. I am not as a rule a note-taker, except in the case of travel books, but on this occasion I was bound to take notes so as to establish an authentic medical background. Even making notes day by day in the form of a journal I made mistakes which had to be corrected at a later stage by my friend Dr Lechat, the doctor of the settlement. As a journal had been forced on me I took advantage of the opportunity to talk aloud to myself, to record scraps of imaginary dialogue and incidents, some of which found their way into my novel, some of which were discarded. Anyway for better or worse this was how *A Burnt-Out Case* started, though it was four months after my return from the Congo before I set to work. Never had a novel proved more recalcitrant or more depressing. The reader had only to endure the company of the burnt-out character called in the novel Querry for a few hours' reading, but the author had to live with him and in him for eighteen months.

The circumstances in which *A Burnt-Out Case* grew in the author's mind are described fully enough in the extracts from the journal I kept, *In Search of a Character*, but I ask myself now, after the interval of many years, why should I have been searching for this particular character? I think the reasons go far back to the period which followed *The Heart of the Matter*.

Success is more dangerous than failure (the ripples break over a wider coastline), and *The Heart of the Matter* was a success in the great vulgar sense of that term. There must have been something corrupt there, for the book appealed too often to weak elements in its readers. Never had I received so many letters from strangers – perhaps the majority of them from women and priests. At a stroke I found myself regarded as a Catholic author in England, Europe and America – the last title to which I had ever aspired. A young man wrote to me from West Berlin asking me to lead a crusade of young people into the Eastern Zone where we were to shed our blood for the Church. (How surprised he would have been to find *The Heart of the Matter* translated into Russian – the Marxist critic is often very perceptive.) To find a reply to his letter was difficult – I could hardly write that my commitments at the moment were too heavy to allow me to shed my blood. A young woman sent me a rather drunken letter of invitation from a Dutch fishing-boat enclosing a photograph, and another wrote from Switzerland suggesting I join her 'where the snow can be our coverlet' – a prospect which was even less attractive to me than martyrdom. A French priest pursued me first with letters of a kind which should only have been addressed to his confessor, and then in person: he even popped up, unannounced and inopportunely, one evening in a narrow lane of Anacapri, as I was catching the bus to Capri with my mistress, trailing a smoke of dust from his long black soutane. Other priests would spend hours in my only armchair, while they described their difficulties, their perplexities, their desperation. An American woman began to telephone across the Atlantic in the early hours of the morning demanding my presence to help in her marriage difficulties; she wore down my resistance till I went accompanied by my greatest friend – the awful little New Jersey house with its too feminine furnishings and an insolent black maid still come vividly to mind. The mistress of the house lay in a drugged sleep at midday with the curtains closed and an eyeshade hiding the face and a pink silk nightdress the body. Our visit was as useless as we had anticipated; only death could save her, and save her it did a year later in London with the help of drink and drugs, abandoned by all but one of the Jesuits she had befriended.

This account may seem cynical and unfeeling, but in the years between *The Heart of the Matter* and *The End of the Affair* I felt myself used and exhausted by the victims of religion. The vision of faith as an untroubled sea was lost for ever; faith was more like a tempest in which the lucky were engulfed and lost, and the unfortunate survived to be flung battered and bleeding on the shore. A better man could have found a life's work on the margin of that cruel sea, but my own course of life gave me no confidence in any aid I might proffer. I had no apostolic mission, and the cries for spiritual assistance maddened me because of my impotence. What was the Church for but to aid these sufferers? What was the priesthood for? I was like a man without medical knowledge in a village struck with plague. It was in those years, I think, that Querry was born, and Father Thomas too. He had often sat in that chair of mine, and he had worn many faces.

I have often noticed that Catholic and Marxist critics are more perceptive than others, their criticism less subjective. I was not a famous Catholic figure as Querry was in the novel, nor had I abandoned my Church and my old mode of life as Querry had done. But there *were* new elements in this book, whether it was a failure or a success. The critic who saw in it nothing but the old crosses on the Easter eggs (he was referring to Querry's fable) was more at sea than the Marxist critic in Poland who welcomed the novel as a renunciation of the Catholic Church, or my dear friend Evelyn Waugh, who realized that Querry was a redraft (perhaps a less satisfactory one) of the old French Catholic writer in my short story 'A Visit to Morin' and was grieved by the book.

I wrote to the Communist paper that as a Catholic I considered myself able to treat loss of faith just as freely as discovery of faith, and I trusted that if I were a Communist writer in his country I would be able to take as a character a lapsed Communist. I asked that the fee they owed me for their extensive quotations, which were mainly from Querry's fable, should be sent to the repair fund of Warsaw Cathedral.

Evelyn Waugh had written to me: 'I know of course how mischievous it is to identify fictional characters with their authors, but . . . this novel makes it plain that you are exasperated by the reputation which has come to you unsought of a "Catholic" writer. I realize that I have some guilt in this matter. Twelve years ago I gave a number of lectures here and in America presumptuously seeking to interpret what I genuinely believed was an apostolic mission in danger of being neglected by people who were shocked by the sexuality of some of your themes. In fact in a small way I behaved like Rycker [an unattractive character in the novel]. I am deeply sorry for the annoyance I helped to cause and pray that it is only annoyance, and that the desperate conclusions of Morin and Querry are purely fictional.'

I replied more frankly to Evelyn than to my Communist critic. 'With a writer of your genius and insight I certainly would not attempt to hide behind the time-old gag that an author can never be identified with his characters. Of course in some of Querry's reactions there are reactions of mine, just as in some of Fowler's reactions in *The Quiet American* there are reactions of mine. I suppose the points where an author is in agreement with his character lend what force or warmth there is to the expression. At the same time I think one can say that a parallel must not be drawn all down the line and not necessarily to the conclusion of the line. Fowler, I hope, was a more jealous man than I am, and Querry, I fear, was a better man than I am. I wanted to give expression to various states or moods of belief and unbelief. The doctor, whom I like best as a realized character, represents a settled and easy atheism; the Father Superior a settled and easy belief (I use easy as a term of praise and not as a term of reproach); Father Thomas an unsettled form of belief and Querry an unsettled form of disbelief. One could probably dig a little of the author also out of the doctor and Father Thomas.'

Evelyn Waugh replied: 'I was not so dotty as to take Rycker as a portrait of myself. I saw him as the caricature of a number of your admirers . . . who have tried to force on you a position which you found obnoxious. You have given many broad hints which we refused to recognize. Now you have made a plain repudiation. You will find not so much "hostility" among your former fellowship as the regrets of Browning for his "Lost Leader" – except, of course, that no one will impute mercenary motives . . . I don't think you can blame people who read the book as a recantation of faith. To my mind the expression "settled and easy atheism" is meaningless, for an atheist denies his whole purpose as a man – to love and serve God. Only in the most superficial way can atheists appear "settled and easy". Their waste land is much more foreign to me than "the suburbia of the *Universe*" [a snobbish phrase I had used in my letter for some Catholic attitudes].'

'Must a Catholic' – I returned to the argument on the lines I had taken with my Communist critic – 'be forbidden to paint the portrait of a lapsed Catholic? Undoubtedly if there is any realism in the character it must come from the author experiencing some of the same moods as Querry, but surely not necessarily with the same intensity . . . If people are so impetuous as to regard this book as a recantation of faith I cannot help it. Perhaps they will be surprised to see me at Mass.

'What I have disliked in some Catholic criticism of my work, particularly some of the books which have been written about it in France, is the confusion between the functions of a novelist and the functions of a moral teacher or theologian.

'I will match your quotation from Browning with Bishop Blougram:

> All we have gained then by our unbelief
> Is a life of doubt diversified by faith,
>   For one of faith diversified by doubt:
> We called the chessboard white, – we call it black.'

I felt the discussion was becoming too serious. Evelyn's reference to the Lost Leader had surprised me and even shocked me a little, for had I not always regarded him as *my* leader? To bring the correspondence to a close I sent him a flippant postcard – I think one of Brighton pier – 'My love to Milton, Burns, Shelley and warn them that Spender and Day Lewis are on the way. I shall be grateful for all your coppers. A voice from the Rear and the Slaves' to which he replied in kind, 'Mud in your mild and magnificent eye. Hoping for a glad and confident morning.' The cloud had passed. Browning had served us both well.

It was very true all the same that Evelyn Waugh and I inhabited different waste lands. I find nothing unsympathetic in atheism, even in Marxist atheism. *My* waste land is inhabited by the pious 'suburbans' of whom I had too carelessly written – I had not meant the piety of simple people, who accept God without question, but the piety of the educated, the established, who seem to own their Roman Catholic image of God, who have ceased to look for Him because they consider they have found Him. Perhaps Unamuno had these in mind when he wrote: 'Those who believe that they believe in God, but without passion in their hearts, without anguish of mind, without uncertainty, without doubt, without an element of despair even in their consolation, believe only in the God Idea, not in God Himself.' I would not look for Querry in that waste land; I would seek him among those – Unamuno describes them – 'in whom reason is stronger than will, they feel themselves caught in the grip of reason and haled along in their own despite, and they fall into despair, and because of their despair they deny, and God reveals Himself in them, affirming Himself by their very denial of Him'.

Querry like my other character Morin was a victim of theology. Morin said to his non-Catholic interviewer: 'A man can accept anything to do with God until scholars begin to go into details and the implications. A man can accept the Trinity, but the arguments that follow . . . I would never try to determine some point in differential calculus with a two-times-two table. You end by disbelieving the calculus . . . I used to believe in Revelation, but I never believed in the capacity of the human mind.'

I had not known Unamuno's *A Tragic Sense of Life* when I wrote 'A Visit to Morin' or later *A Burnt-Out Case*, but when I came to read his book, I found there the same distrust of theology that Morin felt: 'The Catholic solution of our problem, of our unique vital problem, the problem of the immortality and eternal salvation of the individual soul, satisfies the will, and therefore satisfies life; but the attempts to rationalize it by means of dogmatic theology fail to satisfy the reason. And the reason has its exigencies as imperious as those of life.' And again, 'The traditional so-called proofs of the existence of God all refer to this God Idea, to this logical God, the God by abstraction, and hence they really prove nothing or rather they prove nothing more than the existence of this idea of God.'

Thirty years before I had read Unamuno's *Life and Death of Don Quixote* with no particular interest – it left no memories. But perhaps the book which I so quickly forgot had continued to work its way through the cellars of the unconscious; in the life of which I was fully aware I was making my way with passionate curiosity through works of theology. Yet *The Heart of the Matter* offended the moral theologians, *The End of the Affair*, *The Living Room*, *The Potting Shed* caused some uneasiness among those of my faith, and at the end of a long journey, without knowing myself the course which I had been taking, I found myself, in 'A Visit to Morin' and *A Burnt-Out Case*, in that tragi-comic region of La Mancha where I expect to stay. Even my Marxist critics shared a characteristic with Waugh – they were too concerned with faith or no faith to notice that in the course of the blackest book I have written I had discovered Comedy.

4

Alas, it was the last dispute I had with Evelyn Waugh. His death in 1966 came suddenly, without warning, and it was the death not only of a writer whom I had admired ever since the twenties, but of a friend. It was a curious and in a way macabre death, which almost symbolized his work and his problems. It was Easter Sunday; he had been to Communion, he was lunching with his family, a priest was in the house – this can all represent the Catholicism to which he was so deeply attached – and he died in the lavatory: which represents his satire and the comic savagery with which he sometimes describes the deaths of his characters,

352

and brings to mind Apthorpe's thunderbox in *Men at Arms*.

There was always in Evelyn a conflict between the satirist and the romantic. I suppose a satirist is always to some extent a romantic: but he doesn't usually express his romanticism. Perhaps romanticism was a weak point in Evelyn's life and work, and in the end it helped to kill him. He had too great expectations of his fellow creatures, and too great expectations even of his Church. I think the old expression 'a broken heart' comes near to the truth, when one thinks of his reaction to the changes in the liturgy of the Catholic Church.

The disillusionment was not only with his Church; it was also a disillusionment with the Army. He had been a very courageous officer, but not a successful one; and he expresses that disillusionment in his war trilogy, *Men at Arms, Officers and Gentlemen,* and *Unconditional Surrender*. At the end – or what, to my mind, should have been the end – of *Officers and Gentlemen* (and perhaps even should have been the end of the trilogy) he wrote: 'He was back after less than two years' pilgrimage in the Holy Land of illusion – in the old ambiguous world, where priests were spies and gallant friends proved traitors, and his country was led blundering into dishonour.'

I would date the satirist, and the serious undertones to his most amusing books, from the break-up of his first marriage. In his early books he himself was thoroughly enjoying what he satirized. *Decline and Fall*, Evelyn's first book, which I admire as much as any – I must have read it half a dozen times at least – is, to me, pure fun. So is the less successful *Vile Bodies*. He made fun out of the 'bright young things' of the twenties, but he was one of them himself. He doesn't take his characters seriously enough to satirize them. Perhaps with *Black Mischief* – tale of a black emperor's attempt to modernize his country, based on Evelyn's experience in Ethiopia – the serious satire begins to be visible below the fun. In *A Handful of Dust*, his most painful book, there is no fun at all.

A writer of Evelyn's quality leaves us an estate to walk through: we discover unappreciated vistas, paths which are left for our discovery at the right moment, because the reader, like the author, changes. And I, for one, had been inclined to dismiss *Brideshead Revisited*. When he had written to me that the only excuse for it was Nissen huts and spam and the blackout I had accepted that criticism – until the other day when I reread all his books, and to my astonishment joined the ranks of those who find *Brideshead* his best, even though it is his most romantic. I had always remembered a passage at the beginning, describing the railway journey of the young officer to the place where he is to be billeted – Brideshead. I used to think that was the best part of the book; but when I came to reread it, I found that the railway journey only took up three pages. This, I'm inclined to think, is genius.

My earlier favourite was that very courageous book, *The Ordeal of Gilbert Pinfold*: a novel based on the time when he himself went temporarily off his head. It happened after writing *Men at Arms* and *Officers and Gentlemen*. I remember walking with him in his garden and asking him why it was that on the jacket of *Officers and Gentlemen* he had not repeated the fact that this work was intended to be a trilogy, and his reply was, 'It's because I don't know if I shall ever write the third book. I may go off my head again.'

In *Pinfold* he draws a character study of himself. It reminds one a little of Freud bravely doing his own self-analysis: 'He had made no new friends in late years; sometimes he thought he detected a slight coldness among his old cronies. It was always he, it seemed to him, who proposed a meeting; it was always they who first rose to leave. It sometimes occurred to Mr Pinfold that he must be growing into a bore. His opinions certainly were easily predictable. His strongest tastes were negative – he abhorred plastics, Picasso, sunbathing and jazz; everything in fact that had happened in his own lifetime. The tiny kindlings of charity which came to him through his religion sufficed only to temper his disgust and change it to boredom . . .'

But in this strange book he has left out all his fine qualities: physical courage, private generosity, loyalty to friends. *Pinfold*, I think, shows him technically almost at his most perfect. How well he faces the problem of linking passages between the scenes. There is almost a complete absence of the beastly adverb – far more damaging to a writer than an adjective. These are points a novelist notices, but one can't underestimate what Trollope calls in his autobiography 'the unconscious critical acumen of the reader'. What the novelist notices the reader probably notices too, without knowing it.

Evelyn's diaries have been joyfully exploited by the media, a word that has come to mean bad journalism. Journalists have always been intent on transforming a fine writer into a 'character'. If they succeed the legend will supersede the work. The 'character' will be safely mummified: the actions and remarks which once offended will now amuse because they form part of the fictional character. Robert Louis Stevenson received this treatment, helped by the letters from Vailima, though in his day literary journalists were of a rather higher standard. Conrad suffered the same fate and D. H. Lawrence too, until the writers were rescued from legend by Dr Leavis. Who will save Waugh, the writer?

So I write unwillingly of the 'character'. I was for many years puzzled by his reputation for rudeness and cruelty – I must have known him well for nearly a dozen years without seeing any example to justify it. I had even stayed with him several times in the country (a feat regarded as extraordinary by some of his friends) and had seen only an excellent and witty host, one who disguised his own inner torment in drollery rather than disturb his guest.

It was not until the middle fifties that I saw the cruel Evelyn in action. We were dining at Carol Reed's house and our fellow guests were Alexander Korda and the young girl he was later to marry. Suddenly Evelyn leaned across the table and launched an attack on Korda of shocking intensity, killing all the conversation around. Korda bore it with exemplary patience and courtesy. Next day Evelyn and I were sharing a taxi and I demanded an explanation, for I was very fond of Alex. 'What on earth induced you to behave like that?'

'Korda,' he said, 'had no business to bring his mistress to Carol and Pempe's house.'

'But I was there with my mistress,' I said.

'That's quite different,' he replied, 'she's married.' Fornication more serious than adultery? It was not the orthodox Catholic view. I gave the problem up, and we were driven on in silence.

But those who have built Evelyn up as a sort of sacred monster have left out the other side: they have ignored the man who gave

up from work which was essential to him time to stay with the
dying and no longer amusing Ronald Knox in the kind of hotel
and the kind of resort he hated, who attended the deathbed of
his friend Alfred Duggan and against all obstacles brought him
the help he needed. When I come to die, I shall wish he were
beside me, for he would give me no easy comfort. Our politics
were a hundred miles apart and he regarded my Catholicism as
heretical. What indeed had made us friends? He wrote to me in
October 1952, 'I am just completing my forty-ninth year. You
are just beginning yours. It is the grand climacteric which sets
the course of the rest of one's life, I am told. It has been a year of
lost friends for me. Not by death but by wear and tear. Our
friendship started rather late. Pray God it lasts.' It did.

A few years ago I reread his letters to me – a sad memorial –
and for the first time I realized what a lonely man he had been.
Over and over again he suggests that I visit him and only three
times I responded. It was always impossible. I was travelling, I
was otherwise occupied, no, it was impossible this month . . . I
regret the lost occasions now.

In October 1944 he wrote in his diary in Yugoslavia, 'My
forty-first birthday and the glummest I have had for eleven years
. . . It has been a good year – a daughter born, a book written, a
narrow escape from death. I pray God that next year I am at my
own home, at my own work, and at peace.' Peace he was not
granted – only a long despair which he passed off with the lighter
word, boredom.

The other day I was rereading James's *The Bostonians* and I
came on Verena's description of the principal character, Basil
Ransom. Evelyn came immediately to mind.

Brought up, as she had been, to admire new ideas, to criticize the
social arrangements that one met almost everywhere, and to disapprove
of a great many things, she had yet never dreamed of such a wholesale
arraignment as Mr Ransom's, so much bitterness as she saw lurking
beneath his exaggerations, his misrepresentations. She knew he was an
intense conservative, but she didn't know that being a conservative
could make a person so aggressive and unmerciful. She thought
conservatives were only smug and stubborn and self-complacent,
satisfied with what actually existed; but Mr Ransom didn't seem any
more satisfied with what existed than with what she wanted to exist, and

356

he was ready to say worse things about some of those whom she would have supposed to be on his own side than she thought it right to say about almost anyone.

Henry James never analyses what is *behind* Ransom, and I doubt whether Evelyn Waugh's diaries help us to understand Waugh. What is certain is that when they were published they gave an opportunity for many writers of smaller talent to denigrate a man whom they would have feared to criticize when he was alive to answer them.

5

A decade is not neatly ruled off, and my desire to escape London and a writer's enclosed life continued into the 1960s, and was reawoken by an article I read on Papa Doc's Haiti. My first two visits to Haiti in the fifties had been happy enough. That was the time of President Magloire, there was extreme poverty, but there were many tourists and some of the money they brought was allowed to trickle down the social scale. The luxury hotel, El Rancho, in Piétonville, where I stayed when I was in Port-au-Prince, was always full, too full. The Mayor of Miami came over for one night with a horde of boisterous followers and screaming girls, and there were wild scenes in the swimming pool till the not-so-early hours. I met Haitian poets and painters and novelists, and one man I liked above all who was the model for Doctor Magiot in *The Comedians*, a novel I never dreamed then that I would come to write. He was a doctor and a philosopher – but not a Communist. For a time he had been Minister of Health, but he found his hands too tied, so he resigned (something which it would have been very dangerous to do under Doctor Duvalier). Every other year he visited Europe to attend philosophical congresses. He was a very big man and very black, of great dignity and with an old-world courtesy. He was to die in exile – more fortunately than Doctor Magiot? Who can tell? It was during that period I attended the voodoo ceremony I describe in the novel. For those with the means there was complete freedom to travel through the country. I went twice to Cap Haïtien, I visited Jérémie, the scene of a cruel massacre the year of my last arrival in Haiti. No need to wait for hours in the police station to get a pass to leave Port-au-Prince.

Inspired by the article I came to Haiti for the last time in 1963. It was the most critical year of Papa Doc's rule and perhaps the cruellest. There were two dozen guerrillas fighting in the north (I met what were left of them a year later lodged in what had been an old lunatic asylum in Santo Domingo). They were the excuse for the barricades all round the capital manned by ragged militiamen. Impossible to drive to and from one's hotel without being searched twice for arms. Papa Doc, while remaining in American eyes a bastion against Communism in the Caribbean, had shown his power by quarrelling with the West. Barbot, the founder of the Tontons Macoute, had been shot to pieces in a suburb of Port-au-Prince, and snapshots of his body decorated the walls of the police station – he had been in touch with the American marines who were there to guard the Embassy and to help with the military aid programme. The young son of the American commander was kidnapped by the Tontons and rescued, at the last moment as he was being dragged into the palace, by Duvalier's son who attended the same *lycée*. After that incident the marines were withdrawn, the American Ambassador left, the British Ambassador was expelled, Duvalier was excommunicated and the Nuncio stayed in Rome. The South American embassies were crowded with refugees, including the Chief of Staff and most officers above the rank of major. The Tontons pursued refugees into the Santo Domingo Embassy and President Bosch mobilized tanks on the frontier less than a day's march from Port-au-Prince. It was a dark city in which I arrived that summer, and though the curfew had been raised no one ventured abroad after dark. I little thought then that Papa Doc would survive to die a natural death years later, that an American ambassador, suitably named Benson Timmons III, would be kept waiting for hours at the palace before being harangued by the Doctor, and that Nelson Rockefeller would appear on the balcony before the Port-au-Prince mob to shake Duvalier's hand and to hand him a personal letter from the President of the United States.

This time I didn't stay at El Rancho, but I went up the hill once to revisit it. There were no guests in the hotel, only a clerk, and the swimming pool was empty. In my hotel, the Oloffson (I call it the Trianon in *The Comedians*), there were three guests besides myself – the Italian manager of the casino and an old American artist and his wife – a gentle couple whom I cannot deny bore some resemblance to Mr and Mrs Smith of the novel. He wanted to teach the use of the silk screen to Haitian artists, so that they could earn a better living by selling reproductions of their paintings in the States. He had been encouraged to come by the Haitian Consul-General in New York who had promised to send all the necessary material for his teaching after him, but the weeks had passed and nothing had arrived, and no one in the Government displayed any interest at all in a project which would not line his own pocket. One night the three of us braved the dark to visit the brothel I have described as Mère Catherine's. There were no customers except a couple of Tontons Macoute. 'Mr Smith' began to draw the girls who had been dancing together decorously and decoratively, and they gathered round his chair like excited schoolchildren, while the Tontons glared through their dark glasses at this strange spectacle of a fearless happiness and an innocence they couldn't understand.

Every day 'Petit Pierre' would appear for a drink and once he brought with him the Mayor of Port-au-Prince who took me to see the dilapidated and abandoned buildings of the new city of Duvalierville where only the cockfight theatre had been finished. I soon realized it was 'Petit Pierre's' job to see what I wanted and report what I was about.

What I wanted most was to get away from the stifling nightmare city where a few weeks after I left all the schoolchildren were forced to attend the execution of two captured guerrillas in the cemetery, a scene repeated every night for a week on the local television. But to get permission to go anywhere outside the city was not so easy – even to leave the country an exit visa had to be procured. Finally I had an interview with the Foreign Minister himself. Mr Chalmers was about to leave for New York to attend the Assembly of the United Nations and to make a protest that American arms had been found in the hands of the guerrillas (a not unlikely claim since the Haitian army had been furnished with arms by the United States and all their senior officers were dead or in exile or shut in the foreign embassies). Mr Chalmers refused to allow me to go north to Cap Haïtien 'for my own safety', but reluctantly gave his consent to my visiting Aux Cayes in the south, where I wanted to spend the night with some Canadian missionaries. Even with his consent I had to pass hours in the police station, sitting under the snapshots of dead Barbot. The police station faced the white palace of the President. No pedestrians passed the palace – it was thought dangerous to walk under those blank windows through which Baron Samedi, the haunter of graveyards, might be peering down: even taxi-drivers would avoid that side of the square. Looking up from my bench I would see my character Concasseur staring at me through the open door of his office for minutes on end through his dark glasses. I would have been even less reassured if I could have read what they wrote about me later: that I was known to be the 'spy' of an unnamed imperialist power.

The trip to Aux Cayes by 'the Great Southern Highway' was under 180 kilometres, but it was to take me, as I had been warned, more than eight hours, for the road hardly existed half an hour outside the capital. The night before I left I slept little for fear of what might happen. I was under no illusions about my friendly driver – he was certainly an informer of the Tontons, and it seemed to my mind only too easy for a convenient accident to be arranged on that rough route or a yet more convenient murder which could be blamed on the guerrillas, a few of whom were operating in the south. Papa Doc would not be concerned about scandal – there were no tourists to frighten away.

Fear in those weeks must have penetrated deep into my unconscious: Haiti really was the bad dream of the newspaper headlines, and when the time came to leave and I waited at the airport for my Delta plane, I wasn't happy to feel pressed secretively into my hand a letter addressed to a former presidential candidate, an exile in Santo Domingo. Was I to be tricked by an *agent provocateur* at the last minute? No wonder that for years afterwards Port-au-Prince featured in my dreams. I would be back there incognito, afraid to be spotted.

If I had known the way the President regarded me my fears would have seemed even more rational. *The Comedians*, I am glad to say, touched him on the raw. He attacked it personally in an interview he gave in *Le Matin*, the paper he owned in Port-au-Prince – the only review I have ever received from a Chief of State. '*Le livre n'est pas bien écrit. Comme l'œuvre d'un journaliste, le livre n'a aucune valeur.*'

Was it possible that I disturbed his dreams as he had disturbed mine, for five long years after my visit his Ministry of Foreign Affairs published an elaborate and elegant brochure, illustrated, on glossy paper, dealing with my case? A lot of research had gone into its preparation, with many quotations drawn from the introductions I had written for a French edition of my books. Printed in French and English and entitled 'Graham Greene Démasqué Finally Exposed', it included a rather biased sketch of my career. This expensive work was distributed to the Press through the Haitian embassies in Europe, but distribution ceased abruptly when the President found the result was not the one he desired. 'A liar, a *crétin*, a stool-pigeon . . . unbalanced, sadistic, perverted . . . a perfect ignoramus . . . lying to his heart's content . . . the shame of proud and noble England . . . a spy . . . a drug addict . . . a torturer.' (The last epithet has always a little puzzled me.)

I am proud to have had Haitian friends who fought courageously in the mountains against Doctor Duvalier, but a writer is not so powerless as he usually feels, and a pen, as well as a silver bullet, can draw blood.

Chapter 9

1

DURING the forty years which had passed since I published my first novel I had occasionally written a short story. The short story as a form bothered me when I first began to write and a little bored me. I knew too much about the story before I began to write – and then all the days of work were unrelieved by any surprise. In the far longer work of the novel there were periods of great weariness, but at any moment the unexpected might happen – a minor character would suddenly take control and dictate his words and actions. Somewhere near the beginning, for no reason I knew, I would insert an incident which seemed entirely irrelevant, and sixty thousand words later, with a sense of excitement, I would realize why it was there – the narrative had been working all that time outside my conscious control. But in the short story I knew everything before I began to write – or so I thought.

I was reminded of the kind of essays we were taught to write at school – you were told to make first a diagram which showed the development of the argument, rather as later a film producer would sometimes talk to me of the necessity of 'establishing' this or that and the imaginary value of 'continuity'. When school was safely behind me I began to write 'essays' again. I learned to trust the divagations of the mind. (If you let the reins loose the horse will find its way home.) The shape was something which grew of itself *inside* the essay, during the revision – you didn't have to think it out beforehand.

In the case of the short story I was equally misled. It was only the surface of the story which I knew as I began to write – the surprises might not be so far-reaching as in a novel but they were there all the same. They came in the unexpected shaping of a sentence, in a sudden reflection, in an unforeseen flash of dialogue; they came like cool drinks to a parched mouth.

Now I realize that since the beginning I have really been all the time a writer of short stories – they are not the 'scraps' I called them in the prefatory note to my first volume of short stories. 'The End of the Party' was written in 1929, the year of my first printed novel, and strangely enough, during the period when I was writing my second and third novels, I wrote a short story, 'I Spy', which has the qualities which all my first novels so disastrously lack – simplicity of language, the sense of life as it is lived. It is no great thing – 'I Spy' – but how, if I were able to write a short story of even that modest truth, could I have been so bent on self-destruction with the total unrealities of *The Name of Action* and *Rumour at Nightfall*?

Yet, though I am content with many of these stories (I believe I have never written anything better than 'The Destructors', 'A Chance for Mr Lever', 'Under the Garden', 'Cheap in August') I remain in this field a novelist who has happened to write short stories, just as there are certain short-story writers (Maupassant and Victor Pritchett come to mind) who have happened to write novels. This is not a superficial distinction or even a technical distinction, as between an artist who paints in oil or water-colour; it is certainly not a distinction in value. It is a distinction between two different ways of life.

With a novel, which takes perhaps years to write, the author is not the same man at the end of the book as he was at the beginning. It is not only that his characters have developed – he has developed with them, and this nearly always gives a sense of roughness to the work: a novel can seldom have the sense of perfection which you find in Chekhov's story, 'The Lady with the Dog'. It is the consciousness of that failure which makes the revision of the novel seem endless – the author is trying in vain to adapt the story to his changed personality – as though it were something he had begun in childhood and was finishing now in old age. There are moments of despair when he begins perhaps the fifth revision of Part One, and he sees the multitude of the new corrections. How can he help feeling, 'This will never end. I shall never again be the same man I was when I wrote this months and months ago.' No wonder that under these conditions a novelist often makes a bad husband or an unstable lover. There is something in his character of the actor who continues to play Othello when he is off the stage, but he is an actor who has lived far too many parts during far too many long runs. He is encrusted

363

with characters. A black taxi-driver in the Caribbean once told me of a body which he had seen lifted from the sea. He said, 'You couldn't tell it was a man's body because of all the lampreys which came up with it.' A horrible image, but it is one which suits the novelist well.

And so the short story for the novelist is often yet another form of escape – escape from having to live with a character for years on end, picking up his jealousies, his meanness, his dishonest tricks of thought, his betrayals. The reader may well complain of the unpleasantness of the character, but lucky reader! he has only had to spend a few days in his company. Sometimes in Flaubert's letters you can see him becoming Madame Bovary, developing in himself her destructive passion.

My stories therefore can be regarded as a collection of escapes from the novelist's world – even, if you like, of escapades, and I can reread them more easily because they do not drag a whole lifetime in their wake. I can look at them quickly as I would look at an album of snapshots taken on many different holidays. Of course they contain memories – sometimes unhappy memories, but if I turn the page, the next picture has no connection with the one before. One book, *May We Borrow Your Husband?*, was indeed written, mainly in 1966, in a single mood of sad hilarity, while I was establishing a home in a two-roomed apartment over the port at Antibes. Taking my dinner nightly in the little restaurant of Félix au Port, some of the tales emerged from conversations at other tables (even from a phrase misunderstood).

A story which came to me in sleep appears in the collection called *A Sense of Reality*. It is the tale of a leper patient in Sweden who returns to plead for private treatment with an old medical professor who has condemned him to the publicity of a leper hospital and he finds the doctor's house transformed into a gambling casino for the night to please a senile general. I can still clearly see, as I saw them in sleep, the hired musicians tumbling out of the taxis with their cumbrous instruments. Was I the leper? I think not. I think I was the professor, bemused by the transformation of his house and seeing his patient's face peer in at him from the garden outside.

Dreams, perhaps because I was psychoanalysed as a boy, have always had great importance when I write. The genesis of my novel *It's a Battlefield* was a dream, and *The Honorary Consul* began too with a dream. Sometimes identification with a character goes so far that one may dream his dream and not one's own. That happened to me when I was writing *A Burnt-Out Case*. The symbols, the memories, the associations of that dream belonged so clearly to my character Querry that next morning I could put the dream without change into the novel, where it bridged a gap in the narrative which for days I had been unable to cross. I imagine all authors have found the same aid from the unconscious. The unconscious collaborates in all our work: it is a *nègre* we keep in the cellar to aid us. When an obstacle seems insurmountable, I read the day's work before sleep and leave the *nègre* to labour in my place. When I wake the obstacle has nearly always been removed: the solution is there and obvious – perhaps it came in a dream which I have forgotten.

Looking over my short stories now which stretch in time from 1929 to the eve of the 1970s I am struck by an odd fact – humour enters very late and very unexpectedly. The only three stories I wrote during the war were humorous ones – there again the short story was an escape, an escape from the blitz and the nightly deaths. So perhaps the stories which make up the collection *May We Borrow Your Husband?*, all written during what should have been the last decade of my life, are an escape in humour from the thought of death – this time of certain death. Writing is a form of therapy; sometimes I wonder how all those who do not write, compose or paint can manage to escape the madness, the melancholia, the panic fear which is inherent in the human situation.

2

'Panic fear' – I had felt that once in the East End of London in the 1930s when the police charged the crowd which was obstructing a Mosley march. I had felt it momentarily in Vietnam when I found myself lost between the French parachutists and the Viet Minh outside Phat Diem, but there are situations so absurd that absurdity kills fear. In 1967 I was a tourist visiting Israel for the first time. I wasn't deliberately seeking a troubled place, but lying against a sand dune in the autumn sky under Egyptian fire from anti-tank guns, mortars and small arms, I couldn't help

365

thinking that the phrase 'The Six Days War' was a bit of a misnomer. The war was too evidently still in progress.

Of the six of us lying flat against the dune two were truck drivers, and after an hour they abruptly took off, running doubled up the fifty yards to their truck exposed to the Egyptian shore, which was less than half a mile away. I watched them with selfish apprehension (sooner or later I might have to take the same track), but they made it successfully; one started the engine and they disappeared from sight in the direction in which most of the shells were falling. We weren't tempted to follow them yet.

My companion, the major, lay at right angles to me at the bottom of the slope. Shrapnel had nipped a small piece out of his cheek. When he stopped dabbing it with his handkerchief two horseflies settled on the unimportant wound like cats round a saucer of milk.

It was a quarter to three. I wondered how long it would be before the United Nations observers settled a cease-fire this time.

It was nineteen years since the War of Independence, and the sides of the road from Tel Aviv to West Jerusalem, which was held with such difficulty against odds, were still littered with the remains of battle – small lightly armoured cars, with faded *in memoriam* wreaths lying over them like buoys above a wreck. They are Holy Places which a Christian tourist is apt to ignore, yet this ugly sort of *immortelle* has deeply affected the imagination of Jewish artists, and in the Garden of Statuary at the new National Museum the *objets trouvés* of war, stuck up on pedestals, contrasted grimly with the smooth sensuous Henry Moore sculpture and the pretty, elegant mobile of Alexander Calder, swimming round and round in the cool Jerusalem air. Suddenly Calder and Moore seemed to belong in a gentle, academic, elderly world. There is another mobile by Jean Tinguely – a black, clanking piece of machinery like a bit of a bombed pithead that continues to work for a while with the miners dead or fled: the sound pursues you through the quiet garden.

The garden, so unsuitably named the Billy Rose, was a good preparation for seeing the Sinai Peninsula and following the road to El Arish and the Canal taken by the forces of General Tal. Here were the more recent *objets trouvés* of war.

Hemingway once described the battlefield of the Spanish Civil

366

War as covered with scraps of paper: here it was covered with tin and wood, and next time perhaps it will be with plastic: food tins and petrol tins and shell cases everywhere, ammunition boxes, tracks like discarded snake skins, and of course the burnt-out trucks on their backs or their sides as they were rushed off the road, showing their intestinal coils like medical diagrams of robots. Only an occasional group of Egyptian tanks retained a scorched, upright dignity and sometimes even faced in the direction of their enemy. Some trucks had started through a grove of date palms towards the blue still sea as though their drivers hoped to escape from war. The bouquets of dates hung overhead out of reach, brown, orange, yellow, scarlet; the trucks failed to reach the white beach before they were sent up in flames.

There wasn't much more than that for a tourist to see, yet the tourists were already arriving in coaches at El Arish, disembarking at a smashed building with an improvised soft drink bar. Some of the women wore funny hats marked Israel, and there were formidable matrons with blonde hair who spoke American and probably belonged to book clubs. A man with two cameras round his neck asked a soldier where he could find a rest room and was told to choose any quiet corner. The coaches went no further into Sinai and it was possible to believe that the war was over and only waiting for the refuse trucks to tidy it all away.

But at Kantara nothing was over: this was the frontier as it has always been for Israel, in the south, the west and the north, life under the guns of the enemy. A tall building flew the blue UN flag, the headquarters of the UN observers. The Israeli officers, who liaised with the UN observers, occupied a house behind which had once been a doctor's and the Egyptian flag flew on the other side of the Canal about as far as the Nelson monument from the National Gallery.

'If there's firing,' the colonel said, 'don't go into the street. You see the field of fire – it's a certain way of dying.' On a board was written 'Hilton Hotel, Kantara. First Class Accommodation. All full.' There hadn't been an incident for two weeks, he said, but you never knew. I said to the colonel, 'I have a reputation of bringing trouble with me,' but I didn't mean it seriously.

My companion the major and I shared a room in a building

behind the doctor's house haunted by cats who kept on leaping through gaps in the mosquito wire. There was a trench between and a strongpoint of sandbags in the centre of the doctor's house.

'But if firing starts,' the colonel said, 'get straight into your trench. Don't come to the house. Things escalate here very quickly, but they usually start with small arms.' I thought that perhaps he was trying to create atmosphere for a tourist.

Dinner was not quite up to even the Hilton standard. It seemed unlikely that the Israeli army would be corrupted with either alcohol or hot food. There was a cold pizza, a sort of tomato-coloured smear over rather dry bread, and an equally frigid Welsh rarebit washed down by lemonade; afterwards the officers watched Cairo television, though only one man had a smattering of Arabic. The reception was as bad as the programme. A man sang interminably about love, never changing his profile and there was a drama about family life – nothing military.

The tours of duty were eight weeks and they must have seemed very long without even a nightclub. A sense of danger lent the only savour, but, as the colonel said, there had been no incident for two weeks.

The UN observers on the Israeli side were under an Australian colonel at Kantara. Next day, travelling down the Canal, I met a Burmese officer, a Frenchman, a Swede and a Finn (English was the common language they all spoke). They too, like the Israeli officers, did their own haphazard cooking, but at least they had a little beer. Like civil servants they tried hard to believe in the importance of their own duties, and like civil servants they were subject to Parkinson's Law. A big fleet of white UN cars stood in the yard of the Kantara HQ: one mortar shell could have dispersed them for ever.

From Kantara to Port Tewfik at the end of the Canal there were four permanent posts manned day and night by observers and liaison officers, and there were other points which they had to visit regularly. 'We stay a quarter of an hour here,' the Burmese officer said by a smashed pontoon bridge, and at the end of a quarter of an hour, he grinned happily – 'All peaceful' – and we drove on.

This was the signature tune of our drive: 'All peaceful' at the broken swing bridge, 'All peaceful' opposite Ismalia, where we stood listening to the voices of the Egyptian sentries, 'All peaceful' along the Bitter Lakes, where thirteen ships lay at anchor, the prisoners of the Canal, 'All peaceful' at Port Tewfik.

Suez, like a long grey rubbish dump, lay across the way and at the entrance of Tewfik there was a homemade statue in white stone of an Israeli soldier looking towards the Sinai desert: a very bad statue, but the inscription in Hebrew was imaginative: 'We looked Death in the face, and Death lowered his eyes.'

When an incident occurred an observer reported to his headquarters at Kantara, Kantara reported to the bureau of General Odd Bull in Jerusalem, Jerusalem reported to Ismalia, and then cease-fire negotiations could get under way.

Lunching with the observers at Port Tewfik on baked beans and squares of tepid tinned beef, I asked how long it took for this chain of communications to be completed. 'Not more than three-quarters of an hour,' the Swedish officer said. He had very decorative rank badges and I suppose this was the nearest he was ever likely to come to war; a conscientious man tired of the desert heat who loved the cold and the long nights of northern Sweden.

'And suppose,' I asked, 'you were not here at all, wouldn't things perhaps be arranged more quickly between the Israeli command and the Egyptians?'

'But there is no way for them,' he said, 'to communicate at all without us,' and I couldn't help remembering the white flags which I had seen still dangling from many houses in Gaza. A white flag does not need a UN observer. Its message is clear.

I wanted to say, 'Surely the very fact that a cease-fire will be agreed upon in a matter of hours tempts the Egyptians, especially while the Assembly talks and talks in New York, to create incidents which will be stopped before there are too many casualties or too much danger of serious engagement?' But in Sinai one very quickly adopted the Israeli attitude of kindly protectiveness to these men who had come a long way from home to live in great discomfort and some danger and who had to believe that their function had value.

'Everything peaceful,' the Finnish officer said as we drove away.

Near the Bitter Lakes, where the road ran parallel to the Canal

369

half a mile away, we were stopped by a soldier. He was there to halt traffic. There was firing, he said, further on near Ismalia. Down a branch track, between us and the Canal, a quarter of a mile away, lay a unit of artillery and a couple of tanks. A truck drove up beside the jeep and halted too. It was a little past two and the sun was very hot.

We stood in the road listening until at last we detected a faint bim-bam of guns. Smoke rose in the sky, perhaps above Ismalia. 'We ought to get near cover,' the major said, and we ambled over to a sand dune and then ambled back because no one had followed our example. The sound of gunfire came no closer.

Then without warning there was a whistle overhead and a shell exploded with a mushroom of black smoke perhaps a quarter of a mile beyond us. We ran for the sand dunes and before we were properly down two other shells exploded. The major began to dab his cheek. I remembered how the colonel had said, 'Things escalate very quickly here.'

The sentry, a red-haired young man with a toothy grin, was the only real professional among us. I envied him his steel helmet. He was dissatisfied for some reason with our particular sand-bank, so he led us to another, and after a series of shell bursts to yet a third. I couldn't myself see any difference. In each case we were protected by the dune from the Canal and exposed from behind where the shells were bursting. If the Egyptians were trying to hit the artillery post, I thought, surely sooner or later they will shorten their fire and then we've had it.

Apprehension, except when there was a whistle overhead, gave place after a while to resignation. It was nearly two forty-five and not a shot had been fired from the Israeli side.

Well now, I thought, the observers must be at work. If the incident began at two, the chain of communications must be nearly completed. Perhaps the cease-fire would be at three, but at three there was no change, except now I was aware of a beastly sound, far more demoralizing than the whistle of a low trajectory shell fired by a tank or an anti-tank gun, the gentle secretive whisper, flip-flap-flip, of a mortar shell stealing through the air.

After every explosion we looked back – they were still over-shooting, and at every sound in the air we flattened into the sand. A breeze raised my shirt and I felt more vulnerable. I took silly precautions like taking off my sun glasses in case they broke into my eyes. I remembered the blitz, but the blitz had one great advantage – the pubs remained open.

It was about then that the two truck drivers made off. I was inclined to follow their example, but small-arms fire opened from the Canal and put paid to that idea. And at last, nearly three-quarters of an hour after the first Egyptian shell, the Israeli artillery went into action.

Like the first barrage over London, it was an encouraging sound, until the little devil of fear whispered in our ears, 'They've disclosed their position now. The Egyptians will shorten their range,' and when the tanks joined in, 'After every burst they changed position. Perhaps at this moment they are approaching the other side of our dune and making us a major objective for the Egyptian anti-tank guns.'

I found it encouraging to see the apprehension in my companions' eyes and the tension of their bodies. It would have been lonely to share the sand dune with heroes.

At the beginning we lay in silence. We only began to talk to each other when fire slackened – except for the sentry, who at every new sound overhead gave a definition of the shell, sometimes erroneous as when he thought for a moment we were being bombed from the air. Social life began only when the artillery fell silent and then stopped again abruptly at the whistle of a shell or a flip-flap of a mortar as though all our attention had to be directed towards altering its course.

Four o'clock came and no cease-fire. I began to analyse the emotional stages of a man under fire if only to understand better those kibbutz workers who had suffered this for nearly twenty years. First reaction was fear, but certainly not panic fear which is felt in a crowd or in solitude, and this developed gradually into resignation ('Well, if this is the end, it's the end. At least I shan't die of cancer or be humiliated by senility').

When the ceasefire failed to arrive at four and again at four fifteen (we had been lying on the dune now in the heat of the afternoon sun for two hours) irritation began to set in. I felt like Henry James listening to an anecdote at the dinner table that went on too long for his purpose. The fatuous words of our provincial politicians came to mind. I thought of all the empty

371

speeches in the Assembly of the United Nations: these bombardments were debating points to be made there.

At four forty-five fire slackened, and then in the silences which
were always interrupted sooner or later, apprehension returned
again – it would be an absurd chance to be killed by the last
mortar shell. How often Shimon X or Ygael Y must have felt
that, and for them this shelling was an everyday fear, not allevi-
ated as in my case by a professional interest. By five fifteen the
artillery had ceased and there were only occasional bursts of
small-arms fire, so we made a run for the jeep and took the next
five exposed kilometres at a speed which would have been
reckless if it had not been prudent.

At Kantara when we arrived after dark there were now ruins
which hadn't been there when we drove out, but the doctor's
house had only lost a little plaster and the UN house still stood.
The Egyptian flag had disappeared across the Canal and there
were flames in eastern Kantara which burned till five in the morning. Artillery had opened up nearly the whole length of the Canal,
the greatest incident in two months, but in Kantara of four dead
one was an Arab child of three and another an Arab criminal.
Lives cost a lot of ammunition.

The UN observers were busy making out their report over
their tepid meal. All knew very well which side had broken the
cease-fire, but papers must be made out in due form and filed.
Parkinson's Law applies to the multiplication of files as well as
personnel. In my small area of observation I knew that the
Egyptians had fired first and the Israeli artillery had not replied
for nearly three-quarters of an hour (my sole occupation on that
dune had been noting on my watch the passage of time), but that
was not what the UN would consider to be reliable evidence.

There is the story of an Israeli sentry shot dead on the border,
and the UN observer who demanded proof of the incident.

'Proof? But here's the body.'

'Yes, but the man might have shot himself.'

'Through the forehead? With a rifle?'

'One of his companions might have done it accidentally. This
isn't what we call proof.'

The odds against an observer himself being present at the
opening of an incident were heavy, and so the paper work went

happily on. An actual incident was finally so swathed in paper that all its reality was lost. It became no more than a series of contradictory reports from either side of the Canal, filed for lack of 'proof'.

Back from the Sinai desert I opened my paper the next day. Secretary-General U Thant complained that both sides had neglected to use the 'UN cease-fire observation machinery' and had not complained directly to the UN military observers 'for remedial action' (that long chain of communication, Kantara – Jerusalem – Ismalia and back) and had 'reacted impulsively by immediately shooting in case of alleged breaches of the cease-fire'.

Three hours of fire by artillery mortars and small arms remained, in that fairyland of UN investigation, 'alleged' like a crime in a British court of justice, but I couldn't help feeling that 'impulsive' was not the right word to use for the Israeli reaction when I remembered the long three-quarters of a long hour as we lay on the sand dune waiting for any reply to the Egyptian fire.

3

If *A Burnt-Out Case* in 1961 represented the depressive side of a manic-depressive writer, *Travels with my Aunt* eight years later surely represented the manic at its height – or depth. The novel followed naturally enough *May We Borrow Your Husband?*, indeed, a number of tales I had only noted down as possible ideas at the time of that collection now found a place as 'my aunt's' anecdotes in Henry Pulling's narrative. I had opened my notebook for his inspection and he left it almost empty.

I had finished *A Burnt-Out Case* with the depressing certitude that this would be my last novel. My depression was caused in part by living for several years in company with my characters. It was not helped by a serious pneumonia which I had developed in Moscow in 1961 and a specialist's suspicion that I had lung cancer, though the unpleasant experience of a bronchioscopy I was happily able to use in a short story, 'Under the Garden'. What swung me out of the depression into the manic condition in which I wrote most of the stories in *May We Borrow Your Husband?* and then started work on *Travels with my Aunt*? I can only suppose it came from making a difficult decision in my private life and leaving England to settle permanently in France in 1966. I burned a number of boats and in the light of the flames I began again to write a novel.

Travels with my Aunt is the only book I have written for the fun of it. Although the subject is old age and death – a suitable subject to tackle at the age of sixty-five – and though an excellent Swedish critic described the novel justly as 'laughter in the shadow of the gallows', I experienced more of the laughter and little of the shadow in writing it. When I began with the scene of the cremation of Henry Pulling's supposed mother and his encounter with Aunt Augusta I didn't believe for a moment that I would continue the novel for more than a few days. I didn't even know what the next scene was likely to be – I didn't know that Augusta was Henry's mother. Every day when I sat down before the blank sheets of foolscap (for as a symbol of my new freedom I had abandoned the single-lined variety where the lines seemed to me now like the bars on a prison window) I had no idea what was going to happen to Henry or Augusta next. I felt like a rider who has dropped the reins and left the direction to his horse or like a dreamer who watches his dream unfold without power to alter its course. I felt above all that I had broken for good or ill with the past.

I was even irresponsible enough to include some private jokes which no reader would understand. Why not? I didn't expect to have any readers. So I christened 'Detective-Sergeant Sparrow, John' after that elegant scholar the ex-Warden of All Souls, Augusta's black lover 'Wordsworth' after a villainous District Commissioner whom I had met more than thirty years before in Liberia, Mr Visconti's son 'Mario' after my friend Mario Soldati who once greeted me and gave me lunch in Milan station with similar flamboyance on my way to Istanbul. I remember I even found room for Kingsley Amis's surname which I gave to a character on whom I can't at the moment lay my finger. The name Visconti for Aunt Augusta's lover was adapted from my favourite character in Marjorie Bowen's *The Viper of Milan* which I had loved as a boy, and it gave me an innocent amusement when I heard Detective Sparrow describing him as a viper. Some critics have found in the book a kind of résumé of my

374

literary career – a scene in Brighton, the journey on the Orient Express, and perhaps a hint of this did come to my mind by the time Aunt Augusta arrived at the Pera Palace, but what struck me with some uneasiness, when I reread the book the other day, were the suggestions I found in it of where the future was going to take me. The boat which carried Henry Pulling from Buenos Aires to Asunción stopped for half an hour during the night in the little river harbour of Corrientes in northern Argentina, but I had no idea that I would be landing there from a plane some years later in search of the right setting for *The Honorary Consul*. And Panamá – the smuggling by the route Panamá–Asunción–Argentina played a minor role in the story of 'my aunt' and Mr Visconti, and no thought entered my head that nearly ten years later I would become so attached to that country of the five frontiers, poor, beautiful, bizarre Panamá.

I came to Paraguay by a writer's instinct. I had realized that Henry's travels with his aunt had to reach as climax some destination more removed and less familiar than Brighton, Paris, Istanbul, Boulogne. I knew nothing of the city, but I believed I would find in Asunción some mingling of the exotic, the dangerous and the Victorian which would appeal to Aunt Augusta. How right I proved to be: a street named after Benjamin Constant, 'a little white castellated Baptist church, a college built like a neo-Gothic abbey' – these were the things which Henry Pulling, retired bank manager, and I noticed as we drove from the quay-side into town.

As for the exotic and the dangerous we had come to a country ruled by the rough hand of General Stroessner, the protector of Nazi war criminals. One of the first friends I made, a charming and cultured man who spoke English well and was always ready to accompany me for an excursion or to a party, inadvertently let me see that he was carrying a police card. He quickly explained it away – he carried it only because he lectured sometimes at the police college. I pretended to believe him, for after all perhaps he had been allotted to me for my protection. Once I asked Luis Fernandez, the driver whom I had hired to take me on a country journey, 'Motor accidents?' as I wondered at the many small shrines for the dead lining the road on which we had encountered far more horsemen than cars. He replied, ambiguously, 'Paraguayans hold life very cheap. If one comes from the city to a country place it is best to stay very quiet in a corner – there are always those who like to pick a quarrel with a knife or a gun. Of course to seem too withdrawn may look insulting. Like speaking Spanish, as though you consider Guarani a low language. But then if you speak to them in Guarani they may think you take them for uneducated fellows.'

I was fortunate to be in Asunción like my character Henry Pulling when the National Day was celebrated by the ruling party, the Colorado. In a country where Communism is a crime and even the Jesuits have their telephones tapped and where no criticism of the United States was allowed in the Press it surprised me to find when I woke that the whole of Asunción had gone Red – red banners, red skirts, red scarves, red flowers, red ties, red handkerchiefs; poor Henry Pulling was thoughtless enough to use his red handkerchief for blowing his nose – an appalling insult to the Colorado Party and the President. I was wiser, but then I had been properly warned.

None the less I was aware a few days later of having somehow transgressed. The man from the Foreign Office who came nearly every evening to my hotel for a drink ceased to turn up; the transport to the Chaco which had been promised me never materialized; only my friend with the police card remained faithful and friendly to the last. I could only assume that what offended the General had been this: the sixteen-year-olds at the local *lycée* asked to visit me, and the hotel provided an interpreter – a Belsen type of woman who smelt like an informer. She was irritated to find her services were not really necessary, for I could understand the students' questions and most of them could understand my answers. She couldn't control what was said. I chose to speak about Fidel Castro of whom the students knew nothing (Cuba was a banned subject in the Press), and to criticize Pope Paul's encyclical on birth control, *Humanae Vitae*, which had been recently published. I doubt if the General minded my opinion of the encyclical, but he certainly would not have cared for my favourable portrait of Fidel Castro.

Ten years later in Washington, at the party given in 1977 by the Organisation of American States for the signing of the Panamá Treaty, I was standing as a Panamá delegate a few feet away from General Stroessner who looked in civilian clothes like the proprietor of a German *bierstube*, and I was introduced by my companion to someone passing by. 'This is Señor So-and-so, one of General Stroessner's Ministers.' The minister at the sound of my name quickly withdrew his hand and spat his reply, 'You passed once through Paraguay,' before turning abruptly on his heel to join the General. I felt some pride – as I had when Papa Doc so furiously attacked me – that a mere writer could irritate a dictator so irremovable, and a regret for that sad and lovely land to which I could never return as long as these men lived.

4

The origin of my next novel, *The Honorary Consul*, written between 1970 and 1973, lies in the cave of the unconscious. I had a dream about an American ambassador – a favourite of women and a good tennis player whom I encountered in a bar – but in my dream there was no kidnapping, no guerrillas, no mistaken identity, nothing to identify it with *The Honorary Consul* except the fact that the dream lodged inexplicably in my head for months and during those months the figures of Charley Fortnum and Dr Plarr stole up around the unimportant ambassador of my dream and quietly liquidated him.

It remained for me to discover the scene of the action. Of Uruguay I knew nothing and the Tupamaros were far too efficient an organization to make the mistake of kidnapping an unimportant English honorary consul in place of an American ambassador. Paraguay was quite another matter. Under the heavy rule of Stroessner no guerrilla organization had been able to grow, and it seemed plausible that a small inexperienced group working across the border into Argentina might make the blunder which I needed for my story. I was certainly right about the Tupamaros who almost at the same time as I was finishing my novel succeeded most efficiently in kidnapping the British Ambassador in Montevideo. His story when he came to write it contained some interesting parallels to my own. There was even, he believed, a priest among his kidnappers.

My choice of setting was an easy one. For some reason Corrientes had penetrated my imagination like the first injection of a drug. Indeed there is a tradition in that proud little city, founded long before Buenos Aires by the *conquistadores* coming from the north, that anyone who once sees it will always return. My boat to Asunción stopped for only half an hour – a few lights along the quay, a solitary sentinel outside a warehouse, a small public garden with something resembling a classical temple, and the slow tide of the great river – those were all on which I based my expectations.

In Buenos Aires when I stopped on my way north I encountered a serious problem. My story needed a brothel where Charley Fortnum, the Honorary Consul, would find the girl he married, but when I sought information I was reminded that there were no longer legal brothels in Argentina – only clandestine houses in Buenos Aires for the rich. The kind of public brothel I desired, I was told, could no longer be found anywhere in Argentina. There was a certain character – a friend of a friend – who would certainly know if any such brothel existed anywhere, and from his appearance I felt certain of his authority on sexual matters. I borrowed his features for one of my minor characters, Gustavo Escobar: 'his face, brick-red as laterite, resembled a clearing which had been hacked out of the bush and his nose reared like the horse of a *conquistador*', but that description was all he contributed to my story, for the only information he could give me was of a brothel which existed on the Uruguayan border four hundred kilometres from Corrientes.

None the less the brothel proved the least of my problems and the soonest solved. Corrientes, a very independent state with a military station, was a law to itself, and I had not been forty-eight hours in the city before I was able to describe the friendly establishment of Señora Sanches with its little patio, where Fortnum discovered a wife and the novelist Saavedra a character.

A more serious problem arose on my first morning as I lay in bed and looked at the local paper *El Litoral*. On the main news page I read what was very nearly the story I had come there to write – a Paraguayan consul from a town near Corrientes had been kidnapped in mistake for the Paraguayan Ambassador and a demand for the release of political prisoners had been delivered to General Stroessner, who was on a fishing holiday in the south of Argentina.

All day I thought how wasted my journey had been. How could I continue to plan a novel so clearly anticipated by reality and what was the use of staying in Corrientes? However, a few days later the General replied to the kidnappers that they could do what they liked with their prisoner – he wasn't interested in anything but his fishing – and the consul was released and forgotten. I was encouraged to go on with my story. I had been right to choose Paraguayans to organize so inefficient a kidnapping.

I passed two happy and interesting weeks in Corrientes. My friends in Buenos Aires couldn't understand my interest in a city which I had seen so briefly from a boat. They said it was the wrong time of year in Corrientes, it was still hot and humid summer in the north – and the city had no interest at all. Nothing, they assured me, really *nothing*, ever happened in Corrientes. As day followed day I remembered with amusement what they had told me.

My second day there a third-world priest working in the *barrio* of the poor had been turned out of his church by the Archbishop, and a Mass was said that Sunday by a strange priest in an empty church while the congregation stood outside carrying banners – 'Give us back our priest.' Next day the Archbishop himself was put under house arrest by the Governor. After all something was happening in Corrientes.

Perhaps it was on my fourth day in the city that I took up an invitation from the director of the airport to go for a walk with him. We began to walk across the fields near the airport; he wanted to show me where the rafts of timber were floated south on their journey of two thousand kilometres to the sea. He said to me as we started off, 'Every day when I arrive at the airport I ask my manager, "Any robberies? Any murders?" This morning he said to me, "No robberies, but one murder."'

At the edge of the field ahead of us two policemen stood guard over what looked like a large brown paper parcel. 'There,' the director said.

A piece of brown paper had been spread over the body: only the feet protruded at one end. I wanted to photograph the strange package, but a policeman with too friendly zeal took off the brown paper and left only an uninteresting corpse. We took a small path down through the trees to the waterside: a trickle of blood had not yet been dried by the sun. The director said, 'I came out here and met the murderer. I said to him, "He was your friend. Why did you do it?" He said, "He was stronger, but I had a knife."'

I asked the director, 'Weren't you scared? You were unarmed.'

He smiled. 'No, no. These are my people. I told him I must go back to the airport and telephone the police, and he disappeared into the woods.'

The incident stayed in my mind, destined to find a place in the novel I was planning. I spoke of it later to my friend Mario Soldati and he gave me some advice which corresponded with the experience I had when I wrote *The Quiet American*. 'You must never when you write a novel include something which has happened to you without in some way changing it.' So it was with this incident. The words of the director, 'These are my people,' I put into the mouth of Colonel Perez, the chief of police, in *The Honorary Consul*, and the body I deposited on one of the rafts across which with trepidation I now followed the director, the logs sinking and heaving at every step.

Certainly my friends in Buenos Aires had exaggerated the dullness of Corrientes. In my first week there had been the abortive kidnapping, the expulsion of the third-world priest from his church, the arrest of the Archbishop, the murder near the airport, and a few days after that a small and unimportant bomb was discovered in the cathedral. On the day I left I noticed a crowd of people bunched on the parapet above the Paraná. I asked my driver what they were doing there. He said they were waiting for the frogmen.

'The frogmen?'

'Yes. Ten minutes ago a family committed suicide. A man drove his wife and children off the jetty where the river is deepest. The windows of the car were closed and the doors locked.'

The Honorary Consul was one of the novels I found hardest to write. In my experience, after a few months, an author usually feels that his novel is taking control. There has been the drive at increasing speed of the plane along the runway, then the slow lift and you feel that the wheels no longer touch the ground. But with *The Honorary Consul* it was only in the last chapter that I found myself at last in the freedom of the air. Now when I read the

book again I have the impression that I must have been dozing at
the controls, for the plane had taken to the air on the very first
page when Doctor Plarr stood at night in the small port 'among
the rails and yellow cranes', as I might have observed him years
before while I stared through the darkness at the same scene from
the deck of the Asunción boat and the passenger whom I had
identified as a smuggler told me with a sceptical smile that 'the
people here' always said that those who once saw Corrientes
returned.

5

1929 to 1978 is a long lifetime of work, but, before I could
consider retiring, there was one engagement I had made with
myself. My ambition after the war was to write a novel of espionage free from the conventional violence, which has not, in spite
of James Bond, been a feature of the British Secret Service. I
wanted to present the Service unromantically as a way of life,
men going daily to their office to earn their pensions, the background much like that of any other profession – whether the
bank clerk or the business director – an undangerous routine, and
within each character the more important private life. When I had
spent a few years in the Service during the war, first in West
Africa and then in London, I had certainly found little excitement
or melodrama coming my way.

There were some conflicts of personalities under the shadow
of the enormous conflict – that time, for instance, in my one-man
station in Sierra Leone when I had been for a while cut off from
supplies by my boss a thousand miles away in Lagos; or when I
had watched with sympathy the Commissioner of Police in
Freetown, who had survived twenty years of hard life and a dose
of blackwater fever, driven into a nervous breakdown by a young
puppy from MI5. Melodrama was sadly lacking – one last-
minute scramble to persuade the Navy to stop a Portuguese liner
outside territorial waters in order to arrest a Swiss suspected of
being a German spy, but in that affair I was only a glorified
messenger-boy.

When I returned to London it was a question of files, files,
endless files. I had been responsible in London, as I have written
earlier, for counter-espionage in Portugal under Kim Philby, who,

when he defected much later, in 1963, to the Soviet Union, was ironically dubbed 'the Third Man'. No melodrama or violence disturbed us: only a certain boredom and lassitude induced by the closed-in life, since the nature of our occupation forced our small sub-section of five men to live too closely together – there were few meetings with strangers outside the Service who might want to know what we were doing in this so-called 'branch of the Foreign Office'. The only relic I left behind me when I resigned (my 'hero' in *The Human Factor* makes a passing reference to it) was a Who's Who, limited to twelve copies, if I remember right, compiled by myself, of German agents in the Azores with two introductory essays – very much at second hand – on the administration and agricultural aspect of the islands and a contribution by Kim Philby on radio communications – this for the use of our invasion forces. Does a copy exist still somewhere on the files? It would have a certain value today.

The Secret Service, of course, has changed much since those days, so in writing my novel I based my picture on rather outdated material. I began *The Human Factor* more than ten years before it was published and abandoned it in despair after two or three years' work. I thought it would join all those other unfinished projects which had littered my desk (three abandoned novels lie there even today). I abandoned it mainly because of the Philby affair. My double agent Maurice Castle bore no resemblance in character or motive to Philby, none of the characters has the least likeness to anyone I have known, but I disliked the idea of the novel being taken as a *roman à clef*. I know very well from experience that it is only possible for me to base a very minor and transient character on a real person. A real person stands in the way of the imagination. Perhaps a trick of speech, a physical trait may be used, but I can write no more than a few pages before realizing that I simply don't know enough about the character to use him, even if he is an old friend. With the imaginary character I am sure – I know that Doctor Percival in *The Human Factor* admires the painting of Ben Nicholson, I know that Colonel Daintry will open a tin of sardines when he returns from the funeral of his colleague.

Years passed and during those years I wrote *The Honorary Consul*, perhaps the novel I prefer to all the others. Ahead of me,

I thought, were only blank years, and all the time *The Human Factor*, which didn't even have a title, hung like a dead albatross around my neck. My imagination seemed as dead as the bird. And yet there were some good things in the twenty thousand words which I had written – I liked especially the shooting party at C's country house. The memory of it nagged me. I couldn't settle to any other work, and so reluctantly and doubtfully I took the novel up again, telling myself that the Philby affair belonged now sufficiently to the past.

Perhaps the hypocrisy of our relations with South Africa nagged me on to work too. It was so obvious that, however much opposed the governments of the Western Alliance might pretend to be to apartheid, however much our leaders talked of its immorality, they simply could not let South Africa succumb to black power and Communism. If Operation Uncle Remus did not exist, it would certainly come into existence before long. It was less an invention than a prediction.

The novel at last was written and I was free of the incubus, but that did not mean it had to be published, and for a long while I thought of leaving it in a drawer for my children to publish after my death. I am never satisfied with a novel, but I was more than usually dissatisfied with this one, I had betrayed my purpose. There *was* violence – the death of Davis – and Doctor Percival was hardly a typical figure of the British Secret Service. It wasn't as realistic a picture as I had intended, and the novel was saved only by the human factor of the title. As a love story – a married-love story of an elderly man – I think it may have succeeded.

I sent a copy of the book to Moscow, to my friend Kim Philby, and his reply interested me. His criticism was valid. I had made Castle's circumstances in Moscow, he wrote, too bleak. He himself had found everything provided for him, even to a shoehorn, something he had never possessed before. (It was true, he added, that he was a more important agent than Castle.) As for Doctor Percival, Philby commented with justice that he must have been recruited from the CIA. Doctor L, whom we had both known, was hardly capable of deliberately poisoning a man, even though his diagnoses were notoriously inaccurate. (He had tried to prevent me going to West Africa by diagnosing me as a diabetic. A more reliable specialist found a small sugar deficiency.)

Another friend of mine in Moscow, Professor Valentina Ivasheva, pointed out that the days of the Russian stove were over – there was central heating everywhere now, so I altered 'stove' to 'radiator' when the book was reprinted. I didn't however improve the other furnishings of Castle's flat, for as I pointed out in my reply to Philby I had based these on the account given by his wife, Eleanor Philby, in her book *The Spy I Loved*.

Nearly twenty years before I had assumed, after *A Burnt-Out Case*, that my writing days were finished – at any rate as far as the novel was concerned – and I assumed the same again now, but a writer's imagination, like the body, fights against all reason against death. So it was that at lunch on Christmas Day, 1978, in Switzerland with my daughter and my grandchildren nine months after the publication of *The Human Factor*, a new book, *Dr Fischer of Geneva*, came without any warning to my mind. At the age of seventy-five I found my future still as unpredictable as when I sat down at my mother's desk in Berkhamsted and began to write my first novel: 'He came over the top of the down as the last light failed . . .'

Epilogue

The Other

THIS book has not been a self-portrait. I leave such a portrait to my friends and enemies. All the same, I did find myself for many years in search of someone who called himself Graham Greene.

When I bought Edward Thomas's *Collected Poems* more than fifty years ago, one poem called 'The Other' haunted me, though I didn't know why. It was not one of Thomas's best poems. It told of a traveller who along his road, at this inn or that, continually stumbled on the trace of someone exactly like himself who had preceded him along the same route.

> I learnt his road and, e'er they were
> Sure I was I, left the dark wood
> Behind, kestrel and woodpecker,
> The inn and the sun, the happy mood
> When first I tasted sunlight there.
> I travelled fast, in hopes I should
> Out run that other, what to do
> When caught, I planned not, I pursued
> To prove the likeness, and if true
> To watch until myself I knew.

The poem ends,

> He goes: I follow: no release
> Until he ceases. Then I also shall cease.

Some quarter of a century after I first read that poem, I came myself on the Other's tracks, and few years have passed since without signs of his passage: letters from strangers who remember me at a wedding I never attended or serving a Mass I never served – once a telephone call from a woman in Rome, even photographs in a Geneva newspaper and a Jamaican one. The Other calls himself Graham Greene, perhaps his name is Graham Greene – there's no copyright in names – though there are reasons to suppose in one of his appearances that he was a certain John Skinner, a notorious jail-breaker, or according to the Indian police someone with the improbable name of Meredith de Varg. He may be both – for there is no resemblance between the two blurred photographs I possess, both claiming to be me.

It was a little case of blackmail which brought the Other first to my attention. My friend Alex Korda rang me up one afternoon in London. 'Have you been in trouble?' he asked.

'Trouble?'

'The editor of a film magazine in Paris has telephoned me. He's very distressed because he has found that one of his employees has tried to blackmail you.'

'But I haven't been in Paris and I haven't been blackmailed.'

I remembered our conversation the next time I was in Paris when my friend and literary agent, Marie Biche, said, apropos of nothing, 'If anyone tried to blackmail you, you'd come to me, wouldn't you? You wouldn't pay up.'

'Blackmail me about what?'

'Oh, something about photographs with women – I don't know – there's a story going round.'

It was the year 1955–6. The Other was very active that year. Stray bits of his past gathered round me – they could so easily have been bits of my own past. The editor of *Mondanités* ('*Revue de l'élite française*') wrote to me reminding me of our meeting at the Cannes Film Festival (which I had never attended) and praising my talent for tennis which I haven't played since I was a schoolboy. '*J'ai eu la joie de vous voir fréquemment sur les courts de tennis, car votre talent littéraire ne cède en rien à vos qualités sportives.*' A woman wrote to me from Montevideo: 'You once took me to have coffee in a Belgian pastry shop on a corner of Oxford Street (does it still exist?) and you introduced me to a girl from up North with whom you were very much in love. Did you marry her? You came to my wedding in November 1935 and I left for S. America soon after.' The Other certainly seemed to leave strong impressions behind, particularly on women.

It was a woman's voice which spoke to me on the telephone at the Grand Hotel, Rome (I had gone to bed early after a long flight from Calcutta). 'Hullo, Graham, this is Veronica.'

'Oh yes, how are you?' Who the hell, I wondered, was Veronica?

'I rang up the George V in Paris and they said you had left for

Rome. I know you always stay at the Grand' – which was true enough.

'Yes, I've just arrived. What are you doing?' I asked, to delay the conversation in hope of a clue. I had forgotten the Other and thought it just possible that I had once known someone called Veronica.

'I am lying in bed and reading the *Odyssey* in the new Penguin translation.'

'I'm in bed too. What about a drink tomorrow? I'm so sorry, but I'm fixed for meals,' I added with caution.

Next evening I went with a friend and waited in the bar. He agreed to speak to her if she were unknown to me and not attractive. A woman in her forties entered in a long evening dress, with the extended face of an upper-class horse. I left her for my friend to deal with. He told me later that she was American and had met Graham Greene in Arabia.

It was that summer, I think, that the Other hit the headlines. I had been in Brighton for a few days and returning to London I found an inquiry from *Picture Post*. They had received a telegram signed Graham Greene, dated from Assam, asking for a hundred pounds because the sender was in a kind of imbroglio with the Indian police as he had lost his passport. The editor had sent someone to Albany, off Piccadilly, where I had chambers, to inquire whether I was, in fact, in India. The porter replied with wise caution that he had not seen me for several days, so perhaps I was, and *Picture Post* telegraphed a hundred pounds to India. Then, of course, the news began to break. Indian Press stories percolated through – 'Graham Greene Convicted. Sentenced to Two Years RI [rigorous imprisonment].' as well as the only authentic letter I have seen from the Other himself. With its quiet assumption that he was on a mission for *Picture Post* it must have been written to convince the police – he could never have expected it would convince *Picture Post*.

The Other wrote in a breezy Sapper style from Duklingia, Assam.

Gentlemen,

Possibly by this time, swarms of flatfooted policemen, intelligence agents in false beards and other peculiar characters have been swarming over the building asking questions about me. Graham Greene has

387

suddenly become NEWS. A few days ago someone most unkindly pinched my bags, cash and passport. I accordingly as in duty bound telegraphed the information to the UK REP, the High Commission in Calcutta, asking them to make arrangements for my passage to Calcutta. They, in turn, having nasty minds, asked the local police to check up, which was, under the circumstances, a most stupid thing to do. This is a DISTURBED area and finding they had in their midst an unidentifiable foreigner, they were delighted, classed me as an agent of a foreign power engaged in assisting and advising the hostile NAGAS, and promptly locked me up. This, when I have recovered, will make an excellent supplement to the article as yet unborn on the NAGA PROBLEM. Two local tea planters, with infinite kindness, came along to court this morning and bailed me out, otherwise I should have remained there for God-knows how long.

You have probably by this time received OIL and FLOOD. Father Christmas has gone up to Amritsar to snap the local temples and bearded Sikh gentlemen. He has missed the scoop of the century by failing to record for posterity – British Correspondent behind bars. I don't intend to give him another opportunity!

I now, very desperately, need some money. Please forward to this address, forthwith (or sooner) a hundred or so. Make sure there are no snags as to exchange control, otherwise it might be possible to arrange something through Orient Longmans at Calcutta.

There doesn't seem to be much else. JUNGLE RECLAMATION will have to wait until I have taken a deep breath. The NAGA PROBLEM is still a problem – to me anyway. Everyone assures me that everything is now under control and that the bad boys are behaving themselves. I being a born cynic feel otherwise. It is extremely difficult to persuade the powers that be that I am simply a newsman after the truth. Much as I wish to write what promises to be the most fascinating article, the difficulties are stupendous. Perhaps after all, they do NOT wish the truth to be published.
Sincerely, Graham Greene

I suggested to *Picture Post* that they might send me to interview the Other in his Assam prison, but I was deterred by the thought that it was the monsoon season and by a conversation I had on the telephone with an official at the High Commissioner's office in London. He warned me to give him advance notice of my leaving for Calcutta, otherwise I would be in danger of arrest on arrival as the Other had broken his bail. Not only had he broken bail, but he had gone off with a typewriter, a wrist watch and

388

some clothes of the tea planters who had befriended him. An Indian friend wrote me further details: 'It appears that he calls himself at times Graham Greene and at other times Graham Green – without the "e". He's supposed to be an Australian by birth, but this is only a conjecture (from his accent) for he has no identity papers with him. For a long time he has been moving about from one tea estate to another, living on charity, living the life of a tramp and claiming to be a professional writer.'

Re-arrested, the Other disappeared for a time into an Indian prison, but even in these straits he had a woman to speak up for him, although she had not seen him for a dozen years. She wrote to me from Bournemouth asking me to help him. 'Mr Graham Greene is a man of courage and is not indifferent to principles, and although he may have been in a forbidden place, due to his roving adventurous spirit, I do feel sure that the charge against him is without much foundation.' Adventurous spirit indeed. 'The accused was wanted,' the *Statesman* of Calcutta reported, 'in a series of cases in Calcutta, Patna, Ranchi, Lucknow, Meerut, Poona, Bombay, Delhi and other places.' A lot for one man: perhaps he was both John Skinner and Meredith de Varg.

, For nearly two years I heard nothing more of the Other; he went out of my mind until one day I was booking a passage to New York in the BOAC office. 'Are you staying only one night in New York?' the girl asked me with surprise.

'No. I'm not sure how long . . .'

'But we have you booked next day on the return flight New York – London.'

Could the other passenger be the Other returning from jail in India? One thing is certain, that in December 1959 he had come back into circulation. Marie Biche wrote to me that month to tell me that an attractive young Frenchwoman had gone to apply for a job with an American businessman staying at the Hotel Prince de Galles. After being interviewed by him in the lobby and having failed to get the job because she didn't have English short-hand, she was stopped on the way out by another American who gave his name as Peters or something similar. He told her that he had overheard part of the conversation and understood she was looking for a job; he was on the lookout for a secretary for his friend and partner, the writer Graham Greene, who was coming to Paris to work for two months before going on a trip of several months across the United States, where he would be renting a house here and there as he travelled around, a habit of his as he couldn't work in hotels. Would she like to be offered the post?

The girl was working part-time in a Paris bookshop, and feeling that the job sounded too good to be true she called up my publisher, who put her on to Marie. In between she had checked with the Prince de Galles and learned that they had no one by the name of Peters staying there. Marie suggested it would be worth going to the appointment to try and lead the man on to volunteer a little more about himself and his partner, but the girl wouldn't go as she was convinced that Peters was a scout for a white slavery gang. He had said that, if she had a nice friend who would like to come along as a housekeeper for Graham Greene on his American tour, it would be possible to arrange it as he was looking for someone to fill that post too.

It was the last big intrusion of the Other into my life – the rest have been only passing appearances: for example a photograph in a Jamaican paper of 'Famed Novelist Graham Greene and Missus drink with the Scudders (centre) at Galleon Club.' Everyone is laughing, glass in hand; the Other with Pompidou eyebrows is very debonair in a white jacket, and Missus is an attractive woman. Neither corresponds with a photograph in *La Tribune de Génève* of Mr and Mrs Graham Greene at the airport of Cointrin – a man much older than I was then, a bit travel-worn and wearing an absurd little tweed hat, an out-of-focus woman in a toque and dark glasses. 'Thick set, a pipe between his teeth, the British writer Graham Greene arrived yesterday afternoon [7 July 1967] at Cointrin. Coming from Paris where he lives now the author of *The Third Man* has begun his wandering holidays at Geneva.' Asked whether he was writing a new book, he said no, he was taking a true holiday.

Was the lady with him Claudine, or was Claudine the more glamorous woman in Jamaica drinking with the Scudders? It was in 1970 I first learnt of Claudine in a letter addressed to her (as Mrs Graham Greene) from Cape Town. 'I called in at the club yesterday ... By subtle steering I learnt that you had forsaken the steamy parts of Africa and had married a really distinguished author ... Being an author's wife will be right down

390

your street and I am sure you must be of enormous assistance to your husband.' Nearly twenty years had passed since the blackmailing in Paris: the Other seemed to be settling down.

> He goes: I follow: no release
> Until he ceases.

Some years ago in Chile, after I had been entertained at lunch by President Allende, a right-wing paper in Santiago announced to its readers that the President had been deceived by an impostor. I found myself shaken by a metaphysical doubt. Had *I* been the impostor all the time? Was I the Other? Was I Skinner? Was it even possible that I might be Meredith de Varg?

FOR THE BEST IN PAPERBACKS, LOOK FOR THE 🐧

In every corner of the world, on every subject under the sun, Penguin represents quality and variety – the very best in publishing today.

For complete information about books available from Penguin – including Puffins, Penguin Classics and Arkana – and how to order them, write to us at the appropriate address below. Please note that for copyright reasons the selection of books varies from country to country.

In the United Kingdom: Please write to *Dept E.P., Penguin Books Ltd, Harmondsworth, Middlesex, UB7 0DA.*

If you have any difficulty in obtaining a title, please send your order with the correct money, plus ten per cent for postage and packaging, to *PO Box No 11, West Drayton, Middlesex*

In the United States: Please write to *Dept BA, Penguin, 299 Murray Hill Parkway, East Rutherford, New Jersey 07073*

In Canada: Please write to *Penguin Books Canada Ltd, 2801 John Street, Markham, Ontario L3R 1B4*

In Australia: Please write to the *Marketing Department, Penguin Books Australia Ltd, P.O. Box 257, Ringwood, Victoria 3134*

In New Zealand: Please write to the *Marketing Department, Penguin Books (NZ) Ltd, Private Bag, Takapuna, Auckland 9*

In India: Please write to *Penguin Overseas Ltd, 706 Eros Apartments, 56 Nehru Place, New Delhi, 110019*

In the Netherlands: Please write to *Penguin Books Netherlands B.V., Postbus 195, NL–1380AD Weesp*

In West Germany: Please write to *Penguin Books Ltd, Friedrichstrasse 10–12, D–6000 Frankfurt/Main 1*

In Spain: Please write to *Alhambra Longman S.A., Fernandez de la Hoz 9, E–28010 Madrid*

In Italy: Please write to *Penguin Italia s.r.l., Via Como 4, I-20096 Pioltello (Milano)*

In France: Please write to *Penguin Books Ltd, 39 Rue de Montmorency, F-75003 Paris*

In Japan: Please write to *Longman Penguin Japan Co Ltd, Yamaguchi Building, 2–12–9 Kanda Jimbocho, Chiyoda-Ku, Tokyo 101*

BY THE SAME AUTHOR

The Honorary Consul

In a provincial Argentinian town a group of revolutionaries kidnap the wrong man. 'The tension never relaxes, and one reads hungrily from page to page' – Auberon Waugh

England Made Me

The themes and personal morality of Graham Greene's most ambitious pre-war novel remain as relevant today as they were in the depression years.

The Confidential Agent

He was sent to England to buy coal . . . at almost any price. Failure meant defeat – defeat for a continental government with a civil war on its hands. And this man carried the war with him, trusted by no man, trusting nobody.

Travels With My Aunt

Through his septuagenarian Aunt Augusta, a veteran of Europe's hotel bedrooms, retired bank manager Henry Pulling joins a shiftless twilight society: mixing with hippies, war criminals and CIA men, smoking dope . . . coming alive after a dull suburban lifetime.

A Gun for Sale

Assassinating an idealistic War Minister to boost the armaments industry was just a job to Raven. But when he is paid in stolen notes he becomes determined to revenge himself against his corrupt employers . . .

The Tenth Man

The masterpiece – written while Greene was under contract to MGM – that lay forgotten for forty years. 'The discovery of *The Tenth Man* is one of the undoubted literary pleasures of the year' – Anthony Burgess

BY THE SAME AUTHOR

Our Man in Havana

'As comical, satirical, atmospherical an "entertainment" as he has given us' – *Daily Telegraph*

Monsignor Quixote

A wonderfully picaresque and profoundly moving tale of innocence at large amidst the shrines and fleshpots of modern Spain. Like Cervantes's seventeenth-century classic, this novel is a brilliant fable for its times.

Doctor Fischer of Geneva or The Bomb Party

'Manages to say more about love, hate, happiness, grief, immortality, greed and the disgustingly rich than most contemporary English novels of about three times the length' – *The Times*

The Man Within

Greene's key themes of betrayal, pursuit and the search for peace resound throughout his first published novel. Begun when he was twenty-one, it retains all its grip, tension and freshness of impact.

Stamboul Train

As the Orient Express crosses Europe, it draws with it a trail of lust, murder, revolution and intrigue from Ostend to Constantinople . . .

Loser Takes All

Bertram, a conspicuously unsuccessful accountant, is wafted by another man's whim to Monte Carlo. Inevitably he goes to the casino – and loses. Then suddenly his system starts working . . .

BY THE SAME AUTHOR

Brighton Rock

Set in the pre-war Brighton underworld, this is the story of a teenage gangster, Pinkie, and Ida, his personal Fury who relentlessly brings him to justice.

The Power and the Glory

This poignant story set during an anti-clerical purge in one of the southern states of Mexico 'starts in the reader an irresistible emotion of pity and love' – *The Times*

The Comedians

Set in Haiti under a corrupt dictatorship, this is a graphic story about the committed and uncommitted.

The Quiet American

This novel makes a wry comment on European interference in Asia in its story of the Franco-Vietminh war in Vietnam.

The Heart of the Matter

Scobie – a police officer in a West African colony – was a good man but his struggle to maintain the happiness of two women destroyed him.

The End of the Affair

This frank, intense account of a love-affair and its mystical aftermath takes place in a suburb of war-time London.

Yours Etc.

'An entertaining celebration of Graham Greene's lesser-known career as a prolific author of letters to newspapers; you will find unarguable proof of his total addiction to everything about his time, from the greatest issues of the day to the humblest subjects imaginable' – Salman Rushdie in the *Observer*

Conversations With Graham Greene

In 1979, over a period of weeks at his Antibes home, Graham Greene talked to Marie-Françoise Allain about his life and work in a remarkable series of interviews. 'A collective portrait mixing frankness and evasion with considerable art' – Norman Shrapnel in the *Guardian*

also published:

In Search of Character
The Lawless Roads
May We Borrow Your Husband?
   and Other Comedies of The Sexual Life
Getting to Know the General
Collected Plays
The Ministry of Fear
A Burnt-Out Case
It's a Battlefield
The Captain and the Enemy
in one volume:
The Third Man
The Fallen Idol

The Human Factor
A Sense of Reality
Journey Without Maps
Lord Rochester's Monkey
Twenty-One Stories
Collected Essays
Collected Short Stories

and forthcoming:

The Last Word and Other Stories